Praise Praise Praise for Gardening For Dummies!

"*Gardening For Dummies* offers the perfect map for this new generation of gardeners."

> — William Raap, President,
> Gardener's Supply Co.

"These guys are no dummies. Using a world class cast of garden experts, they have assembled a first rate book for beginning gardeners. Dig in and start digging."

> — Shepherd Ogden, President and Founder
> The Cook's Garden

"If *Gardening For Dummies* had been available 50 years ago, I would have grabbed it. Back then, most of the garden books were written by gardeners from the big cities on the east or west coasts. I would have given my right arm for a solid reference book that included input from all parts of the country, as does *Gardening For Dummies*."

> — Jim Wilson
> Co-host PBS series *The Victory Garden*

Praise Praise Praise for NGA and Their Educational Programs!

"GrowLab has given my students absolute enthusiasm for their plant explorations and a zest for science, questioning, and initiating new projects that I haven't seen before."

> — Sixth Grade Teacher
> Massachusetts

"The wonderful thing about GrowLab is that it's a hands-on learning experience where my students and I learn together. A tremendous boost in self-esteem, use of science skills, and genuine fascination have resulted from exploring and nurturing plants."

> — Fifth Grade Teacher
> Connecticut

"The GrowLab curriculum and other resources NGA has produced are innovative, high-quality, and enormously popular with users here in the Twin Cities. The *Growing Ideas* newsletter is the best newsletter we receive on any topic in science."

> — Arboretum Education Manager
> Minnesota

"Your newsletter, *Growing Ideas*, is inspirational and full of good information. The format is excellent. It shows me what can be done and that I'm not alone."

> — Eighth Grade Garden Advisor
> Massachusetts

"I have given every teacher I come in contact with information on GrowLab, including the Growing Ideas newsletter. The materials are well thought out, flexible, fun, and enriching. I looked everywhere trying to find ideas — yours are the best."

> — Science Supervisor
> Texas

"Your newsletter is great! We are using the activity on herbs with our 4-H Junior Garden Club this month. Thanks."

> — 4-H Leader
> Colorado

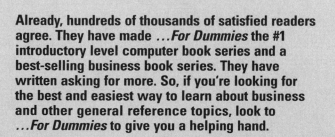

Gardening For Dummies™

BUSINESS
BOOK SERIES
FROM IDG

Quick Reference Card

Gardener Jargon

Annual. A plant that germinates, blooms, fruits, and dies in the course of one year.

Bedding plant. Foliage or an ornamental plant suited for habit by growing in beds or masses.

Biennial. A plant that requires two seasons of growth to produce its flowers and fruit and then dies after the second year.

Botanical name. The Latin or "scientific" name of a plant, usually composed of two words, the genus and the species.

Bulb. A term commonly used for a whole category of spring- or summer-blooming perennial plants that may grow from underground stems, corms, rhizomes, tubers, and tuberous roots.

Compost. A mass of decomposed, rotted organic matter (such as yard and garden wastes).

Deciduous. A plant that drops its leaves in winter and resprouts in spring.

Evergreen. A plant that holds some foliage throughout the year.

Ground cover. Low-growing, usually spreading plants that, when planted close together, form a layer of uniform foliage.

Hardening off. The process of gradually acclimating greenhouse- or indoor-grown plants to outdoor growing conditions.

Hardiness. The ability of a plant to withstand low temperatures without artificial protection. Hardiness zone maps divide the world into climatic zones, based on average winter minimum temperatures.

Hybrid. A cross between any two plants that are not genetically the same. Hybrids rarely breed true.

Native plant. A plant that occurs naturally in a specific region or locality.

Open-pollinated. Plant varieties that have the ability to cross-pollinate among themselves by natural means and to produce plants that resemble the parent variety.

Perennial. A plant that renews its top growth seasonally and lives year after year.

The Most Fragrant Plants

Arabian jasmine	Lilac
Carnations	Michelia
Chocolate cosmos	Mignonette
Common heliotrope	Plumeria
Dames rocket	Roses
Daphne	Stock
Flowering tobacco	Sweet olive
Gardenia	Sweet peas

Your Growing Zone

These plant hardiness zones are based on average annual minimum temperatures (U.S. Department of Agriculture data). See Chapter 5 for more about plant-growing zones.

Temperature C	Zone	Temperature F
–45.6 and below	1	Below –50
–42.8 to –45.5	2a	–45 to –50
–40 to –42.7	2b	–40 to –45
–37.3 to –39.9	3a	–35 to –40
–34.5 to –37.2	3b	–30 to –35
–31.7 to –34.4	4a	–25 to –30
–28.9 to –31.6	4b	–20 to –25
–26.2 to –28.8	5a	–15 to –20
–23.4 to –26.1	5b	–10 to –15
–20.6 to –23.3	6a	–5 to –10
–17.8 to –20.5	6b	0 to –5
–15 to –17.7	7a	5 to 0
–12.3 to –14.9	7b	10 to 5
–9.5 to 12.2	8a	15 to 10
–6.7 to –9.4	8b	20 to 15
–3.9 to –6.6	9a	25 to 20
–1.2 to –3.8	9b	30 to 25
1.6 to –1.1	10a	35 to 30
4.4 to 1.7	10b	40 to 35
4.5 and above	11	40 and above

... For Dummies: Bestselling Book Series for Beginners

Positive Thinking for Beginning Gardeners

There's no such thing as a "brown" thumb.

Making a perfect garden is complicated and difficult. Making a garden is easy.

The more you plant, the more success you'll have. Corollary: Everyone has failures.

Don't expect an instant garden. The best kinds happen gradually, over time.

Trust us on this: The food you grow yourself will taste better than anything you can buy. Most likely, it's more nutritious, too.

Don't be shy about asking questions. Most gardeners love to explain. Ask a neighbor, local nursery, botanical garden, or an Extension agent.

Plants are forgiving. They'll cover bad architecture and usually blend enough to blur the edges of a mediocre garden design.

The Basic Hand Tools of Gardening

Garden hose	Lawn rake
Hand trowel	Pruners
Stiff-tined rake	Shovel
Hoe	

Quick Pronunciation Guide to Common Plant Names

Abies	<u>aa</u>-bees
Acer	<u>aa</u>-sir
Betula	<u>bet</u>-you-la
Cercis	<u>kerr</u>-kiss (or "<u>sir</u>-sis")
Chamaecyparis	ka-mee-<u>qu</u>-pa-ris
Cotoneaster	ko-<u>tone</u>-ee-aster
Dianthus	dee-<u>anth</u>-us
Echinacea	ee-kee-<u>nah</u>-kee-a
Eleagnus	e-lee-<u>egg</u>-nus
Floribunda	flor-a-<u>bun</u>-da
Hemerocallis	hay-mee-row-<u>kay</u>-lis
Heuchera	<u>hew</u>-kee-ra
Lagerstroemia	law-ger-<u>strom</u>-ee-a
Lathyrus odoratus	<u>lay</u>-thi-rus
Lilium	<u>lee</u>-lee-um
Liquidambar	li-quid-<u>am</u>-bar
Liriope	lee-<u>ree</u>-o-pay
	(or "<u>lear</u>-ee-ope")
Muscari	mus-<u>kah</u>-ree
Parthenocissus	par-then-o-<u>kiss</u>-us
Quercus	<u>kwer</u>-kus
Raphiolepis	raf-ee-o-<u>lep</u>-is
Rudbeckia	rude-<u>beck</u>-ee-a
Trachelospermum	tra-kay-low-<u>sperm</u>-um
Trillium	<u>tril</u>-lee-um

... For Dummies: Bestselling Book Series for Beginners

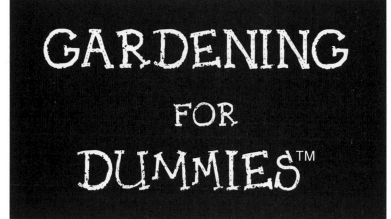

GARDENING

FOR

DUMMIES™

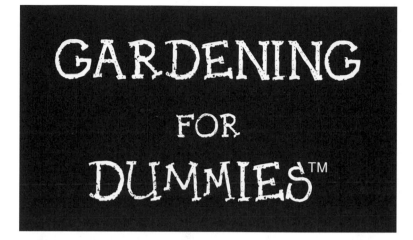

GARDENING FOR DUMMIES™

by Michael MacCaskey
Editor-In-Chief of *National Gardening* Magazine
& the Editors of The National Gardening Association

Foreword by Jim Wilson
Co-host PBS series *The Victory Garden*

IDG Books Worldwide, Inc.
An International Data Group Company

Foster City, CA ♦ Chicago, IL ♦ Indianapolis, IN ♦ Southlake, TX

Gardening For Dummies™

Published by
IDG Books Worldwide, Inc.
An International Data Group Company
919 E. Hillsdale Blvd.
Suite 400
Foster City, CA 94404

http://www.idgbooks.com (IDG Books Worldwide Web site)
http://www.dummies.com (Dummies Press Web site)

Library of Congress Catalog Card No.: 96-75401

ISBN: 1-56884-644-4

Printed in the United States of America

10 9 8 7 6 5

1A/RV/QU/ZX/IN

Distributed in the United States by IDG Books Worldwide, Inc.

Distributed by Macmillan Canada for Canada; by Transworld Publishers Limited in the United Kingdom and Europe; by WoodsLane Pty. Ltd. for Australia; by WoodsLane Enterprises Ltd. for New Zealand; by Longman Singapore Publishers Ltd. for Singapore, Malaysia, Thailand, and Indonesia; by Simron Pty. Ltd. for South Africa; by Toppan Company Ltd. for Japan; by Distribuidora Cuspide for Argentina; by Livraria Cultura for Brazil; by Ediciencia S.A. for Ecuador; by Addison-Wesley Publishing Company for Korea; by Ediciones ZETA S.C.R. Ltda. for Peru; by WS Computer Publishing Company, Inc., for the Philippines; by Unalis Corporation for Taiwan; by Contemporanea de Ediciones for Venezuela. Authorized Sales Agent: Anthony Rudkin Associates for the Middle East and North Africa.

For general information on IDG Books Worldwide's books in the U.S., please call our Consumer Customer Service department at 800-762-2974. For reseller information, including discounts and premium sales, please call our Reseller Customer Service department at 800-434-3422.

For information on where to purchase IDG Books Worldwide's books outside the U.S., please contact our International Sales department at 415-655-3023 or fax 415-655-3299.

For information on foreign language translations, please contact our Foreign & Subsidiary Rights department at 415-655-3021 or fax 415-655-3281.

For sales inquiries and special prices for bulk quantities, please contact our Sales department at 415-655-3200 or write to the address above.

For information on using IDG Books Worldwide's books in the classroom or for ordering examination copies, please contact our Educational Sales department at 800-434-2086 or fax 817-251-8174.

For press review copies, author interviews, or other publicity information, please contact our Public Relations department at 415-655-3000 or fax 415-655-3299.

For authorization to photocopy items for corporate, personal, or educational use, please contact Copyright Clearance Center, 222 Rosewood Drive, Danvers, MA 01923, or fax 508-750-4470.

is a trademark under exclusive license to IDG Books Worldwide, Inc., from International Data Group, Inc.

About the Authors

Michael MacCaskey's passions in life (after his family) are magazines, books, and growing plants. He started gardening in the early 1970s when he "discovered" the connection between good food and good health. By the mid-1970s, he was studying horticulture at California State Polytechnic University at San Luis Obispo, and by 1977 was researching and writing books about gardening. A native of California, he became immersed in Western gardening as a writer for *Sunset* magazine. Since becoming Editor-in-Chief of the Vermont-based *National Gardening* magazine in 1994, his gardening horizons have broadened considerably. He still believes in the connection between good food and good health and is more aware every day of the transformative power of gardening for both individuals and communities.

The **National Gardening Association** is the largest member-based, nonprofit organization of home gardeners in the United States. Founded in 1972 (as "Gardens for All") to spearhead the community garden movement, today's National Gardening Association is best known for its bimonthly magazine, *National Gardening*. Reporting on all aspects of home gardening, each issue is read by some half-million gardeners worldwide. These publishing activities are supplemented by online efforts, such as the Gardening Forum on CompuServe.

Other NGA activities include:

- **Growing Science Inquiry and GrowLab** (funded in part by the National Science Foundation). Provides kindergarten through grade 8 science-based curricula.
- **National Gardening Survey** (conducted by the Gallup Company). Has continued since 1972 as the most detailed research about gardeners and gardening in North America.
- **Youth Garden Grants**. Awards annual grants of gardening tools and seeds worth more than $500 each to schools, youth groups, and community organizations.

Mission statement: "The mission of the National Gardening Association is to sustain the essential values of life and community, renewing the fundamental links between people, plants, and the earth. Through gardening, we promote environmental responsibility, advance multi-disciplinary learning and scientific literacy, and create partnerships that restore and enhance communities."

For more information about the National Gardening Association, write to 180 Flynn Ave., Burlington, VT 05401, U.S.A. You can also contact them at 76711.417@compuserve.com or at 800-LETSGRO.

ABOUT IDG BOOKS WORLDWIDE

Welcome to the world of IDG Books Worldwide.

IDG Books Worldwide, Inc., is a subsidiary of International Data Group, the world's largest publisher of computer-related information and the leading global provider of information services on information technology. IDG was founded more than 25 years ago and now employs more than 8,500 people worldwide. IDG publishes more than 275 computer publications in over 75 countries (see listing below). More than 60 million people read one or more IDG publications each month.

Launched in 1990, IDG Books Worldwide is today the #1 publisher of best-selling computer books in the United States. We are proud to have received eight awards from the Computer Press Association in recognition of editorial excellence and three from *Computer Currents'* First Annual Readers' Choice Awards. Our best-selling *...For Dummies®* series has more than 30 million copies in print with translations in 30 languages. IDG Books Worldwide, through a joint venture with IDG's Hi-Tech Beijing, became the first U.S. publisher to publish a computer book in the People's Republic of China. In record time, IDG Books Worldwide has become the first choice for millions of readers around the world who want to learn how to better manage their businesses.

Our mission is simple: Every one of our books is designed to bring extra value and skill-building instructions to the reader. Our books are written by experts who understand and care about our readers. The knowledge base of our editorial staff comes from years of experience in publishing, education, and journalism — experience we use to produce books for the '90s. In short, we care about books, so we attract the best people. We devote special attention to details such as audience, interior design, use of icons, and illustrations. And because we use an efficient process of authoring, editing, and desktop publishing our books electronically, we can spend more time ensuring superior content and spend less time on the technicalities of making books.

You can count on our commitment to deliver high-quality books at competitive prices on topics you want to read about. At IDG Books Worldwide, we continue in the IDG tradition of delivering quality for more than 25 years. You'll find no better book on a subject than one from IDG Books Worldwide.

John J. Kilcullen

John Kilcullen
CEO
IDG Books Worldwide, Inc.

Eighth Annual Computer Press Awards ≥ 1992

Ninth Annual Computer Press Awards ≥ 1993

Tenth Annual Computer Press Awards ≥ 1994

Eleventh Annual Computer Press Awards ≥ 1995

IDG Books Worldwide, Inc., is a subsidiary of International Data Group, the world's largest publisher of computer-related information and the leading global provider of information services on information technology. International Data Group publishes over 275 computer publications in over 75 countries. Sixty million people read one or more International Data Group publications each month. International Data Group's publications include: **ARGENTINA:** Buyer's Guide, Computerworld Argentina, PC World Argentina; **AUSTRALIA:** Australian Macworld, Australian PC World, Australian Reseller News, Computerworld, IT Casebook, Network World, Publish, Webmaster; **AUSTRIA:** Computerwelt Osterreich, Networks Austria, PC Tip Austria; **BANGLADESH:** PC World Bangladesh; **BELARUS:** PC World Belarus; **BELGIUM:** Data News; **BRAZIL:** Annuario de Informática, Computerworld, Connections, Macworld, PC Player, PC World, Publish, Reseller News, Supergamepower; **BULGARIA:** Computerworld Bulgaria, Network World Bulgaria, PC & MacWorld Bulgaria; **CANADA:** CIO Canada, Client/Server World, ComputerWorld Canada, InfoWorld Canada, NetworkWorld Canada, WebWorld; **CHILE:** Computerworld Chile, PC World Chile; **COLOMBIA:** Computerworld Colombia, PC World Colombia; **COSTA RICA:** PC World Centro America; **THE CZECH AND SLOVAK REPUBLICS:** Computerworld Czechoslovakia, Macworld Czech Republic, PC World Czechoslovakia; **DENMARK:** Communications World Danmark, Computerworld Danmark, Macworld Danmark, PC World Danmark, Techworld Denmark; **DOMINICAN REPUBLIC:** PC World Republica Dominicana; **ECUADOR:** PC World Ecuador; **EGYPT:** Computerworld Middle East, PC World Middle East; **EL SALVADOR:** PC World Centro America; **FINLAND:** MikroPC, Tietoverkko, Tietoviikko; **FRANCE:** Distributique, Hebdo, Info PC, Le Monde Informatique, Macworld, Reseaux & Telecoms, WebMaster France; **GERMANY:** Computer Partner, Computerwoche, Computerwoche Extra, Computerwoche FOCUS, Global Online, Macwelt, PC Welt; **GREECE:** Amiga Computing, GamePro Greece, Multimedia World; **GUATEMALA:** PC World Centro America; **HONDURAS:** PC World Centro America; **HONG KONG:** Computerworld Hong Kong, PC World Hong Kong, Publish in Asia; **HUNGARY:** ABCD CD-ROM, Computerworld Szamitastechnika, Internetto online Magazine, PC World Hungary, PC-X Magazin Hungary; **ICELAND:** Tolvuheimur PC World Island; **INDIA:** Information Communications World, Information Systems Computerworld, PC World India, Publish in Asia; **INDONESIA:** InfoKomputer PC World, Komputek Computerworld, Publish in Asia; **IRELAND:** ComputerScope, PC Live!; **ISRAEL:** Macworld Israel, People & Computers/Computerworld; **ITALY:** Computerworld Italia, Macworld Italia, Networking Italia, PC World Italia; **JAPAN:** DTP World, Macworld Japan, Nikkei Personal Computing, OS/2 World Japan, SunWorld Japan, Windows NT World, Windows World Japan; **KENYA:** PC World East African; **KOREA:** Hi-Tech Information, Macworld Korea, PC World Korea; **MACEDONIA:** PC World Macedonia; **MALAYSIA:** Computerworld Malaysia, PC World Malaysia, Publish in Asia; **MALTA:** PC World Malta; **MEXICO:** Computerworld Mexico, PC World Mexico; **MYANMAR:** PC World Myanmar; **NETHERLANDS:** Computer! Totaal, LAN Internetworking Magazine, LAN World Buyers Guide, Macworld Netherlands, Net, WebWereld; **NEW ZEALAND:** Absolute Beginners Guide and Plain & Simple Series, Computer Buyer, Computer Industry Directory, Computerworld New Zealand, MTB, Network World, PC World New Zealand; **NICARAGUA:** PC World Centro America; **NORWAY:** Computerworld Norge, CW Rapport, Datamagasinet, Financial Rapport, Kursguide Norge, Macworld Norge, Multimediaworld Norge, PC World Ekspress Norge, PC World Nettverk, PC World Norge, PC World ProduktGuide Norge; **PAKISTAN:** Computerworld Pakistan; **PANAMA:** PC World Panama; **PEOPLE'S REPUBLIC OF CHINA:** China Computer Users, China Computerworld, China InfoWorld, China Telecom World Weekly, Computer & Communication, Electronic Design China, Electronics Today, Electronics Weekly, Game Software, PC World China, Popular Computer Week, Software Weekly, Software World, Telecom World; **PERU:** Computerworld Peru, PC World Profesional Peru, PC World SoHo Peru; **PHILIPPINES:** Click!, Computerworld Philippines, PC World Philippines, Publish in Asia; **POLAND:** Computerworld Poland, Computerworld Special Report Poland, Cyber, Macworld Poland, Networld Poland, PC World Komputer; **PORTUGAL:** Cerebro/PC World, Computerworld/Correio Informático, Dealer World Portugal, Mac*In/PC*In Portugal, Multimedia World; **PUERTO RICO:** PC World Puerto Rico; **ROMANIA:** Computerworld Romania, PC World Romania, Telecom Romania; **RUSSIA:** Computerworld Russia, Mir PK, Publish, Seti; **SINGAPORE:** Computerworld Singapore, PC World Singapore, Publish in Asia; **SLOVENIA:** Monitor; **SOUTH AFRICA:** Computing SA, Network World SA, Software World SA; **SPAIN:** Communicaciones World España, Computerworld España, Dealer World España, Macworld España, PC World España; **SRI LANKA:** Infolink PC World; **SWEDEN:** CAP&Design, Computer Sweden, Corporate Computing Sweden, Internetworld Sweden, it branschen, Macworld Sweden, MaxiData Sweden, MikroDatorn, Nätverk & Kommunikation, PC World Sweden, PCaktiv, Windows World Sweden; **SWITZERLAND:** Computerworld Schweiz, Macworld Schweiz, PCtip; **TAIWAN:** Computerworld Taiwan, Macworld Taiwan, NEW ViSiON/Publish, PC World Taiwan, Windows World Taiwan; **THAILAND:** Publish in Asia, Thai Computerworld; **TURKEY:** Computerworld Turkiye, Macworld Turkiye, Network World Turkiye, PC World Turkiye; **UKRAINE:** Computerworld Kiev, Multimedia World Ukraine, PC World Ukraine; **UNITED KINGDOM:** Acorn User UK, Amiga Action UK, Amiga Computing UK, Apple Talk UK, Computing, Macworld, Parents and Computers UK, PC Advisor, PC Home, PSX Pro, The WEB; **UNITED STATES:** Cable in the Classroom, CIO Magazine, Computerworld, DOS World, Federal Computer Week, GamePro Magazine, InfoWorld, I-Way, Macworld, Network World, PC Games, PC World, Publish, Video Event, THE WEB Magazine, and WebMaster; online webzines: JavaWorld, NetscapeWorld, and SunWorld Online; **URUGUAY:** InfoWorld Uruguay; **VENEZUELA:** Computerworld Venezuela, PC World Venezuela; and **VIETNAM:** PC World Vietnam.   2/14/97

Dedication

We dedicate this book to the person who sows a packet of seeds for the first time and connects with the mysteries of a growing plant.

Acknowledgments

Risking understatement, without the initiative and support of the IDG Books Worldwide team — Kathy Welton, Sarah Kennedy, Stacy Collins, and especially our editor, Melba Hopper — there would be no book at all.

Primary credit for this book goes to the NGA staff, present and past, that accumulated the resources, relationships, library, and information archives that are the heart of NGA (and, we hope, this book). Current NGA staff that contributed to this book includes David Els (President), Jack Ruttle (senior editor), Linda Provost (art director), Charlie Nardozzi (horticulturist), and Ann Pearce (assistant editor).

To write and edit this book, the National Gardening Association called upon some of its most stalwart contributors. First, we thank Emily Stetson, a former managing editor of our magazine, for her organizational and editing expertise throughout the project. In a similar vein, we thank Vicky Congdon (also a former managing editor) for her help during the final editing stages.

To these contributing authors, we extend our deepest gratitude:

Vicky Congdon, Baltimore, MD — Chapter 17, "Lawns and Lawn Care"

Robert Kourik, Occidental, CA — Chapter 16, "Maintaining Your Garden"

David Lyon, Cambridge, MA — Appendix B, "Gardening Online"

Susan McClure, Chagrin Falls, OH — Chapters 1, 2, and 3, plus Chapters 14, 15 (exclusive of "Getting Plants for Free"), and 18

Lynn Ocone, Burlington, VT — book plan, Chapter 4 (exclusive of power tools), "Getting Plants for Free" (in Chapter 15), "Wildflower Fantasies" (in Chapter 20), and Part VI ("The Part of Tens")

Barbara Pleasant, Huntsville, AL — Part V: "Creating Special Gardens"

Jack Ruttle, Alburtis, PA — Introduction and Chapter 13, "Making Places for People"

Lance Walheim, Exeter, CA — Part II: "Which Plants for You?"

Sally Williams, Boston, MA — Appendix A: "Books and Magazines about Gardening"

For his eagle eye and encyclopedic mind, we thank consulting reviewer Richard Dunmire. Also, thanks to Kevin Reichard for his review and thorough checking of "Gardening Online."

Thanks also to artist (and gardener) Jean Carlson Masseau of Hinesburg, VT, for creating the delightful color illustrations of gardens you'll find in this book.

Publisher's Acknowledgments

We're proud of this book; please send us your comments about it by using the Reader Response Card at the back of the book or by e-mailing us at feedback/dummies@idgbooks.com. Some of the people who helped bring this book to market include the following:

Acquisitions, Development, & Editorial

Project Editor: Melba Hopper

Executive Editor: Sarah Kennedy

Copy Editors: Diane L. Giangrossi, Diana R. Conover, William A. Barton

Consulting Reviewer: Richard Dunmire

Editorial Manager: Mary Corder

Editorial Assistants: Chris H. Collins, Ann Miller

Production

Project Coordinator: J. Tyler Connor

Layout and Graphics: Brett Black, Linda M. Boyer, Cheryl Denski, Maridee V. Ennis, Angela F. Hunckler, Jill Lyttle, Tom Missler, Drew R. Moore, Mark C. Owens, Anna Rohrer, Gina Scott, Michael A. Sullivan

Proofreaders: Sharon Duffy, Christine Meloy Beck, Gwenette Gaddis, Dwight Ramsey, Carl Saff, Robert Springer

Indexer: Sharon Hilgenberg

Special Help

Gray Scale Illustrator: John Padgett

General and Administrative

IDG Books Worldwide, Inc.: John Kilcullen, CEO; Steven Berkowitz, President and Publisher

IDG Books Technology Publishing: Brenda McLaughlin, Senior Vice President and Group Publisher

Dummies Technology Press and Dummies Editorial: Diane Graves Steele, Vice President and Associate Publisher; Judith A. Taylor, Brand Manager; Kristin A. Cocks, Editorial Director

Dummies Trade Press: Kathleen A. Welton, Vice President and Publisher; Stacy S. Collins, Brand Manager

IDG Books Production for Dummies Press: Beth Jenkins, Production Director; Cindy L. Phipps, Supervisor of Project Coordination, Production Proofreading, and Indexing; Kathie S. Schutte, Supervisor of Page Layout; Shelley Lea, Supervisor of Graphics and Design; Debbie J. Gates, Production Systems Specialist; Tony Augsburger, Supervisor of Reprints and Bluelines; Leslie Popplewell, Media Archive Coordinator

Dummies Packaging and Book Design: Patti Sandez, Packaging Specialist; Lance Kayser, Packaging Assistant; Kavish + Kavish, Cover Design

◆

The publisher would like to give special thanks to Patrick J. McGovern, without whom this book would not have been possible.

◆

Contents at a Glance

Foreword .... *xxix*

Introduction *1*

Part I: Planning Your Garden *7*
Chapter 1: A Garden Makes Your Life Better 9
Chapter 2: Evaluating Your Property's Potential 15
Chapter 3: Making Your Plan 23
Chapter 4: Gardening Tools You Will Need 33

Part II: Which Plants for You? *43*
Chapter 5: Which Plant Where? 45
Chapter 6: Trees 57
Chapter 7: Shrubs 67
Chapter 8: Vines 77
Chapter 9: Perennials 83
Chapter 10: Annual Flowers 91
Chapter 11: Flowering Bulbs 99
Chapter 12: Ground Covers, Prairies, and Meadows 109

Part III: Making Your Garden *115*
Chapter 13: Making Places for People 117
Chapter 14: It's All Happening in the Soil 129
Chapter 15: How to Plant 141

Part IV: Caring for Your Garden *155*
Chapter 16: Maintaining Your Garden 157
Chapter 17: Lawns and Lawn Care 173
Chapter 18: Pests and Diseases 183

Part V: Creating Special Gardens *201*
Chapter 19: Gardens for Food and Flavor 203
Chapter 20: Gardens for Color and Cutting 215
Chapter 21: Gardens for Birds and Butterflies 223
Chapter 22: Gardens in Containers 229
Chapter 23: Rose Gardens 235

Part VI: The Part of Tens *245*
Chapter 24: Composting and Recycling Yard Waste 247
Chapter 25: Ten Quick "Garden" Projects 255
Chapter 26: Ways to Stretch the Garden Season 263
Chapter 27: How to Support Climbing Plants 269
Chapter 28: Tips for Gardeners without Much Garden 273
Chapter 29: Best Plants for a Perfumed Garden 279

Part VII: Appendixes **287**
Appendix A: Books and Magazines about Gardening 289
Appendix B: Gardening Online 297
Appendix C: Where to Find It 307

Index *317*
Reader Response Card .... *Back of Book*

Table of Contents

Foreword .... *xxix*

Introduction *1*

How to Use This Book 1
Part I: Planning Your Garden 2
Part II: Which Plants for You? 2
Part III: Making Your Garden 3
Part IV: Caring for Your Garden 3
Part V: Creating Special Gardens 3
Part VI: The Part of Tens 3
Part VII: Appendixes 4
A Word about Plant Names 4
Icons Used in This Book 5

Part I: Planning Your Garden *7*

Chapter 1: A Garden Makes Your Life Better **9**

Keeping It Private 9
Party Time! 11
Where Are Those Kids? 12
Creating a Practical Work Area 12
Being Your Own Supermarket 13
Being Your Own Flower Shop 13
Here, Doggy! 13
Using the Sun and the Shade 14
This Path Was Made for Walkin' 14
Sitting for a Spell 14

Chapter 2: Evaluating Your Property's Potential **15**

Making a Site Inventory 15
Drawing Goose Eggs 16
Let There Be Light 17
Checking Out Your Dirt 18
Controlling Water Movement 20
Enjoying Gardens with a View 21
Meeting Your Potential 22

Chapter 3: Making Your Plan **23**

Planning: You Gotta Do It 23

A Garden Is More than Plants 24

Making a list 24

Heavy jobs for hire 25

Picturing your property 26

Getting Your Plan on Paper 26

Creating a Scaled Plan of Your Property 26

Sketching in the existing features 27

Using your computer 27

Elements of a Plan 29

Plants 29

Hardscape 31

Chapter 4: Gardening Tools You Will Need **33**

Hand Tools 33

The seven essential tools that every gardener needs 33

. . . And five more tools to buy 34

More Power 35

Cutting grass 36

String trimmers 38

Tilling soil 39

As the tines turn 40

Mini-tillers 40

Jobs mini-tillers do well 41

Where to Shop for Garden Tools 41

Nurseries 41

Other sources for tools and garden supplies 42

Part II: Which Plants for You? **43**

Chapter 5: Which Plant Where? **45**

Putting Plants in Their Place 46

Getting Zoned 46

What Else Does a Plant Need? 52

Sun or shade 52

Soil and water 52

Room to grow 53

Using Native Plants 53

Shady Business 53

Stuck between a rock and shady place? 54

Made in the shade 55

Fifteen flowering perennials for shady sites 55
Fourteen annuals for shady sites 55
Six evergreen shrubs for shady sites 56
Five deciduous shrubs for shady sites 56
It's a Matter of Choice 56

Chapter 6: Trees 57

Choosing the Right Tree 57
Getting Cool with Trees 58
Keep your cool 59
Lower your heating bills 59
Make you look marvelous 59
Don't Try This at Home 60
Our Favorite Trees 62

Chapter 7: Shrubs 67

Cozying Up to Shrubs... 67
Choosing and Using Shrubs 68
Design considerations 68
Our Favorite Shrubs 69
Top Dwarf Conifers 74

Chapter 8: Vines 77

Let's Play Twister 77
Lean on me 78
Using Vines Effectively 79
Don't let vines grow where they shouldn't 79
Provide sturdy support 79
Prune for healthy vines 80
Our Favorite Vines 80

Chapter 9: Perennials 83

Creating a Perennial Border 83
Tips on designing a perennial border 84
Planting perennials 85
Caring for perennials 85
Our Favorite Performance Perennials 87

Chapter 10: Annual Flowers 91

What Is an Annual? 91
Cool dudes 92
When it's hot, they're hot 92
Go for a Riot of Color 92

Landscaping with Annuals 93
    Getting annuals together 93
    Containing annuals 94
    Treating them with care 94
The Best of the Annuals 94
    Cool-season annuals 94
    Warm-season annuals 96

Chapter 11: Flowering Bulbs 99

What Are Bulbs? 99
    Getting down and dirty 99
    Going natural: "You're not getting older; you're getting better!" 100
Where Should I Plug In My Bulbs? 100
Buying Bulbs 101
Planting Bulbs 101
Caring for Bulbs 102
Dividing and Propagating Bulbs 103
Bulbs in Containers 104
Best Bulbs 105

Chapter 12: Ground Covers, Prairies, and Meadows 109

Over in the Meadow 109
The Ground-Cover Alternative 110
Planting Ground Covers 110
Top Ground-Cover Choices 112

Part III: Making Your Garden 115

Chapter 13: Making Places for People 117

Paving, Fences, and Other Expensive Stuff 117
D.I.Y. (Do It Yourself) or Hire Help 118
Walking along Paths 119
    Side by side: determining width 119
    Naturalistic walks: lawn or mulch 119
    The gardener's edge 120
    Bark and gravel 121
    Brick, stone, and concrete 121
    Step by step: making slopes easier to climb 121
Cool Things on Posts 123
    Don't fence me in: property and privacy fences 123
    Keeping Peter Rabbit out 124
    Prefab fencing: pickets to stockades 125
Putting a Living Room Outdoors: Patios, Terraces, and Decks 126
    How big to make it 126

Patios (and terraces) 127
Hitting the deck 127
Now Showing: Private Screenings 127

Chapter 14: It's All Happening in the Soil 129

Dig Here: Clearing the Site 129
Stripping sod 130
Applying black plastic mulch 131
Using the repeated tilling/cover cropping method 131
Checking Your Soil 131
Texture 132
Ribbons and bows 133
The jar test 133
Structure 133
"I'll have mine perked, please" 134
The direct approach: the metal-rod method 134
Sweet and sour: pH tests 135
For more 135
Amending Soil 136
Good soil 136
Bad soil 136
Changing pH 137
Adding nutrients 137
Fertilizers 137
Compost 137
Green manures and cover crops 138
Loosening the Soil 138
Simple raised beds 139
Double digging 140
Finishing Touches 140

Chapter 15: How to Plant 141

When to Plant What 141
Making a Planting Plan 142
Sowing Seeds in Your Garden 142
Transplanting Seedlings 144
Planting Trees and Shrubs 146
Planting Bulbs 148
Getting Plants for Free 149
Dividing 149
Taking cuttings 150
Softwood stem cuttings 150
Water-rooted stem cuttings 151
Starting Seeds Indoors 151
Getting on the (red) wagon: hardening plants 152

Part IV: Caring for Your Garden 155

Chapter 16: Maintaining Your Garden 157

Pruning Smart 157
Pruning Basics 159
  Details on these kindest cuts 159
  Pruning in winter 160
  Pruning in summer 160
  Pruning tools 161
Watering Just Right 162
  Watering in furrows 162
  Sprinklers simplified 162
  Oscillating sprinklers 163
  Oozing hoses 163
  How much water do plants need? 164
Weeding Made Easy 164
  Beware hitchhikers 165
  Weeding by hand and by tool 165
  Mulches 166
    Inorganic mulches 166
    Fertile mulches 166
Plant Nutrients 168
Fertilizer Types and How to Use Them 169
  Common fertilizer forms 169
  Kinds of fertilizers for various plants 170
  Organic fertilizers 171

Chapter 17: Lawns and Lawn Care 173

More Lawn or Less Lawn? 173
Putting In a New Lawn 174
  Which grass is best? 174
  Turfgrass short list 175
    Cool-season grasses 175
  Before you plant 176
Seeding a Lawn 177
  Shopping for seed 177
  Planting day 177
Lawns from Sod 179
  Buying sod 179
  Laying sod 179
  Planting plugs and sprigs 179
Overseeding to Improve Your Lawn's Looks 180
  Lawn color where winters are mild 180
  Don't like the lawn you've got? 180

The Care and Feeding of Lawns 181
  Weeding and mowing 181
  Fertilizing 182

Chapter 18: Pests and Diseases 183

Preventing Pests and Diseases 183
  Gardening to prevent pest problems 184
  Encouraging "good" insects 185
Managing Pests 186
  Dealing with pests in the vegetable garden 187
  Insect pests you're most likely to encounter 188
  Nine safe and effective pest remedies 193
    Bt 193
    Diatomaceous earth (DE) 193
    Horticultural oils 194
    Insecticidal soaps 194
    Neem 195
    Pyrethrins 195
    Sabadilla 196
    Rotenone 196
    Sevin (carbaryl) 197
Preventing Plant Diseases 198
  A dozen dirty diseases: what to do 198

Part V: Creating Special Gardens 201

Chapter 19: Gardens for Food and Flavor 203

Growing a Vegetable Garden 203
  Choose a sunny location 203
  Make the garden the right size 204
  Stake and weed the garden 204
  Raise the beds 205
  Feed the soil 205
  Decide what to grow and when 205
  Time it right 205
  Tough or tender? 206
  Raise them right 207
  Put it together 207
  Have a happy harvest 208
Is There Fruit in Your Future? 208
  Six steps to a fruit tree harvest 209
  Planning a fruit garden 211

Fruits for the home garden 211
    Apples 211
    Peaches 212
    Pears 212
    Sweet cherries 212
    Plums 212
    Strawberries 213
    Grapes 213
    Blueberries 213
    Bramble fruits 213
Sneaking Edible Plants into Your Landscape 213

Chapter 20: Gardens for Color and Cutting **215**
    Rooms with a View 215
    Swinging with the Seasons 216
    Don't Be Square 216
    Combining Congenial Flowers 217
    Coloring Your World 218
    Planting Your Rainbow 219
    Wildflower Fantasies 220
        Growing wildflowers 221

Chapter 21: Gardens for Birds and Butterflies **223**
    Making Birds an Offer They Can't Refuse 223
    Keeping Pest Birds at Bay 225
    Beckoning Butterflies to Your Garden 226
        Designing for butterflies 227
        Mixing a butterfly cocktail 228

Chapter 22: Gardens in Containers **229**
    Choosing the Right Pots 229
    Making a Garden in a Pot 230
        A primer on soil for pots 231
        Fill 'er up 232
    Deciding What to Grow 232
        Annuals all summer 232
        How many will fit? 233
        Perennial accents 233
        Delectable edibles 234
    Is Everybody Happy? 234

Chapter 23: Rose Gardens **235**

Kinds of Roses 236

Trying out teas 236

Fun with floribundas 236

Here comes the queen 237

Climbing high with roses 237

"Honey, I shrank the roses!" 237

"...Honey, now I've stretched the roses" 237

Shrub varieties proliferate 238

David Austin roses 238

Old-fashioned roses 239

Roses by many other names. 239

Landscaping with Roses 240

Buying, Planting, and Growing Roses 241

Pruning Roses 243

Helping roses survive winter 244

Part VI: The Part of Tens .... **_245_**

Chapter 24: Composting and Recycling Yard Waste **247**

How the Piles Stack Up 247

From refuse to riches: composting 248

Bin or no bin? 249

To build or buy? 249

Composting aids . . . who needs them, anyway? 251

Heap it on 252

Treasures from Twigs 253

Mulching Matters 254

Chapter 25: Ten Quick "Garden" Projects **255**

Cooking Up Herb Vinegars 255

Making a Flowering Centerpiece 256

Creating a Water Garden in a Tub 256

Forcing Narcissus Indoors 258

Cleaning Containers 259

Preparing a Salad Basket 259

Drying Flowers 260

Creating an Autumn Harvest Wreath 261

Making Cut Flowers Last 262

Chapter 26: Ways to Stretch the Garden Season 263

Planting Earlier in the Year 263
Extending the Season into Autumn (and Beyond?) 266
Gardening All Year 266

Chapter 27: How to Support Climbing Plants 269

Raising Canes 269
    Bamboo teepees 270
    Chain-Link Fences 270
    Metal Trellises 271
    Latticework Trellises 271
    Fan Trellises 271
    Plastic Netting 272
    Pillars 272
    Wall-Mounted Supports 272
    Arbors 272

Chapter 28: Tips for Gardeners without Much Garden 273

Simple Pleasures 273
Details Make the Difference 274
Illusions of Grandeur 274
Outer-Space Exploration 276
Diamonds in the Rough 277

Chapter 29: Best Plants for a Perfumed Garden 279

Getting the Most for Your Whiff 280
Flowers Most Possessed with Scent 280
Fragrance after Dark 282
Heavenly Scented Trees, Shrubs, and Vines 283
Best Bulbs for Fragrance 284
Redolent Roses 286

Part VII: Appendixes *287*

Appendix A: Books and Magazines about Gardening 289

Books 289
    Beyond basic books 292
    A word about British books 293
    Sources of books 294
Magazines, Newsletters, and Newspapers 294

Appendix B: Gardening Online 297

    Commercial Online Services 298
        America Online 298
        CompuServe 299
    The Internet 300
        Talking (or typing): Usenet newsgroups for gardeners 300
        Cutting through the clutter 301
        Mailing lists 302
    Web Sites 303

Appendix C: Where to Find It 307

    Bulbs 307
    Flowers and Vegetables 308
    Herbs 310
    Fruits and Berries 311
    Perennial Plants 311
    Roses 313
    Tools and Supplies 313
    Trees, Shrubs, and Vines 315
    Water Garden Plants and Supplies 315
    Wildflowers 316

Index *317*

Reader Response Card .... *Back of Book*

Foreword

· ·

*H*ere I am, one of the most visible gardeners in the United States, writing the Foreword to *Gardening For Dummies*. However, while writing, I must immediately acknowledge that during each and every one of my 50 years of gardening, I have made at least one monumental goof. Talk about poetic justice!

I would have made even more mistakes, but I cheated. Early on, I figured that no one can ever learn everything there is to know about gardening. So I bit off a small chunk of information every few years, digested and practiced it, and then wrote books and articles about it. One by one, I specialized in food gardens, then in annual flowers, herbs, container gardening, native plants, and, of late, home habitats for birds and butterflies. I didn't abandon my first loves but added to them as I expanded my gardens and vagabonded about this big country.

Looking back, I can see that my way was the hard way. If *Gardening For Dummies* had been available 50 years ago, I would have grabbed it. Back then, most of the garden books I found were written by gardeners from the big cities on the east or west coasts. I would have given my right arm for a solid reference book that included input from all parts of the country, as well as information about gardening around the world, as does *Gardening For Dummies*.

I know personally many of the writers who contributed to this book, and the others I know by reputation. Collectively, we have made about every mistake there is in gardening.

But cheer up! There is a saving grace in gardening. The Great Architect arranged things so that we can make outrageous mistakes and still have good gardens. Being human, we will never graduate from being gardening *dummies;* rather, we will gradually age from young to old dummies. The challenge of gardening is not to eliminate mistakes and misjudgments but to diminish their impact on our self-esteem and on the equally fragile earth.

Jim Wilson
South Carolina, USA

Jim Wilson has served as co-host of the PBS television series The Victory Garden *for ten years. As a speaker, he has journeyed to just about every gardening hamlet in the U.S. and several abroad, and he is an author of numerous books and magazine articles. Last year, Jim received an infrequently bestowed honor, when he was inducted into the Hall of Fame of the Garden Writers Association of America.*

Introduction

• •

*T*he meaning of the word *garden* is changing in a big way these days. It used to be that when people talked about their garden or somebody else's garden, they meant a rectangular patch of ground — usually somewhere out back — where people grew their vegetables or flowers to cut for bouquets.

Now when people talk about gardening, they may be talking about cutting a hedge, mowing the lawn, snipping some flowers for indoors, or planting a patch of hostas in the shady strip between the house and the garage. But gardening is even more than this. Gardening is good for the body and soul, and it's good for families. Gardening is good for the environment.

The point is, gardening has moved out of the vegetable patch and the flower beds. Gardening now encompasses our lives. And this means that if you have a yard — even a very tiny one — you are a gardener. Gardening has become the least exclusive hobby of all. Everybody is doing it.

This universalizing may not fit well with the snobbish stereotype — the gardener as someone who calls every plant by its proper Latin name or pampers perfect rosebuds in order to take home the gold medal at the flower club meeting or state fair. To be sure, there is truth in the stereotype: Gardening can be a high-class hobby that borders on competitive sport. As you are reading these very words, hundreds of hard-core horticulturists are laboring over their beloved specimens. But millions of other people are simply enjoying their time outdoors and striving to make their little corner of the world more peaceful and beautiful — a better place to live. And that's what this book is about.

How to Use This Book

You have in your hands a gardening encyclopedia in miniature — all you need to know to get off to a good start. No matter what area of gardening interests you — growing roses or perennials or just cutting the grass — you'll find good advice here. And when you outgrow the level of information that we've provided, you can turn to the appendixes for pointers on where to look next.

In every chapter, our basic goal is to give readers who know almost nothing at all about gardening the information that they need to go out and plant or prune what they want. But that doesn't mean that only novices will find the book useful. Gardening is such a huge topic that no one ever comes close to knowing everything about it. That's one reason why it has become the most popular hobby of all time.

If, for example, you (or a friend or relative) are a seasoned rose grower but know next to nothing about how to start a salad garden or make a better garden path, you (or they) can find excellent advice in Chapter 19 or Chapter 13, respectively.

Part I: Planning Your Garden

Before you buy your first six-pack of flower seedlings in spring, you need to decide just where to start digging. Part I gets you to thinking about what and where your gardening areas should be.

Chapter 1 gives a quick overview of the wide range of garden areas that you can make, based on the way you want to use them.

Chapter 2 helps you evaluate the suitability of different parts of your yard for garden-making.

Chapter 3 gets into the details of a preliminary plan, with emphasis on making a rudimentary written record that you can refer to and refine later.

Chapter 4 gives you the gardening tool basics.

Part II: Which Plants for You?

Here's where the real fun starts! This part is the heart of the book because for most people, the essence of gardening is putting in plants and watching them grow.

Chapter 5, a sort of Botany 101 class, tells you about the basic requirements of plants.

Chapters 6, 7, and 8 are about the trees, shrubs, and vines that give your garden shape over the long haul — cool shade in summer, deep green in winter, and beautiful flowers plus colorful foliage throughout the growing season.

Flowers, flowers, flowers! You can find out all about perennials, annuals, spring bulbs, and more in **Chapters 9, 10, and 11. Chapter 12** covers the wide range of ground covers available.

Part III: Making Your Garden

This section is the nitty-gritty — literally. These three chapters are all about working in the ground.

Chapter 13 tells you how to put in all kinds of walkways, patios, and decks. It also covers fences, screens, and arbors.

In **Chapter 14**, you find the basics of soil preparation, from getting rid of grass or weeds to testing soil and preparing garden beds.

Chapter 15 focuses on the entire planting process in great detail: planting the trees and other transplants that you buy, starting your own plants from seed, and even propagating your own plants by growing cuttings and divisions.

Part IV: Caring for Your Garden

In a nutshell, this section covers long-term garden maintenance.

Chapter 16 is the heart of the matter: watering, weeding, pruning, and fertilizing. Lawn care is covered in detail in **Chapter 17,** while **Chapter 18** offers commonsense methods of pest control.

Part V: Creating Special Gardens

It's back to the fun stuff — plants and planting — in this section!

Sweet corn, strawberries, lettuce, tomatoes, and other edibles are featured in **Chapter 19**. **Chapter 20** is about making gardens that will fill bouquets for the house all season long. **Chapter 21** tells you what to plant to attract butterflies, hummingbirds, and other wildlife. **Chapter 22** is devoted to flower gardening in miniature with container gardens and window boxes.

Roses — the queens of any flower garden — take center stage in **Chapter 23**. Anybody can grow roses, in our opinion, and this chapter proves it!

Part VI: The Part of Tens

No ...*For Dummies* book would be complete without this compendium of expert tips for achieving interesting, low-care gardens. We collected some of our best ideas here: ways to compost (**Chapter 24**), quick garden projects (**Chapter 25**), ways to stretch the season (**Chapter 26**), ways to support climbing plants (**Chapter 27**), tips for gardeners without much garden (**Chapter 28**), and the best fragrant plants (**Chapter 29**).

Part VII: Appendixes

One exciting feature about gardening is the endless amount of information available about whatever aspect of gardening you find most compelling. The three appendixes that we've compiled here are intended to help you in that effort.

Books and magazines. Here we recommend a few (including the book that you're holding right now) for your permanent library. But more important, we offer tips to help you choose the book or magazine that will serve you best.

Gardening online. Going online can be a quick and cheap way to get your questions answered. We should know. The National Gardening Association has hosted CompuServe's Gardening Forum for five years, and greatly expanded it just this year. In this appendix, you'll find some of our favorite gardening Web sites and automatic mailing lists. If you have any questions or comments after reading this book, you can contact us at 76711.417@compuserve.com.

Mail-order gardening. The variety of plants, seeds, and tools that you can buy through the mail and have delivered the next day (if you like) is astounding. The list that we assembled here is not exhaustive — that would be impossible. But it does offer many of our favorite suppliers.

A Word about Plant Names

Like any hobby or pastime, gardening has its own jargon. Although most words are straightforward and down to earth (most of us wouldn't have any trouble figuring out *watering, fertilizing,* or *composting,* for example), one area is a bit trickier: the names of specific plants. To ensure that we all know which plant we're talking about, gardeners have a system of plant naming based on Latin and Greek.

So following conventional garden nomenclature, we listed the common name of plants in normal type, usually lowercased (sweet peas, for example). From there, it gets a bit more complex. Every plant is a member of a larger horticultural family, sharing general characteristics with other family members. For sweet peas, it's the *Leguminosae* family. Common garden peas share the same family. These plant families are divided into groups of closer relatives, indicated by a group or "genus" name. This genus name is always written in italics and with the first letter uppercased. Thus, the genus name for sweet peas is *Lathyrus,* the Greek name for "pea."

The next name is the species name. Like the genus, it is written in italics, but the first letter is lowercase. Usually, a plant's species name tells something about the plant's shape, color, leaf form, fragrance, or some other peculiarity. Sweet peas are *Lathyrus odoratus,* which describes their wonderful scent. (A genus name followed by the word "species" means we are referring to numerous species of that group, such as *Lathyrus* species.)

The final common part of a plant's name that we used throughout this book is the variety name. We won't bore you with all the reasons why, but these are enclosed in single quotation marks. An example is *Lathyrus odoratus* 'Little Sweetheart'.

Hortus Third, compiled by the staff of the L. H. Bailey Hortorium at Cornell University and published by Macmillan Publishing Co. in 1976, is our reference.

Icons Used in This Book

 Suggests ways to save money.

 Points out ecological tips and ways to be earth friendly.

 Flags information that even some experienced gardeners may not know.

 Marks tips that experienced gardeners live by.

 Offers international gardening advice and data.

Demystifies gardening lingo. (Although we've made this book as jargon-free as possible, you need to know some terms.)

 Gives addresses and/or phone numbers for ordering special gardening equipment. (You can also find sources in the appendixes.)

 Watch out! Alerts you to avoid bad gardening experiences, including some that may cause injury.

Part I
Planning Your
Garden

In this part . . .

A garden is made of plants. (You probably already knew that.) But it's also a place to walk and relax. Think of designing a garden as designing an outdoor room for your house, which means, of course, that you need a plan. You don't necessarily need to call an architect. You just need to figure out what you want your garden to do for you (within reason, of course — don't expect Versailles overnight!).

Then determine how you can do that with the yard (or dirt or concrete) you're currently looking at. (Okay, so maybe you can't create Versailles at all. Don't lose hope.)

What should you get rid of and how can you hide that ghastly view? Then when you're ready to dig, where do you get all the plants, tools, and supplies that you'll need to make a garden?

This part helps you with these preliminaries and what it takes to start gardening!

Chapter 1

A Garden Makes
Life Better

In This Chapter

▶ Creating privacy

▶ Entertaining, playing, and working

▶ Growing food

▶ Supplying your own cut flowers

▶ Making a place for pets

▶ Using sunny and shady areas

▶ Imagining a path for walking

▶ Including a nook for sitting

A garden makes your life more comfortable, healthier, more colorful, and more convenient. It lets you expand your living area outdoors, harvest fresh food, and pick your own flowers. But you already suspected that, or you wouldn't be reading this book. To get the most from your garden, you need to understand everything a garden can do. Once you've got a sense of the possibilities, you can begin to decide what you want to include in your own garden.

Begin by drawing your yard and loosely dividing it into different areas, based on how you'd like to use your outdoor space (as shown in Figure 1-1). Chapter 2 has more details on making the "goose-egg" sketches and planning your yard's design. This chapter gives you some basic suggestions for creating these areas and may open your eyes to other ways that a garden can give you greater pleasure in your yard.

Keeping It Private

Imagine taking a vacation in your own backyard or relaxing in a shady spot, secluded from the hustle and bustle of ordinary life. This dream can be yours, if you begin by creating a private area for your own pleasure.

For privacy, you'll need to have garden walls — either constructed or planted — that shelter you from the rest of the world. These kinds of walls are called *screens* (see more about screens in Chapter 13). You can make them with clumps of shrubs, hedges, a vine-covered trellis, a fence, or a wall. You can choose from different kinds of screens — literal or psychological. A literal screen can rise over your head, blocking out everything except the sky. But that kind of tall barrier can make you feel hemmed in, especially if you have a small yard. For sitting areas where the neighbor's yard is level or lower than your own, a 4- or 5-foot-high screen provides psychological privacy. You have a barrier between your garden and beyond, but you can still see the sky and trees.

You may not need to enclose your entire yard to achieve the feeling of privacy. If you use your front yard primarily as a public area for greeting visitors, you won't need a screen there. Keep it open and welcoming. But if an area of your yard has an especially unattractive view that you would rather not see — the neighborhood playground, perhaps, or the neighbor's old cars — put your privacy screen there.

In your backyard, or any other private area, you can use screens to line the edge of your property. You also can use them internally, perhaps to close off your sunbathing area but leave the kids' ball field open. There are certain areas that you should not screen — places with great views, for example.

Here are some screens that you can use in your yard:

- **Deciduous hedge.** Shrubs that drop their leaves in winter provide a screen during the growing season, the time when people are most likely to linger outdoors. Many deciduous shrubs have the extra bonus of lovely flowers and handsome autumn color. (See Chapter 7 for more on shrubs.)

- **Evergreen hedge.** For most screens, evergreens that reach 4 or 5 feet high work well. You can leave them unpruned in a low-maintenance, informal hedge or clip them into a time-consuming, formally sheared hedge. Be patient at first; even quick-growing shrubs take several years to fill in before they can work as a screen.

- **Fences.** You can install a variety of fences — such as board on board, picket fences, and brick walls — to provide instant privacy (see Chapters 3 and 13). Tall fences create shade that limits your planting options; moderate-sized fences are most versatile.

- **Tall perennials.** You can develop a quick-growing screen to fill a modest-sized opening by planting clumps of eulalie grass and other ornamental grasses, delphiniums, or other tall perennials. These plants create a flowing, less solid screen that may die back to the ground in winter. (See Chapter 9 for more on perennials.)

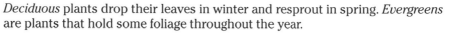

✔ **Vine-covered trellis (or fence).** Climbing roses, clematis, grapes, and other handsome vines climb up a trellis to give you a partial screen. Few vines produce a solid wall of greenery (and many are deciduous), so you end up with some openings that provide tantalizing glimpses of the world beyond. (See Chapter 8 for more on vines.)

Deciduous plants drop their leaves in winter and resprout in spring. *Evergreens* are plants that hold some foliage throughout the year.

Figure 1-1:
Make a
rough
sketch of
your
property
and include
existing and
desired
features.

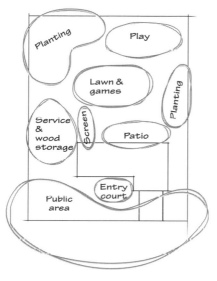

Party Time!

Whether you like large get-togethers with the extended family or business associates or a quiet dinner with a few friends, your garden can provide an ideal atmosphere. You'll need a few key ingredients to make your garden perfect for entertaining.

✔ **Flooring.** Establish an all-weather flooring for a patio or sitting area, a place where you can put tables and chairs and walk in comfort, even when the soil is wet. If you go for more formal entertaining, build a solid patio floor of brick or interlocking tiles that won't trap high heels. For casual entertaining, you can have something as simple as a couple of inches of gravel beneath picnic tables. If you like to grill outdoors in the summer, put your grill or barbecue pit nearby. (See Chapter 13 for more details on flooring.)

> ✔ **Flower garden.** If you want to impress your guests with the beauty of your garden, consider planting a flower bed nearby. For evening entertaining, try white flowers that reflect moonlight in the most enchanting way. Or plant a formal herb garden, which is beautiful and provides a bountiful source of herbs for cuisine or fragrance. See Part V for more details on special gardens.
>
> ✔ **Shade.** If you intend to entertain during the heat of summer, you'll want some shade. Put your entertaining area beneath a shade tree (but not a tree that drops messy nuts or berries) or build a gazebo or vine-covered arbor for some relief from the sun. For entertaining at night, place some lights in the garden. See Chapter 6 for more on trees.

Now your outdoor play area can be as beautiful and functional as one indoors!

Where Are Those Kids?

Children have no better place to play than outdoors when the weather is nice. You can use your yard as a ball field or find a corner for a swing set, playhouse, or sandbox. If you have younger children, put the play area close to the house so you can watch from a window or the patio. Older children may appreciate the freedom of having the play area farther from the house, where their imaginations can run wild.

If you don't have room for a separate children's area, incorporate children's activities throughout the entire yard. Consider letting your children have a corner of a vegetable garden for peas, radishes, or cherry tomatoes that they can grow and pick themselves. Or look at a shade tree as a fine place for climbing or for hanging a swing. A shrub bed can make a perfect place for hide-and-seek. You may find yourself enjoying your yard even more as you watch your kids playing in it.

Creating a Practical Work Area

There's more to the outdoors than fun and games. You may need a place in your yard to keep your garden tools, heating oil tank, firewood, clothesline, or garbage cans. Organize all of these less-than-attractive outdoor necessities into the same out-of-the way location, a work station separate from your entertaining and play areas. Ideally, the location should be handy, near the garage or driveway, but far enough away from handsome views or gardens so that it won't be a distraction from them. Use screens to hide your work area (see "Keeping It Private" earlier in this chapter) or blend it in at the far edge of the lawn.

Being Your Own Supermarket

One of the most delicious aspects of your garden is that it can produce wonderful vegetables, fruits, and herbs. You can grow expensive gourmet produce, as much as you want for less money than you may imagine. You can have access to rare and special crops — cinnamon basil, heirloom tomatoes, French sorrel, Turkish eggplants — food you just can't buy. You can harvest vine-ripened tomatoes, peaches, and strawberries for the ultimate in flavor. Better yet, you can choose to grow the food organically so that you're sure it's healthy for your family.

Food gardens grow best in a sunny part of your yard. You also can grow many vegetables, herbs, and even fruits such as citrus or figs in pots or tubs on a sunny step or patio. Try to place the culinary garden near your house, where you can easily run out to harvest or pull over a hose for watering. You can even use a decorative garden design to make the food garden as handsome as a flower garden. See Chapter 19 for more on food gardens.

Being Your Own Flower Shop

It is so satisfying to cut an armful of flowers from your own garden and bring them indoors. If you like freshly cut flowers, be sure to leave a little space to grow your own. You can grow traditional favorites, such as carnations and daisies, or expand into more unusual flowers, such as Texas bluebell and *Patrinia*. You can grow your cut flowers right in your vegetable garden, harvesting every last bloom. Or you can blend them in with other flowers and plants, taking a flower here and there but also leaving some to decorate the garden. See Parts II and V for more on flowers.

Here, Doggy!

Make sure that your pets have an outdoor area where they can enjoy the weather without getting into trouble in the garden. Some dog owners build a separate kennel and dog run area that is fenced or screened off from the rest of the yard, rather like a work area. One advantage of keeping your dogs in a separate area is ease of flea control. If fleas are a problem for you from time to time, you can treat the soil with parasitic nematodes (see Chapter 18 for definition), which are an effective and safe way to eliminate outdoor fleas.

Another option is to adapt the landscape so that it's pet-friendly. For example, you can create a path that encircles your lawn and build tall raised beds beside it. Teach your dogs that they are free to romp on the path or the lawn but are not to go into the raised beds to dig, roll, or cause other trouble. Make the distinctions clear so that everyone can enjoy the yard.

Using the Sun and the Shade

Use your open sunny areas and your shady tree- or fence-lined areas for gardens of very different ambience. Sun is great for high-impact gardens full of productive vegetables or bright flowers or for a lush lawn. Use your shady spots for a quiet sitting bench, spring wildflowers, or a subdued garden of ferns and hostas.

If you prefer the atmosphere of shade gardens but have an open yard, you can gradually transform it by planting shade trees. If you want the excitement of growing a wide range of sun-loving plants but have a shady yard, you'll have to remove some of the trees to let the sun show through.

This Path Was Made for Walkin'

Paths can have a remarkable effect on the garden. They let you travel through a vegetable or flower garden without stepping on your plants. They take you across your yard without wearing out your lawn. They draw you into the woods to reveal a handsome scene. And they can be beautiful in themselves, creating formal or sweeping lines that complement your plantings.

Consider where you usually walk and whether a path with all-weather footing — gravel, mulch, brick, or stone — will make your life easier. Make it a wide one so several people can walk side by side to your front door. Or use a narrower one to get to the middle of a broad garden without stepping in the soil or on the plants. (For more on walks or paths, see Chapters 3 and 13.)

Sitting for a Spell

Anywhere that seems cozy and pleasant is a great place to put a sitting nook. It doesn't have to be a fancy area; it can be a place for you to relax and, perhaps, watch the kids play. Start with a comfortable bench or chair and position it in shade beneath a magnificent oak, at the end of your vegetable garden, or at the back of your yard near the swing set. If you put in all-weather footing — gravel or mulch, for example — you can sit outside regardless of the soil conditions.

The possibilities for your garden are almost endless. Take some time to jot down everything you may possibly want in your yard. Chapter 3 shows you how to pull this all together in a garden plan.

Chapter 2

Evaluating Your Property's Potential

● ●

In This Chapter

▶ Taking an inventory of your garden

▶ Figuring property dimensions and making goose-egg sketches

▶ Understanding light levels and changing sunlight

▶ Looking at soil possibilities

▶ Providing proper drainage

▶ Making way for scenic views

▶ Figuring out your existing landscape potential

● ●

Developing your yard and landscape can be like creating a work of art that unfolds as you plan, plant, and watch it grow. But unlike the artist's blank canvas, your yard has many special features that will shape the kind of garden you can plant and the kind of look you will achieve. This chapter shows you how to take a careful inventory of your yard's natural features before you begin to plan your landscape.

Making a Site Inventory

You've got to come to grips with what you've got. Besides knowing where your property line is, you need to determine what major features currently exist in your yard so that you can begin to decide what to keep and what to replace with new landscaping. Look for major items such as the following:

✔ **Plants:** Trees and shrubs, hedges, large patches of *ground cover* (see Chapter 12), and flower, herb, or vegetable gardens

✔ **Structures:** Fences, walks, arbors, patios, decks, sculptures, fountains, laundry lines, work sheds, storage areas, utility lines (above and below ground), septic systems, property lines, and easements

✔ **Natural features:** Banks, ditches, hills, rocks, creeks, ponds, and wooded areas

List every feature, starting in the front yard at the street and moving progressively backward through the backyard. Put a comment beside each item. Do you like it or not? Does it add to or detract from your landscape? Is the item in good shape? If you're looking at a plant, is it healthy with firm bark, even branching, and attractive green leaves? Is the shape pleasing, or has age or crowding made a shrub or tree lopsided or awkwardly barren?

Simple though this step may sound, this list is a valuable starting point for future planning, in both this chapter and Chapter 3. This list lets you put sentiment aside and evaluate each item for its true worth. For example, you may have noticed that the shrubs around the foundation have grown so large that they block the windows. By looking closely at them, you can determine whether to keep them. If they have a nice shape and some vigorous new growth emerging near the ground, they can be *thinned* (see Chapter 16) and returned to good order. If the shrubs are unhealthy or aged, with old, gnarled wood and no new, interior growth, they may need replacement rather than pruning.

Drawing Goose Eggs

No, we're not talking about your bank account. Now you're ready to begin sketching some of the features of your yard and jotting down preliminary ideas of what you may want to do with the space. Begin by documenting property size and shape. You can get exact dimensions of your property from the plot or building plan developed when your house was built. If you can't find a plan, ask at your municipality's building or zoning department; the folks there may have a copy in their records.

The plot plan shows the shape and size of your property as well as the location of your house, which saves you from having to fight your way into perimeter thickets to measure yard dimensions. Make a dozen photocopies of your original plot plan so you can use them to record your ideas as you read through this chapter and Chapter 3. If you can't find the plot plan, you can find out how to measure to scale in Chapter 3.

The size of your yard helps you determine how you use it. For example, large properties need larger beds of flowers or masses of shrubs to look substantial in the expanse of the yard. Warm colors, used in the rear of a large yard, seem to advance and give the planting more impact. Smaller properties look good with smaller beds, planted so that you can focus on the special beauty of more petite plants that won't overwhelm the space. But if you enjoy gardening and want more gardening space, you may choose to replace lawn areas entirely and turn your small yard into a large garden. You can enjoy cool blues and purples that are soft and comforting when viewed up close (but may be lost if viewed from a distance).

Many yards are square or rectangular, which makes determining public, entertaining, work, and play areas (see Chapter 1) relatively straightforward. But you need to think creatively to make the landscape soft and natural rather than stiff and geometric. Irregularly shaped properties can take more planning to fit everything necessary into a convenient and attractive place. Figure 2-1 shows the same basic layout on differently-shaped lawns.

Figure 2-1:
How you use your property is not determined by its shape. In these examples, two differently shaped properties are organized similarly.

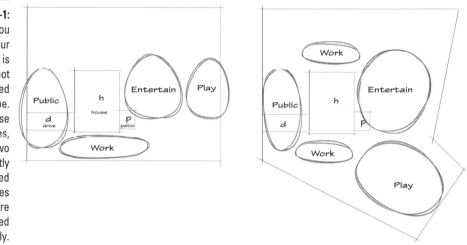

To help you organize the different areas of your yard in advance, make goose-egg studies, as we did in Figure 2-1. Take a copy of your plot plan and use a pencil to circle broad areas (*goose eggs*) that you think will work well for different purposes. After you finish the first, do several more to consider alternatives and decide which will work best. If you plan carefully, you will have a unique garden with a special character all its own.

Let There Be Light

Of course, your ideal layout may not be practical, given the natural forces at work on your garden. The sun has a big say in the design. Take note of how much sun different parts of your property receive so that you can determine which kinds of plants will grow well there. Here are some examples:

- ✔ **Areas with full sun — at least six hours a day.** Good for growing sun-loving lawns, vegetables, flowers, herbs, and many shrubs and trees.

- ✔ **Areas with light shade — four to six hours of sun a day.** Supports a more limited group of plants, including some vegetables (such as lettuce and mint), some flowers (such as impatiens and daylilies), some shrubs (such as hydrangeas and rhododendrons), and some trees (such as native dogwoods).

> ✔ **Heavy shade — less than four hours of sun a day.** Limited in the kinds of plants it can grow — ferns, spring wildflowers, ivy, and pachysandra being some possibilities. (For more details on gardening in shade, see Chapter 5.)

One good way to keep track of sunlight is to sketch sunny and shady areas on a copy of your plot plan, as shown in Figure 2-2. Note which parts of your yard have full sun, light shade, or heavy shade. If you're working on this project over a period of several months, check sun exposure every now and then and note the number of hours you find at any given time; be as specific as you can. File the plan away so that it's easy to find when you're deciding where to use sun and shade plants.

Checking Out Your Dirt

Gardeners hate the word *dirt.* The proper word is *soil.*

The soil in your yard is more than something to walk on. It provides nutrients, moisture, and support for plants. Not all soil is the same. It comes in a huge range of different textures and pH (acidity or alkalinity) and has different amounts of organic matter, nutrients, and moisture (see Chapter 14). Learn about your yard's soil characteristics so that you can choose plants that will thrive there.

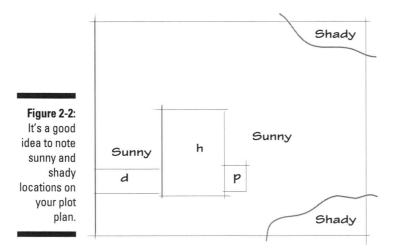

Figure 2-2: It's a good idea to note sunny and shady locations on your plot plan.

Changes in latitude, changes in light

When checking sun exposure, counting the number of hours the sun reaches a garden on any particular day is not enough. You also have to estimate how much more or less sun will reach that space as the seasons change. Make sure that on an autumn day, when shadows are long and daylength is short, your sunny garden will still receive at least 6 hours of sun.

Daylengths change as spring turns to summer and autumn — quite dramatically in northern climates and less dramatically closer to the equator. In some places, summer days get to be 16 hours long but shrink to only 10 hours in the winter. This means that a garden in your yard that receives 6 hours of sun during the long days of June will have less than full sun when the days grow shorter in autumn. If you've planted that garden with sun-loving plants such as roses, you'll find that they begin to suffer.

The position of the sun in the sky may also affect how much light your garden receives. The sun is high overhead in early summer, casting minimal shadows. But other times of the year, it hangs lower in the sky, sending long shadows from nearby trees, buildings, and fences to cast shade over a garden that was in full sun in midsummer. This can be an advantage of sorts. If you live in an area with hot summers, you can put a shadow-casting tree to the west of your patio or salad garden. Once you get a good feel for changing sun levels, you'll be well on your way to being a great gardener.

You can have your soil tested to determine fertility and structure. Contact the nearest Extension Service office for more information. You also can do some simple at-home tests (see Chapter 14). But be sure to evaluate samples of soil from different parts of your yard, from the surface and from lower down. It's not unusual for soil characteristics to change. Often, when homes are built, all the *topsoil* (the richer soil that lies on top of the less fertile layers below) is removed near the house. As a result, you may find only stiff clay in some areas, and that can make gardening difficult. Elsewhere, construction crews may have brought in topsoil that differs in character from the native earth. Because you can't necessarily see these variations, find them by testing before going any further.

Jot down different soil types (see Chapter 14) on your plot plan, right alongside possible landscape uses and light levels, as in Figure 2-3. Your plot plan is starting to show the real possibilities of the property.

Here are the different soil types:

- **Sand.** These soils are loose, warm, and airy but can be dry and low in fertility. You can usually work in sandy soils much sooner in spring than other soils, which makes them great for nurseries or avid gardeners who can't wait to get started. However, in summer, they need watering. These soils benefit from the addition of organic matter for nutrients and water retention.

LEARNING THE LINGO

✔ **Clay.** These soils are thick, heavy, and dense but rich in nutrients and able to hold large amounts of moisture. Clay soils often have poor air circulation because of their density, which you can correct by adding organic matter. You can also prevent packing by walking on garden paths rather than in the planting bed.

Organic matter is the decomposed version of anything that was once alive. Compost, manure, and peat moss are common kinds of organic matter that gardeners use. You find more about organic matter in Chapter 14.

✔ **Silt.** These soils contain over 80 percent silt particles, which are primarily small sand fragments. Unlike sandy soils, silt can compact and needs extra organic matter to stay fluffy.

✔ **Loam.** These soils mix roughly equal amounts of sand, silt, and clay for a nice blend of characteristics — a little looseness from sand and a little richness from clay. This kind of balance produces a soil that farmers dream of and plants luxuriate in.

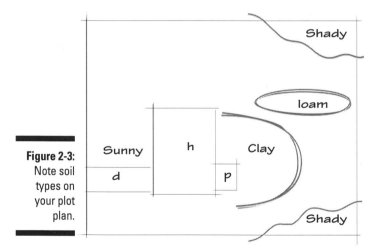

Figure 2-3:
Note soil types on your plot plan.

Controlling Water Movement

Water is always on the move in your yard. Keep an eye out for it to determine how it will affect your landscaping. After a downpour or spring snow melt, some water will run across the surface of your soil without soaking in. It can create streams and puddles in the low areas. If the water stagnates there, it can damage your garden.

Your yard also can develop stagnant puddles if water from watering or normal rainfall can't drain down through the soil. Water usually moves freely through sandy or loam soils, unless impeded by hard and impenetrable underground soil layers. It moves more slowly, sometimes hardly at all, through thick clay soils. Where underground water movement is stifled, surface water will puddle and make it hard for you to grow plants. Note on your plan where water collects and determine how to correct the problem; some solutions follow.

If drainage is poor in one isolated place, a broken water or sewer pipe or a submerged spring beneath the ground may be letting water seep up. Poor drainage also can be a result of a hard layer of compacted soil underground, which could be a natural sheet of bedrock or clay or simply soil compacted from the pressure of heavy equipment driving over that area. You may need to dig down a bit to find the source of your problem and break up the hard area or fix the leaky pipe. If you find a natural spring, you may be able to turn the soggy area into a little bog or water garden instead of draining the water off.

Some plants not only live in wet or soggy soil but also *thrive* in it. In special ways, they are adapted to life in water. These are the plants of bog and water gardens. Directions on how to make your own water garden in a tub are in Chapter 25.

If drainage is a problem over most of your yard, you may want to install drainage pipes beneath the entire area. *Drainage tiles* — perforated plastic pipes that pick up excess moisture — shuttle water underground to the sewer system or street.

Drainage systems are big and sometimes complicated jobs. Consider consulting with a landscape architect or engineer with water drainage experience, especially if you live on or near a hillside.

Enjoying Gardens with a View

A few lucky homeowners are blessed by scenic views — a hillside clad in autumn leaves, a majestic waterfall, a rolling meadow. Make the most of the view by planning your landscape around it. Even if you don't have a mountain range to gaze at, you may still be able to find an interesting view — a magnificent street tree or a small creek lined with cattails and wildflowers. Even small scenes of beauty are worth preserving and framing in your landscape.

Circle the location of the scenic area on your plot plan. Now identify where you usually sit or stand when you look at that scene. Do you usually see it from the patio, from your family room window, or from your front step? Note on your plan the pathway that needs to stay clear of tall vegetation to keep your favorite view open.

Meeting Your Potential

Now that you've surveyed your site and made notes on a site plan, pull out your landscape inventory. (See "Making a Site Inventory" at the beginning of this chapter.) Pencil in the existing features that appeal to you and are in good shape. They form the framework of the landscape that you will expand on as you develop new areas in Chapter 3. Cut down and eliminate any existing features that just won't work.

Figure 2-4 shows a completed site analysis — with topical features, drainage problems, desired views, potential view problems, and existing landscape features all mapped out.

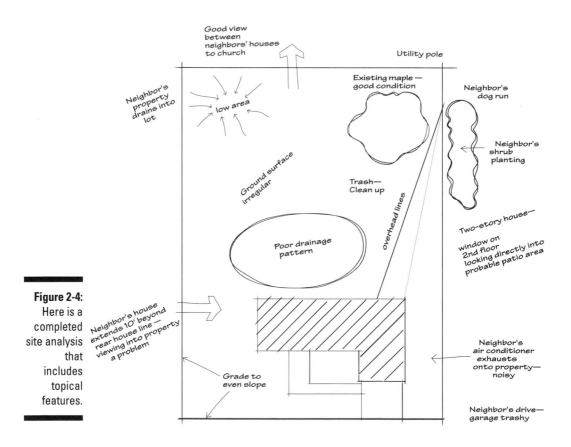

Figure 2-4: Here is a completed site analysis that includes topical features.

Be sure to keep your plot plan sketches in a handy place; you need them for Chapter 3.

Chapter 3
Making Your Plan

● ●

In This Chapter

▶ Doing things right by planning

▶ Seeing your garden as a "place"

▶ Making lists and setting priorities

▶ Documenting with photographs

▶ Putting it to paper

▶ Drawing to scale

▶ Designing with a computer

▶ Understanding hardscape and plant characteristics

● ●

*P*lanning is important whether you want to have one special garden or landscape your entire yard. The forethought that you apply now will make any garden project work well, tomorrow and in years to come. This chapter shows you how to develop a plan and what kinds of elements you may want to include in it.

Planning: You Gotta Do It

If you don't plan ahead, you'll run short of plants or supplies, or you'll put a plant or patio in the wrong place. Doing the job right the first time not only saves you money in the long run, but is also the only way to ensure satisfaction.

You began to think about how to use your yard in the first two chapters of this book. Now you need to firm up some specifics on paper. If you get bogged down in this process and want another opinion, consult a landscape designer or landscape architect, professionals who specialize in planning and designing.

By planning, you can organize the following:

- ✔ **Quality plants.** Plan ahead to make sure that you have the best-quality plants you can at a time when the weather is ideal for planting. Remember to order special plants ahead of time — the most desirable varieties often sell out early.

- ✔ **Labor.** You may need extra people to help you muscle the landscape into place. If so, it's smart to schedule them several months in advance to ensure that they come during prime planting time.

- ✔ **Budget.** It costs money to hire help, build decks, or buy plants and garden tools. Because few of us have an unlimited budget, you can prioritize your landscape needs as you plan.

A Garden Is More than Plants

Think of your garden as an outdoor room, not just a place to grow plants. In Chapter 1, you saw how your landscape can be a great place to work, play, relax, or entertain. In Chapter 2, the inventory that you took of your yard's assets showed you what natural potential it has for future landscape development. Now you can take all these ideas and put them together as you develop a plan.

Making a list

Here are the steps for making a list of landscape priorities. Expand on the goose-egg diagram that you made in Chapter 2 to fill in this information.

1. **Identify areas of your yard that are unsuitable for growing plants, perhaps because the soil is very poor or the drainage is bad.**

   Plan to cover such areas, for example, with a deck or patio, or assume that conditions will require fixing before any planting work can go on. Or find special plants that will grow in unsuitable conditions. (For more about soils and planting, see Chapters 14 and 15.)

2. **Look at existing landscape features. Remove any trees, shrubs, or structures that are damaged, sick, or dangerous as soon as possible.**

3. **Get all the heavy equipment and workers in and out before planting.**

   Whether you're installing a new deck or fixing up your house, you need to attend to construction before you can do any planting. Once that's out of the way, you can repair the damage done by piled-up supplies and large trucks running across the yard and then begin new plantings.

4. Decide what and where to plant first.

Let your personal preferences guide you. Are you most concerned with how your house looks from the street? Or is it more important to have a comfortable, private living space in the backyard?

- **If the front yard is a priority.** Plan to make your yard and home appear more beautiful from the street and to improve the visitor's route of approach. Sometimes simpler is better. An effective planting scheme may include a healthy green lawn sweeping across much of the front yard and some trees and shrubs to frame the house and blend it into the yard. A front walk — at least 4 feet wide — should move gracefully and sensibly from the driveway or street to your door. (See Chapter 13 for more details on paths.)

- **If your yard's living area is more important than the public area.** Start by creating privacy with fencing or hedges. You should also develop any arbors or other shelters now. Plant your shade trees as soon as possible; they'll take time to grow. Then develop your walkways and paths. When the main structure of the garden is in place, you can begin to fill other areas with beds of decorative shrubs and flowers, vegetable and herb gardens, and other pleasurable touches.

Heavy jobs for hire

Many garden jobs can be done by anyone, regardless of age or physical condition. You can plan your landscape, shop for plants, and supervise construction. But even an athletic gardener may not be strong enough to accomplish the heaviest garden jobs single-handedly. This is especially true if you have health problems that limit your activities. Consult your physician and consider having someone else do the more strenuous work. Here are a range of activities that you will have to deal with:

- ✔ **Heavy work.** Digging, rototilling, moving large plants, carrying heavy supplies or equipment (such as bales of peat moss), pushing wheelbarrows of soil, pruning large branches

- ✔ **Moderately strenuous work.** Hoeing, hand weeding, planting (seeds, seedlings, and small nursery plants), harvesting, pruning shrubs and small trees, dividing and transplanting perennial flowers, mowing the lawn with a push mower

- ✔ **Light work.** Cutting back flowers, mowing the lawn with a riding mower, spreading fertilizer or lightweight mulch, planting and tending raised planters

Picturing your property

As you're planning, you may want to have some photographs of your yard in spring, summer, or autumn to refer to, especially when you're planning during winter. The photos allow you to look closely at any area and keep fresh in your mind how you'd like it to look. Even if you're planning during the growing season, photographs let you concentrate on the job at hand instead of running outside to look around. They also allow you to keep an inventory of the existing plants that you want to keep or move around — and they're fun to look at later as your landscaping develops. You'll be amused by how far you've come.

Photograph your yard from a variety of different angles, catching every inch of it. Document the front yard as seen from the street, from the center of the yard, and from both side yards, for example. You also may want to photograph the front yard and backyard from your picture windows or from your patio. Take closeups of complicated beds. Label all your photographs and file them away so that they'll be easy to find.

Getting Your Plan on Paper

Now create a pencil plan that shows your ultimate goal for your property. You'll be surprised at the ideas that become clear to you when you see your yard compressed on a piece of paper rather than spread out before your eyes. Each landscape feature is reduced to a symbol and a representative size, so you can evaluate its worth in the overall plan without being sidetracked by sentimentality or guilt.

On paper, you can eliminate the existing features that you no longer want, creating a blank slate on which to draw new features. You can adapt, change, and reorganize with a flick of an eraser. To help you visualize your new yard, make tracing paper overlays to show different scenarios for your landscape, moving your patio behind the garage or close to the kitchen door, for example. Set overlays on top of the original plot plan and secure them with masking tape so that they're easy to move and change. Other overlays can show the color of the garden as it changes by season or the size of trees and shrubs as they grow. Still other overlays can show how your landscape will develop if you divide the entire project into several phases.

Creating a Scaled Plan of Your Property

In Chapter 2, you used a builder's plot plan to evaluate your site. You can use copies of the same plan to start your landscape design, sketching in existing landscape features that you intend to keep, using your site analysis as a reference point. If you can't find your plot plan, you'll have to measure your entire yard. Either way, make your plan to scale so that it gives a precise representation of your yard. See the sidebar, "Making a scale drawing of your property," for tips on drawing to scale.

A *scale drawing* is a reduced-size replica of your yard that uses proportions such as 1 foot of yard space equals $^1/_4$ inch of plan space.

Sketching in the existing features

When you have your plot plan, follow these steps to sketch in the existing landscape features, starting with the front yard and then moving on to the side yards and the back yard:

1. **Take the graph paper and measuring tape out into the yard with you. Note on the paper which directions are north and south and what scale you're using.**

2. **Plot each landscape feature that you intend to keep.**

   Find its depth in the length of the yard by measuring from either the house or the street. Make a pencil mark to show its location. Then measure its distance from the side of the property. Move the pencil mark to indicate the correct spacing from the side property line.

   If the landscape feature is a tree, measure the limb spread of the tree and indicate it with a circle around the mark. If the tree is young, you may want to use a dotted line to show the ultimate shady, mature spread.

   If you plan to eliminate existing features, don't bother to sketch them in. Not including them will save you time and trouble as you plan new developments for your yard.

3. **When the entire yard is penciled in, go back and check the accuracy of the drawing.**

   When you eyeball the plan and look at the yard, does it appear that everything is in the right place? Pull out your measuring tape and check several sample distances. Are they the same distance shown on your plan? If so, your plan probably is accurate. If not, pull out your eraser and correct the plan. Now you're ready to develop your plan by adding new features, either by hand or by computer.

Using your computer

Once you have your scale plot plan, you can input it into your computer and develop your design electronically. Here are the benefits of using a computer:

✔ Saves you the time and trouble of drawing all changes and updates by hand.

✔ Lets you explore the way a landscape may look when viewed from different angles, at different times of the year, or at any time in the future.

✔ Some computer programs include detailed plant encyclopedias. You may be able to indicate your landscape needs and have the program select suitable plants.

Making a scale drawing of your property

Here are some tips on drawing your property to scale if you don't have a plot plan.

✔ **Start by using graph paper.**

The easiest kind of graph paper has 5 squares per inch of paper space, which allows you to easily record the garden in units of 5 and 10 (that is, 1 inch can equal 5 or 10 feet). Some kinds of graph paper come with 4 squares per inch, which requires more mathematical manipulating. In that case, 1 inch can equal 4 or 8 feet. Graph paper also comes in a variety of sizes. The standard 8½ x 11-inch paper may not be large enough to accommodate an entire landscape. You can find oversized graph paper, as large as 17 x 22 inches, at better office or art supply stores.

✔ **Find a proportional scale that's suitable for your drawing and landscape complexity.**

If you're going to have a simple landscape planted with trees and shrubs, you can make an inch of plan space represent 8 or 10 feet of landscape space. But, if you're going to be planning complicated flower, herb, and vegetable gardens, you may want to be able to include more detail by making an inch represent 4 or 5 feet — even less if necessary.

✔ **Always use a measuring tape to calculate distances.**

Eyeballing or estimating is not precise enough. At the minimum, you need a 50-foot-long measuring tape.

✔ **Start your measuring in the front yard, taking down the length and the width. Then do the side yards and the backyard.**

The front yard ends at an invisible line that cuts across the width of your property and runs along the front of your house. Draw the front yard perimeters on the plan. For example, if you measure the front yard as 50 feet long and wide and you use a scale of 5 feet equals 1 inch, then your front yard will be a 10-inch square on your plan. Do the same for the side yards and back yard.

The key to success is to find good software and have access to a color printer. Unfortunately, many software programs are constrained by bad graphics, limited variety information, cumbersome design constraints, and poor manuals. Look for software that is simple and user friendly, yet detailed enough for your needs. Anything else won't be time effective.

Elements of a Plan

All of the above-ground elements of your garden plan can be categorized as either plants or *hardscapes.* (Hardscapes are built surfaces and structures that give a sense of permanence and order to your garden.) As you put together your design, keep the following basics about each in mind.

Plants

Plants come in a rainbow of sizes, shapes, and colors. (For information about how to use specific plants, see Part II.) Some characteristics point out architectural highlights. Others are as handsome as sculptures. Some harmonize; others contrast. Consider the varying design characteristics of plants before you finalize your design.

- ✔ **Size.** The tallest trees can frame or shade your house or sitting area. Medium-tall plants, such as tall shrubs and small ornamental trees, can provide height in a small yard or be used as screens. Medium-sized shrubs can help blend the house into the landscape. If you're planting them around the foundation, stick with plants that are naturally dwarf, not growing much over 3 feet tall, so that they won't overwhelm the site and require regular pruning. Smaller plants — flowers, vegetables, low shrubs — can fill in openings between larger plants or create gardens of their own.

- ✔ **Form and shape.** Plants come in a variety of shapes that you can blend and balance for maximum beauty. A conservative way to start your landscape is to use a majority of rounded shapes, accented occasionally by other forms such as the following:

  - *Horizontally spreading plants,* such as junipers and native dogwoods, blend strongly vertical architecture — including the corners of your house — into the landscape.

  - *Upright or spiky plants,* such as columnar arborvitae, stand out like exclamation points. Use them near an important part of the yard — on either side of the front door, for example. But be careful that you don't use too many upright plants, or they'll be overwhelming.

- *Naturally rounded or mound-shaped plants,* such as viburnums and boxwood look neat, smooth, and comfortable but can be a little plain if not jazzed up with other forms.

- *Low and spreading plants* such as creeping junipers and ivies cover the ground like a carpet, filling space with greenery to help tie the landscape together.

✔ **Texture.** Some plants, such as oak leaf hydrangea and sheared yew, have a bold, eye-attracting texture because of large leaves, dense branching, or a dark appearance. These plants are strong and can stand on their own or visually anchor a garden bed. But too many bold plants can look somber or overwhelming.

Other plants, such as shasta daisies and spiraeas, have medium texture with moderate-sized leaves, average shapes, and a moderately loose growth habit. These plants look comfortable in the garden but, without other textures, can become boring.

Fine-textured plants, such as astilbe and flax, have small or finely cut leaves or open, fine-stemmed shapes that allow light to shine through. They can be intricate and invite a closer look but can also appear insubstantial and, in large quantities, chaotic.

✔ **Color.** Plants provide color with their foliage, flowers, berries or cones, or even stems, as in the case of red-twigged dogwood. Choose a color scheme that emphasizes one color in addition to green. Make sure that the color looks good with your yard's hardscape — for example, pink flowers are attractive near a red brick walk. And drop in small amounts of different colors as accents. You may have a small garden of blue or purple flowers with highlights of yellow. Hot colors, such as yellow, orange, and red, are strong and work well in a large yard or a faraway bed. Cool colors, such as blue and purple, recede and are best used in a small yard or a close-up bed.

✔ **Order.** Your garden needs dominant features with similar characteristics — plants of like shapes, sizes, textures, or colors — to create a sense of order. One way to achieve order is to mass identical varieties into natural-looking groups. But you also need some variety or accent, which you achieve by adding plants with different characteristics.

✔ **Repetition and rhythm.** In each garden and elsewhere throughout your landscape, repeat the same plants and building materials so that the yard appears to be part of a whole. Repetition gives the garden *rhythm*, which people find comforting and enjoyable.

✔ **Style.** You can choose from a great number of garden styles, including formal with symmetrical and geometric beds and informal with sweeping lines and asymmetrical beds.

Hardscape

Hardscapes solve problems by providing all-weather footing, shade, privacy, or support for climbing plants. Fences, walks, trellises, and arbors are examples of hardscape. You can use fencing of all styles for screening or to separate spaces.

If you're planning to put up a new fence, check with your local municipality or homeowners association. Sometimes rules govern the type and height of fence that you can use. Here's one common-sense rule: Never put a tall fence near the foot of the driveway — it can block your view of oncoming traffic.

Trellises, depending on how they are built, can provide a symbolic doorway to a garden or can be stretched over a sitting area as a symbolic ceiling. Better yet, these structures can support flowering vines or climbing roses, creating a romantic setting in any garden. (See Figure 3-1.) Also see Chapter 13 for the specifics on creating these hardscapes.

Figure 3-1:
Create an entrance to your garden with a vine-covered, arching trellis.

In Chapter 13, you will read more about constructing paths, walkways, steps, and fencing. *Walkways* are more structured than paths and able to bear more traffic. You may want to consider steps where you have a slope or rise to a deck or door. You can use fencing of all styles for screening, to separate spaces. Just remember to choose a style that best fits your landscape aesthetics and the architecture of your house.

Chapter 4
Gardening Tools You Will Need

· ·

In This Chapter

▶ Hand tools: the seven essential ones and five handiest ones

▶ Finding the right lawn mower

▶ Using string trimmers

▶ Tilling soil

▶ Where — and how — to shop for garden tools

· ·

Gardening really doesn't require a shed full of tools. In fact, we recommend starting with just a few essential tools and then building your collection as specific jobs call for more-specialized tools. But having the right tool for the job often makes the difference between a pleasurable and a frustrating experience, or between a job well done or not. That's what this chapter is all about: choosing the right tool for the job.

Hand Tools

To save money over the long haul, buy high-quality, durable tools. Generally, forged-steel tools hold up better than welded types. Relatively new on the market are tools with fiberglass handles, which are stronger than wood. Hardware stores and garden centers offer what you need to get started. Mail-order garden supply catalogs, such as A. M. Leonard, Inc., offer more-specialized tools. (See Appendix C.)

The seven essential tools that every gardener needs . . .

Following is a list of the tools that you absolutely must have:

- ✔ **Garden hose.** Buy a top-quality hose with a lifetime guarantee. It will coil easily, resist kinking, and remain flexible, even in cold weather. Choose one long enough to reach all corners of your garden.

- ✔ **Hand trowel.** A hand trowel is important for transplanting seedlings, scooping soil into containers, and doing close-up weeding jobs. Buy one that fits your hand and is light enough to be comfortable.

- ✔ **Hoe.** Forgo the conventional garden hoe designed to chop at the soil, and buy a scuffle hoe instead. It's easier to use; instead of chopping, you push it along the soil's surface. It's indispensable for weeding on packed, level surfaces such as garden paths. Although scuffle hoes vary in design, all work with a push-pull motion. Some cut and scrape the tops off weeds on both strokes. Our favorite, the *oscillating* or *action* hoe, has a hinged blade that moves back and forth as it cuts.

- ✔ **Lawn rake.** Nothing works better than a bamboo (see Figure 4-1), polypropylene, or metal rake with long, flexible tines for gathering up lawn clippings, leaves, and even small rocks on both paved and natural surfaces.

- ✔ **Pruners.** Once you own a pair of pruners that you can hold comfortably and that produce a clean cut with little effort, you'll find it hard to imagine gardening without them. Pruners cut soft and woody stems up to about $^1/_2$ inch. Use them to clip flowers, harvest vegetables, groom shrubs, and prune trees. (See Chapter 16 for specific recommendations.)

- ✔ **Shovel.** A regular round-nose shovel (see Figure 4-1) is the single most versatile tool you'll own. You need it for digging, turning, and scooping. When used in a chopping motion, the shovel effectively breaks up clods of earth. Choose a length and weight that's comfortable.

- ✔ **Stiff-tined rake.** Start with a *stiff-tined* or *steel bow* rake. (See Figure 4-1.) It's an important tool for spreading and leveling soil and for collecting organic materials. The rake is also a good tool for breaking up small clods of earth. Use both the *tines* (the thin, pointed prongs) and the back edge of the rake for building and smoothing raised garden beds: Keep the tines facing downward when breaking up lumps of soil or collecting stones and keep the flat edge of the head downward when leveling.

. . . And five more tools to buy

After you've accumulated the seven essential tools — if you still have space in your shed or garage — here's what to buy next. While not as essential as the previous seven, these all-purpose tools are most useful to most gardeners. (Special tools for garden construction are described in Chapter 13.) Again, which tools to own depends entirely upon the jobs that you're trying to accomplish. If, for example, you've just moved into a home with a garden that includes massive, overgrown shrubs, buy loppers before a trowel.

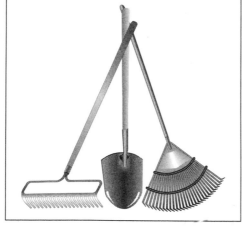

Figure 4-1:
Steel bow rake, for leveling soil; round-nose shovel, for digging; and bamboo lawn rake, for raking leaves.

✔ **Garden cart.** A lightweight, well-balanced cart that maneuvers easily makes daunting tasks a cinch. With a cart, a gardener can easily haul big, heavy loads of soil, compost, plants, containers, or wood with little effort. (See Figure 4-2.)

✔ **Gardening gloves.** Sooner or later, you'll wish you had a good pair of gloves. Gloves should fit well and be thick enough to protect your hands, yet not so clunky that you can't maneuver small objects. Cloth gloves with leather reinforcement generally hold up well to garden tasks. Gloves with cuffs help protect your wrists from branches and thorns.

✔ **Lopping shears.** When you get serious about pruning trees and shrubs, loppers are a must. They cut easily through branches an inch or more in diameter. (See Chapter 16 for specific recommendations.)

✔ **Tape measure.** A metal tape measure is essential for laying out garden beds and helpful in spacing plants. When staking out an entire landscape, a 100-foot length helps you measure precisely.

✔ **Water wand.** This hose-end attachment is great for watering containers, garden seedlings, and seedbeds. Choose one with a shut-off valve. It should provide a full but gentle flow that won't wash away soil and seeds.

More Power

Which is it for you: "That cursed internal combustion contraption!" or "Praise be the internal combustion!" Does anyone really *need* power equipment of some kind? In our experience, most gardeners make use of at least one of these tools from time to time.

Figure 4-2:
Garden
carts are
handy tools
for moving
heavy loads.

Cutting grass

Lawns may not be the most politically correct corner of the garden, but most of us have one — or wish we did. (For more about lawn care, see Chapter 17.)

One of the reasons that people get fed up with lawns is that lawns require this regular, monotonous maintenance called *cutting the grass,* which, for some of you, may conjure up memories of noisy, dirty, hard-to-start engines. We're here to tell you that times have changed! You have so many more choices now that you're more likely to find the mower that's right for you. New lawn mowers are quieter, better working, less polluting, and safer to use.

Pick a lawn mower according to the size of your lawn, the type of grass, your tolerance (or not) of noise, and your desire for exercise. Allow about an hour to mow 2,500 square feet of grass with a 20-inch-wide rotary mower. The wider the mower or the faster it moves, the more quickly you can get the job done.

Push-reel mowers

The original teenage nightmare, push-reel mowers have been rediscovered, reinvented, and improved. Guess what? They're good for the environment and for your body, too. Push-reel mowers are quiet and completely nonpolluting. They give your body a workout at least the equivalent of a session with a tread-mill. If your lawn is 1,000 square feet or less and composed mostly of soft grasses such as fescue, Kentucky bluegrass, or ryegrass, this type of mower is a serious option. Most cost around $100, but fancy ones can be twice that.

Power-reel mowers

The power-reel mower is the type of mower that professional gardeners and greenskeepers use. In all cases, the engine drives both the cutting blades and the wheels, but some throw clippings to the front, while others throw to the rear. These mowers are much more expensive ($300 and up), but they are unexcelled at providing a close, even cut, even of dense, thick grasses such as Bermuda grass or zoysia.

Push rotary power mowers

Push rotary power is the type of mower that America uses to cut its grass. You provide the push power, but the engine and the spinning blade do the grass cutting. This type is relatively inexpensive ($200 to $400, depending upon features) and easy to operate. One choice you'll have to make is between *side* or *rear bagging*. Side-baggers are cheaper. They are slightly less convenient (because you can cut close on one side of the mower only) but work just as well.

 Don't buy a push rotary power mower that doesn't include a blade break system, colorfully termed a *deadman switch*. This device makes the spinning blade stop within three seconds after the operator releases a lever on the handle, which makes power mowers more complicated (and expensive) but reduces mower-caused injuries.

Self-propelled and mulching rotary mowers

Self-propelled and mulching rotary mowers are basically the same as the push rotary power mower but with added features. Naturally, the price is steeper — $500 to $700, usually. The *self-propelled* feature is plain enough: The engine is linked by pulleys and gears to the front wheels. The mulching concept is a bit more involved: The mower is basically the same, but the cutting blade and deck are redesigned to cut and recut the grass and leaves, resulting in smaller pieces, and there's no exit chute on the side or rear (or it's optional).

Mulching mowers chop grass blades small enough that the grass filters back down into the lawn. As the cut blades decompose, they release nutrients to the growing lawn, and you don't have to bag and send clippings to the landfill.

Electric rotary mowers

We think that electric rotary mowers are great, especially if you live next to a hospital or absolutely refuse to deal with anything gasoline powered. You turn a switch, and the blade spins. They're virtually silent, too — all you hear is the low hum of the spinning blade. Downsides: A long cord, usually of a maximum length, restricts your movements (and how much lawn you can cut); the umbilical-free, battery-powered kinds are a bit heavy and pricy. A variety of solar-powered mowers is available now, but these are expensive and not practical in many situations.

Lawn mowers that you can sit on

This category is broad. The simplest are correctly called *riding mowers*. This is the type that does nothing but cut grass. Typically, the engine is in the rear, the mowing deck out in front, and you sit somewhere in between. The mowing deck is 30 to 42 inches wide, and engines are 8 to 13 horsepower. Prices range from $700 to $1,000.

Lawn and garden tractors

Lawn and garden tractors are somewhat larger than sit-down lawn mowers and look a bit more like real farm tractors. You sit and look out over a hood that covers the engine, and the mowing deck is right below your chair. Most have a channel steel frame and front axle, and most have 12 to 18 horsepower. They cut 38 to 48 inches of grass in one swipe. Some models take attachments such as tillers and snowblowers. Some even offer cruise control! The lawn and garden tractor is the type for a homeowner with a large property. Cost? Expect to pay anywhere from $1,000 to $4,000.

Don't buy more horsepower than you need. Lawn and garden tractors with 14 horsepower are enough to cut several acres of grass and occasionally till the soil.

Garden tractors

Garden tractors are actual scaled-down versions of farm tractors. Equally heavy-duty as their full-size brethren, their frames are heavy, 10-gauge steel, and both front and rear axles are cast iron. They use anywhere from 12 to 20 horsepower and cut 38 to 60 inches of grass at once. The benefit of a garden tractor over a lawn tractor is that the garden tractor can accept a variety of attachments, such as rototillers, clippers, and snowblowers. A good tool for weekend farmers who need lots of chores done — expect to pay at least $3,000 and as much as $10,000.

String trimmers

The string trimmer is (after lawn mowers) the most widely used power tool. Some are electric (power cord or battery), and some are gas powered. Most of the gas-powered kinds utilize two-stroke engines. This type of engine requires that you mix special oil into the gasoline; it's also louder in operation. One company, Ryobi, makes a trimmer with a four-cycle engine. It's much quieter and less polluting.

Choose a trimmer with an automatic or semiautomatic "feed" system for the nylon whip. Some trimmers force you to stop the engine and lengthen the whip by hand every time it's worn down.

If you don't like to fuss with the pull-start cords on small engines, look for the Homelite *trigger start* trimmer — a gas-powered trimmer that starts with a pull on a switch.

Electric trimmers

Electric trimmers with power cords are the cheapest kind. They allow you to work 50 to 100 feet from an outlet, they're lightweight, and they're quiet. Prices start at about $50. Models powered by batteries allow you to roam more freely but limit you to about 45 minutes of continuous trimming. They cost a bit more, about $100.

Gasoline-powered trimmers

Trimmers with gas power work roughly the same as the electric models, but they give you more power, need more maintenance, make more noise, and let you do more work in less time.

Even though the spinning whip of cord is safer than a whirling blade, it can damage the bark of young trees and shrubs. If you use this type of trimmer around trees, protect the lower trunk with a heavy plastic collar (available at garden centers).

Tilling soil

A typical rotary tiller is a good-size machine. Weight begins at about 70 pounds and goes up to a few hundred. Engine horsepower begins at 3, but some have 8 or more. The cost begins at around $500 and ranges upward to $1,600. As big and heavy as they are, rotary tillers are big time savers. If you regularly garden a quarter-acre or more of vegetables, a rotary tiller is an essential investment.

A tiller consists of an engine providing the power to a transmission that channels the power to the wheels and the tiller. Tillers with the tines in front don't have powered wheels, so the transmission only has to drive the tiller.

All rotary tillers are categorized as either *front tine* or *rear tine*. Front-tine rotary tillers are lighter in weight and cheaper; consider them medium duty. If the soil you're tilling is relatively loose, these are very effective. It's different if the soil is compacted or rocky — because the tiller is pulled forward by the tines, if the tines connect with a big stone or root, the machine lurches forward. The other downside of front-tine tillers is that you must walk directly behind them, through the freshly fluffed soil.

Heavy-duty tillers have the engine in front and the tines in the rear. Expert gardeners prefer rear-tine tillers because they're much easier and less jarring to operate (even though heavier), because the tines dig down into the soil rather than force the machine to lurch forward, and because the operator doesn't need to walk through freshly tilled soil.

As the tines turn

Most tines rotate in the direction of travel. The resistance of the soil on the blades causes the tiller to drive itself forward. You need to restrain this driving force to ensure even tilling of the soil.

Tillers offer several kinds of tines, with many different functions. By far the most common kind of tine is the *bolo* tine, which is shaped like an *L* and is sharpened on the cutting edge. The bottom of the *L* is twisted slightly so that the soil is lifted up and away as the tine turns. Some tines are further bent so that they can enter the soil more easily.

The higher the tine speed, the more easily and more finely you prepare the seedbed. A higher tine speed is also necessary to adequately chop up crop residues or compost and incorporate them into the soil. The common tine speed for front-tine tillers is 100 to 175 RPMs. Commercial tillers often allow you to vary the tine speed for different uses. Tine speed is also affected by the throttle setting.

Mini-tillers

Also referred to as *lightweight tiller/cultivators, hand-held tiller/cultivators,* and *power cultivators,* mini-tillers are 20- to 30-pound, gasoline-powered (usually two-cycle) machines. In most designs, the horizontally mounted engine (1 to 1$^1/_2$ horsepower) sits directly above the tines. Connected to this engine and tine unit are handlebars with a lever for throttle control and an on/off switch. The cost of mini-tillers varies with the number of attachments you buy, but expect to pay around $300.

Mini-tiller tines are made of sharper-edged spring steel and spin faster than the heavier tines of large tillers. The patented Mantis tines are star-shaped, so they tend to slice into the soil. The others have conventional, L-shaped tines that dig like a hoe.

On small patches of ground that are in good condition, hand tools are probably just as quick and efficient. Additionally, hand tools are not as damaging to soil structure as tillers, which tend to pulverize particles more than plants need for good root growth. Tillers of any kind may create a layer of packed and hardened soil at the bottom of their cultivating depth — the so-called plow sole. But on larger stretches of relatively stone-free ground, the mini-tillers can be worthwhile. They dig about twice as fast as a person skillful with a fork and spade and require much less bending than working the soil with hand tools does.

Forward motion is controlled by the tines, and they are activated by an automatic clutch. A lever on either the right or left handlebar controls engine speed. At idle, the tines don't move. As you squeeze the lever, the engine speeds up, and the tines engage.

Don't carry the machine while the engine is running.

Tines work soil to a depth of 3 to 10 inches. An average working depth after two passes through an average soil is probably about 6 inches, but by working the machine back and forth, you make it dig deeper. Some gardeners use mini-tillers for digging trenches and planting holes for trees.

Jobs mini-tillers do well

Here's what you should use a mini-tiller for:

- ✔ Tilling loamy, stone-free soil
- ✔ Tilling soil in small or raised beds
- ✔ Cultivating compacted, weedy soil between rows of vegetables
- ✔ Cultivating soil in narrow, tight locations
- ✔ Weeding in compacted walkways
- ✔ Mixing compost and amendments into planting beds
- ✔ Digging planting holes for trees, shrubs, and perennials

Where to Shop for Garden Tools

All plants are not created equal, nor are tools, potting mixes, and most gardening implements. So in order to get what you want for your garden — the best quality, a true bargain, or something really strange (like an electric bulb-planting drill) — you need to know where to shop.

By the way, you can order an electric bulb-planting drill from Park Seed Co. (See Appendix C for the address.)

Nurseries

In addition to plants and information, larger nurseries offer seeds, bulbs, soil amendments, bark mulches, containers, fertilizers, pesticides, tools, irrigation supplies, and even garden ornaments.

Other sources for tools and garden supplies

Shop at hardware stores and home-building centers for garden tools. Also look to these places for materials to build garden structures, such as lumber, nails, and twine for trellises.

Farm and feed stores are found in rural areas. These stores are a great source for seeds, tools, soil amendments, fertilizers, pesticides, fencing, and irrigation supplies.

If you know a quality product by brand name or know how to judge the quality of a product, then you are well positioned to find a true bargain at a discount store. But just because something is cheap doesn't mean it's a bargain. Heed this warning: Know what you're paying for.

Shopping by mail greatly broadens your choice of seeds, plants, tools, and supplies. However, besides having to wait for delivery, the downside of shopping by mail is not being able to see what you're buying. That's why it's especially important to know that your sources, especially nurseries, are reliable. Appendix C lists some reliable mail-order catalogs. Look for the Source icon throughout this book for more.

Part II
Which Plants for You?

In this part . . .

Plants are what your garden's really all about, so we devoted an entire section to them. To begin, you need a sense of what plants grow where, and why (as well as why not). So we explain the idea behind "plant hardiness zones" and show you how to figure out the zone you live in.

Once you're "zoned," you can start to choose actual plants. Because you can't grow *all* of them, we selected some of our favorites to get you growing.

Chapter 5
Which Plant Where?

In This Chapter

▶ Which plants are best for your garden?

▶ Don't gamble: check your region's climate

▶ North American Zone Map

▶ Western European Zone Map

▶ Garden hardiness around the world

▶ Using native plants

▶ Adjusting sun and shade plants

*L*ike other living things, plants have certain requirements for good health. For example, plants require the right amounts of sunlight, moisture, and nutrients. Plants also require an equitable range of temperatures — temperatures that are neither too hot nor too cold.

When selecting plants, you can meet plant requirements in one of two ways. The first way involves picking out your favorite plants and then doing your best to alter the growing conditions at the planting site to meet their needs. You can alter the growing conditions by adding sprinkler irrigation, incorporating fertilizer, hauling in fresh topsoil, pruning some trees, or covering plants with blankets in winter. But this first way is the backward approach.

A better way to make sure that plants grow well — and need less care in the process — is to learn about the conditions at the planting site first and then choose plants that grow under the conditions found at the planting site. Oh, sure, some of the plants that you want to put in are accustomed to different conditions than are found in your yard, and those plants are going to need some attention to stay happy. But the better you match plants and planting site, the longer the plants will live, the better the plants will look, and the less work (watering, pruning, fertilizing, and controlling pests) you'll have to do to care for them.

Putting Plants in Their Place

Matching a plant to a planting site needs to be done on both a large and a small scale. On a large scale, a plant needs to be adapted to the general climate of the area in which it lives. (Can the plant withstand winter's low temperatures and summer's high temperatures? Is the annual rainfall enough to keep the plant alive, or will it need supplemental irrigation?)

On a smaller scale, can the plant grow well in the localized climate of your yard or the planting site? Smaller climates, called *microclimates*, can be quite a bit different from the overall climate of your area. For example, because of the shadows cast by your house, the northern side of your house is cooler and shadier than its southern side. Or a planting site located beside a white, west-facing wall can be several degrees warmer than the rest of the yard because of the heat reflected by the wall.

Getting Zoned

All plants have a certain tolerance to cold temperatures. Below these temperatures, plant tissues are damaged or destroyed. If cold temperatures are prolonged, plants may die. The ability of a plant to withstand a certain minimum temperature is called its *hardiness*. Hardiness can vary depending on growing conditions, so the hardiness numbers are not always precise, but they are still very useful.

In 1990, the U.S. Department of Agriculture published a zone map that covers all of North America, Alaska, and Hawaii. Based on *average* winter minimum temperatures collected from 125,000 weather stations, the continent is divided into 11 zones. The warmest, zone 11, has an average winter minimum above 40°F. Each succeeding zone down to zone 1 averages 10° colder. Zones 1 through 10 are further divided into "a" and "b" regions in order to distinguish zones where average winter minimum temperatures differ by 5°.

In its original 4'×4' published format, the 1990 USDA Zone Map shows considerable detail when compared with earlier versions of the map. But any attempt to divide all of North America into zones is bound to have limitations. The 1990 USDA Zone Map is shown in Figure 5-1 (Canada) and Figure 5-3 (United States and Alaska). Despite their limitations, zone systems based upon average minimum temperatures have also been developed for Western Europe (see Figure 5-2), South Africa, Australia, New Zealand, Japan, and China.

Plants mentioned in *Gardening For Dummies* (and those plants sold in most nurseries) are identified by zone according to the lowest winter temperatures that they can withstand. For example, a tree that is recommended as being hardy to USDA zone 5 indicates that the tree can be reliably grown in areas where temperatures do not fall below -20°F. (These areas include zones 5a through 11.)

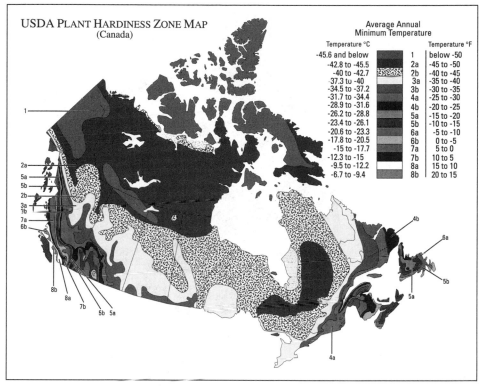

Figure 5-1: Plant hardiness zones for Canada.

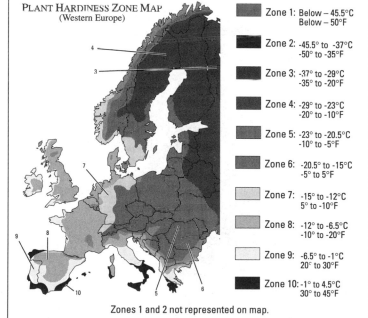

Figure 5-2: Plant hardiness zones for Western Europe.

USDA Plant Hardiness Zone Map

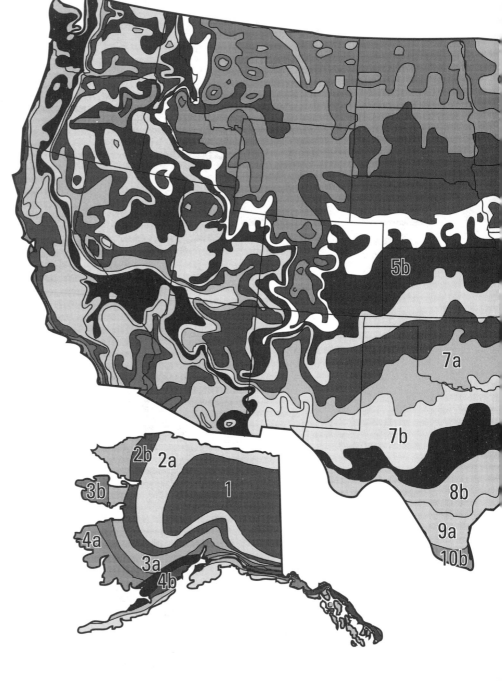

Figure 5-3:
Plant hardiness zones for the United States. Map shows the extreme low temperatures you can expect in an average winter. Map developed by the USDA in 1990.

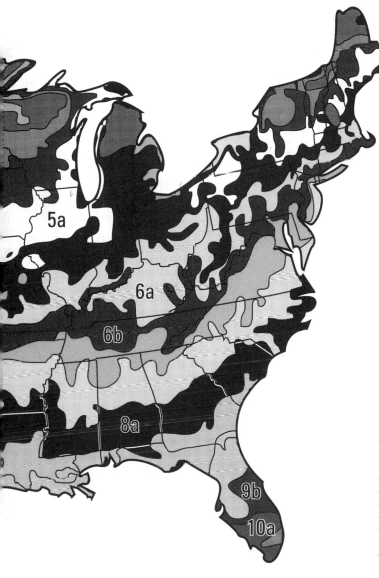

Average Annual Minimum Temperature

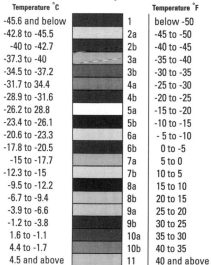

Temperature °C			Temperature °F
-45.6 and below		1	below -50
-42.8 to -45.5		2a	-45 to -50
-40 to -42.7		2b	-40 to -45
-37.3 to -40		3a	-35 to -40
-34.5 to -37.2		3b	-30 to -35
-31.7 to 34.4		4a	-25 to -30
-28.9 to -31.6		4b	-20 to -25
-26.2 to 28.8		5a	-15 to -20
-23.4 to -26.1		5b	-10 to -15
-20.6 to -23.3		6a	- 5 to -10
-17.8 to -20.5		6b	0 to -5
-15 to -17.7		7a	5 to 0
-12.3 to -15		7b	10 to 5
-9.5 to -12.2		8a	15 to 10
-6.7 to -9.4		8b	20 to 15
-3.9 to -6.6		9a	25 to 20
-1.2 to -3.8		9b	30 to 25
1.6 to -1.1		10a	35 to 30
4.4 to -1.7		10b	40 to 35
4.5 and above		11	40 and above

Zone 11 not represented on map.

Unfortunately, minimum temperature is only one of many factors that determine whether a plant will grow in your area. And if you compare climates *within* certain USDA zones, you can see that the USDA Zone Map has its weaknesses. For example, compare zone 9 in California to zone 9 in Florida. Both zone 9 in California and zone 9 in Florida have average winter minimums in the 20° to 30° range, but other differences in their climates are dramatic. Most notably, Florida receives most of its rainfall in summer, while in California rainfall occurs primarily in the winter. This difference in seasonal moisture has a profound effect on the kinds of plants that will grow well.

Widely used in the western United States, "The West's 24 Climate Zones" was developed by Sunset Publishing Corporation and published in their *Sunset Western Garden Book* (Sunset Publishing Corporation, 80 Willow Road, Menlo Park, CA 94105; 800-759-0190). Sunset's climate zones are very specific (Sunset offers 24 zones for the 11 states west of the Rocky Mountains). Sunset's zones also accommodate more of the other factors, such as summer temperatures and humidity, that affect plant growth.

So, although USDA zone recommendations are useful, you need more than USDA zone recommendations in order to choose plants wisely. Luckily, most nurseries carry only plants that perform well in their specific areas, so you can't go too wrong by shopping locally. You can also find more information on plant adaptation in the books listed in Appendix A.

Check your temperature

Plant hardiness in this book is rated according to the 1990 USDA Plant Hardiness Zone Map, a plant map based on average winter minimum temperatures. The minitable in this sidebar indicates extreme winter temperatures (°F/°C) in key world cities, which occur in January in the northern hemisphere and in July in the southern hemisphere. To identify and equate the USDA zone in which you live, match the temperatures shown in the following table to the temperature ranges of the USDA zones. (Also, see Figures 5-1 and 5-3 for North American maps and Figure 5-2 for Western European Zone Map.)

Because USDA zones are based on average minimum temperatures and the following are typical extreme minimums, this table is really only an estimate. Use this table to get an idea of your USDA zone equivalent, but also check with local plant authorities and other kinds of local information.

North America (see Figures 5-1 and 5-3 for minimum temperatures and zone equivalents)

Central and South America	Minimum Temperatures (°F/°C)	USDA Equivalents
Bogotá	40/5	Zone 11
Buenos Aires	22/-6	Zone 9a
Caracas	47/8	Zone 11
Goiás	41/5	Zone 11
Lima	49/10	Zone 11
Rio de Janeiro	52/11	Zone 11

San José	49/10	Zone 11
Santiago	24/-4	Zone 9a
Europe	*Minimum Temperatures (°F/°C)*	*USDA Equivalents*
Athens	24/-4	Zone 9a
Berlin	-6/-21	Zone 6a
Budapest	-9/-23	Zone 6a
London	15/-10	Zone 8b
Madrid	14/-10	Zone 8a
Marseilles	13/-11	Zone 8a
Moscow	-25/-32	Zone 4b
Munich	-20/-30	Zone 5a
Paris	10/-12	Zone 8a
Rome	24/-4	Zone 9a
St. Petersburg	-25/-32	Zone 4b
Stockholm	-19/-29	Zone 5a
Vienna	7/-14	Zone 7b
Warsaw	-20/-30	Zone 5a
Middle East and Africa	*Minimum Temperatures (°F/°C)*	*USDA Equivalents*
Istanbul	18/-8	Zone 8b
Jerusalem	26/-3	Zone 9b
Cairo	35/2	Zone 10b
Riyadh	19/-7	Zone 8b
Nairobi	43/6	Zone 11
Dakar	56/13	Zone 11
Lagos	63/17	Zone 11
Kinshasa	58/15	Zone 11
Pretoria	24/-4	Zone 9a
Cape Town	28/-2	Zone 9b
Tehran	-5/-20	Zone 6b
Karachi	40/4	Zone 11
Far East	*Minimum Temperatures (°F/°C)*	*USDA Equivalents*
Bangkok	55/13	Zone 11
Beijing	-9/-23	Zone 6a
Brisbane	36/2	Zone 10b
Calcutta	44/7	Zone 11
Chongjin	29/-2	Zone 9b
Delhi	31/-1	Zone 10a
Hong Kong	32/0	Zone 10a
Madras	57/14	Zone 11
Manila	58/15	Zone 11
Perth	34/1	Zone 10a
Singapore	68/20	Zone 11
Sydney	36/2	Zone 10b
Tokyo	17/-8	Zone 8b
Vladivostok	-22/-30	Zone 4b
Wellington	29/-2	Zone 9b

What Else Does a Plant Need?

In addition to climate, here are some other factors that you should consider when analyzing planting sites.

Sun or shade

All plants need light to grow properly. However, the amount of light that plants need varies.

Many plants require full sun for at least six to eight hours per day. Plants that don't get enough sunlight become *leggy,* as if stretching out for more light. Plants that don't get enough sunlight also tend to flower poorly and are subject to diseases.

Some plants prefer shady conditions for the entire day (or for at least part of the day). Many different types of shade exist, and each type of shade creates a different microclimate. For example, consider the area on the east side of your house. For at least half a day — in the morning — this area is sunny and warm. In the afternoon, the same area is shady.

The west side of the house is usually just the opposite — shady in the morning but hot and sunny in the afternoon. Heavy, all-day shade is found on the north side of the house, and filtered shade is found under trees. To further confuse the matter, shade can change with the seasons as trees lose their leaves and as the sun moves on the horizon. And in the hottest climates, some normally sun-loving plants prefer at least partial afternoon shade. More information on shade gardening can be found later in this chapter and in the color illustration of a city shade garden later in this book.

Soil and water

The kind of soil in your garden — heavy clay or porous sand, for example — and soil moisture are closely related. The importance of these two factors and the ways in which they affect plant growth and cultural practices are discussed at greater length in Chapters 14 and 16. Just remember plants that are well-adapted to almost every situation are available. Wet, soggy clay soil is very difficult to correct but, certain plants can grow (and even thrive) under those conditions. Choosing plants to fit existing soil conditions is usually a great deal easier than altering the soil conditions themselves.

Room to grow

Planting too close together is one of the most common mistakes gardeners (even experienced ones) make. When you plant, space your plants based upon the size that they may be at maturity. Give them room to grow and develop fully so that they can attain their true character. Giving plants an appropriate amount of space helps to ensure that you'll have healthy plants (and it saves you a great deal of pruning).

Using Native Plants

Native plants are plants that are found naturally in a specific region or locality. Over hundreds (probably thousands) of years, these plants have become superbly adapted to the exact conditions of the areas to which they are native. In those areas or in similar areas, native plants grow with health and vigor and without the help of gardeners. These factors can make native plants very valuable as landscape plants.

Native plants are becoming very popular in many areas, particularly in arid regions of the western United States where thirsty non-native plants are impractical because they use too much of a precious resource — water. Local native plants can get by on what nature provides. And conserving natural resources always makes sense.

Using native plants also helps the native fauna — the birds, butterflies, squirrels, and other local animals that depend upon native plants for food and shelter.

Many retail nurseries can help you select native plants. Some mail-order catalogs also specialize in native plants, especially wildflowers. (See Appendix C.)

Shady Business

On sultry summer afternoons, a cool, refreshing shade garden has a welcoming ambience that's hard to resist. And it's possible, with just a little green-thumb finesse, to turn a dull, shady corner into a tranquil summer haven.

Here's one very important rule for gardening in the shade: Put *shade-loving* plants in the shade. Sun-worshipping plants just won't make it. (It's a bit like forcing a round peg into a square hole: easy enough to do, but not a good fit.) Don't fret. Hundreds of incredible shade-loving plants (some with showy flowers and others with attractive foliage and form) are available to choose from. Among the shade-loving plants are annuals, perennials, shrubs, vines, and trees.

To make matters just a little complicated, a plant's shade tolerance varies both by region and by specific garden conditions. For example, many plants that need full sun in cool northern climates (or in coastal areas) tolerate (or actually require) some afternoon shade when they are grown in warm southern climates.

Check a reliable nursery or garden center in your area to see which shade plants can work best for you. In better nurseries, shade plants are often displayed together.

Also, peruse mail-order catalogs for shade plants. Most catalogs note plants' light requirements. Catalogs that specialize in shade plants, such as the catalog from Shady Oaks Nursery (listed in Appendix C), actually have a rating system that describes, in detail, just how much shade a plant can tolerate. Some suggestions to get you started are listed below.

Stuck between a rock and shady place?

We've all been counseled, at one time or another, on turning challenges into opportunities. Here's another chance: If you have a real shady nook with soil that feels like modeling clay — and your nook's best view features your neighbor's garbage cans — why not turn this problem site into a private retreat?

Give up on elaborate planting schemes. Instead, cover the ground with an attractive stone mulch or pavers.

1. **Use a light-colored material to brighten up the place.**
2. **Put up a fence for quick screening.**
3. **Soften the fence with a shade-tolerant vine like star jasmine (in warm climates) or wisteria (in colder regions).**

   Consider shade plants, such as English ivy or pachysandra, as ground cover. (See Chapter 12.)
4. **Add the coziest garden furniture that you can afford. (Start with a recliner.)**
5. **Accent the nook with containers overflowing with shade-thriving annuals.**
6. **Install a water feature to deliver soothing sounds.**
7. **Finally, grab a book and a glass of ice tea (or whatever). Sweet dreams!**

Made in the shade

Here's a list of plants that shun the sun. USDA hardiness zones are listed to the right of the name; where not listed, plants are hardy in all zones. Actually, some of these plants prefer shade, and others simply tolerate it. For most of the following plants, the light, filtered shade of a high tree limb is ideal.

Fifteen flowering perennials for shady sites

Bear's breech *(Acanthus mollis)*	Zone 6a
Lady's mantle *(Alchemilla mollis)*	Zone 3a
Columbine *(Aquilegia)*	Zone 3a
False spiraea *(Astilbe)*	Zone 4a
Bergenia *(Bergenia crassifolia)*	Zone 4a
Bellflower *(Campanula portenschlagiana)*	Zone 5a
Bleeding heart *(Dicentra spectabilis)*	Zone 3a
Hosta *(Hosta)*	Zone 3a
Siberian iris *(Iris sibirica)*	Zone 4a
Bee balm *(Monarda didyma)*	Zone 4a
Primrose *(Primula)*	Various
Lungwort *(Pulmonaria)*	Zone 3a
Meadow rue *(Thalictrum)*	Zone 5a
Spiderwort *(Tradescantia virginiana)*	Zone 5a
Globeflower *(Trollius)*	Zone 3a

Fourteen annuals for shady sites

These are hardy in all zones during the growing season:

Waxleaf begonia *(Begonia semperflorens-cultorum)*

Amethyst flower *(Browallia)*

Canterbury bells *(Campanula medium)*

Coleus *(Coleus)*

Impatiens *(Impatiens wallerana)*

Lobelia *(Lobelia erinus)*

Monkey flower *(Mimulus hybridus)*

Forget-me-not *(Myosotis sylvatica)*

Nicotiana *(Nicotiana alata)*

Love-in-a-mist *(Nigella damascena)*

Scarlet sage *(Salvia splendens)*

Black-eyed Susan vine *(Thunbergia alata)*

Wishbone flower *(Torenia fourneiri)*

Pansy *(Viola wittrockiana)*

Six evergreen shrubs for shady sites

Andromeda *(Andromeda polifolia)*	Zone 2b
Korean boxwood *(Buxus microphylla koreana)*	Zone 6a
Camellia *(Camellia japonica)*	Zone 8a (with exceptions)
Inkberry *(Ilex glabra)*	Zone 4a
Mountain laurel *(Kalmia latifolia)*	Zone 4a
Rhododendron *(Rhododendron)*	Various

Five deciduous shrubs for shady sites

Allspice *(Calycanthus)*	Zone 4a
Summersweet *(Clethera alnifolia)*	Zone 3a
Red-osier dogwood *(Cornus sericea)*	Zone 2
Smooth hydrangea *(Hydrangea arborescens)*	Zone 3
Japanese snowball *(Viburnum plicatum)*	Zone 5a

It's a Matter of Choice

If you've gotten one thing out of this chapter, we hope that it's this: The key to selecting plants for a healthy, long-lived garden is to choose plants that are well-adapted to the conditions at the planting site. The better you choose well-adapted plants, the better your garden looks and the less care it requires.

To help get you started in the selection process, we describe many of our favorite plants in the following chapters. But you still have to plant these plants in the right spot and care for them properly to get the best results. To help you with that task, we've included a list of good gardening books and magazines in Appendix A.

Chapter 6
Trees

• •

In This Chapter

▶ Choosing the right tree

▶ Seeing what a tree can do for you

▶ Avoiding mistakes with trees

▶ Our favorite trees

• •

o home or neighborhood should be without trees. Trees bring a home into scale with the surrounding landscape and give a neighborhood a sense of place. They provide protection from the elements, buffering strong winds and blocking hot summer sun. In our crowded world, trees can also provide privacy, screening you from neighbors or unpleasant views.

But more than anything else, trees offer beauty. Beauty in flowers held high among the branches, or simply beauty in their canopies in the leafy green canopy. Beauty in colorful berries and seedpods dangling among the limbs. Beauty in dazzling hues created by their autumn leaves. Even beauty in winter, when the texture of their bark and the structure of their branches add strength and permanence to the landscape. Beauty in diversity, too — after all, without trees, where will the birds perch or the squirrels dash?

Choosing the Right Tree

People who know trees like to say that there is no perfect tree, and they're right. You have so many trees to choose from that many of them can probably do the job for you. But as with people, every tree's personality has its good and bad aspects. Before you plant one, you need to learn everything you can about the tree, both the good and the bad. Most trees get big and live a long time (possibly longer than you), so if you make a mistake and plant the wrong one in the wrong place, it may be very costly to remove or replace. Removing it may even be dangerous to people and property.

So get to know the tree before you commit to it.

✔ How fast does it grow?

✔ How tall and wide will it get?

✔ Is it adapted to your climate and the sun, soil, and water conditions at the proposed planting site?

✔ Does it have any common problems — invasive roots, weak limbs, insects, diseases?

✔ Does it need any special maintenance, such as pruning?

✔ How messy is it? Does it drop excessive amounts of flowers, fruits, or leaves?

A local nursery is a good place to find out how a tree performs in your area; so are city or county parks departments. Extension offices can help you with information about trees, and parks and university campuses often have fine plantings to study. Botanical gardens and arboretums are especially good places to observe a wide variety of trees.

Contact your city or county planning or parks department before planting trees along streets. The officials there may have a list of suitable street trees. If you plant something not on their list, they may make you remove it.

To help get trees planted in the public areas of your community or in forests damaged by fire or abuse, contact Global ReLeaf, a campaign of *American Forests*. For $10, this organization will plant ten trees in your name and return a personalized certificate; call 800-873-5323 to order. For more information, write P.O. Box 2000, Washington, DC, or call 202-667-3300.

Getting Cool with Trees

In our fast-paced world of concrete, asphalt, and hazy sky, trees are the great equalizers. They shade our streets and cool our cities and neighborhoods, they absorb dust and air pollution, and their roots hold the soil in place and prevent erosion.

You should feel good about planting a tree. The following sections show you how to maximize trees' effectiveness and make them particularly hardworking.

Keep your cool

Providing cooling shade is one of a tree's greatest assets, especially in regions where summers are hot and dry. If you plant *deciduous* trees on the warmest side of your house (usually the south or west side, but the east side can also be warm), the shade that they provide keeps your house cooler in summer and reduces your air-conditioning expenses. The best shade trees spread wide and tall enough to shade a one- or two-storied home.

Deciduous trees drop all their leaves in autumn (or, sometimes, in some other season) and so are leafless for a period of time.

Of course, you don't have to worry about overcooling in winter: Trees lose their leaves — right when you need them to — so the warm sun is able to get through, thus reducing heating costs.

Lower your heating bills

You can save energy by planting trees as windbreaks. Planted close together and at right angles to prevailing wind, upright, dense-growing trees can reduce the chilling effects of winter winds and lower heating bills. (Energy conservation aside, planting trees is just a good way to create a comfortable and inviting place in the garden.)

Make you look marvelous

Once you decide on the kind of tree that you need in terms of size, shape, and adaptation, you have a wealth of ornamental characteristics to choose from. Here are some points to consider:

- ✔ **Seasonal color.** Many trees, including flowering fruit trees, bloom on bare branches in early spring. Others bloom later in spring, and some, like crape myrtles, in midsummer. And you can choose almost any color.

  With trees such as liquidambars, stunning autumn color is possible even in warm-winter climates. And these trees offer a whole palette of colors to choose from. (See Figure 6-1.)

- ✔ **Colorful fruit.** Trees such as crab apples and hawthorns follow their blooms with colorful fruit, which can (if the birds don't eat it) hang on the tree into winter after the leaves have fallen.

  Don't overlook trees that produce edible fruit when you're making your choices. Many fruit and nut trees are exceptional ornamentals and have the added bonus of bringing food to the table.

- ✔ **Attractive bark.** The white bark of birch trees is familiar to most people, but many other trees have handsome peeling or colorful bark.

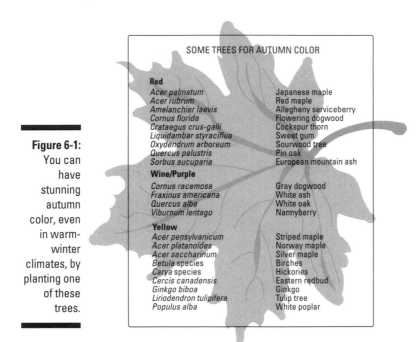

SOME TREES FOR AUTUMN COLOR

Red

Acer palmatum	Japanese maple
Acer rubrum	Red maple
Amelanchier laevis	Allegheny serviceberry
Cornus florida	Flowering dogwood
Crataegus crus-galli	Cockspur thorn
Liquidambar styraciflua	Sweet gum
Oxydendrum arboreum	Sourwood tree
Quercus palustris	Pin oak
Sorbus aucuparia	European mountain ash

Wine/Purple

Cornus racemosa	Gray dogwood
Fraxinus americana	White ash
Quercus alba	White oak
Viburnum lentago	Nannyberry

Yellow

Acer pensylvanicum	Striped maple
Acer platanoides	Norway maple
Acer saccharinum	Silver maple
Betula species	Birches
Carya species	Hickories
Cercis canadensis	Eastern redbud
Ginkgo biboa	Ginkgo
Liriodendron tulipifera	Tulip tree
Populus alba	White poplar

Figure 6-1:
You can have stunning autumn color, even in warm-winter climates, by planting one of these trees.

Don't Try This at Home

The following sections point out some things that you should *not* do when planting a tree, for practical and aesthetic reasons. (See Chapter 15 for more about planting trees.)

- ✔ **Planting too close to buildings.** Even smaller trees should be planted at least 5 to 10 feet away from the side of a house or building. Larger trees should be even farther away. Otherwise, the trees don't have room to spread and develop their natural shape. Also, aggressive roots can damage the foundation; falling limbs can damage the house.

- ✔ **Planting a tree that's too big at maturity.** Some trees can get huge — more than 100 feet tall and almost as wide. These belong in parks and open spaces where they can spread out. But even smaller trees can be too big for a planting site, eventually crowding houses or shading an entire yard. For example, horse chestnut and weeping willow will overwhelm a small garden in only a few years. Choose something that's in scale with your house and won't become overcrowded and cramped-looking at maturity. See Figure 6-2 for an illustration of how big some trees get at maturity.

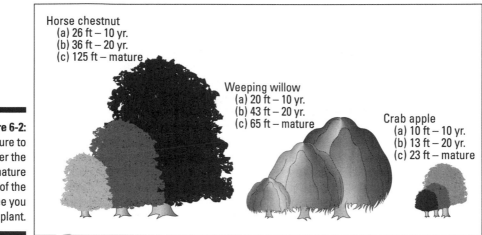

Horse chestnut
(a) 26 ft – 10 yr.
(b) 36 ft – 20 yr.
(c) 125 ft – mature

Weeping willow
(a) 20 ft – 10 yr.
(b) 43 ft – 20 yr.
(c) 65 ft – mature

Crab apple
(a) 10 ft – 10 yr.
(b) 13 ft – 20 yr.
(c) 23 ft – mature

Figure 6-2:
Be sure to consider the mature height of the tree you plant.

Don't plant trees where they'll grow into power lines or utilities. Pruning such trees is dangerous and costly and results in misshapen trees. And fallen limbs may cause power outages. Also, don't plant a big tree in a small yard. Not only will it look bad, but branches overhanging the house and walkways can be hazardous.

✔ **Planting too close to paving.** Some trees are notorious for having shallow roots that, as they grow, buckle sidewalks and raise patios. Actually, almost any tree, especially larger species, will cause problems if planted too close to paving. Leave at least 3 or 4 feet between the trunk and the paving. If you live where trees require watering, apply water slowly and for long periods so it can soak deeply into the soil. This practice encourages roots to grow deep and not near the surface.

✔ **Planting a messy tree in the wrong place.** All trees shed some leaves at one time or another, but certain species are messier than others. Don't plant trees that drop wet fruit or excessive flowers near patios or sidewalks. They will not only make a mess but can also make the surface slippery, causing a passerby to fall.

✔ **Planting too many fast-growing trees.** Fast-growing trees are valuable for providing quick shade, but they are often also weak-wooded and short-lived. Consider planting a mixture of slow- and fast-growing types and then removing the less desirable trees when the slower ones reach functional size.

Our Favorite Trees

As we've said, you have many good trees to choose from. We divided the following lists of trees into two main groups: *deciduous* and *ever-green*. Evergreen trees include both conifers, such as pine and fir, and broadleaf evergreens, such as the Southern magnolia (see Figure 6-3 later in chapter). To make your final choice, you'll need more information than we can provide here — see Appendix A for gardening books that discuss trees or consult the experts at nurseries that specialize in trees. (See Appendix C.)

Unlike *deciduous* trees, *evergreen* trees retain their leaves for more than one growing season.

To learn what zone you live in and how to choose the right plant, see Chapter 5.

Here's our list of favorite deciduous trees.

- ✔ **Maples.** *Acer* species. The maples are a large group that includes many trees known primarily for their wonderful autumn color. Most are hardy to at least zone 5a (–20°F). The sugar and Norway maples (*A. saccharum* and *A. platanoides*) are hardy to zone 3a (–40°F).

  Most maples perform poorly in areas with very mild winters or hot, dry summers, including large, upright species like the red maple, *A. rubrum,* which can reach up to 50 feet high, and some very useful smaller types, like the spreading Japanese maple, *A. palmatum.*

  The Japanese maple is one of the most popular small trees (ranging from 5 to 25 feet high, depending on the variety). It comes in dramatic weeping forms with finely cut leaves and bright autumn color, mostly in shades of red, orange, and yellow. Some varieties, like 'Bloodgood', have purplish leaves the entire growing season. In hot, dry-summer areas, Japanese maples are best planted in partial shade.

- ✔ **European white birch.** *Betula pendula.* Loved for its papery white bark, multiple trunks, and yellow autumn color. Hardy to zone 3a (–40°F) but not well adapted to areas with hot, dry summers or to areas where birch borers are prevalent. Call your Extension office or local nursery to find out about birch borers.

- ✔ **Redbuds.** *Cercis* species. Most popular is the eastern redbud, *C. canadensis,* which reaches 20 to 30 feet high and spreads almost as wide. It is hardy to zone 4a (–30°F). 'Alba' has white flowers; 'Forest Pansy' has maroon foliage.

  The western redbud, *C. occidentalis,* is a multitrunked, small (12 to 15 feet), drought-tolerant tree particularly well adapted to dry-summer areas. It is hardy to zone 8a (10°F).

GOOD ADVICE

Choosing a healthy tree at the nursery

Here are some tips for buying a healthy tree:

✓ Avoid trees that have been in a nursery container too long or are unhealthy and growing poorly — they'll probably be disappointing once in the ground.

Examine the top of the rootball. Avoid specimens that have large, circling roots near the surface — that's a sure sign that the tree has been in the container too long.

✓ Avoid trees that are the smallest or largest of a group. Select ones that are well proportioned.

✓ Select trees that can stand on their own without being tightly tied to a stake (tightly tied stakes can be like crutches, preventing a tree from developing a strong trunk).

✓ Ideally, pick a tree whose trunk is evenly tapered from bottom to top.

✓ Look for healthy, even-colored foliage.

✓ Pick a tree that's free of insects and disease. (See Chapter 18 for more about common pests and diseases.)

✓ **Flowering dogwood.** *Cornus florida.* Key attributes are deep-red autumn color and large white or pink midspring flowers followed by bright-red fruit. A fine small (20 to 30 feet) tree. Hardy to zone 5a (–20°F). Not well adapted to hot, dry climates but can often be grown successfully in partial shade. Anthracnose and borers can be serious problems. Hybrids 'Aurora', 'Galaxy', 'Constellation', and 'Stellar Pink' are less prone to anthracnose disease.

✓ **Hawthorns.** *Crataegus* species. These small trees (most are 20 to 25 feet high) offer a long season of color: white, pink, or red flowers in midspring, bright-orange-to-red berries in autumn and winter, and usually orange-to-red autumn leaf color. Most are hardy to at least zone 5a (–20°F). Fireblight can be a serious problem.

✓ **Russian olive.** *Elaeagnus angustifolia.* Tough, single-trunked or multi-trunked tree with narrow, silvery leaves. Fragrant — but not showy — spring flowers. Small, yellow fruit. Excellent hedge or screen in difficult situations. Grows 30 to 35 feet. Hardy to zone 2a (–50°F).

✓ **Ash.** *Fraxinus* species. Mostly large, spreading-to-upright trees, many reaching well over 50 feet high, with divided leaves. They're good, fast-growing, tough shade trees able to thrive under a variety of conditions. Most are hardy to at least zone 4a (–30°F). Many have excellent autumn color. Anthracnose and borers can be problems.

Our favorite ash is the Raywood ash, *Fraxinus oxycarpa* 'Raywood'. It is a full-size (30 to 40 feet) but not huge tree, and its leaves turn a striking purple color in autumn.

✔ **Crape myrtle.** *Lagerstroemia indica*. Beautiful, summer-blooming, small trees (usually 10 to 20 feet high but can also be grown as a multitrunked shrub), hardy to zone 7a (0°F). Flowers are huge, crinkly, and crapelike, in shades of white, pink, red, and purple. Crape myrtles also have shiny, peeling brown bark and orange-red autumn color. Grow best in areas with hot, dry summers. Elsewhere, plant mildew-resistant varieties, which usually have Native American names, such as 'Cherokee' and 'Catawba'.

✔ **Liquidambar.** *Liquidambar styraciflua*. Tall (40 to 50 feet and higher), narrowly upright trees prized for their bright autumn colors, in shades of yellow, orange, red, and purple. Some are multicolored. Named varieties differ in autumn colors. They also have interesting seedpods, which can be messy. Hardy to zone 5a (–20°F).

✔ **Magnolia.** *Magnolia* species. The deciduous magnolias bloom stunningly on bare branches in early spring. Flowers are huge, often more than 10 inches across, and come in shades of white, pink, and purple. Some are bicolored. Leaves are large and leathery. Trees usually grow 15 to 25 feet high, are often multitrunked, and are hardy to at least zone 6a (–10°F). One of the best is the saucer magnolia, *M. soulangiana*, which bears large, cup-shaped flowers, usually white on the inside, purplish on the outside.

✔ **Flowering crab apples.** *Malus* species. Crab apples differ from apples in that they have fruit less than 2 inches in diameter. You have many species and varieties to choose from, ranging in tree size and shape. Spring flowers come in white, pink, or red and are followed by colorful red, orange, or yellow edible fruit that often hangs on the bare branches into winter. Most are hardy to at least zone 5a (–20°F) and grow best where winters are cold. Subject to severe diseases, including fire blight, powdery mildew, and scab. Ask for disease-resistant varieties such as 'Dolga', Japanese flowering crab apple (*M. floribunda*), 'Pink Spires', 'Royalty', Sargent crab apple (*M. sargentii*), 'Snowdrift', and *M. zumi calocarpa*.

✔ **Chinese pistache.** *Pistacia chinensis*. A wonderful, spreading shade tree with stunning yellow, orange, or red autumn color. Grows 30 to 35 feet high, has divided leaves, and is hardy to zone 6a (–10°F). Drought tolerant.

✔ **Flowering fruit.** *Prunus* species. A large family of early-spring-blooming trees that includes flowering cherries and plums. Flowers are usually fragrant and come in shades of white, pink, or red. Most are hardy to at least zone 5a (–20°F) and range in height from 15 to 20 feet. Favorite fruitless types include Kwanzan flowering cherry, *P. serrulata* 'Kwanzan', with drooping clusters of double pink flowers. Another favorite is Krauter's Vesuvius purple-leaf plum, *P. cerasifera* 'Krauter Vesuvius', which has pink flowers and bronzy-purple leaves.

✔ **Aristocrat pear.** *Pyrus calleryana* 'Aristocrat'. Upright oval tree (30 to 40 feet high) with white spring flowers. Shiny green leaves turn bright orange, red to purple in cold-winter climates. Other good varieties include 'Capital', 'Cleveland Select', 'Earlyred', 'Redspire', and 'Whitehouse'. Hardy to zone 5a (–20°F).

✔ **Oaks.** *Quercus.* A large family of varied trees, many of them very large and suitable for open areas only. Some have good autumn color. Natives — such as the red oak, *Q. rubra,* in the eastern United States, the English oak, *Q. robur,* throughout western Europe, the cork oak, *Q. suber,* of northern Africa and southern Europe — are often good choices. However, many species are widely adapted. (See also Oaks in the following list of evergreen trees.)

We divided evergreens into two groups: *conifers* and *broadleaf* evergreens. (The broadleaf group consists of all the varieties listed after "conifers.")

✔ **Conifers.** The pines, junipers, spruces, firs, hemlocks, and cedars are a diverse group of evergreens, most with needlelike leaves. They are widely grown throughout the world and are especially valuable for year-round greenery and as windbreaks and screens. Most are large trees and need room to grow, but many dwarf forms are available. The overall pyramidal appearance of these varieties is often similar, but foliage density, color, and texture varies. Adaptation also varies. Check with a local nursery for species adapted to your climate.

✔ **Camphor.** *Cinnamomum camphora.* Dense-foliaged tree with light green, aromatic leaves. Grows 40 to 50 feet high with a round head. Hardy to zone 8a (10°F). Withstands drought. Has aggressive surface roots.

✔ **Eucalyptus.** *Eucalyptus* species. Large group of fast-growing, drought-tolerant plants native to Australia. Most valued in dry-summer and mild-winter climates; few can be grown north of zone 8a (10°F). Some are too large for home landscapes. All have heavily aromatic leaves. Many have very colorful flowers and interesting seed capsules. Lower-growing species include Nichol's willow-leaf peppermint, *E. nicholii.* It grows to about 40 feet high, but with languid branchlets that droop like those of a willow tree. Interestingly, leaves are peppermint-scented. Another is the coolibah, *E. microtheca,* also reaching about 40 feet high, with one trunk or several and "willowy" blue foliage.

✔ **Southern magnolia.** *Magnolia grandiflora.* Huge (up to 12 inches across), fragrant, white summer flowers held among bold, deep green leaves make this tree one of the all-time favorite evergreen trees for mild-winter climates. The species gets large, upwards of 80 feet high. Dwarf varieties, such as 'Saint Mary', grow a quarter to a third as high. Hardy to zone 7a (0°F). (See Figure 6-3.)

✔ **Evergreen pear.** *Pyrus kawakamii.* This tree adapts well to home gardens. Its mature height and root system fit well into most home gardens. Leaves are shiny and bright green. White flowers come in spring. Hardy into zone 8a (10°F), but will drop its leaves (which often turn a beautiful red before falling) in coldest areas. Grows 15 to 25 feet high with a wide-spreading canopy.

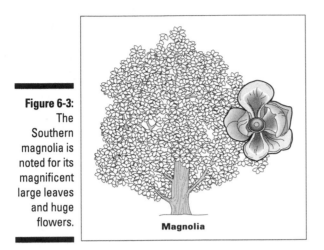

Figure 6-3:
The
Southern
magnolia is
noted for its
magnificent
large leaves
and huge
flowers.

Magnolia

✔ **Oaks.** *Quercus* species. Evergreen oaks come in many species, most of which get quite large and spreading. Widely adapted species include the southern live oak, *Q. virginiana,* which grows 40 to 60 feet high, is wide spreading, and is hardy to zone 7a (0°F). Another one is the holly oak, *Q. ilex,* which reaches 20 to 35 feet high and is hardy to zone 8a (10°F). The coast live oak, *Q. agrifolia,* is a California native oak that's widely planted in that state.

We hope the preceding lists include trees that will further enhance your landscape. If you remember one thing from this chapter, perhaps it should be that few plants can have such a positive effect on your surroundings as trees can.

Chapter 7

Shrubs

- -

In This Chapter

▶ Identifying shrubs

▶ Using shrubs effectively

▶ Our favorites

- -

Both versatile and hardworking, shrubs are the backbone of the landscape. They tie the garden together, bringing unity to all the different elements, from tall trees to low-growing ground covers.

Simply put, shrubs bring together the voices of many different plants and garden features and turn them into the song of a well-planned landscape.

Cozying Up to Shrubs

The term *shrub* covers a wide variety of plants. They can be deciduous or evergreen, and they provide a variety of ornamental qualities, from seasonal flowers to colorful fruit to dazzling autumn foliage color. But equally important, shrubs offer diversity of foliage texture and color, from bold and dramatic to soft and diminutive. As the backbone of the landscape, shrubs are always visible, whether or not they're in bloom. So you should always consider the foliage and form of the plant when selecting shrubs and deciding how to use them.

Technically, a shrub is a woody plant that branches from its base. But that's actually too simple a definition. Shrubs can range from very low-growing, spreading plants that are ideal ground covers (see Chapter 12 for shrubs that are also ground covers) to tall, billowy plants that you can prune into multi-trunked trees. In general, shrubs cover themselves with foliage from top to bottom. Try to pigeonhole all shrubs into an absolute size range, and you'll run into many exceptions, but for our purposes, most shrubs fall into the 1- to 15-foot range.

Choosing and Using Shrubs

Like trees, shrubs are large and long-lived plants, so it is essential to select ones that can thrive in your region and at your specific site. Consider the advice offered in Chapter 5 regarding climate and hardiness and also be mindful of soil types and quantity of light or shade.

No matter what the condition of the soil in your garden, so many shrubs are available that you are sure to find several that will thrive. However, if you make even modest improvements in your soil, such as improving the drainage of heavy soils or the moisture retention of sandy soils, adjusting pH, or increasing the fertility of poor soils, the number of shrubs that will grow well dramatically increases. You can read more about improving your soil in Chapter 14.

As with trees (see Chapter 6), you can buy shrubs in containers, bare-root, or balled-and-burlapped. The vast majority of shrubs that are sold in the United States are in containers. Examine the container-grown shrub carefully to be sure it is not damaged. Slide the rootball out — this is easy if the shrub is in a plastic pot. Look for young, white roots — these are essential for efficient uptake of water and nutrients. Older, darker roots function primarily to stabilize the plant.

Design considerations

Shrubs serve so many functions in gardens that categorizing them is useful to better understand them. As you consider your garden design, use these following categories to understand how to best use shrubs.

- ✔ **Foundation plantings.** Traditionally, one of the most common uses of evergreen shrubs is to plant them around the base of a house to conceal the foundation and soften the transition between the lawn and the building. This use of shrubs also gives the landscape winter appeal.

  However, using too many of one species of plant leads to monotony and an unnatural look. Try mixing groups of plants with different sizes and textures. And don't plant too closely to the house. Bring the plantings out some distance to gain a smoother transition and to give the shrubs more growing room.

- ✔ **Unity.** Repeating small groupings of plants in different parts of a landscape ties everything together and gives the yard a feeling of order and purpose. Similarly, shrubs serve well when planted among shorter-lived perennials in border plantings. Because they are usually larger and more substantial, shrubs provide a foundation for the more extravagant perennials and a structure for the garden when the perennials are dormant. For more about perennial plants, see Chapter 9.

✔ **Accent.** Some shrubs, such as azaleas and rhododendrons, are spectacular bloomers. Others have stunning berries or autumn color. Just a plant or two in a special place can light up a whole yard. And don't forget the foliage — a bold hydrangea with diversely colored leaves can make a stunning statement among plants with smaller leaves, like azaleas.

As you're selecting shrubs for your garden, be sure to note the season of the shrub's peak interest. For example, many shrubs produce flowers in early spring, but others — such as several of the hollies — are showy in winter, particularly against a backdrop of snow. By mixing shrubs with different seasons of peak interest, you can be sure to have plants worth admiring in your garden any time of the year.

✔ **Hedges, screens, and ground covers.** Many shrubs can be planted close together and maintained as hedges and screens. Some, including boxwoods and euonymus, can be clipped regularly into the rigid shape of a formal hedge to give a garden very organized look. Many others can be left to grow more naturally, creating screens for privacy. Many prostrate (lowgrowing) shrubs make excellent ground covers. For more information, see Chapter 12.

✔ **Background and barriers.** Shrubs can be the perfect backdrop for flower beds. A consistent, deep green background is one of the best ways to highlight blooming plants. If you want to keep pets (or people) out of a certain area, plant a line of thorny Pyracantha or barberries. They'll get the "point."

Our Favorite Shrubs

Here are the shrubs that we consider to be foolproof. All are widely available, and most are broadly adapted. Regarding specific soil needs, please refer to Chapter 14 to see how to adjust soil as needed for certain plants. Likewise, see Chapter 18 to read more about the pests to which some shrubs are prone. Also, see Chapter 5 for more about hardiness zones.

✔ **Glossy abelia.** *Abelia grandiflora.* Evergreen. Handsome, arching plant with bright green, glossy foliage. New growth is bronzy red. Leaves turn reddish purple in winter. Small, fragrant, white flowers in summer. Loses its leaves in colder areas. Can be grown as a hedge. Plant in full sun or light shade. Hardy to zone 6a (–10°F).

✔ **Barberries.** *Berberis* species. Evergreen and deciduous shrubs known for their thorny stems, red berries, and tough constitution. Some have showy yellow flowers and colorful foliage. Upright-growing barberries make excellent hedges and barriers. The deciduous Japanese barberry, *B. thunbergii,* is generally 4 to 6 feet high with arching stems. However, you have many varieties from which to choose, varying in height and foliage color. Most have good autumn color. 'Atropurpurea' has reddish-purple foliage during the growing season. It is hardy to zone 4a (–30°F). Evergreen barberries include *B. mentorensis,* a compact, dense plant growing 6 to 7 feet high. It is hardy to zone 6a (–10°F). Most barberries can grow in sun or partial shade and thrive under a variety of growing conditions.

✔ **Boxwoods.** *Buxus* species. Evergreen. The boxwood is one of the finest plants for a tightly clipped, formal hedge. Small, dark green leaves densely cover the branches. The Japanese boxwood, *B. microphylla japonica,* is one of the most popular types. Unpruned, it grows about 4 to 6 feet high. 'Winter Gem' and 'Green Beauty' are two varieties that stay bright green all winter. Others pick up a brownish tinge. Grow in full sun to partial shade. Hardy to zone 5a (–20°F). The English boxwood, *B. sempervirens,* is the classic boxwood of the mid-South. Many named varieties are available. It is hardy to zone 6a (–10°F).

✔ **Camellias.** *Camellia* species. Evergreen. With its glossy, deep green leaves and perfectly formed flowers, it is one of the finest shrubs for shady conditions. Flowers come in shades of red, pink, and white, with some bicolors. Most types bloom in winter and early spring.

The Japanese camellia, *C. japonica,* is most commonly grown, usually reaching 6 to 12 feet high. Many varieties are available, varying by color and flower form. Most are hardy into zone 8a (10°F).

Sasanqua camellias, *C. sasanqua,* has smaller leaves and earlier flowers (often in autumn). They range from small shrubs to more spreading, vine-like plants. Hardy to zone 8a (10°F).

New varieties are more cold hardy, to zone 6a (–10°F). These are hybrids of the Japanese camellia and *C. oleifera.* Named varieties include 'Winter's Beauty', 'Winter's Interlude', 'Winter's Star', and 'Winter's Waterlily'.

✔ **Cotoneaster.** *Cotoneaster* species. Evergreen and deciduous. There are many types from which to choose, ranging from low-growing ground covers to tall, upright shrubs. Most share a profusion of white spring flowers followed by red berries and are tough, widely adapted plants. Deciduous kinds often have good autumn color. Taller types include the evergreen Parney cotoneaster, *C. lacteus,* which reaches about 8 feet high and equally as wide, and *C. watereri,* which reaches up to 20 feet high with arching stems. Deciduous *C. divaricatus* has stiff, arching branches to 6 feet high and bears a heavy crop of berries.

Most cotoneasters are hardy to zone 5a or 6a (–15°F to –5°F). Plant in full sun. Fireblight can be a problem. Ground-cover types are described in Chapter 12.

✔ **Euonymus.** *Euonymus* species. Evergreen and deciduous. Euonymus are workhorse foliage plants. Deciduous kinds, such as winged euonymus, *E. alata,* are hardy to zone 4a (–30°F) and are grown for their convenient size and shape and their stunning red autumn color. The European spindle tree, *E. europaea,* grows to about 20 feet high and produces attractive red berries in autumn.

Evergreen euonymus, such as *E. japonica* and *E. fortunei,* are hardy to zones 5a to 7a (–20°F to –5°F), depending on the variety. Varieties with colored leaves, like 'Silver King' (white with green) and 'Aureo-variegata' (yellow with green), are very popular. They range in height from 6 to 20 feet and make fine hedges. Plant euonymus in sun or light shade. *E. japonica* is often troubled by powdery mildew.

↙ **Gardenia.** *Gardenia jasminoides.* Evergreen. Intensely fragrant, pure-white summer flowers and beautiful deep green leaves make gardenias a favorite shrub wherever they can be grown. Plants usually grow 3 to 6 feet high and must have acid soil and consistent moisture. Plant in full sun in cool climates, partial shade in warmer areas. 'Mystery' is a popular, large-flowered variety. Hardy to zone 8a (10°F).

↙ **Hydrangea.** *Hydrangea* species. Deciduous. The big, bold leaves and huge summer flowers of these unique plants put on a great show in shady gardens. The bigleaf hydrangea, *H. macrophylla,* is most commonly grown. Flower clusters are up to a foot across and are light to deep blue in acid soil, pink to red in alkaline soil. Plants usually grow 4 to 8 feet high and must be pruned heavily to encourage compactness and heavy bloom. Hardy to zone 7a (0°F).

↙ **Hollies.** *Ilex* species. The most commonly grown hollies are evergreen plants known for their bright-red berries and clean-looking, spiny, often multicolored leaves. Many make excellent hedges. The most familiar holly is the English holly, *Ilex aquifolium.* It generally grows 15 to 25 feet high but can get larger. Varieties such as 'Argenteo-marginata', with leaves of diverse shades of white, make excellent accents. Other popular types include the compact 'Burfordii' and 'Dazzler', varieties of *I. cornuta.* They grow 8 to 10 feet high. 'Nellie Stevens' is a hybrid that grows at least 15 feet high. Plant hollies in full sun. Most are hardy to at least zone 5a (–20°F).

↙ **Junipers.** *Juniperus* species. Evergreen. The low- and wide-spreading growth pattern of most junipers makes them most useful as ground covers (see Chapter 12). However, there are many more upright, shrubby types, including forms of the Chinese juniper, *J. chinensis,* such as 'Pfitzerana' and 'Torulosa'. There are also very columnar varieties, like 'Wintergreen' and 'Spartan'. Plant in full sun. Hardiness varies; most can be grown into at least zone 5a (–20°F).

↙ **Heavenly bamboo.** *Nandina domestica.* Evergreen. Light and airy in appearance, heavenly bamboo has divided leaves and straight, erect stems of a small bamboo. However, it is much more ornamental. New growth is bronzy red when the plant is grown in full sun. The entire plant turns red in winter. White spring flowers are followed by bright red berries. Grows 6 to 8 feet high, but many dwarf forms are available. Hardy to zone 6a (–10°F).

↙ **Oleander.** *Nerium oleander.* Evergreen. Oleander is a tough plant that puts on an incredibly long show of color throughout summer and into autumn. The flowers are born in large clusters in shades of white, pink, and red. The plants are low maintenance and thrive in hot summers. Oleanders are densely foliaged and generally grow 10 to 20 feet high but can be kept lower with annual pruning. You can also choose dwarf varieties. Plant in full sun. Hardy to zone 8a (10°F).

All parts — leaves, stems, flowers, and seeds — of all types of oleander are toxic.

✔ **Photinia.** *Photinia* species. Mostly evergreen. Several species of useful shrubs that show bronzy-red new growth in spring followed shortly by clusters of small, white flowers and often black or red berries. *P. fraseri,* which reaches 10 to 15 feet high, is popular because of its resistance to powdery mildew, but it does not have berries. Japanese photinia, *P. glabra,* is slightly lower growing and has red berries that gradually turn black. Plant photinias in full sun. They are hardy to zone 6a (–10°F).

✔ **Mugho pine.** *Pinus mugo mugo.* Evergreen. A neat, compact pine that rarely exceeds 4 to 8 feet in height. Easy to care for as a specimen or in group plantings. Plant in full sun. Hardy to zone 3a (–40°F).

✔ **Bush cinquefoil.** *Potentilla fruticosa.* Deciduous. Particularly valuable in cold-winter climates, bush cinquefoil is a handsome little shrub with bright green, ferny foliage and colorful wild-roselike blossoms. Plants bloom from late spring into autumn in shades of red, yellow, orange, and white. Yellow varieties, such as 'Katherine Dykes', are most popular. Ranges in height from just under 2 feet up to 5 feet. Plant in full sun. Hardy to zone 3a (–40°F).

✔ **Firethorn.** *Pyracantha* species. Evergreen. Colorful and dependable, firethorn come in a wide range of forms, from low-growing ground covers (see Chapter 12) to upright, spreading shrubs. All cover themselves with clusters of small, fragrant, white flowers in spring followed by showy, orange-to-red berries lasting into autumn and winter. Branches are sharply thorned. Popular types include the very hardy *P. coccinea* 'Lalandei', which grows 8 to 10 feet high and has red berries (see Figure 7-1). Fireblight can be a serious problem; hybrids 'Mojave' and 'Teton' are fireblight resistant. They grow about 12 feet high, with orange-red and yellow-orange berries, respectively. Plant firethorn in full sun. Most are hardy to zone 5a or 6a (–20°F to –5°F).

✔ **Indian hawthorn.** *Rhaphiolepis indica.* Evergreen. It's hard to go wrong with Indian hawthorn. Compact and carefree, the plants bloom profusely from late winter into spring. The pink-to-white flowers are followed by blackish-blue berries. New growth is tinged bronze. Plants generally grow 3 to 6 feet high. *R.* hybrid 'Majestic Beauty' is taller, growing up to 15 feet high, and has large leaves. Plant Indian hawthorn in full sun. Hardy to zone 7a (0°F).

✔ **Azaleas and rhododendrons.** *Rhododendron* species. Evergreen and deciduous. Huge family of much-loved flowering shrubs. Many types to choose from, but all grow best in acid soil. Most prefer moist, shady conditions and soil rich in organic matter. Some can take full sun. Hardiness varies.

Figure 7-1:
Branch tip
of firethorn
*(Pyracantha
coccinea)*
with berries.

Azaleas are generally lower-growing, compact plants that cover themselves with brightly colored spring flowers in shades of pink, red, orange,
yellow, purple, and white. Some are bicolored. Favorite evergreen types
include Belgian Indicas, Kurumes, and Southern Indicas. Deciduous kinds
include Knap Hill-Exbury Hybrids, Mollis Hybrids, and the very hardy
Northern Lights Hybrids.

Rhododendrons are usually taller with larger flower clusters. They come in
basically the same color range but are not as well adapted to hot-summer
climates as are azaleas.

Rhododendrons include some of the most cold-hardy evergreen shrubs, a
few of which tolerate winters in zone 4a (–30°F). Deciduous azaleas share
the rhododendron's cold tolerance. The Northern Lights series is also
hardy to zone 4a (–30°F). Evergreen azaleas are much less tolerant of cold.
Belgian Indicas are hardy to zone 9a (25°F), and Kurumes to zone 8a (10°F).

✔ **Roses.** *Rosa* species. Deciduous. Many roses are outstanding landscape
shrubs. Among the best are the hardy rugosa roses, which are notable for
the "quilted" look of their leaves. They flower in spring and produce large,
edible rose hips in autumn. Roses rightfully deserve their own chapter —
which we give them, in Chapter 23.

✔ **Spiraea.** *Spiraea* species. Deciduous. You have many types of spiraeas to
choose from. Many are mounding, fountainlike shrubs with an abundance
of tiny, white flowers in mid-spring to late spring. Included among these
is the bridal wreath spiraea, *S. vanhouttei,* which grows about 6 feet high
and at least 8 feet wide. Its small, dark green leaves turn red in autumn.
Other spiraeas, like *S. bumalda* 'Anthony Waterer', have clusters of
pink-to-red blooms later in summer. 'Anthony Waterer' has upright stems
reaching about 4 feet high. Plant spiraeas in full sun. Hardiness varies, but
most grow in zones 4a and 5a (–30°F and –20°F).

- **Common lilac.** *Syringa vulgaris.* Deciduous. Wonderfully fragrant clusters of spring flowers make lilacs a favorite wherever they grow. Most bloom in shades of lavender and purple, but some are white or rosy pink. Plants usually grow 8 to 15 feet high and have dark green leaves. Plant in full sun. Lilacs grow best where winters are cold; they're hardy to zone 3a (–40°F). The newer Descanso Hybrids will flower where winters are milder.

- **Viburnum.** *Viburnum* species. The viburnums represent a large family of evergreen and deciduous shrubs that are wonderful additions to the landscape. They offer great variety of form and function, and their ornamental characteristics include colorful flowers, brightly colored berries, and, often, autumn color. Favorite evergreen types include the neat-growing *V. tinus,* which grows 10 to 12 feet high and has pink-to-white spring flowers followed by metallic-blue berries. The variety 'Variegatum' has leaves colored with white and creamy yellow. 'Compactum' is lower growing than is typical for the species. All make good unpruned hedges and are hardy to zone 7a (0°F).

  Choices among deciduous types include the Korean spice viburnum, *V. carlesii,* which has very fragrant clusters of white flowers in spring followed by blue-black berries. Leaves turn red in autumn. Plants grow about 8 feet high, spreading just about as wide. The horizontal-branching *V. plicatum* is also distinctive, with rows of white spring flowers and red autumn color. It grows about 15 feet high. Deciduous viburnums are generally hardy to at least zone 5a (–20°F). Plant viburnums in full sun or partial shade.

Top Dwarf Conifers

Many kinds of dwarf conifers are available. Here's a list of our favorites. See Figure 7-2 to get an idea of the classic shapes dwarf conifers.

- **Firs.** *Abies* species. *A. koreana* is not truly miniature, but it's so slow growing that it's regarded as such. *A. koreana* 'Aurea' grows to 6½ feet tall; has green needles with silvery undersides and appealing bluish cones. *A. nordmanniana* 'Golden Spreader' is compact and irregularly shaped. Grows to 20 inches. Hardy to zone 5a (– 20°F).

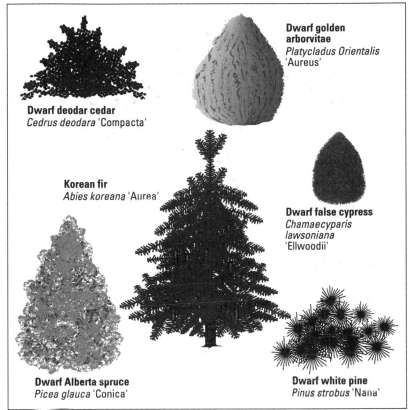

Dwarf deodar cedar
Cedrus deodara 'Compacta'

Dwarf golden arborvitae
Platycladus Orientalis 'Aureus'

Korean fir
Abies koreana 'Aurea'

Dwarf false cypress
Chamaecyparis lawsoniana 'Ellwoodii'

Dwarf Alberta spruce
Picea glauca 'Conica'

Dwarf white pine
Pinus strobus 'Nana'

Figure 7-2:
Some classic shapes of dwarf conifers.

- ✔ **Cedars.** *Cedrus* species. *C. deodara* 'Compacta' forms a 30-inch mound of weeping, green-gold foliage. Hardy to zone 7a (0°F).

- ✔ **Cypresses.** *Chamaecyparis* species. *C. lawsoniana* 'Ellwoodii' is pillar-shaped and grows to 30 inches high, with blue-green leaves. *C. lawsoniana* 'Minima Aurea' is bushy and golden yellow; grows to 24 inches high. Both are hardy to zone 6a (–10°F).

- ✔ **Junipers.** *Juniperus* species. *J. communis* 'Compressa' is columnar, grows to 18 inches high; has blue-green foliage. Hardy to zone 3a (– 40°F).

✔ **Spruces.** *Picea* species. *P. glauca* 'Conica' is a neat, conical shrub with bright-green needles; grows to 4 feet. Hardy to zone 3a (– 40°F).

✔ **Pines.** *Pinus* species. *P. strobus* 'Nana' grows 3 to 4 feet high with dense; has blue-green needles. Hardy to zone 3a (– 40°F).

✔ **Red Cedars.** *Platycladus* species. *P. orientalis* 'Aureus' is a vivid golden green; round and grows to 30 inches. Hardy to zone 5b (– 15°F).

✔ **Yews.** *Taxus* species. *T. cuspidata* 'Nana' grows to 3 feet high and wide; has dark green foliage. Hardy to zone 5a (– 20°F).

GOOD ADVICE

Evergreen shrubs

Broadleaf evergreen shrubs are likely to be less tolerant of intense cold than deciduous shrubs. To protect the evergreens, be sure to do the following:

Plant them in wind-sheltered locations.

Protect them with a burlap wind screen or spray with an antidesiccant (a lacquerlike material that won't damage leaves but slows evaporation of water from them, thus reducing winter injury).

Chapter 8

Vines

● ●

In This Chapter

▶ Understanding how vines climb

▶ Using vines effectively

▶ Avoiding mistakes with vines

▶ Our favorites

● ●

*V*ines are constantly on the move. Usually very vigorous, these plants sprawl over, twine around, climb up, or attach to whatever gets in their way.

They're also very useful plants for gardeners. As long as you keep them within bounds and under control, they can be used as ground covers (see Chapter 12), as a covering for a fence or blank wall, or as shading on an arbor or trellis to cool a patio or deck.

Let's Play Twister

Vines need to grow on something, either another plant or a trellis you provide. Before deciding what kind of support to provide for your favorite climbers, you need to know exactly how the climbers will hold on. Vines can be grouped into several types, according to the way they climb, as illustrated in Figure 8-1.

✔ **Clinging vines.** Examples are English ivy and Boston ivy. These vines have specialized growths — like little suction cups or claws — along their stems that can hook onto any surface they touch.

✔ **Sprawling vines.** An example is a climbing rose. These vines are often just very vigorous, spreading plants. In order for them to climb, they need to be tied to a trellis or support.

✔ **Twining vines.** These vines come in two types. Some, like star jasmine, wrap around anything that falls in their way. Others, like grapes, have small, twining *tendrils* at the bases of their leaves. The tendrils grab and wrap around anything they can reach.

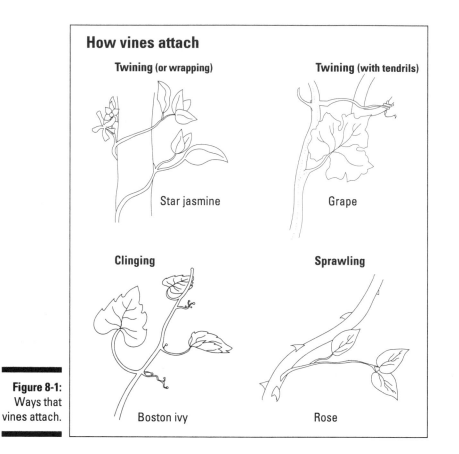

How vines attach

Twining (or wrapping) — Star jasmine

Twining (with tendrils) — Grape

Clinging — Boston ivy

Sprawling — Rose

Figure 8-1:
Ways that
vines attach.

Lean on me

You have many ways to support a vine, from arbors to lath trellises to wires strung between secure anchors. The important thing is to plan the supporting device in advance, make it strong, and design it to fit the growth habit of the vine.

Probably the simplest way to support a vine is to let it climb up and ramble through a companion tree or shrub — the way many vines grow in nature. This display can be enchanting in a garden if the two plants are good companions. Moderate growers like clematis happily associate with large shrubs. Vigorous growers like ivy or wisteria need a sturdy tree.

Heavy fences or the walls of outbuildings are another place to plant climbers, and these supports require little work from you. A chain-link fence can be transformed from an eyesore to a wall of color with a handsome climbing rose or Virginia creeper.

The classic structure for any vine is an arbor. The simplest of these may be a pair of posts with a timber or arch spanning the top. You train the vine to grow up the posts and over the arch. You can use a series of these arches to make a shady outdoor tunnel or to cover an entire patio. Attach wire to the posts to help the young vine find its way to the top. (See Chapters 3, 13, and 27 for more about arbors and vines.)

Using Vines Effectively

Like other plant groups (trees, shrubs, and so on), vines offer a variety of ornamental characteristics, including seasonal flower color, bright berries, and autumn color. Because most grow vertically, you can use them in tight spots where few other plants would fit. And they are versatile — they can create privacy, provide shade, and conceal unattractive landscape features.

Because of their hasty growth rate and the way they attach to structures, some vines can cause problems as they mature. The following sections give you tips on avoiding problems with vines.

Don't let vines grow where they shouldn't

Clinging vines, such as English ivy and Virginia creeper, can attach so firmly to walls and fences that getting them off without damaging the structure becomes almost impossible. And sometimes the attaching parts of the plant work their way into cracks and crevices. As they enlarge and grow, they can lift shingles and damage even the sturdiest materials, such as concrete and brick.

Letting a vine attach directly to the walls of your house usually isn't a good idea, unless the house is made of brick, stone, or aluminum siding. And even then you can have problems. Instead, build a trellis a few feet away from the side of the house and let it support the vine. That way, you can also paint the wall if you need to.

Don't let vines climb into the tops of trees. The health of the tree is almost always compromised by the vigorous vine.

Provide sturdy support

As vines grow, the branches enlarge, and the plant gets heavier. If the supports aren't strong enough, they can buckle under the weight. Build supports that are sturdy and long lasting. Two-inch galvanized pipe and pressure-treated 4 x 4 lumber are both good choices. (See Chapter 27 for more on supports.)

Prune for healthy vines

Pruning prevents vines from getting out of control, becoming too heavy, or growing into places where they're not wanted. Prune with vigor to keep the vine healthy and attractive. (For more on pruning, see Chapter 16.)

Winter is a traditional time for pruning. But you can prune in any season to keep a rampant vine in check. Prune flowering vines like wisteria immediately after the plants drop their blooms. The best time to do your major pruning of vigorous-growing fruiting plants, such as grapes and kiwi, is during their dormant season (winter). But you can nip back plants of any kind whenever they begin to grow out of the bounds that you set for them.

Our Favorite Vines

You can choose from dozens of vines to adorn the sides of buildings or fences as well as ramble through your shrubs and trees. If your space is limited, look for kinds that offer more than one "pleasure," usually those with handsome foliage as well as beautiful flowers or delectable fruit. Some vines provide handsome bark in winter, and others offer superb autumn color.

Plant encyclopedias are a good place to start digging deeper into the world of vines. You can also find a good selection of vines at botanical gardens and quality nurseries. Meanwhile, here are a few of our favorites. The temperatures given indicate the average winter minimum temperature that the plant can tolerate.

- ✔ **Bougainvillea.** *Bougainvillea* species. Evergreen or partially deciduous. Bougainvilleas are one of the most spectacular flowering vines. Stunning flowers in electric shades of purple, red, pink, orange, yellow, and white cover the plant all summer and beyond. Leaves are an attractive bright green. Plants are shrubby and must be tied to a sturdy support and given room to grow. Plant in full sun or, in the hottest climates, partial shade. Plant carefully, being sure not to disturb the roots. Needs little water once established. Can be grown in mild-winter areas with only light frosts (zones 10a and 11, 30°F to 40°F) or protected areas in zone 9b (25°F).

- ✔ **Clematis.** *Clematis* species. Mostly deciduous. A diverse family of eye-catching flowering vines, with hundreds of selections available. Large-flowered hybrids, with summer blooms up to 10 inches across in shades of white, pink, red, blue, and purple, are most popular. (See Figure 8-2.) Delicate plants can twine more than 10 to 15 feet high. Plant where the roots are cool and shaded but where the top can grow into full sun. For example, set the plant at the base of a large shrub and let it ramble through to the sunny top. Or plant it anywhere and cover the roots with a thick mulch. Hardy to zone 5a (–20°F).

Figure 8-2:
Clematis.

✔ **Evergreen clematis.** *C. aramandi.* Bears masses of fragrant white flowers in early spring and has handsome, shiny, dark green leaves. It grows under similar conditions as other clematis but quickly reaches 20 feet high and is hardy to only zone 8a (10°F).

✔ **Creeping fig.** *Ficus pumila.* Evergreen. A very compact foliage vine that tightly adheres to any surface it touches. Good-looking, small, heart-shaped leaves. Best grown on stone or masonry. Plant in sun or shade. Hardy to zone 8a (10°F).

✔ **English ivy.** *Hedera helix.* Evergreen. Fast-growing, tenacious, and adaptable, English ivy comes in many varieties differing in foliage size, shape, and color. The species has deep green, heart-shaped leaves and is very vigorous. (See Figure 8-3.) Clings with small aerial rootlets and takes over open areas in a minute — you have to keep your eyes on this one! It will damage all but the hardest surfaces. 'Hahn's Self-Branching' is a small-leaved type with more restrained growth. 'Baltica', whose leaves are a mixture of white and green, is one of many varieties with colorful, variegated leaves. Plant in sun or shade. Generally hardy to zone 5 (–20°F), although hardiness of some varieties varies.

✔ **Chinese jasmine.** *Jasminum polyanthum.* Evergreen. The wonderfully fragrant flowers of Chinese jasmine perfume the air for months in spring. The small blooms are borne in clusters, white on the face, pink on the back. The twining stems hold bright green, divided leaves and are very fast growing to 20 feet high. Good choice to cover a fence, trellis, or arbor. Prefers partial shade. Hardy to zone 8a (10°F).

✔ **Virginia creeper and Boston ivy.** *Parthenocissus* species. Deciduous. Two vines grown for their dramatic red and gold autumn color. Virginia creeper, *P. quinquefolia,* has leaves divided into 5 leaflets. Boston ivy, *P. tricuspidata,* has glossy, three-lobed leaves. Both climb vigorously, clinging to surfaces with their small adhesive discs. Plant in sun or shade. Hardy to zone 4a (–30°F).

Figure 8-3:
English ivy.

✔ **Climbing roses.** *Rosa* species. Many types of vigorous-growing roses can be used like vines. (Turn to Chapter 23 for more details on roses.)

✔ **Star jasmine.** *Trachelospermum jasminoides*. Evergreen. One of the most attractive and well-behaved vines for mild climates. Showy clusters of fragrant white flowers almost obscure the shiny, dark green foliage in late spring to summer. Twining stems reach up to 20 feet high; they're not invasive but need support. Great for climbing through lattice or on fences. Plant in full sun or light shade. Hardy to zone 8a (10°F).

✔ **Grapes.** *Vitis* species. Deciduous. The sprawling grapevine is one of the best choices for covering an arbor or trellis. Besides gnarled trunks, good-looking leaves, and autumn color, you also get edible fruit. Hardy to zone 3b (–30°F) to zone 9a (20°F), depending on type of grape.

✔ **Chinese wisteria.** *Wisteria sinensis*. Deciduous. Purely elegant — that's about the best way to describe one of the finest vines you can grow. Beautiful, large (often over 12 inches long), dangling clusters of fragrant purple blooms hang among bright green, divided leaves in spring. The twisting, twining shoots will keep growing almost indefinitely. As they mature, they take on the classic "muscular" appearance. Casting just the right shade, wisteria is the perfect cover for a sturdy arbor or trellis. It also looks great on fences. Requires annual pruning to look its best and bloom prolifically. Plant in full sun. Hardy to zone 5a (–20°F).

However you choose to use vines — as temporary or permanent screens, shade providers, for color, and so much more — their benefits can be unequaled. And, remember too, you can plant them alone or in combination with other plants.

Chapter 9

Perennials

In This Chapter

▶ Designing a perennial border

▶ Planting perennials

▶ Caring for perennials

▶ Our favorites

*P*erennial plants, grown for their flowers, their foliage, or both, are with us like the seasons — perennials return with their beauty, year after year. Compared with annuals (which have to be replanted every year), *perennials* are left in place to grow, to look better, and to bloom more, season after season.

The plants known as perennials are a diverse group. Perennials include some of the best-loved flowering plants, such as daisies, mums, and carnations. Spectacular foliage plants, such as ornamental grasses, hostas, and lamb's ears, are also perennials.

Perennials can be planted in containers or worked in among trees and shrubs for seasonal color. Many perennials make excellent ground covers. (See Chapter 12.)

Creating a Perennial Border

The classic use of perennials is to combine many of them in a large planting bed, known as a *perennial border*. A well-designed perennial border has something in bloom throughout the growing season. It not only has a well-thought-out color scheme, but also relies on plant texture for visual interest. Designing a spectacular planting can take years of experience, but even beginning gardeners can create a workable, pleasing border, adding to it over the years as their knowledge increases.

For most gardeners, a perennial border is constantly evolving, which is part of the fun of creating it. If certain plants don't work, you can replace them with something else. If the border has some downtime when nothing is in bloom, add some flowering annuals to fill in the gap, or plant some flowering shrubs, such as floribunda roses, which bloom over a long season. (Chapters 7, 10, and 23 cover shrubs, annuals and roses, respectively.)

Many gardening books give specific plans for perennial borders. Some nurseries even sell plants or seeds that fit predesigned borders. Although the use of these plans and designs may be a good way to start a perennial border, blooming times and growing conditions vary so much from place to place that you'll probably end up making changes to the border. In any case, you'd want to make changes to such predesigned plans because designing your own, unique garden is part of the fun.

Tips on designing a perennial border

Even though individual experience is the best teacher, here are some things that we've found useful in designing a perennial border.

- ✔ **Start with a plan and keep records.** Draw your bed out on paper, making sure to give plants the room that they need to grow. Work with a simple color scheme, such as three of your favorite colors, and plant only things that bloom in those shades.

- ✔ **Plan for a succession of bloom.** Think seasonally, aiming for something always in bloom. Keep records of blooming times so that you'll know where there are gaps to be filled the next planting season. And don't forget winter. Even in cold climates, you can use shrubs that have colorful berries or attractive bark.

- ✔ **Prepare the soil carefully.** You won't be remaking this bed every year. Dig deep, add organic material, and, most important, eliminate perennial weeds.

- ✔ **Plant in groups.** One plant, alone, gets lost in the masses. We find that grouping plants in odd numbers — 3s, 5s, and 7s — looks the most natural.

- ✔ **Don't forget the foliage.** Use plants with dramatic foliage to set off the flowers. Ornamental grasses or bold-textured shrubs make excellent focal points.

- ✔ **Use grays and whites.** Gray foliaged plants (such as lamb's ears) and plants with white flowers highlight other colors and can be used to tie everything together. These plants also reflect light and look great on those nights when the moon is bright.

- ✔ **Consider the background.** A dark green background enriches the color of most flowers. Consider planting a hedge (possibly of flowering shrubs or evergreens) at the back of the border.

Planting perennials

Before planting, prepare the garden site as described in Chapter 14.

Perennial plants are usually sold in six-packs, 4-inch pots, or 1-gallon pots. Many mail-order suppliers ship a wide selection of plants bare-root.

 Container-grown perennials can be planted any time that you can work the ground. However, the best time to plant such perennials is in the autumn or early spring because the plants have time to get established before hot weather begins.

For more details about transplanting and planting, see Chapter 15.

Caring for perennials

Many perennials benefit from being cut back at various times during their growth cycles. To stimulate branching on lower stems and make the plant bushier, for example, pinch out new growth at the top of the plant. (See Figure 9-1.)

Figure 9-1: Pinching out new growth at the top of the plant helps it develop lower branches and become bushier.

 Deadheading is the process of pinching or cutting off faded flowers while the plant is in bloom. Deadheading forces the plant to spend its energy on developing more flowers instead of setting seed. The result of deadheading is usually a longer bloom cycle. (See Figure 9-2.)

Figure 9-2:
Deadhead spent flowers to offset seed production and divert plant energy to producing new blooms.

Some perennials, such as coreopsis and gaillardia, rebloom if cut back by about one-third after the initial bloom cycle.

Most perennials (some shrubbier types are an exception) should be cut back to a height of 6 to 8 inches at the end of the growing season. This cutting back rejuvenates the plant and results in a better bloom next season. Where the ground freezes in winter, mulch plants with at least 6 inches of organic matter.

Taller perennials, such as delphiniums, and bushy types, such as peonies, may need to be staked to prevent the flowers from falling over. Figure 9-3 shows two types of staking: loops (for bushy plants) and ties (for taller perennials).

Figure 9-3:
Support plants as they grow with either metal loops or bamboo stakes and ties.

If older plants become overcrowded or bloom poorly, they can be rejuvenated by *dividing*. In fact, division is a good way to increase plant numbers. (For more about plant division, see Chapter 15.)

Our Favorite High-Performance Perennials

Here are our favorite perennials. A few others, which are often grown as annuals, are described in Chapter 10. Some perennials are technically *biennials*, meaning that they mostly grow foliage the first year, bloom the second year, and then die.

- **Yarrow.** *Achillea* species. A useful group of easy-care, summer-blooming perennials with ferny gray foliage and tight, upright clusters of yellow, red, or white blooms. Yarrows range in height from low-growing ground covers to tall plants (up to 5 feet high). One favorite is *A. filipendulina* 'Moonshine', with bright yellow flower clusters atop 2-foot stems. Plant in full sun. Most are hardy to zone 3a.

- **Artemisia.** *Artemisia* species. Very useful group of mounding, silver-foliaged plants that are great for highlighting other plants. One of the best is the hybrid 'Powis Castle' with lacy, silver foliage on a mounding plant about 3 feet high. Plant in full sun. Hardy to zone 5a.

- **Columbine.** *Aquilegia* species. Widely adapted perennials with fernlike foliage and beautiful, spurred flowers. Columbine blooms in spring and early summer in many single colors and multicolors. Many natives are included in wildflower seed mixes. The plants range in height from about 18 inches to 3 feet. Columbine is easy to grow from seed and will reseed. Plant in full sun to light shade. Hardy to zone 3a.

- **Asters.** *Aster* species. Colorful, late-blooming perennials with daisylike flowers, mostly in shades of blue, purple, red, pink, and white with yellow centers. Asters usually bloom in the late summer to autumn. Some begin flowering in early summer or late spring. *A. frikartii* produces blue flowers almost year-round in mild-winter climates. Asters grow about 2 feet high. Plant in full sun and divide every two years. Hardy to zone 4a.

- **Basket-of-gold.** *Aurinia saxatilis*. Brilliant gold blooms cover the gray foliage in spring. Basket-of-gold grows about 12 to 15 inches high and spreads. The plant also withstands drought. Plant in full sun. Use in foreground. Hardy to zone 3a.

- **Bellflower.** *Campanula* species. Much-loved family of mostly summer blooming perennials with bell-shaped flowers in shades of blue, purple, or white. There are many species, varying from low-growing spreading plants to taller types, some of which are 6 feet high. Flower size and shape also vary.

Favorites include the Serbian bellflower, *C. poscharskyana* (a low, mounding plant, 4 to 8 inches high, with blue flowers). Another favorite is the peach-leaf bellflower, *C. persicifolia,* which is also spreading, can reach up to 3 feet high, and has blue or white blooms. Campanulas grow best in light shade but can take sun in cool-summer climates. Hardy to zone 3a.

✔ **Chrysanthemum.** *Chrysanthemum* species. A very diverse, useful group of perennials. This group includes the familiar garden mums, so useful for autumn bloom, and types such as *C. coccineum* (the painted daisy), *C. frutescens* (the marguerites), and *C. superbum* (the Shasta daisies), all of which are well known as daisies. All chrysanthemums are wonderful cut flowers. Although chrysanthemum plants vary in height, flower color, bloom season, and hardiness, one exists for almost every garden and situation. Most grow best in full sun. Hardy to all zones.

✔ **Coreopsis**. *Coreopsis* species. Easy-to-grow plants known for their sunny yellow, daisylike flowers borne from spring through summer. *C. grandiflora* is one of the most common. This variety grows about 3 feet high and has single or double flowers. Plant in full sun. Hardy to zone 5a.

✔ **Dianthus.** *Dianthus* species. Lovely family of usually fragrant, spring- and summer-flowering plants that includes carnations, *D. caryophyllus.* Many varieties of dianthus can be grown as annuals. Favorites include sweet William, *D. barbatus* (which grows 6 to 18 inches high and has tight clusters of white, pink, red, purple, and bicolored flowers), and cottage pinks, hybrids that have very fragrant, frilly, rose, pink, white, or bicolored flowers on stems reaching about 18 inches high above a tight mat of foliage. Plant in full sun or light shade (in hot-summer areas). Hardy to zone 3a.

✔ **Purple coneflower.** *Echinacea purpurea.* Tall, purple or white, daisylike flowers top this fine, long-lasting perennial. Purple coneflower reaches 3 to 5 feet high and blooms in summer. Plant in full sun. Hardy to zone 3a.

✔ **Blanketflower.** *Gaillardia grandiflora.* These sunny-colored, daisylike flowers are a combination of red and yellow or are straight red or yellow. Blooms heavily in summer and grows 2 to 3 feet high. Plant in full sun. Hardy to zone 2a. (See Figure 9-5.)

Figure 9-5:
Blanketflower.

✔ **Blood-red geranium.** *Geranium sanguineum.* One of the best of the species *geraniums,* which is a large group of fine perennials. Dainty-looking, purplish-pink, red, and white flowers appear in abundance above good-looking, deeply cut leaves that turn red in the autumn. Blood-red geranium blooms spring to summer and mounds to about 18 inches high. Many varieties are available. Plant in full sun to light shade. Hardy to zone 4a.

✔ **Daylilies.** *Hemerocallis* species. A dependable group of summer-flowering perennials with stalks of large, trumpet-shaped flowers in single and bicolored shades of yellow, orange, pink, red, and violet. Some daylilies are fragrant. Lilies have grassy foliage that reaches 12 to 24 inches high. Plant in full sun. Hardy to zone 3a.

✔ **Coral bells.** *Heuchera sanguinea.* Wiry spikes of tiny, bell-shaped, white, pink, or red flowers are held 12 to 24 inches above lovely, lobed leaves. Coral bells bloom in the spring. Plant in light shade, although they can take sun in cool-summer climates. Hardy to zone 3a.

✔ **Plantain lily.** *Hosta* species. Very useful foliage plants that make a nice contrast to shade-loving flowers. Plantain lily leaves are usually heart-shaped and are often crinkled or variegated. Flower spikes appear in summer. Plants and leaves range from small to large. One favorite is the blue-leaf plantain lily, *H. sieboldiana,* which has large (10 to 15 inches), crinkled, blue-green foliage and pale purple flowers; it grows 3 feet high. Hardy to zone 3a.

✔ **Candytuft.** *Iberis sempervirens.* In early spring, snow-white flowers completely cover this dainty, compact plant. Candytuft grows from 4 to 12 inches high and makes a wonderful edging. Plant in full sun. Hardy to zone 4a.

✔ **Ornamental grasses.** The term *ornamental grasses* designates a large group of wonderful plants grown for their grassy foliage and feathery, plumelike flowers. Ornamental grasses make stunning focal points among other blooming plants. The dried flowers often look good well into winter. Some favorites include purple fountain grass, *Pennisetum setaceum* 'Rubrum', with purplish-red leaves and plumes that reach over 6 feet high; the huge (often more than 8 feet) variegated eulalia grass, *Miscanthus sinesis* 'Zebrinus', with yellow-striped leaves and broomlike plumes; and blue oat grass, *Helictotrichon sempervirens,* with gray-blue foliage 2 to 3 feet high. Growing conditions and hardiness vary.

Beware! Some ornamental grasses get very large and can become invasive.

✔ **Garden penstemon.** *Penstemon gloxinioides.* Spring-blooming, mounding plants that grow 2 to 4 feet high. Garden penstemon features spikes of tubular flowers in many single and bicolored shades of white, pink, red, and purple. Plant in full sun. Hardy to zone 8a. Check nursery catalogs for other species that are hardier.

- **Summer phlox.** *Phlox paniculata.* Large clusters of small white, pink, red, salmon, and purple flowers bloom in mid- to late summer. The plants grow 2 to 4 feet high. Plant in full sun. Hardy to zone 3a.

- **Gloriosa daisy; Black-eyed Susan.** *Rudbeckia hirta.* Free-blooming, easy-to-grow perennial or biennial. These plants have large yellow, orange, maroon, or mahogany daisylike flowers with dark, domelike centers. Some kinds are bicolored. These plants bloom from summer to autumn. The plants grow 2 to 4 feet high, are easily grown from seed, and reseed themselves heavily. The plants can be invasive. Plant in full sun. Hardy to zone 4a.

- **Salvias.** *Salvia* species. So many excellent perennial salvias are available that we could write a book about them alone. Most are best adapted to dry-summer areas with mild winters. Many are shrublike; others are perennials that are usually grown as annuals. (See Chapter 10.)

  Still others are valuable herbs. Favorite flowering types include *S. superba,* with violet-blue summer flowers reaching 2 to 3 feet high, and *S. azurea grandiflora,* with 4- to 5-foot-high, rich gentian-blue flowers in late summer. Plant in full sun. Hardy to zone 6a.

- **Lamb's ears.** *Stachys byzantina.* A lovely, low-growing foliage plant with soft, fuzzy, silver-gray leaves. It grows 6 to 12 inches high and has purplish-white flowers in summer. Lamb's ears is a fabulous edging plant for flowering perennials. Plant in full sun. Hardy to zone 4a.

By now, we imagine that you're sold on the idea of using perennials. Because they are reliable and, in many cases, low maintenance, you can count on them to grow year after year, and they ask little in return.

Chapter 10
Annual Flowers

In This Chapter
▶ What is an annual?
▶ Getting a riot of color
▶ Landscaping with annuals
▶ Our favorites

*A*nnuals are the workhorses of the flower garden. If you want flower color, if you want your garden to be bright and showy, and if you want your garden to look good right now, annuals are the answer.

What Is an Annual?

Technically, an *annual* is a plant that lives for one gardening season and dies. Annual-flowering plants grow quickly, put on a spectacular flower show for several months, and then expire. When the plants die, they are usually removed and replaced.

However, this definition of *annual* is a bit misleading for two reasons. First, some plants that are actually *perennials* (that is, the plants live on from year to year) are often used as annuals in climates where they can't survive year-round because of extreme heat or cold. Some flowering plants, such as geraniums and primroses, are long-lived in some climates, but because their bloom is so spectacular in a particular season, they are planted for that seasonal bloom and are then removed from the garden when their bloom is finished.

Our definition of annual plants is also a bit misleading because two kinds of annuals exist: cool-season and warm-season annuals. The distinction between these two types is important because it determines when you plant these plants and when the plants bloom.

Cool dudes

Cool-season annuals (such as pansies, violas, and primroses) thrive in spring and autumn. Planted in late summer or early spring, these plants grow quickly and bloom while the weather is still on the cool side. When the days get longer and hotter, most cool-season annuals stop blooming. At that time, take them out of the garden, even though they may live a while longer.

In mild-winter climates, many cool-season annuals that are planted in late summer bloom throughout winter. In general, cool-season annuals can withstand mild frosts.

When it's hot, they're hot

Warm-season annuals (such as zinnias, marigolds, and petunias) prefer the hot months of summer. Planted after the last frost in spring, these plants grow quickly and bloom when the weather is hot. Warm-season annuals usually continue to flower until the first frost in autumn, but because they bloom poorly in cool weather, we often pull them out before a frost does them in.

Some overlap in bloom time between cool- and warm-season annuals exists, so if you orchestrate your planting just right, you may never be without blooms.

Go for a Riot of Color

When it comes to planting annuals, you have three choices. Some annuals can be planted from seed that is sown directly where the plants are to grow and bloom. Other annuals can be started from seed indoors and transplanted to the garden later. Or transplants of varying sizes (from small plants in six-packs to larger ones in gallon cans) can be purchased at nurseries and planted in the garden.

A nice thing about buying transplants at the nursery is that many annuals can give you instant color because they are already in bloom. You can wake up in the morning to a dull green landscape and turn it into a riot of color before noon by simply visiting your nursery or garden center. We describe planting techniques for each method (from seed, from homegrown transplants, and from nursery stock) in Chapter 15. Make sure that you prepare the soil properly before you plant, and make sure that you match the requirements of the plant — sun or shade — with the conditions at the planting site.

Many plants that bloom easily from seed can reseed themselves and come back year after year on their own. Most annual wildflowers reproduce themselves this way. Leave annuals such as alyssum, calendula, cosmos, forget-me-nots, marigolds, pansies and violas, sunflowers, vinca, and zinnias to go to seed for a garden full of "volunteers" next season.

Landscaping with Annuals

The group of flowering annuals is incredibly diverse. Annual plants come in all shapes and sizes, from low-growing alyssum (which rarely gets more than 6 inches high) to the tallest sunflower (which can be more than 10 feet high).

Getting annuals together

The diversity among flowering annuals makes them very useful in the garden. For the brightest blast of color, we like to plant annuals en masse. Low-growing types usually work best for this type of planting, and you can go with just one color or mix a number of colors. But the important thing is to plant many annuals and plant them close (usually 6 to 8 inches apart). We usually start with six-packs and space the transplants evenly in staggered rows. (See Figure 10-1.) The plants will grow quickly and fill in the spaces to give you a solid bed of bright color.

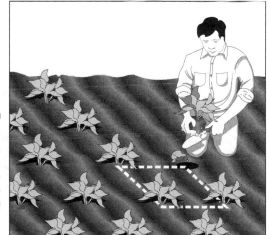

Figure 10-1: Set annuals in staggered rows, evenly spaced, for a bed of color.

If you prefer a less-regimented look, try mixing many different types of annuals together in one bed. In general, we like to keep the lower-growing plants in front and the taller ones in back, but no hard rules about plant placement exist. We also like to keep to a particular color scheme, such as mixing only complementary colors, but you can go with whatever color scheme you like.

Low-growing annuals, such as alyssum and lobelia, are very useful as edgings. You can plant these low-growers along walkways or in front of other annuals, in front of perennials, or even in front of flowering shrubs, such as roses.

Containing annuals

Flowering annuals are especially at home in containers, making it easy for you to insert a touch of color into visible, highly used areas. Match the plant's habits with the pot. Spreading annuals, such as alyssum, cascade over the sides of containers and really look nice in hanging baskets or window boxes. Lower-growing, compact varieties are usually best suited to container growing, but you can use taller types as well. By planting many pots with many different annuals, you'll always have some at peak bloom to put in your most visible spots, like porches or patios.

Treating them with care

Some annuals have unique habits that call for special treatment, but these plants also present special opportunities. Most sweet peas are climbing vines that need some kind of a support, such as a trellis. (See Chapter 13 for information about trellises.) Place the trellis right by a window so that the sweet peas' sweet fragrance can waft through the house. Tall sunflowers are spectacular focal points for any spot where you have room for them, but they also make a beautiful tall "wall" around a vegetable garden or along a back fence.

Really, the best way to use annuals is to put them wherever you have room. Just one or two plants can turn a blank spot into a colorful focal point. Simply scattering some seed in open areas, where newly planted ground covers have yet to fill in, for example, can result in a colorful mulch that changes with the seasons.

No real tricks are needed to grow annuals. Just buy healthy transplants, plant them at the right time, and make sure that the young plants are watered and fertilized regularly. For the longest season of color, pick off faded blossoms to encourage new bloom. (See Chapter 9 for more on this technique, called *deadheading*.)

The Best of the Annuals

Here are some of the most reliably colorful annuals, divided into cool-season and warm-season types. (See Chapter 15 for details on planting methods.)

Cool-season annuals

✔ **Snapdragon.** *Antirrhinum majus.* Plants with wonderfully colorful spikes of white, yellow, orange, red, purple, and multihued flowers. The common name comes from the hinged blossom, which opens and shuts like jaws when squeezed on the sides. Varieties range from 12 to 36 inches high. Plant them in full sun from transplants.

✔ **Flowering cabbage or kale.** *Brassica* species. These vegetable relatives look very much alike. They are grown for their brightly colored, ruffled or frilly foliage arranged in a head like a cabbage. The foliage is usually green with purple, pink, or white markings. Plants grow 12 to 18 inches high. Plant in full sun from seed or use transplants.

✔ **Pot marigold.** *Calendula officinalis.* Easy-to-grow annuals with yellow or orange (or sometimes white) daisylike flowers. Pot marigold is a nice cut flower. The compact plants reach 12 to 30 inches high. Plant in full sun from seed or use transplants.

✔ **Dusty miller.** *Centaurea cineraria.* One of the most valuable gray-foliaged plants; useful for highlighting other colors. Dusty miller makes other garden plants look better and brighter. It is perennial in mild climates and produces yellow flowers in summer, starting when the plant is in its second season. The plants have finely cut leaves and a mounding habit, and they grow about 18 inches high. Plant in full sun from transplants. *Senecio cineraria* is another gray-foliaged plant that is often sold as dusty miller. *Senecio cineraria* grows slightly taller (to about 2½ feet high) than *Centaurea cineraria.*

✔ **Annual chrysanthemum.** *Chrysanthemum paludosum.* A glorious miniature bloomer from seeds or transplants. Small white-and-yellow daisylike flowers cover the plant. Annual chrysanthemums grow best in full sun and reach 12 to 18 inches high.

✔ **Larkspur.** *Consolida ambigua.* Wonderfully delicate spikes of spurred flowers in pastel shades of white, blue, pink, and purple. Larkspurs grow 12 to 48 inches high, depending on variety. The plants are easy to grow from seed and do best in light shade.

✔ **Chinese forget-me-not.** *Cynoglossum amabile.* Wispy clouds of tiny, deep blue, pink, or white flowers; a classic for shady gardens. Chinese forget-me-nots grow 12 to 18 inches high. The plants are easy to grow from seed and reseed readily. *Myositis sylvatica*, the common forget-me-not, is very similar and is equally good in shady gardens.

✔ **California poppy.** *Eschscholzia californica.* The much-loved California wildflower; easily grown from seed (and they'll reseed readily). California poppies bloom mostly in shades of yellow and orange (or sometimes white). The plants reach 10 to 24 inches high. Grow in full sun.

✔ **Sweet peas.** *Lathyrus odoratus.* Much-loved annual vining plant with intensely fragrant blooms. Sweet peas come in single colors and multicolors — almost every hue except true blue and green. Sweet peas make a wonderful cut flower. Most varieties need something like a fence or trellis for support (see Chapter 13 for more about fences and trellises), but bushier, low-growing types, such as 'Little Sweetheart', do not need supports. Plant in full sun from seed.

✔ **Sweet alyssum.** *Lobularia maritima.* Ground-hugging (usually under 6 inches high) annual that covers itself with tiny, bright white, purple, or pink blooms. Alyssum flowers best in cooler weather and is quite hardy, but it often blooms into summer, too. Alyssum is one of the finest edging and container plants. Easy to grow from seed and reseeds readily. Plant in full sun.

✔ **Stock.** *Matthiola incana.* One of the most deliciously fragrant annuals, with intense, spicy scents. Flower spikes reach 12 to 30 inches high (depending on variety) in shades of white, pink, purple, and red. Stocks are best started from transplants. Grow in full sun.

✔ **Geranium.** *Pelargonium* species. Old-time favorites that are often used as perennials in mild-winter climates. Geraniums have huge clusters of white, pink, red, purple, orange, or bicolored flowers in spring and summer. The plants grow from 8 to 36 inches high, and some have variegated leaves. Start from transplants and grow in full sun to light shade.

✔ **Primroses.** *Primula* species. Perennials in many mild climates, but usually grown as annuals. Primroses have brightly colored flower clusters atop straight stems that seldom reach more than 12 to 18 inches high. Many colors of primroses are available to choose from. Fairy primrose, *P. malacoides,* produces airy clusters of white, pink, and lavender blooms above hairy leaves. English primrose, *P. polyantha,* has brighter, often multicolored flowers above deep green, crinkled leaves. Plant in full to partial shade and start with transplants.

✔ **Nasturtium.** *Tropaeolum majus.* Sprawling annual with neat round leaves and bright orange, yellow, pink, cream, or red flowers. Nasturtiums grow about 15 inches high on the ground, but the plants can climb up to 10 feet when given proper supports. Nasturtiums are easy to grow from seed; plant in full sun or light shade.

✔ **Pansies and violas.** *Viola* species. Flowers often resemble colorful little faces. Imagining prettier flowers than pansies and violas is hard. These annuals bloom in almost every single color and multicolor except green. Pansies have slightly larger (but fewer) blooms than violas. Both feature neat, compact plants that seldom grow more than 8 inches tall. Pansies and violas can be grown from seed, but they are usually started from transplants. Plant in full sun or light shade.

Warm-season annuals

- **Bedding begonia.** *Begonia semperflorens.* Versatile annuals that are most useful in shady gardens (although some types can take more sun). The flowers of bedding begonias come in shades of white, pink, and red. Red-flowering plants, which can take more sun, have bronzy-red leaves. Most varieties grow about 12 inches high. Bedding begonias are best started from transplants.

- **Madagascar periwinkle.** *Catharanthus roseus.* (Also known as annual vinca.) These cheery plants are workhorses in the summer garden. Compact with deep green leaves, Madagascar periwinkles produce an abundance of white, pink, red, or lavender blooms that often have a pink or white spot in the center. They grow 12 to 20 inches high and are best in full sun (but can take some shade). These plants can be grown from seed, but are more easily grown from transplants.

- **Coleus.** *Coleus hybridus.* Grown for its intensely colored foliage, which comes in a variety of color combinations and different leaf shapes. Coleus grows best in the shade and is best planted from transplants. It can also be grown as a houseplant. Pinch off the flowers to keep the plant compact.

- **Cosmos.** *Cosmos bipinnatus.* Bright green, airy plants with a brilliant bloom of white, pink, lavender, purple, or bicolored daisylike flowers. Most types grow tall (upwards of 5 feet high), but dwarf varieties stay more compact. Easy to grow from seed or transplants, and the plants reseed. Plant in full sun.

- **Sunflower.** *Helianthus annuus.* Few annuals make a statement the way that sunflowers do. Most sunflowers reach 8 to 10 feet high and are topped with huge, sunny, yellow blooms. But sunflowers also come in small-flowered forms in shades of red, orange, and white. Some dwarf varieties, such as 'Sunspot', stay under 2 feet tall. All sunflowers have edible seeds. Plant from seed in full sun.

- **Impatiens.** *Impatiens wallerana.* The stars of the shady garden and one of the most popular annual flowers. The 1- to 2-inch-wide blooms come in bright shades of white, red, pink, and lavender. Bicolored varieties of impatiens are also available. Impatiens plants have dark green or bicolored leaves and grow 12 to 30 inches high. Grow from transplants.

- **Lobelia.** *Lobelia erinus.* Low-growing (and often spreading) plants covered in deep to light blue blooms. Few blues are as bright as those of lobelia, but white- and pink-flowering forms are also available. All lobelias reach about 4 to 6 inches high. They can be grown from seed but are more easily started from transplants. Plant in full sun to light shade.

- **Flowering tobacco.** *Nicotiana alata.* Small, tubular, often-fragrant blooms in shades of white, pink, red, and purple. Flowering tobacco plants grow 12 to 48 inches high, depending on variety. Plant flowering tobacco in full sun or light shade. Can be grown from seed or from transplants.

- ✔ **Petunia.** *Petunia hybrida.* Much-loved annuals with single and double, usually trumpet-shaped flowers in a myriad of single and bicolored shades. Petunias are compact plants that range from 10 to 24 inches high. Start from transplants and plant in full sun.

- ✔ **Sage.** *Salvia* species. Tall spikes of bright white, red, blue, or purple flowers atop compact, sun-loving plants. Some types of sage are perennials in mild-winter climates. Sages range in height from 10 to 36 inches. Plant in full sun and use transplants.

- ✔ **Marigold.** *Tagetes* species. Marigolds are one of the most popular summer annuals, with blooms in the sunniest shades of yellow, orange, and red. Many varieties are available. Blossoms can be big or small, as can the plants. Plant in full sun. Easy to grow from seed or transplants.

- ✔ **Verbena.** *Verbena hybrida.* Brightly colored clusters of white, pink, red, purple, or blue flowers on low-growing, spreading plants. Verbenas grow 6 to 12 inches high. Plant in full sun. Easiest to start from transplants.

- ✔ **Zinnia.** *Zinnia elegans.* A cut-flower lover's dream. Zinnias come in a huge range of flower colors (except blue), flower shapes and sizes, and plant heights. Small types, such as 'Thumbelina', stay under 12 inches high. 'State Fair' grows up to 5 feet high and has long stems for cutting. Plant in full sun. Easy to grow from seed or transplants.

If you're an unabashed lover of show and color, liven up your garden each year by reaching for your hand trowel and planting some of your favorite annuals.

Chapter 11

Flowering Bulbs

In This Chapter

▶ Buying and planting bulbs

▶ Caring for bulbs

▶ Dividing and propagating bulbs

▶ Forcing bulbs

▶ Our favorites

*F*or many people, especially people who have never had much luck growing any plants, bulbs are a dream come true. Think of bulbs as flowering powerhouses: plants that have packed most of what they need for a season's worth of growth into some type of below-ground storage device — the bulb. Plant a bulb at the right time of year and at the proper depth, and you're almost guaranteed a spectacular bloom.

What Are Bulbs

When you think of bulbs, you probably think of daffodil or tulip bulbs — brownish things that look something like an onion. And all those bulbs are true bulbs, including the onion. But the term *bulb* as used in gardening refers to a great number of different plant bulbs. Besides the true bulbs, such as tulip bulbs, there are corms, rhizomes, tubers, and tuberous roots. Each one of these looks different. Some are underground stems surrounded by modified fleshy leaves, and others are swollen underground stem bases. Some are thickened, branching storage stems, and others are swollen roots. We could bore you with more botanical information about what makes a true bulb and what makes a corm, and so on, but we won't. For starters, all you really need to know is which bulbs to plant, where and how deeply to plant them, and — most important of all — which end is up!

If you don't bore easily and want to know more, try one of the gardening encyclopedias listed in Appendix A. The information can be important, particularly if you intend to propagate more bulbs from your initial plantings. (See "Dividing and Propagating Bulbs" later in this chapter.)

Going natural: "You're not getting older; you're getting better!"

Some bulbs naturally get better, year after year.

You can separate bulbs into two groups. One group of bulbs (including the daffodils, some tulips, and grape hyacinths) is called *naturalizers*. Bulbs that naturalize are left in the ground, year after year. Over time, the bulbs increase, and their bloom gets better and better.

Some bulbs, such as tulips, need more cold than others to naturalize. In climates where the ground freezes, the bulbs bloom on forever. If the ground rarely freezes, which is the case in many mild-winter climates — zones 9a to 11b (see Chapter 5 for information about zones) — the blooms get smaller each year and eventually stop coming altogether.

A second group of bulbs (which includes begonias and dahlias) has to be replanted every year. Bulbs may need to be replanted for many reasons. Some bulbs may not be hardy enough to survive over winter in your climate, while other bulbs may rot in wet soils. Still other bulbs may not get enough chilling to rebloom year after year.

Although some bulbs have to be replanted every year, you don't have to buy new bulbs every year. Most bulbs can be dug up after blooming, properly stored, and then replanted at the appropriate time to bloom again next season.

Where Should I Plug In My Bulbs?

Plant bulbs wherever you want to see them bloom: in the smallest little spot by the front door, in pots, in large swaths under trees, or among other flowering plants. Some bulbs, such as the English bluebell, look particularly good in woodland settings, while others, such as tulips, do well in formal gardens.

One of our favorite designs involves planting large beds of tulips or daffodils. We then plant low-growing annuals or perennials (such as sweet alyssum, pansies, violas, or iberis) right on top of these bulb beds. The bulbs come up through the other flowers and create wonderful combinations. And after the bulbs are through blooming, the other flowers cover up the leftover foliage of the bulbs.

Plan for a long season of color from bulbs. Even though some of the most familiar bulbs (such as daffodils and tulips) bloom in spring, other bulbs (such as dahlias) bloom in summer and autumn.

Bulbs work especially well in containers. With containers, you can really pack bulbs in tight for a spectacular bloom (*but* the tighter you pack the bulbs, the less likely they'll bloom the following year).

If you really want to have fun, try forcing bulbs to bloom indoors. (See "Bulbs in Containers," later in this chapter.)

Buying Bulbs

Bulbs are sold through the mail and at local nurseries. Hardy bulbs, such as daffodils and tulips, are best planted in autumn. Tender bulbs, such as begonias and dahlias, should be planted a few weeks before the last frost date in spring. Nurseries should have the best supplies at the appropriate planting time for your area.

Always purchase fine-quality bulbs — they give you more bang for your buck. Never forget that, with bulbs, bigger is better. Larger bulbs, although more expensive, give you more bloom. Bargain bulbs are often poor performers. Avoid bulbs that are soft and mushy or have obvious signs of decay.

If you live in a warm-winter climate, you may have to refrigerate bulbs that require winter chilling (such as hyacinth and tulip) before planting. Check the bulb package for such a recommendation or ask at your nursery. To chill bulbs, place them in the refrigerator (not the freezer) for six to eight weeks prior to planting.

Planting Bulbs

The two most important things that you should know about planting a bulb are to set the bulb at the right depth and to make sure that you put the bulb in the hole rightside up.

The chart in Figure 11-1 shows the recommended planting depths and proper positioning for common bulb types. As a general rule, most bulbs should be planted at a depth equal to three times their diameter. Remnants of roots on the bottom should tell you which side of the bulb should go down. If you have any doubts, ask at your local nursery.

You can plant bulbs individually by using a hand trowel or bulb planter. If you are planting many bulbs, digging one big trench or hole and lining up the bulbs in the bottom is usually easier.

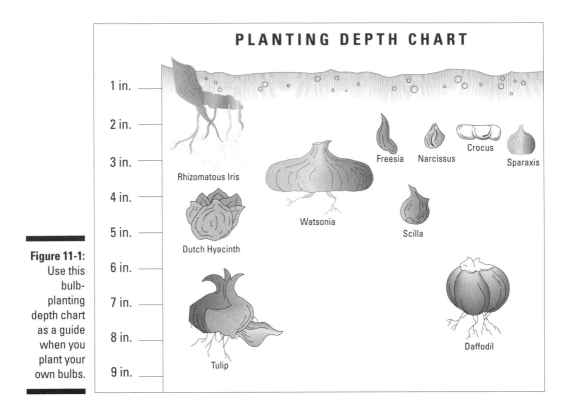

PLANTING DEPTH CHART

1 in.
2 in.
3 in.
4 in.
5 in.
6 in.
7 in.
8 in.
9 in.

Rhizomatous Iris

Freesia Narcissus Crocus Sparaxis

Watsonia

Dutch Hyacinth

Scilla

Daffodil

Tulip

Figure 11-1:
Use this bulb-planting depth chart as a guide when you plant your own bulbs.

Most bulbs require well-drained soil. (Bulbs can rot in soggy, overly wet ground.) Before planting your bulbs, mix a slow-release, complete fertilizer into the soil in the bottom of the hole. You can find appropriate fertilizers (labeled *bulb food*) in nurseries and garden centers. After planting the bulbs, water them thoroughly.

Caring for Bulbs

With many bulbs (especially those bulbs that bloom in spring), you won't have much else to do. Plant the bulbs and forget them. The bulbs grow, bloom, die back, and come back again the following year. Summer-blooming bulbs, like dahlias and begonias, however, need to be watered and fertilized regularly during their growth cycle. Most bulbs, in fact, benefit from a once-a-year application of nitrogen fertilizer during their growing season.

With bulbs, you should pinch off faded blooms just as you would for most flowers. But after the bloom is finished, don't cut down the bulbs' foliage. Let the foliage die down naturally so that it can continue to feed the bulb and build next year's bloom.

Digging and storing bulbs is necessary for begonias, dahlias, and tender bulbs that are grown in cold-winter climates. Wait until the foliage is almost dried out and gently dig the bulbs up. (A spading fork works well.) Brush the dirt off the bulbs and allow them to dry for a week in a cool, dark place. After drying the bulbs for a week, discard any damaged or rotting bulbs and dust the remaining bulbs with sulfur or another fungicide. Finally, pack the dusted bulbs in dry peat moss or perlite and store them in a cool, dark place until replanting time.

If digging and storing bulbs is too much work, just treat bulbs like annuals and plant new ones every year.

Dividing and Propagating Bulbs

Some bulbs, particularly smaller types of bulbs (such as crocuses and daffodils), can be left undisturbed for years. But other bulbs multiply so rapidly that they become too crowded and deplete the nutrients in the soil around them. Few blossoms, unusually small, are a sure sign that your bulbs need more room.

Dividing is done just after the foliage turns yellow and begins to die back. Dig up the clump by using a garden fork, being careful not to injure the bulbs. Then break off the individual bulbs, keeping the roots intact. Replant the bulbs immediately or store them in a dry place until autumn planting time. Water the area well and allow any foliage to mature and die before removing it. The newly planted bulbs should bloom the following spring.

Larger bulbs (for example, lily) or corms (for example, gladiolus) develop small, immature offspring at the base of the bulb. Remove these offsets after the plant has bloomed and the leaves have died; then plant them in a container or in an inconspicuous area where they can grow for a year or two until they are big enough to bloom. (See Figure 11-2.)

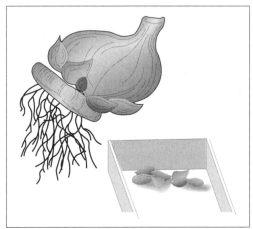

Figure 11-2:
Proper way to remove offsets from the mother bulb.

Tuberous-rooted plants, such as dahlias, are propagated a little differently. After the plant blooms (as the leaves fade), dig the plant up. A clump of fat, tuberous roots is attached to the stalk. Cut the roots into several groupings, leaving part of the stalk intact on each of the clusters. Each cluster should include at least one growth bud at the base of the section of stalk. Then replant the clumps in various spots; plant the clumps at approximately the same depth that they were planted before they were dug. Or store them in peat or sawdust until you are ready to plant.

True bulbs, such as lilies, are propagated by using yet another method. Most true lilies resemble artichokes, with many swollen, scalelike sections. These individual "scales" can be removed and grown to form new bulbs, for planting the following spring. This process is somewhat involved, however, and best left to the more advanced gardener.

Bulbs in Containers

Forcing bulbs — bringing them indoors and getting them to bloom before their normal season — is easier to do than you probably think (and it's not nearly as mean as it sounds). Virtually any spring bulbs — hyacinths, crocuses, dwarf daffodils, and tulips — are good choices for indoor flowering. Generally, the larger grades of bulbs are better for forcing because they produce more and bigger flowers. (Again, avoid the bargain bulbs.)

You can also grow bulbs in containers and *not* force them for early bloom. Plant them in autumn, about the same time you'd plant bulbs in the open soil, and then move the container to an out-of-the-way location for the winter. (In cold winter areas, cover the pot with mulch or store in an unheated garage or basement.) Come spring, the bulbs will begin their growth. That's when you move the pot to the "display" location. One of the color illustrations in this book shows a good way to plant a container of spring bulbs.

If you aren't ready to pot the bulbs when they arrive, store them in a cool (35°F to 50°F), dark place with good ventilation. Don't store the bulbs in airtight plastic bags, or you're likely to find a mushy, moldy mess when you come back in a few weeks.

Shallow clay or plastic pots called *bulb pans* are the best containers for forcing bulbs because they require less potting mix than ordinary pots and are less likely to tip over. The general rule of thumb for forcing bulbs is to have the pot at least twice as deep as the bulb is tall.

Any soilless mixture of peat moss and perlite or vermiculite works well for forcing bulbs. Don't bother buying expensive *bulb bark,* a special mix for forcing bulbs. In the autumn, fill the chosen pot ³/₄ full with the soilless mix and place the bulbs, ¹/₂ inch apart, on top of the mix, with the bulb's pointed end facing up. When forcing several kinds of bulbs together in one container, place the largest bulbs in the center and fan out the smaller bulbs around the largest ones. Gently press the bulbs into the mix so that the tips of the bulbs are level with the rim of the pot. Then fill the pot with more of the soilless mix and water the pot until the soil is evenly moistened.

Set the potted bulbs in a cool, dark place for 8 to 15 weeks to allow the bulbs to grow roots. Smaller bulbs may need a little less time; larger bulbs may need slightly more time. The idea is to try to mimic the natural autumn cycle of temperatures, starting at 50°F for a few weeks and then cooling down to 35°F.

After the required cooling period, check your pots. You should begin to see evidence of shoots emerging from the soil mix. To gradually reintroduce the pots to light and warmth, place the pot in a cool room with indirect sunlight. By the end of one week, move the pot into direct sun with temperatures to 65°F. Within a month of being brought into warmth, the bulbs should begin to flower.

Best Bulbs

Here are a few of our favorite kinds of bulbs. For more information, consult some of the reference books in Appendix A. Perhaps even better, get some bulb catalogs — one of the easiest ways to do this is to subscribe to a gardening magazine, such as *National Gardening,* which contains coupons for many gardening catalogs, including some bulb specialists.

- **Lily-of-the-Nile.** *Agapanthus orientalis.* Very dependable, summer-blooming bulb with tall stalks of bright blue flowers reaching from 4 to 5 feet high. Lily-of-the-Nile's straplike foliage is evergreen in mild climates. Dig and store the bulbs over winter in cold-winter climates. Lily-of-the-Nile gets by on little water. 'Peter Pan' is a compact variety, reaching only 8 to 12 inches high, so it's excellent in containers. Varieties with white flowers are also available. Plant in full sun or light shade. Hardy to zone 9a.

- **Begonias.** *Begonia tuberhybrida.* One of the most beautiful of all flowering plants. Many varieties of begonias are available to choose from. Some varieties have large flowers (up to 8 inches across). Other flowers are smaller and are borne on "weeping" plants. Few begonias grow more than 12 to 18 inches high. Begonias bloom in summer, and their flowers come in almost all shades except blue and green. Foliage is good-looking and succulent. They make ideal container plants and grow best in light shade. Hardy to zone 9a. Dig up and store the bulbs over winter in all regions.

- **Fancy-leaved caladium.** *Caladium hortulanum.* Brightly colored foliage plant for shady situations. Caladiums feature large leaves, which are tropical looking and painted with shades of green, white, pink, and red. The plants grow from 12 to 24 inches high and are great in containers. Hardy only in zone 10a but can be dug up and stored or grown as an annual anywhere.

- **Canna.** *Canna* species. Upright, summer-blooming plant with showy flowers in shades of yellow, orange, salmon, pink, and red. Some have bicolored flowers. The plants have large, tropical-looking leaves. Some cannas grow more than 5 feet high, but many are lower growing. Plant in full sun. South of zone 7a, cannas can be naturalized with little care. Elsewhere, dig and store them over winter.

- **Lily-of-the-valley.** *Convallaria majalis.* Small, dainty clusters of very fragrant, bell-shaped flowers. Blooms in summer. The plants grow from 6 to 8 inches high. Plant in light shade and acid soil and keep the soil moist. Naturalizes in cold-winter climates and is hardy to zone 4a.

- **Dahlia.** *Dahlia* species. A huge, diverse family of hybrids with an incredible array of flower form and sizes. Some dahlia blossoms are tiny balls; other blossoms are huge, star-shaped blooms more than 8 inches wide. Summer-blooming in almost every color but blue, dahlia plants range in size from 6 inches high to more than 5 feet high. Plant in full sun and water regularly. Hardy to zone 9a, but they grow anywhere as long as tubers are dug and stored over winter. Smaller varieties are often grown as annuals.

- **Freesia.** *Freesia* species. Dependable spring-blooming bulb that naturalizes freely in mild climates. Freesia's arching clusters of trumpetlike flowers come in almost every color. Some freesias are fragrant. The plants grow to about 18 inches high. Plant in full sun or light shade. Hardy to zone 9a, but the bulbs must be dug or used as an annual elsewhere.

- **Snowdrops.** *Galanthus* species. Lovely, drooping, bell-shaped white flowers. Bloom in very early spring and naturalize nicely in cold-winter climates. Snowdrops grow from 8 to 12 inches high. Plant in full sun or partial shade (snowdrops are great under trees). Hardy to at least zone 4a. The giant snowdrop, *G. elwesii*, naturalizes farther south, into zone 9a.

- **Gladiolus.** *Gladiolus* species. Much-loved cut flower with tall spikes of trumpetlike flowers. Comes in almost all shades except blue. Most bloom in summer and grow to 4 to 5 feet high, but smaller types are available. Plant in full sun. Hardy to zone 9a, but dig the bulbs or use the plants as annuals elsewhere. Baby gladiolus, *G. colvillei,* is lower growing and hardier. Baby gladiolus bulbs can be left in the ground and can naturalize in most areas.

- **Common hyacinth.** *Hyacinthus orientalis.* Wonderfully fragrant spikes of white, red, pink, yellow, blue, or purple bell-shaped flowers in early spring. Common hyacinth grows to about 12 inches high. Hyacinths look best when planted in masses or containers. Plant in full sun or light shade. Hyacinths do best in cold-winter climates, but they need chilling elsewhere. Hardy to zone 4a.

✐ **Iris.** *Iris* species. A huge group of elegant, spring-to-summer–blooming plants. You can choose from many different types. Favorites include the bearded iris, which has huge blooms and gracefully arching petals. Irises come in many shades and reach from 2 to 4 feet high. The plants spread freely. Plant in full sun or light shade. Most need to have water regularly. Hardiness varies, but most survive into at least zone 5a, some to zone 3a.

✐ **Snowflake.** *Leucojum* species. Very similar to snowdrops (see "Snowdrops" earlier in this list) with white, drooping flowers in early spring. Snowflake plants naturalize in cold-winter climates. Plant in full sun or light shade. Hardy to zone 5a.

✐ **Lilies.** *Lilium* species. Large family of beautiful, mostly summer-blooming bulbs. Most have large, trumpet-shaped flowers, but a great diversity of lilies exists. Colors come in almost every shade but blue, and plant heights range from 2 to 6 feet. Plant lilies so that the roots are in the shade but the tops can reach for the sun. Water regularly during summer. Most are hardy to zone 4a.

✐ **Grape hyacinth.** *Muscari* species. Wonderful little bulbs that form carpets of fragrant, mostly blue, spring flowers and grassy foliage. Grape hyacinths grow from 6 to 12 inches high and naturalize freely. Plant in full sun or light shade. Hardy to zone 3a.

✐ **Daffodils and Narcissus.** *Narcissus* species. Carefree bloomers that flower spring after spring, even in mild climates. If you plant only one type of bulb, this should be it. Narcissus plants generally bear clusters of small, often fragrant, flowers. Daffodils have larger blooms. You can choose from many daffodil and narcissus varieties (mostly in white and yellow shades). 'King Alfred' is one of the all-time favorite, large-flowered, yellow trumpet types. Plant daffodils and narcissus in full sun to light shade. Hardy to zone 4a.

✐ **Persian buttercup.** *Ranunculus asiaticus.* Bright-colored, spring-to-summer flowers in shades of white, yellow, orange, red, and purple. Some Persian buttercups are multicolored. The plants grow from 12 to 24 inches high and have deeply cut leaves. Plant in full sun or light shade. Hardy to zone 8a but dig and store the bulbs in autumn.

✐ **Tulips.** *Tulipa* species. Much-loved, spring-blooming bulbs with the familiar cup-shaped flowers in almost all shades (including multicolors) except blue. Tulips usually grow from 10 to 24 inches high and are best planted in full sun. They rebloom only in cold-winter climates; they're hardy to zone 3a. Elsewhere, the bulbs must be dug and chilled before replanting. However, many species of tulips, such as *T. clusiana*, naturalize even in mild-winter areas. Most tulips thrive as far south as zone 8a.

✔ **Calla lily.** *Zantedeschia* species. Spectacular, tropical-looking plants with large, usually white, cup-shaped summer flowers and bright green, arrow-shaped leaves. Yellow, pink, and red shades are also available. Calla lily plants generally grow from 2 to 3 feet high, but dwarf forms are also available. Best grown in light shade, but can take sun in cool climates. They need regular watering and are hardy to zone 8a.

Now you know some of the specifics for gardening with bulbs. So, if you've been less than successful with plants, let bulbs be your first step to becoming a triumphant gardener.

Chapter 12

Ground Covers, Prairies, and Meadows

In This Chapter

▶ Opting for alternatives to lawn

▶ Putting in native grasses and meadows

▶ Planting and maintaining ground covers

▶ Our favorites

*I*f you measure popularity by acreage, a lawn is by far the most popular ground cover of all. So we mention lawns briefly here at the start of our discussion of ground covers (see Chapter 17 for more on lawn grasses). But lawn is not a good choice of ground cover in many situations. Lawn grasses do not grow well in deep shade, and few kinds of lawn truly thrive in hot, dry regions. Lawns are hard to establish and to maintain on steep pieces of ground. If you have lots of space to cover, the mowing and maintenance of a lawn will eat up your time. And in parts of the world where water is scarce, traditional lawn grass isn't an environmentally sound choice. If any of these situations applies to you, then you want to plant ground cover rather than a traditional lawn.

The most appealing aspect of all the other ground-cover plants — meadow and prairie grasses, wildflowers, woodland perennials, and low-growing shrubs — is that they give your landscape a natural look and require very little maintenance. The selection of good ground-cover plants is so broad that you can find several to fit any landscaping style or regional climate.

Over in the Meadow

One trend in lawn alternatives is the new interest in using native grasses and other low-growing, prairie-type plants. These create meadowlike landscapes that can be beautiful year-round.

Native grasses are superbly adapted to their native ranges and are often well adapted to other areas, too. Native grasses can survive on less water than traditional lawn grasses and can be left unmown (or mown infrequently) and so are low maintenance. Common types of native grasses include wheat grass (a very drought-tolerant native grass of the Rocky Mountains) and blue grama grass and buffalo grass, both native to the Great Plains. (These grasses are described in Chapter 17.) Certain wildflower mixes (see Appendix C for sources) composed of low-growing plants can also be used for meadowlike lawns. Meadow lawns are less formal-looking than most grass lawns but can be walked or played on and have a wild beauty all their own.

The Ground-Cover Alternative

Ground covers are usually low-growing, often spreading plants that, when planted close together, form a uniform layer of foliage. Ground covers range from very low-growing plants that are just a few inches high to more shrubby types that are several feet high. Some of the lowest-growing ground covers, such as chamomile and creeping thyme, can take a little foot traffic; you can plant these types between stepping-stones or in other areas where people occasionally walk.

Ground covers have an artistic side, too. You can create a nearly infinite variety of contrasts with ground covers, and you can mix in other shrubs, vines, annuals, and perennials for a variety of effects. Foliage textures can range from grassy to tropically bold, and colors can range from subtle shades of gray to vibrant seasonal colors. Ground covers provide a naturalistic appearance, so look to the local wild areas for ideas. Choose plants that mimic what you see in wooded areas, in unmown fields, in meadows, or on steep slopes.

Planting Ground Covers

Plants sold as ground covers usually come in small containers or in flats, depending on their growth habit. Those ground-cover plants that are grown in flats are cut into individual sections before planting.

For best results, ground covers should be planted in staggered rows. Plant spacing is very important. If you space the ground-cover plants too far apart, they take a long time to fill in. Plant them too close together, and the plants may quickly become overcrowded. Recommended plant spacings are included in the plant descriptions given later in this chapter.

If you are planting your ground covers from containers, you can place the plants into individual holes. To plant small plants from pots or packs, dig a hole just deep enough for the rootball. For larger, container-grown plants, taper the hole outward at the base and create a mound for the rootball.

If planting a ground-cover plant on a steep slope, set the plant on its own terrace (with the top of the rootball slightly above the soil level) and provide a watering basin behind the plant. (See Figure 12-1.)

Figure 12-1: On a steep slope, set the ground-cover plant above the soil line and create a basin in the soil behind the plant to hold water.

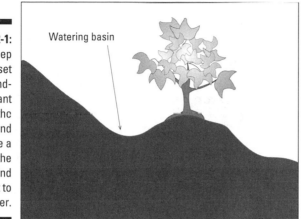

Watering basin

If starting from flats, prepare the whole planting area as if you were planting a lawn (see Chapter 17). As with all plantings, you need to attend to soil needs (see Chapter 14) before introducing your plants to your landscape. Newly set out plants need adequate watering to help get them established; after the plants are growing well, many types need only minimum maintenance.

Plan on controlling weeds between plants until the ground cover is established. We like to use an organic mulch or, for shrubby ground covers, landscape fabric (described in Chapter 16) to control weeds (also see Figure 12-2). One advantage of organic mulches is that they also protect the plants in winter.

Figure 12-2: Use landscape fabric or a blanket of organic mulch to rid new ground cover plantings of weeds.

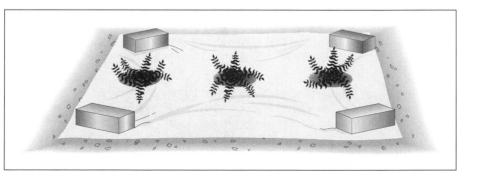

Many spreading, nonwoody ground covers (such as English ivy, St. John's wort, and vinca) can be rejuvenated or kept looking fresh by occasional shearing. Cut the plants back to just several inches above the ground in spring and then fertilize them. Within a few weeks, the plants will regrow and look full, clean, and healthy.

Top Ground-Cover Choices

Although the number of possible candidates is nearly infinite, the following common ground-cover plants have proved themselves in a multitude of situations and environments.

- **Woolly yarrow.** *Achillea tomentosa.* Evergreen. A tough, spreading ground cover that reaches 6 to 9 inches high. Its ferny, gray-green leaves are topped with small yellow flower clusters in summer. Woolly yarrow can take some foot traffic but can also be invasive. Plant 6 to 9 inches apart in full sun. Hardy to zone 3a (–35° F).

- **African daisies.** A group of fairly similar, spreading, evergreen plants with daisylike flowers. Widely grown as ground covers in mild-winter climates. Generally hardy into zone 9a (20° F). Favorites include the trailing African daisy, *Osteospermum,* with white-to-purple spring flowers on 1- to 3-foot-high plants (depending on the species) and gazanias, *Gazania,* with sunny summer flowers in single and multicolored shades of white, red, pink, yellow, and orange borne on 6- to 12-inch-high clumping or trailing plants. Plant 1 to 2 feet apart in full sun.

- **Carpet bugle.** *Ajuga reptans.* Evergreen. Forms a low-growing, spreading ground cover with attractive dark green or purplish-green foliage reaching 2 to 6 inches high. Carpet bugle has blue flowers in summer. Plant in partial to full shade (some types with colored foliage can take more sun), 6 to 12 inches apart. Hardy to zone 4a (–50° F).

- **Kinnikinnick.** *Arctostaphylus uva-ursi.* Evergreen. Several selections of this hardy, shrubby plant make excellent ground covers. Features shiny green foliage. The plants' small urn-shaped, white spring flowers are followed by red berries. 'Point Reyes' and 'Radiant' are two fine choices and generally stay below 12 inches high. Plant in full sun about 3 feet apart. Hardy to zone 2a (–50° F).

- **Barberries.** *Berberis.* Several types of barberries make excellent ground covers. One of the most popular is the deciduous *B. thunbergii* 'Crimson Pygmy'. This variety grows about 18 inches high, has purplish-red foliage (when grown in full sun), bright-red autumn color, and red berries. As a ground cover, plant 'Crimson Pygmy' 15 to 18 inches apart. Hardy to zone 4a (–30° F).

- **Chamomile.** *Chamaemelum nobile.* Evergreen. Chamomile's fine-textured, aromatic foliage can take some foot traffic. Has small yellow flowers in summer. Chamomile stays low and compact in full sun, rarely getting over

6 inches high; plants grow taller in partial shade. You can mow chamomile or plant it between stepping-stones. Plant in full sun, spacing plants about 6 to 12 inches apart. Hardy to zone 7a (0° F).

✔ **Cotoneasters.** *Cotoneaster.* Deciduous or evergreen. Cotoneasters are a large family of shrubs that includes many dependable ground covers known for their bright-green foliage, small flowers, and red berries. Favorites include the evergreen bearberry cotoneaster, *C. dammeri* (which grows only 8 inches high and spreads up to 10 feet), the deciduous rock cotoneaster, *C. horizontalis* (which grows from 2 to 3 feet high and has orange-to-red autumn color), and the evergreen rockspray cotoneaster, *C. microphyllus* (which rarely exceeds 2 to 3 feet in height). Hardiness varies, but most cotoneasters can be grown into zone 5 or 6 (–20° F and –10° F). Plant at least 3 feet apart in full sun. (Some of the widest-spreading types should be spaced 5 feet apart.)

✔ **Winter creeper.** *Euonymus fortunei.* Very hardy, evergreen plant that comes in many fine ground-cover varieties. 'Colorata', the purpleleaf winter creeper, has bright green foliage that turns purple in autumn and winter. 'Colorata' grows about 2 feet high. 'Ivory Jade' has green leaves edged with white and also grows about 2 feet high. 'Kewensis' grows only 2 inches high and makes a very dense ground cover. Plant winter creeper in full sun, spacing the plants from 1 to 3 feet apart. Most are hardy into zone 4 or 5 (–30° F and –20° F).

✔ **Blue fescue.** *Festuca ovina glauca.* A mounding, grassy ground cover with silver-blue foliage. Grows 4 to 10 inches high and gets by on little water. Plant in full sun, spacing the plants 6 to 12 inches apart. Hardy to zone 5a (–20° F).

✔ **English ivy.** *Hedera helix.* Evergreen. With its dark green, lobed leaves, English ivy is one of the most popular ground covers. Grows well under many conditions, including sun or shade. Many varieties (differing in leaf size, texture, and color) are available. English ivy can be invasive, climbing into trees and over structures if not kept under control. Space plants 12 to 18 inches apart. Hardy to zone 5a (–20° F), although some small-leafed types are less hardy.

✔ **Aaron's-beard; Creeping St. John's wort.** *Hypericum calycinum.* Evergreen. These adaptable ground covers thrive under a variety of conditions. They grow 12 inches high and have bright-yellow flowers in summer. The plants spread rapidly and can be invasive. Prefer full sun but will take partial shade. Space the plants 12 to 18 inches apart. Hardy to zone 5a (–20° F).

✔ **Ice plants.** Evergreen. Many different, trailing, succulent ice plants are useful ground covers in mild-winter climates, especially arid areas. Two popular blooming types are rosea ice plant, *Drosanthemum floribundum*, which grows about 6 inches high and has pink flowers in spring and summer; and trailing ice plant, *Lampranthus spectabilis*, which grows 12 to 15 inches high, covering itself with pink, red, or purple flowers in spring. Plant in full sun, spacing them 12 to 18 inches apart. Hardy to zone 9a (20° F).

✔ **Junipers.** *Juniperus.* Evergreen. Many prostrate junipers (differing in height and foliage color) are available. Junipers are tough plants that get by with little care but must have well-drained soil. *J. chinensis* 'San Jose' has grayish-green leaves and grows 2 feet high. *J. horizontalis* 'Bar Harbor' grows about a foot high and spreads up to 10 feet; the gray-green leaves turn bluish in winter. *J. h.* 'Wiltonii' is only 6 inches high and has silver-blue foliage. Plant junipers in full sun. Most should be spaced 2 to 5 feet apart, depending on the variety. Most are hardy into zone 3a (–40° F).

✔ **Mondo grass or lily turf.** *Liriope* or *Ophiopogon.* Evergreen. Mondo grass and lily turf are two similar, grasslike plants that make attractive ground covers in shady situations. *Liriope spicata*, creeping lily turf, is one of the most adaptable, growing 6 to 10 inches high. *L. muscari* grows up to 24 inches high and has blue summer flowers that are partially hidden by the foliage. Some varieties have variegated leaves. *Ophiopogon japonicus* is a common mondo grass with dark green leaves; the plants grow 8 to 10 inches high. Space these plants 6 to 18 inches apart, depending on height. The hardiness of both species varies, but most can be grown into zone 5a (–20° F).

✔ **Japanese spurge.** *Pachysandra terminalis.* Evergreen. Japanese spurge is an attractive spreading, foliage plant for shady, moist conditions. Features rich green leaves on upright 10-inch stems, with fragrant white flowers in summer. Plant in partial to full shade and space them 6 to 12 inches apart. Hardy to zone 4a (–30° F).

✔ **Spring cinquefoil.** *Potentilla tabernaemontanii (P. verna).* Evergreen. This plant's dark green, divided leaves form a soft-textured cover 3 to 6 inches high. Has small clusters of yellow flowers in spring and summer and can take some foot traffic. Plant in full sun to partial shade and space the plants 10 to 12 inches apart. Hardy to zone 4a (–30° F).

✔ **Creeping thyme.** *Thymus praecox arcticus.* Evergreen. A low-growing, creeping herb that is especially useful between stepping-stones. Can take foot traffic and can even be grown as a lawn alternative. Creeping thyme grows 3 to 6 inches high and has white-to-pink flowers in summer. Plant n full sun and space the plants 6 to 10 inches apart. Hardy to zone 3a (–40° F).

✔ **Star jasmine.** *Trachelospermum jasminoides.* Evergreen. This spreading, vining plant has shiny green foliage and fragrant white flowers in spring. Grows about 18 inches high when left to sprawl. Confederate vine, *T. asiaticum*, is similar but grows slightly lower, has dull green leaves, and bears yellowish-white flowers. Plant in full sun and space the plants 2 to 3 feet apart. Hardy to zone 8a (10° F).

✔ **Dwarf periwinkle.** *Vinca minor.* Evergreen. This spreading, deep green ground cover is good for shady conditions. Grows from 6 to 12 inches high and has violet-blue flowers in spring and summer. Can be invasive. Space the plants 6 to 8 inches apart. Hardy to zone 5a (–20° F).

If your landscape — or personality — begs for an alternative to a traditional lawn, go ahead; take the leap and join other happy ground-cover gardeners.

One World of Gardens

Join us on a symbolic "walk" through the world of gardening.

We believe that walking is a particularly apt metaphor. When walking, you can truly notice a garden and appreciate what it offers.

In fact, footprints are the sign of a healthy garden. So walking through your garden frequently will benefit both you and it.

We selected the following eight garden "types" to represent the many. While each one shows a distinct style and form, all eight gardens are generic by intention. Project your own yard and garden onto them. Then visualize what might be and acting on your inspiration, make your vision a reality.

Slow down, relax, and take a walk through the gardens with us.

A Contemporary Kitchen Garden

Flavorful, healthful, homegrown vegetables: Who needs another excuse for a kitchen garden?

We calculated, measured, and designed this garden for a sunny 20 x 20 foot location. You'll need to pick your favorite crops and varieties, of course, but this basic plan has proven to be a good all-region starting point.

The long, central pathway is 3 feet wide, broad enough for a garden cart or wheelbarrow full of compost. Paths between individual beds are 1 ½ feet wide.

All but two of the beds are 3 feet deep. Space hungry corn (top left) takes four rows in a bed 8 ½ x 11 feet. Likewise, sprawling zucchini, winter squash, and nasturtiums (bottom right) need a bed 6 ½ x 8 ½ feet.

For best sun exposure, orient the garden so that the rows run east to west, with the tallest plants on the north end.

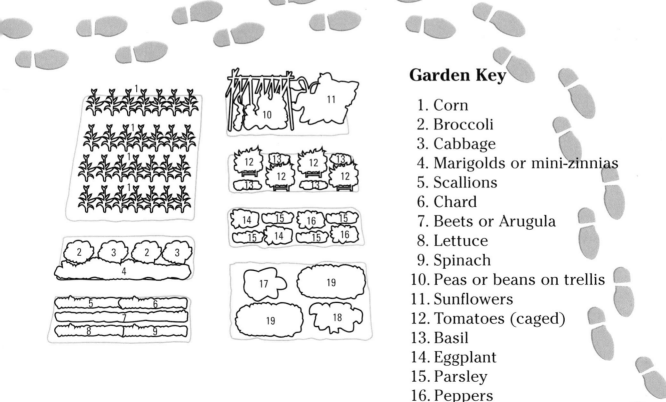

Garden Key

1. Corn
2. Broccoli
3. Cabbage
4. Marigolds or mini-zinnias
5. Scallions
6. Chard
7. Beets or Arugula
8. Lettuce
9. Spinach
10. Peas or beans on trellis
11. Sunflowers
12. Tomatoes (caged)
13. Basil
14. Eggplant
15. Parsley
16. Peppers
17. Zucchini
18. Winter squash
19. Nasturtiums

A Homestead Garden

One-quarter of an acre and independence!

It's a dream isn't it, growing all the food your family needs? With a little planning, you can make it happen, or at least provide most of your own food, even on a small plot of land. Our ¼-acre homestead orchard and garden will help you grow plenty of produce for eating fresh and for "putting-by."

The 40 x 40 foot orchard includes pears, dwarf apples, plums, peaches, and both sweet and tart cherries. Beyond its borders lies plenty of space for strawberries, blueberries, raspberries, grapes, and the same 20 x 20 foot vegetable garden you see on the previous page.

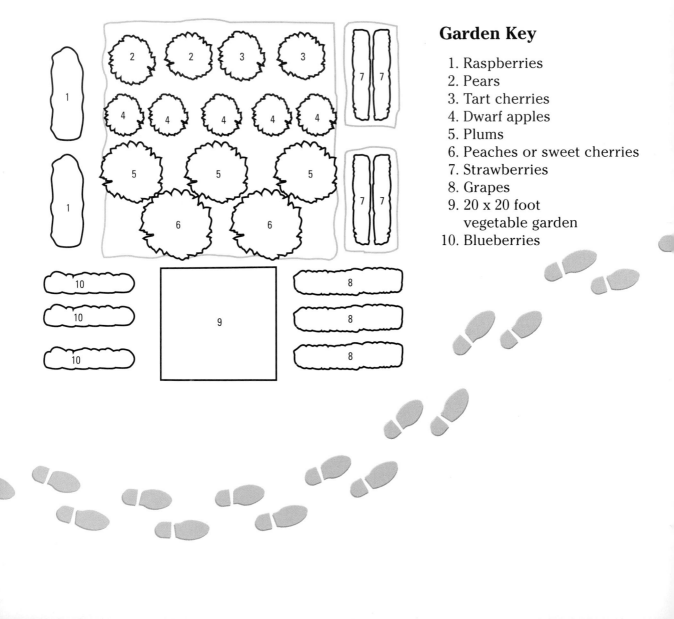

Garden Key

1. Raspberries
2. Pears
3. Tart cherries
4. Dwarf apples
5. Plums
6. Peaches or sweet cherries
7. Strawberries
8. Grapes
9. 20 x 20 foot vegetable garden
10. Blueberries

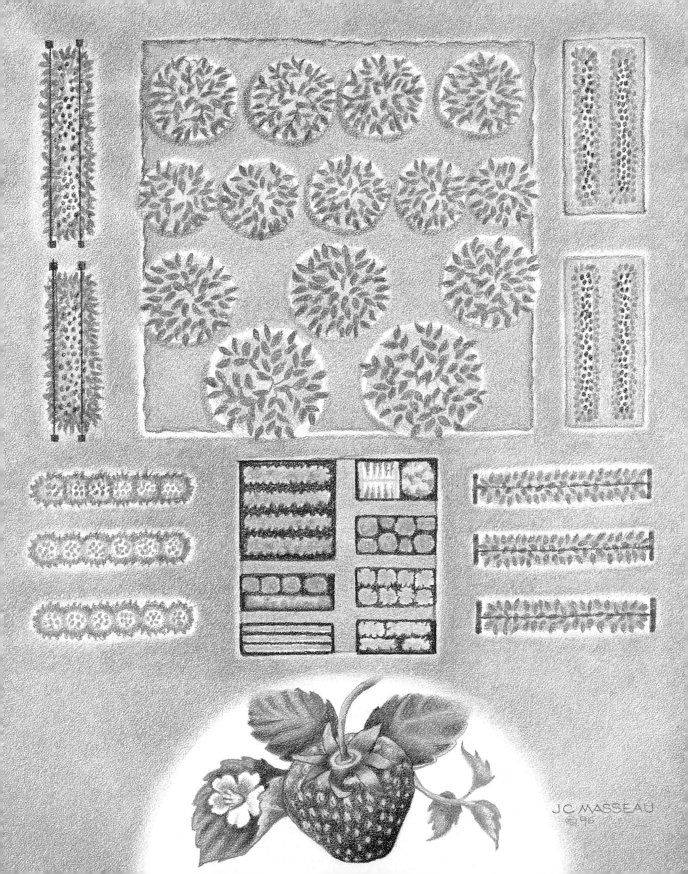

JC MASSEAU
©96

A Garden for Birds and Butterflies

There's nothing too complicated about making a garden "friendly" to birds and butterflies. They like much the same things we do: plenty of flowers, shade, sun, shelter, and water. Just choose your plants and garden techniques with your winged neighbors in mind.

For example, you can choose plants with the berries or nectar that are particularly attractive to these delicate creatures. And there's no law against putting out a feeder or two, especially if the feeders are near the kitchen window and easy to see and enjoy.

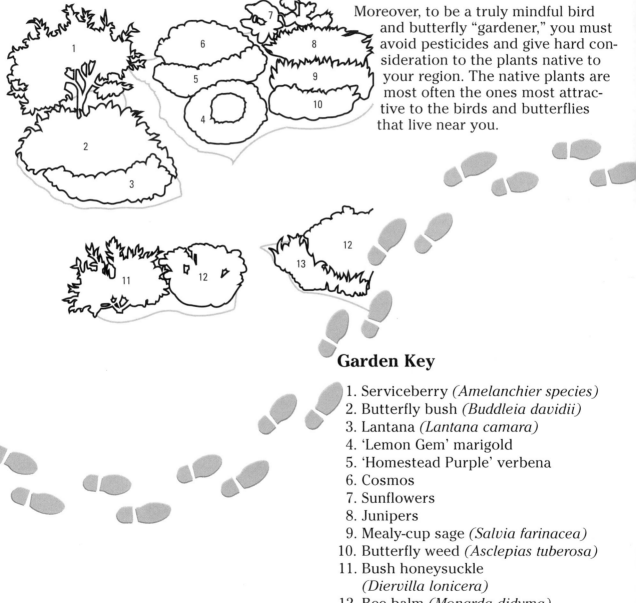

Moreover, to be a truly mindful bird and butterfly "gardener," you must avoid pesticides and give hard consideration to the plants native to your region. The native plants are most often the ones most attractive to the birds and butterflies that live near you.

Garden Key

1. Serviceberry *(Amelanchier species)*
2. Butterfly bush *(Buddleia davidii)*
3. Lantana *(Lantana camara)*
4. 'Lemon Gem' marigold
5. 'Homestead Purple' verbena
6. Cosmos
7. Sunflowers
8. Junipers
9. Mealy-cup sage *(Salvia farinacea)*
10. Butterfly weed *(Asclepias tuberosa)*
11. Bush honeysuckle
    (Diervilla lonicera)
12. Bee balm *(Monarda didyma)*
13. Daffodils

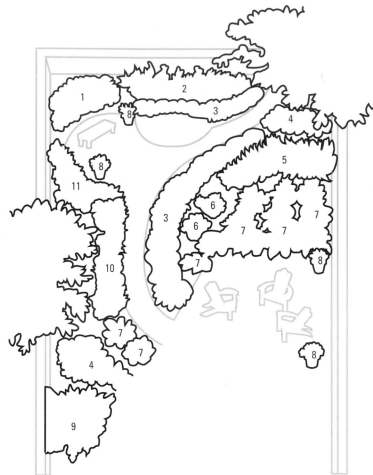

Garden Key

1. Cyclamen *(Cyclamen persicum)*
2. Ferns
3. Impatiens
4. Periwinkle *(Vinca minor)*
5. False spiraea *(Astilbe)*
6. Bleeding heart
   (Dicentra spectabilis)
7. Hostas
8. Caladiums (in containers)
9. Small tree (such as Japanese maple, trident maple, or serviceberry)
10. Coleus
11. Globeflower *(Trollius)*

A City Garden in the Shade

You've got to have shade. No matter where you live, a bench or chair in the shade is the most welcome sight on a midsummer afternoon. (Okay, we can think of a few, a very few, exceptions.)

But sometimes shade isn't a choice. Maybe it's uninvited and comes from surrounding buildings or trees. If your garden is too shaded by overgrown trees, selectively thin the trees to allow more light to pass through.

And don't think of shade as simply "cool." Leaves overhead protect you from heat and light to be sure, but also they protect you from your neighbor's windows. Either way, when shade is your garden destiny, make it a virtue. And despite the shade, you can still have a festive, colorful garden. In fact, plant colors are often most vibrant in shade or filtered light.

Luckily, many plants are well-adapted to growing in shady situations. Several are listed in Chapter 5, but some of our favorites found their way into the garden we planned here.

A Garden for Color . . . and Cutting

Color and color and more color. Our eyes feast on it. It's food for our spirits. We just can't seem to get enough of it.

Our plan combines annuals and perennials so that you'll have color in every season, even winter. Color doesn't always mean "flower." The hollies, for example, show their color in shiny green leaves and vivid red winter berries. You can find more about flowers and ways to combine them in Chapter 20.

Part of producing a colorful cutting garden is enjoying the flowers indoors. Take a look at Chapter 25 where we gathered some of our favorite ways of stretching the indoor life of cut flowers.

Garden Key

1. Sunflowers
2. Celosia
3. *Zinnia angustifolia*
4. Mealy-cup sage *(Salvia farinacea)*
5. Daylilies
6. White summer phlox *(Phlox paniculata)*
7. Holly
8. Shasta daisy
9. Foxglove
10. Mixed zinnias
11. Yarrow *(Achillea filipendulina)*
12. Chrysanthemum

A Garden to Grace Your Home's Entrance

The most convincing way to say "welcome" to your visitors is to make their pathway to your door comfortable and inviting. (Some expert designers say it's the #1 rule of landscaping!) Lining the path and entry with colorful plants is the easiest way to do just that.

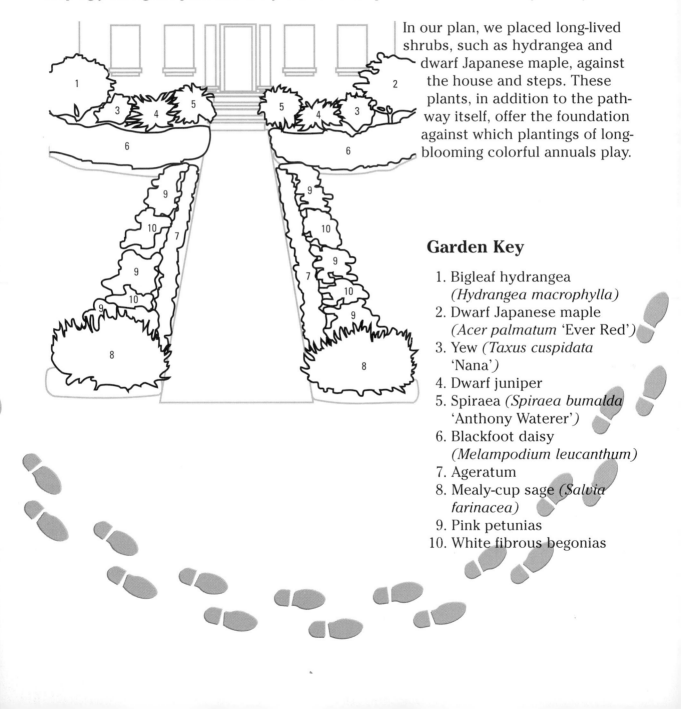

In our plan, we placed long-lived shrubs, such as hydrangea and dwarf Japanese maple, against the house and steps. These plants, in addition to the pathway itself, offer the foundation against which plantings of long-blooming colorful annuals play.

Garden Key

1. Bigleaf hydrangea
   (*Hydrangea macrophylla*)
2. Dwarf Japanese maple
   (*Acer palmatum* 'Ever Red')
3. Yew (*Taxus cuspidata*
   'Nana')
4. Dwarf juniper
5. Spiraea (*Spiraea bumalda*
   'Anthony Waterer')
6. Blackfoot daisy
   (*Melampodium leucanthum*)
7. Ageratum
8. Mealy-cup sage (*Salvia
   farinacea*)
9. Pink petunias
10. White fibrous begonias

A Garden for Roses

Roses have delighted gardeners for generations. More than any other ornamental plant, roses are enjoyed on every continent and coaxed by gardeners in every language. The official flower of the United States, roses are perhaps more rightly the "world flower."

Roses are so diverse that you're bound to find one that suits your needs. Low ones with season-long flowers? Sure. Tall ones as background? Of course. White and disease free? Coming right up. A trailing ground cover? Small enough for a tea cup? Big, almost tree-like? You name it, and there's a rose to fill the bill.

For most gardeners, the key is some combination of rose plants that produces a supply of flowers for cutting, flowers for adding color to the garden, and flowers that are highly scented and not too much trouble. (Although, honestly, gardeners who invest the most time in their roses would never consider their time in the garden "trouble.")

So we laid out this demonstration rose garden, which includes a few of our favorite roses. For more ideas on rose gardens and care, refer to Chapter 23.

Garden Key

1. 'Queen Elizabeth' (pink grandiflora)
2. 'Graham Thomas' (yellow Austin English rose, fragrant)
3. 'Double Delight' (red and white hybrid tea, fragrant)
4. 'Iceberg' (white floribunda)
5. 'Altissmo' (red climber)
6. 'Olympiad' (red hybrid tea)
7. Mealy-cup sage (*Salvia farinacea*)
8. Juniper (*Juniperus scopulorum* 'Blue Creeper')
9. 'Party Girl' (yellow-apricot miniature)
10. Lamb's ears (*Stachys byzantina*)
11. Pink summer phlox (*Phlox paniculata*)

A Stunning Garden in a Pot

Do you have the winter blahs? Or no room for a garden? Then make a garden in a pot! This plan for a single 14-inch (wide and deep) pot of spring-blooming bulbs is just one of many ways to garden in containers, whether for one pot or for your entire balcony or patio.

Instead of only one type of bulb, we combined three of the all-time favorites: tulips, daffodils, and crocuses. The bloom times and colors complement each other in a pot just as they do in a garden.

Cover the drainage hole with a section of screen and add a 1-inch layer of light-weight, fast-draining soil mix as recommended in Chapter 22. Plant the tulips on this layer, and then cover them with more potting soil. Daffodils go on the next layer up, and the crocuses are planted on top in two layers in order to stagger their blooms.

In northern regions (zone 6 and colder), protect bulbs from frost damage by keeping them at least 4 inches from the sides of the container, and move the pots to a protected location (a garage or basement) during the coldest months.

Garden Key

1. Tulips: 20 'Peacock Mixed' (or 'Dutch Fair')
2. Daffodils: 20 'Carlton' (or 'Dutch Master')
3. Crocuses: 40 'Giant Crocus Mixed'
4. Soil
5. Gravel (sand, optional)

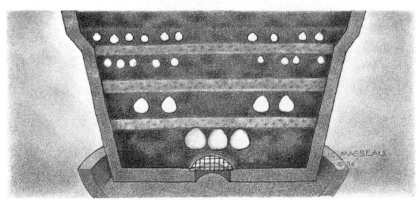

Part III
Making Your Garden

"Well, enjoy everyone! But please don't feed the flytraps –
you give them pate, and they'll never go back to mealworms."

In this part . . .

If by some strange happenstance you read straight through to this point, the logic of the book's organization is no doubt clear: first a plan, then the plants, and finally a garden. Of course, you didn't read straight through (we wouldn't either). In this case, you've just arrived at the fun part: all about garden making and planting.

We begin this part with some of the more elaborate features your garden may include, such as arbors, fences, walkways, and the like. This is important even if you don't do all the work yourself. In fact, we counsel that often it's wiser to work with a professional than to do the task yourself.

Then there's the subject near and dear to every gardener — dirt (or in the proper jargon, *soil*). We tell you how to find out what you've got and how to change it (if necessary).

Finally, you're ready to plant. Chapter 15 walks you through the process of getting down and dirty.

Chapter 13
Making Places for People

In This Chapter

▶ Getting the tools you'll need

▶ Making easy paths and walkways

▶ Building fences and digging postholes

▶ Constructing decks, patios, and terraces

▶ Using lattice screens, gazebos, and arbors

*E*very garden, no matter how small, needs to have a little open space for walking, working, and relaxing. If your garden doesn't include some of these spaces, we suggest that you construct them, at least in rudimentary form, before you plant.

Paving, Fences, and Other Expensive Stuff

Good fences, patios, decks, and well-paved walkways make it possible to be outdoors longer — in more kinds of weather and in more seasons of the year. This aspect of making a garden can be a little more time consuming and expensive than buying and setting out plants — wood, brick, and stone are expensive.

Garden designers often talk about dividing the yard or garden into several "outdoor rooms." It's a useful concept. The idea of rooms lets you contemplate planning the whole yard as a series of smaller, more manageable projects. Start with a picket fence around the vegetable garden or a brick path to the rose beds or compost pile; end with a flagstone patio and swimming pool. If you think big, you'll go farther.

The room idea reminds us to scale the things we make in human terms: Paths in a private garden should be wide enough for either a single person or two people side by side. Patios should be sized to suit the number of people in your family or the number that you ordinarily entertain for dinner.

D.I.Y. (Do It Yourself) or Hire Help

For every gardening project, you face a spectrum of approaches, ranging from low tech and inexpensive to lavish master craftsmanship. Low-tech solutions are easily changed later as your taste changes or finances improve. As the garden evolves, you'll find yourself redoing earlier efforts, at no great loss or inconvenience.

Some projects — like gazebos, decks, retaining walls, and concrete work — require a high level of skill. When you want experienced help in garden construction, the best place to start is with local garden centers and landscapers who employ or know trade workers specializing in outdoor work.

Carpenters are a lot easier to find than good masons, which may be one reason that decks are mushrooming all over suburbia while masonry patios — which are more durable, maintenance free, and often cheaper yet more attractive — are less popular than they used to be. You can learn whether you like garden masonry by building a walkway. But first, read on to see what you'll need.

A tool kit for the most elementary garden-building projects — setting fence posts, installing paving — includes some of the same equipment that you use when you prepare the soil. Here is a list of three such tools. (See Figure 13-1. Also see Chapter 4 for a list of more basic tools.)

- ✔ **Digging bar.** Essential for chiseling a hole into the ground; also good for drilling narrow holes prior to driving large stakes

- ✔ **Pick.** Essential for loosening hard, rocky ground prior to digging

- ✔ **Posthole digger.** Essential for removing earth loosened with a digging bar; good for digging holes in sandy soil

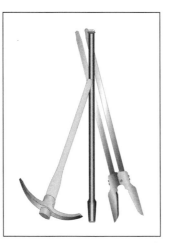

Figure 13-1:
Tools for
setting
posts.

Walking along Paths

Paths and walks get you from one place to another and keep the lawn from being worn to bare ground. And they do something else that's not so obvious: They control where the eye travels as it looks over the garden. So the first step in making a garden that looks good is to make the walkways attractive.

The primary walkways in any garden are the ones that lead out from the doors of the house to other buildings, to garden areas, to the driveway, or to the public walk in front. Chances are that many of these paths have already been built and don't need your immediate attention. On the other hand, keep in mind that the day may come when you want to upgrade them to be of a more generous size, to take more sensible directions, or to include more attractive materials that blend better with your personal garden style.

Side by side: determining width

Don't make any path narrower than 2 feet, the minimum comfortable width for one person. Make it any narrower, and you'll find that turning and reversing direction becomes awkward.

For main paths, 4 feet is the minimum width for two people walking side by side or for a two-wheeled garden cart. When you can afford the space or materials, make paths a little wider than the bare minimum. Shrubs, flowers, and vegetable plants often spill out of their beds and into the paths, which makes them seem smaller. In very small gardens, the path (or a section of it) may need to double as work space and a socializing area; if so, the more generous you can make it, the better.

Your ideas will change as the seasons pass. When time or money is in short supply, a good strategy is to build paths that are intentionally temporary. Walks surfaced with turf, wood chips, or gravel can serve for many years if they're well designed and regularly maintained. And you can change their shape or direction easily. See the next section for more information on naturalistic paths.

Naturalistic walks: lawn or mulch

When making two or more adjacent beds (as for rose gardens or vegetable beds), the simplest way to make a path between them is to leave the lawn in place and keep it mowed. Grass paths are fine for areas that do not get heavy foot traffic. If a bare area becomes worn down the center, you can set a single row of stepping stones into the exposed earth (see Figure 13-2). Notice the plastic edging, which we discuss more in the next section.

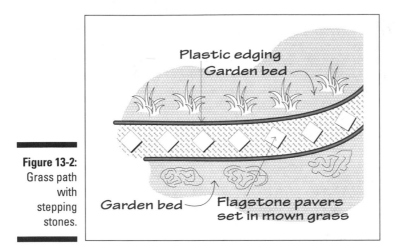

Figure 13-2:
Grass path
with
stepping
stones.

Although grass paths require no installation time, they do require more maintenance than any other kind of walkway. Lawn grasses continually grow into adjacent garden beds, so you must pull or cut lawn grass runner roots several times during the season. You'll also need to trim the grass that creeps over the stones.

Use a spade to recut the edges of grass paths at least once a year. A 2- or 3-inch-deep trench between the lawn path and the garden bed is a traditional way to keep lawn runners from invading beds.

The gardener's edge

A more permanent solution than a grass path — and the first step in upgrading to more formal paths — is to install a permanent edging. Such edgings used to be made of steel, brick, or stone. Today tough, durable black plastic installed below ground level lasts a very long time. It comes in two basic types. The first type, black lawn edging, has a round bead at the top, which gives strength and a more finished look. To install it, cut a narrow trench with a spade and push the edging into place. You can also simply set a single row of brick to make an attractive, moderately priced edging and provide a hard surface for the wheels of the lawn mower.

The other type is made to retain brick, stone, or masonry pavers. To install this type, you excavate a bed to hold the paving. The top of this edging is an inch or so below the top of the paving and almost invisible. The material is often held in place with special nails. You can use this kind to retain bark or gravel paths as well, as long as you excavate a bed for the material — see the next section.

Bark and gravel

Either bark or gravel makes an excellent path where the lawn is poor or absent. The cost and the types available vary widely in different locales. Use metal, masonry, or plastic edging with bark and, especially, gravel paths.

Shredded bark, wood chips, or pine needles make good paths because they decompose slowly. They discourage weed growth more than other organic mulches because they contain very little nitrogen. The moister your climate, the more frequently you will need to replace or replenish these mulches. If weeds begin to grow in the mulch, remove the mulch completely and recycle it through one *hot composting cycle.* (See Chapter 24 for more about composting.) You can use the composted path mulch around shrubs, trees, or perennials and even around vegetables if you don't work it into the soil.

Gravel is the next step up in paving materials. A gravel path lasts many years with minimal upkeep. It is cleaner and drier than organic mulch paths. Excavate the path before installing gravel, digging out a trench 2 to 3 inches deep. Apply the gravel at least 2 inches deep; 4 inches deep is even better.

Some types of gravel, like crushed limestone, may raise the pH (see Chapter 14) and affect nearby sensitive plants, such as rhododendrons and blueberries. Ask about pH at the stoneyard where you buy the gravel.

Brick, stone, and concrete

Brick, cut stone, and concrete pavers are easy to handle and fairly easy to cut with masonry blades and chisels. The work is exacting and slow — perfect if you're the contemplative type and in no great hurry. The bed you dig should be deeper than for a gravel path — 6 or 7 inches. The bottom 4 inches should hold 2 or 3 inches of gravel topped by a 1- or 2-inch bed of fine sand. Use plastic or metal edging to retain the pavers. When you're finished, sweep fine sand into the gaps between pavers.

Poured concrete requires more skill, even more digging, and much heavier equipment. Most times, you'll be better off hiring professional concrete workers. Ask your contractor about special decorative finishes and stains — after all, concrete garden paths don't have to look like city sidewalks!

Step by step: making slopes easier to climb

Wherever garden walkways go up or down a steep grade, steps make the passage safer and the garden more attractive. Any material that you can use to pave a walk can be incorporated into steps. For comfort and safety, the height of individual steps should be at least 5 inches and no more than 9 inches. Steps should be sloped downhill slightly so that they drain quickly, about $1/4$ inch per foot.

Stop all weeds before installing mulch or gravel paths

If the ground contains grass or weeds, you must control them before installing either mulch or gravel paths. You can begin the process by laying down a mulch of black plastic, landscape fabric weed barriers (see Chapter 16), or thick layers of wet newspaper and covering them with a 2- to 4-inch layer of the finished mulch.

But the one-step approach to stopping weeds does not exist. Tenacious weeds (such as quackgrass or wild onions) can eventually pierce porous weed barriers. For the long term, it's better to go a step further and dig out most of the weed roots. Here's what you do:

1. **Lay out the edges of the path with a length of hose or a row of stakes.**

2. **Cut straight edges on both sides of the path with a spade.**

3. **Starting at one end, remove the sod of grass or weeds. Skim off the top 2 to 3 inches.**

4. **Put the weeds or grass out of the way in a pile, cover to exclude light, and let the material rot for a year to kill weed roots.**

5. **Trim the bottom of the path perfectly flat with the spade.**

   You don't have to make it level, but you'll need to even out the small rises and dips.

6. **Install the edging and lay a weed barrier in the bottom.**

   Even though you've cut most of the weeds away, some seeds and bits of root will remain.

7. **Fill the path bed.**

   If you're using an organic mulch, fill the path bed to the top.

   If you're using gravel, get the 1/2-inch size and don't use less than a 2-inch layer of it. If your bed is deeper, you can economize by putting a larger and more inexpensive gravel in the bottom of the trench and then topping it with a 2-inch layer of the finer grade.

On long, shallow slopes, single, widely spaced steps are appropriate. Wide steps should be at least 6 or 7 feet deep to allow people to take at least three full strides as they cross. In naturalistic settings, use split logs or landscape timbers to make the steps. In more formal walks, use risers of concrete, brick, or stone blocks.

Where the grade rises sharply, plan a closely placed series of steps. Design these so walkers take a single step with each stride. The treads (surface of the step) should be about a foot wide. Shallower steps can be wider, but no more than 18 inches.

You can build frames for the steps with landscape timbers filled in with gravel or earth and topped with whatever paving your path is made of: mulch, gravel, stone, or other masonry. Usually, the more formal pavers — brick, cut stone, or cast concrete — are set over a poured concrete base that is best installed by a professional.

Cool Things on Posts

A garden is a protected place. The protection can be from the eyes of strangers, from marauding animals, or from the neighbors' kids and pets. It can be from invading roots of weeds or trees or from harsh winds.

You can achieve this protection with some kind of fence or wall. Today, fences and walls are almost always made of wood or, occasionally, metal (chain-link). Or they're hedges of living plants. (See Chapter 7 for more about hedges.) Small protectors are usually fences of wood or wire mesh.

Don't fence me in: property and privacy fences

Fences that surround the border of a property are usually more symbolic barriers than real ones. Post-on-board or rail fences keep people from taking shortcuts across your property, even though these fences can be easily climbed and present no real barrier to most animals. Often, these barriers are made of various elements — a bit of fence here, a stretch of hedge or a cluster of trees there — and only partially cover the entire perimeter.

Large fences or walls that are able to serve as true privacy or noise barriers or are strong enough to completely exclude people and other forms of wildlife are quite expensive. Prefabricated stockade fencing or chain-link fencing is used extensively in high-density suburban neighborhoods.

See Figure 13-3 for a sample of wooden fences.

Figure 13-3: Types of wooden fences (left to right): stockade (or *grapestake*), post and rail, and post and board.

Perimeter walls are often subject to zoning regulations and require a building permit. If you can afford to, consider hiring a specialist contractor for larger fences and masonry walls.

Building-supply companies carry fence materials of all kinds and have a wide selection of prefabricated wooden fencing. Farm-supply stores stock both wood and wire but have a wider selection of wire fencing, as well as materials for electrical fences.

Keeping Peter Rabbit out

The simplest fences are light-gauge, galvanized or coated-wire barriers that keep rabbits and other animals out of vegetable and flower beds. Chicken wire is the most popular fencing material. It's light, easy to bend and cut, durable, and inexpensive. Chicken wire is good for temporary fences that are quick to take up and move around the yard as needs change.

These fences should be at least 24 inches high, ideally more. To stop burrowing animals like groundhogs, the bottom of the wire mesh should be buried slightly. Here's what you do:

1. **Excavate a strip of sod on the outside of the fence.**

2. **Bend the bottom of the wire out horizontally into the shallow trench.**

3. **Reset the sod.**

For climbing animals (groundhogs, opossums, and raccoons, for example), the best protection is an electric wire at the top of the fence. Or make a three-wire electric fence. Electric fences don't injure animals.

These animals are also put off by a floppy fence. Fasten chicken wire only partway up the stakes, and the top will be very floppy indeed.

To support the wire mesh, use either metal fence posts or wooden stakes. First, drill pilot holes 12 to 18 inches deep into the earth with a heavy iron bar. It's then much easier to drive the stakes into the ground with a heavy hammer or maul. Attach the fence with wire.

Here are some tips for a more permanent or substantial fence:

- ✔ Use heavy-gauge wires or wooden panels. Snow fence is a strong and reasonably priced intermediate option that can give a more rustic look than a plain wire fence.

- ✔ More-substantial fences need bigger posts, either 4 x 4s or 4-inch round posts cut from small-diameter tree trunks. Locust, cedar, cypress, and redwood are among the most rot-resistant species. High-quality, pressure-treated posts are especially long lasting.

Prefab fencing: pickets to stockades

Think of large fence posts as permanent and monolithic. To the posts, you can attach a wide array of decorative and utilitarian wooden panels. And you can dress up homely posts by nailing on face and backing boards, topped with caps and finials from prefab to funky. Think of fence panels as being made of rails that run from post to post with pickets or slats to fill the space in between.

You can buy several kinds of prefabricated fence panels. Panels of picket fence, sometimes already painted white, are available everywhere. So is stockade fence, made of tall, rustic stakes sawn in half and nailed tightly side by side. Basket-weave panels are more formal looking and lightweight.

 You'll see that these are simple designs, easily built with the most basic carpentry skills. But unless you have a special design that you want to duplicate, the cost of the material and the amount of labor required for prefab fence panels are hard to beat.

To avoid ending up with panels that don't fit your posts. Instead, set your first two posts, attach the panel, and proceed one post and panel at a time down the row.

Hole in one

Here are the steps for making a permanent fence:

1. Dig a first-class hole.

It should be 2 to 3 feet deep and as narrow as you can make it. A posthole digger may be the only tool you need in light, stone-free soils. In heavy clay or rocky ground, you'll also need a _digging bar._ (See "D.I.Y. [Do It Yourself] or Hire Help" and Figure 13-1 earlier in this chapter.) Loosen soil and stones with the chisel end of the bar and then excavate with the posthole digger.

2. When the post is in place, place about 6 inches of earth and tamp it firm with the disk end of the bar.

Use a 2-foot level to make sure that the post is vertical.

3. Refill the rest of the way, tamping the fill firmly every 6 inches and checking the post periodically with the level.

Do not set the post in concrete. If the post should ever need to be reset, the concrete base will make doing the job without digging out the heavy base virtually impossible.

Putting a Living Room Outdoors: Patios, Terraces, and Decks

You own only so much space. Use all of it for living, the outside as well as the inside. This is what landscaping is all about.

With that thought in mind, as you consider where to put a patio, terrace, or deck, look first to an area next to the house, ideally adjacent to a major doorway. These paved areas function as an extension of the home and serve best if they are readily accessible to everyone in the household. The wall of the home provides privacy and shelter from one direction. From inside the home, the patio, terrace, or deck is a corridor for views to the garden beyond.

The defining elements of a patio, terrace, or deck are a smooth, flat area and a hard, free-draining surface.

Here are brief definitions:

- ✔ *Patios* and *terraces* are different names for essentially the same thing: a garden area paved with flat stones, masonry, or gravel.

- ✔ *Decks* are made of wood; they're constructed like the floor of a building and rest on posts or pilings.

Decks and patios should be sloped so water drains off them and away from any adjacent buildings. Make the slope the same as for steps: $1/4$ inch per foot. This amount of slope will look and feel flat but will carry rain water away quickly.

How big to make it

All patios and decks incorporate space that serves as a walkway, often intersecting walkways. For example, a very small patio or deck outside the door to a ground-floor bedroom or office might be as small as 4 x 8 feet: a 4 x 4-foot area for a single chair or bench adjoining the 4-foot-wide walkway leading to the door.

On patios next to the kitchen door, you may want to allow extra space for storage containers or a small table. Avid gardeners often incorporate a small work table or potting bench for dealing with flowers, vegetables, and potted plants as they move in and out of doors seasonally.

To plan a space for outdoor socializing, begin your calculations by thinking of the dimensions of your dining room or living room. When in doubt, make the area slightly bigger than might seem necessary for the number of people you ordinarily entertain. Adding patios and decks really is like getting an extra room for your house at a very reasonable cost.

Patios (and terraces)

You make a patio by using the same techniques that we describe for building walks (see "Walking along Paths" earlier in this chapter). Patios are best suited to relatively flat sites. When building on even a shallow slope, retain the edges with edging of concrete, brick, or stone. Where the rise or drop is greater than 6 inches, the patio needs a retaining wall of masonry or heavy landscape timber.

On nearly flat ground, patios made of cut stone, brick, or preformed masonry are relatively easy do-it-yourself projects. The work is slow but satisfying. If you need retaining walls or want poured concrete paving, you're better off hiring a specialist contractor.

Hitting the deck

Decks are best suited to steep sites or where the floor of the house is several feet above the level of the ground outside. Decks are complicated building projects involving expensive materials and advanced carpentry skills. They are usually best left to specialists.

Pressure-treated wood is overused in deck building. It is appropriate only for sections of wood that will touch the ground — the pilings and floor joists. The sawdust is toxic and should not be inhaled. The waste lumber cannot be burned, because it releases very toxic smoke. Buy the exact lengths that you need and avoid cutting completely. Use only galvanized nails, brackets, and other fasteners. For the surface of the deck and seats and railings, use high-quality, rot-resistant wood, like untreated cedar or redwood.

For information about setting pilings that will support the deck, see "Hole in one" earlier in this chapter. Deck frames often rest on concrete piers with metal shoes cast into the top. The shoes hold the bottoms of wooden posts or rafters. For details on building a deck, many good books are available (see Appendix A).

Now Showing: Private Screenings

You can get private screenings in Hollywood — or you can make your own. To create private nooks within your garden, you can build various kinds of rooms within it. They can be a green refuge, like a grape arbor, or a light and airy trellis covered with climbing roses.

If your aim is protection from wind, sun, and noise, a wall and roof made of living vines can serve as well as wood or stone. They're more beautiful, too, with less expense and less work for you.

Gazebos and arbors are two types of screens:

- *Gazebos* are small, wooden houses, always with roofs, usually with open sides or latticework, and often with floors. Many garden centers sell prefabricated gazebos as well as kits.

- *Arbors* are a simpler and very popular way to create almost-instant shade, using roses, grapes, or ornamental vines. They can be as basic as a pair of tall posts spanned with timber or metal. A series of these arbor-arches make a covered walkway called a *pergola*. These screens should be as well made as the best fences because the vines (even with regular pruning, which is essential) become very heavy.

The quickest way to get a little privacy and protection from late-day sun and wind is to put up a screen on one side or more of your patio or deck. It can be as light as a short section of lattice covered with climbing roses or vines, or as formal as a solid wall of wood.

Chapter 14

It's All Happening in the Soil

. . . .

In This Chapter

▶ Preparing your site

▶ Testing and understanding your soil

▶ Improving your soil

▶ Using cover crops

▶ Making raised beds

▶ Double digging

. . . .

*P*reparing your soil is probably the most important step toward bringing your garden to life. Why is it so important? Because of roots. Roots make up half of every plant, sometimes more, but you often forget them because you don't see them — except for the occasional maple root that the lawn mower keeps hitting. But they are there, spreading, digging, questing for nutrients and moisture. Taking time now to create a healthy underground environment for your plants goes a long way toward ensuring a healthy, productive garden.

Begin to prepare the soil for planting by removing existing vegetation and by working the soil well — break it up, check its characteristics, and add organic materials such as compost (called *amending* the soil) as necessary. Your goal is to create an airy soil, rich in oxygen and plant nutrients. If your soil is wet, which squeezes out critical oxygen, raise the bed or improve the drainage. For plants with special soil or nutrient needs, you can add extra organic matter, sand, or fertilizers.

Dig Here: Clearing the Site

Before breaking ground for a new garden, decide where your garden will go and make a plan (see Chapters 2 and 3). Here are the preliminary steps for clearing the site where you intend to place your garden:

1. **Outline the area where you'll go to work.**

   If you're developing a square or rectangular area, you can establish straight-edge lines by stretching a string between two sticks. Leave the string in place or mark the line with a trickle of white ground limestone. For rounded portions of the garden, use a garden hose or rope to lay out the line. Adjust the hose position until the curve looks smooth.

2. **Use a flat spade to dig a small trench that establishes the outline of the garden plot.**

3. **Clear the surface by removing plants, sod, brush, and rocks.**

   Doing this step the season before planting is best, but you can do it at any time.

4. **Mow the site to clear the rough ground.**

5. **Cut down woody plants and grub out the roots with a mattock.**

6. **Once the vegetation is down to a manageable level, you can further remove the sod and other low vegetation.**

You can use several techniques for clearing the site. If the garden is currently lawn, you can strip off the turf, roots and all, using a flat spade. This method is work but does a thorough job.

Watch for thick, white perennial weed roots as you go. When you see some, reach down and pull them up so they won't resprout in the middle of your flowers or tomatoes. Or you can kill grass by covering it with black plastic or rototill the existing vegetation into the soil — see the following sections.

Stripping sod

Here's how to strip sod:

1. **A couple of days prior to digging, water the area to be cleared.**

   Stripping sod is easier when the soil is lightly moist.

2. **If you haven't done so already, mark the edges of the plot.**

3. **Starting at one side of the plot, slip your spade under the grass and slide it under the sod.**

   Don't dig too deep; you want to remove merely the sod and an inch or two of roots.

   Another system is to precut the sod into square or rectangular sections and then loosen each section with the spade.

4. Pivot the tool up, letting the sod flip up over the spade.

5. Slice off the sod section and toss it in a wheelbarrow to take to the compost pile.

6. Gradually continue in this manner until the garden is cleared of sod.

Applying black plastic mulch

An easy way to clear a garden is to cover it with black plastic landscape mulch. After a month under black plastic, existing plants die from lack of sunlight. You must plan ahead to use this method, but it works like a charm.

The process is easy. Just spread the plastic over the entire garden area, securing the edges with spare rocks, bricks, or boards. Let neighboring pieces overlap by several inches so no light can penetrate. Come back in a month to rototill the dead grass into the soil. Wait about ten days for errant weeds to sprout (because you haven't removed weed seeds, you're sure to get some growth). Then cut down any weeds that emerge.

Using the repeated tilling/cover cropping method

If you have plenty of time or a large garden not suited to the methods described previously, consider the repeated tilling method, which adds good organic matter to the soil and kills existing weeds but takes much of the growing season to get into shape. (See Chapter 16 for more on weed control.)

1. In spring, rototill the garden area and broadcast seeds of a cover crop such as buckwheat, sudangrass, or black-eyed peas.

2. Once the cover crop gets to be about 6 inches high, till again to work it into the soil.

3. Let the cover crop decay, which takes a couple of weeks during warm weather. Then till again and prepare to plant.

Checking Your Soil

Now that you've exposed the soil, take a good look to see how well it will perform for your garden. Here are the basics that you'll need to know to become your own do-it-yourself soils expert, plus some easy tests that you can do at home.

Texture

Soil is composed of air spaces, organic matter, and, mostly, mineral particles. Soil minerals come in three types: sand, silt, and clay. The relative percentages of these particles in the soil determine its texture.

The ideal soil texture is *loam*, which is composed of sand, clay, silt, and *humus* (organic matter in the soil). Generally, the darker the soil, the more humus it contains, the richer and warmer it is, and the easier it is to work. Loam retains water without becoming waterlogged and contains a balance of nutrients. (See Figure 14-1.)

✔ **Sand.** Has the largest soil particles. A soil with 70 percent sand particles is "sandy." Water drains through it fast, and it dries quickly. Although sandy soils are less fertile than others, they warm up earlier in spring.

✔ **Clay.** Has the smallest soil particles and the least amount of water and air spaces between particles. A soil with at least 35 percent of clay is a "clay" soil. Water enters and drains from clay soil slowly. Clay soils are very fertile.

✔ **Loam.** Has a mixture of sand, silt, and clay particles. Typically, loam soils contain 40 percent sand, 40 percent silt, and 20 percent clay. Loam soils are ideal for most plants.

Figure 14-1:
The size of the mineral particles determines a soil's texture. Loam is ideal soil for most plants.

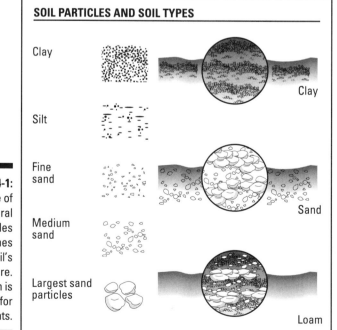

SOIL PARTICLES AND SOIL TYPES

Clay

Silt

Fine sand

Medium sand

Largest sand particles

Clay

Sand

Loam

We've found two methods to be useful in identifying your soil's texture: the *ribbons-and-bows method* and the *jar method*.

Ribbons and bows

You can get a general idea of your soil's texture by taking a handful of moist soil, squeezing it into a ball, and working it out in a ribbon between your thumb and your forefinger. Stand the ribbon straight up in the air.

- ✔ If you can't form a ribbon, the soil is at least 50 percent sand and has very little clay.
- ✔ If the ribbon is less than 2 inches long before breaking, your soil has roughly 25 percent clay in it.
- ✔ If the ribbon is 2 to $3^1/_2$ inches long, it has about 40 percent clay.
- ✔ If the ribbon is greater than $3^1/_2$ inches long and doesn't break when held up, it is at least 50 percent clay.

The jar test

Here's how to use the jar method:

1. **Put 1 inch of dry, crushed garden soil in a tall quart jar.**

2. **Fill the jar $^2/_3$ with water and add 1 teaspoon of a dispersing agent, such as a dish detergent or table salt.**

3. **Shake the jar thoroughly and let the contents settle.**

4. **Measure the depths of the different layers.**

   When the sand settles to the bottom (in about a minute), measure the depth of that layer.

   Silt settles in four to five hours. You should see a color and size difference between the silt and sand layers; if not, subtract the sand depth from the total to determine the silt depth. The clay takes days to settle, and some of the smallest particles may remain permanently in suspension.

   By measuring the depth of each layer, you can figure out the approximate percentages of sand, silt, and clay in your soil. For example, if after settling, the depth of soil is 2 inches and both sand and silt layers are just less than one inch and less than $^1/_2$ inch is clay, then you have loam soil.

Structure

The way in which sand, silt, and clay particles are grouped together is called the *soil structure*. The size and arrangement of these groupings influence the drainage capacity of the soil and its nutrient availability. Without good drainage, your soil will be wet and low in oxygen and your plants prone to rotting.

 ✔ **Ideal structure of topsoil (at least 10 to 12 inches deep):** Granular, crumb-size groupings of soil particles and plenty of pore spaces

 ✔ **Ideal subsoil structure:** Blocky, with cubes of soil and vertical openings

Compacted soil has few air and water pore spaces and tends to be poorly drained.

No matter what kind of soil you have, adding organic matter improves the soil structure. It helps form humus, which enables small clay or silt particles to stick together to form larger aggregates; in sandy soils, humus acts like a sponge to catch and hold moisture and nutrients. Two methods of determining your soil structure are the *percolation method* and the *metal-rod method*.

"I'll have mine perked, please"

The percolation do-it-yourself test evaluates *water drainage* — the ability of water to move through the soil, which is called the *percolation rate.* To evaluate drainage:

1. **Dig several holes 1 foot deep by 2 feet wide in various places in your garden.**

2. **Cover the holes with sheets of plastic to let the soil dry out.**

3. **Once the soil is dry, fill each hole to the top with water and time how long it takes for the water to completely drain.**

   The ideal time is between 10 and 30 minutes.

   • If the water drains in less than 10 minutes, the soil will tend to dry out too quickly in summer.

   • If it takes 30 minutes to 4 hours to drain, you can still grow most plants but will have to water slowly to avoid runoff and to allow the water to soak in deeply.

   • If your soil takes longer than 4 hours to drain, you may have a drainage problem. In sandy soil, dig down a foot or two deep to see whether a hard layer is blocking water movement. If so, break it up. If your soil is clay, raise the bed to get plant roots up out of the soggy soil and into well-drained, elevated soil.

The direct approach: the metal-rod method

In some regions, particularly ones that receive little rainfall, a concretelike layer lies just under the soil. This layer, which is known as *caliche,* prevents normal water movement and root growth.

In addition to caliche, some soils suffer from a layer of dense, clay soil called *hardpan.* Though not as hard as caliche, this dense layer also prevents good plant growth. The simplest way to see whether your soil has a hardpan or compaction layer below the surface is to take a metal rod and walk around your property sticking it into the ground. If you can't easily push the rod into the soil at least 6 to 8 inches deep, you need to improve the structure of your soil. If you push it down and consistently meet resistance at a certain depth, there may be a hardpan layer.

Sweet and sour: pH tests

Just to intimidate the rest of us, chemists use a chemical symbol to represent the relative sweetness (*alkalinity*) and sourness (*acidity*) of the soil. This symbol, *pH,* represents the "negative logarithm of hydrogen ion concentration."

The pH is measured on a scale of 1 to 10. A soil pH below 7.0 is considered acidic. A pH above 7.0 is alkaline.

The correct pH for your plants is important because certain nutrients are available only to plants within a specific pH range. The ideal pH for most plants is 6.0 to 7.0. A few plants (such as acid-loving rhododendrons and blueberries) prefer more extreme conditions. Usually, areas of high rainfall have a low pH, and areas of low rainfall have a high pH.

pH test kits are available in many garden centers. You can also figure out your soil's pH by using a professional soil test. For a quick check of your soil's pH, try the following test:

- ✔ To check whether your soil is severely alkaline, take a tablespoon of dried garden soil and add a few drops of vinegar. If the soil fizzes, the pH is above 7.5. (The "free carbonates" in the soil react with the acid at a pH of 7.5 and above.)

- ✔ To check for acidity in the soil, take a tablespoon of wet soil and add a pinch of baking soda. If the soil fizzes, the soil is probably very acidic (pH less than 5.0).

For more . . .

For most of you, these common-sense soil tests are all that you'll need. But for the definitive word on your soil's chemistry and makeup, a professional test is the next step. Your local Extension office may be able to test your soil or recommend a private lab. These tests can tell you about soil nutrient levels, soil structure, and pH, plus suggest how to make your soil even better.

Keep in mind that the reliability of any soil test depends on the accuracy of the soil sample. Avoid contaminating soil samples with residue from tools, containers, or cigarette ash, for example. The small sample that you send to a lab must also be representative of your garden. Gather soil from several places and fix it together to form a composite picture of the plot. However, don't mix soil from different garden areas where you'll be growing plants with different needs or with soil near foundations or walls where construction residues may remain. Follow the directions from the soil lab or Extension office for best results.

Amending Soil

Once you know what your soil looks like, you can begin to improve it. What you do to amend the soil depends on the kind of condition it's in. Here are some suggestions for good and poor soils, pH changes, and nutrient additives.

Good soil

If your soil is a nice, fertile blend — one that grows good grass — you may not need to do anything special to it to grow most garden plants. But beefing up the organic content never hurts, because organic matter is constantly being broken down. *Organic matter* — such as decaying leaves, hay, grass clippings, compost, and animal droppings — releases nutrients and other chemicals that make soil fertile and productive. It's especially valuable for adding richness to sand and lightness to clay. It makes good gardens great and poor gardens better by making any soil more like the ideal loamy soil.

Before planting, dig in 1 or 2 inches of organic matter, such as compost, peat moss, decayed livestock manure, shredded leaves, or decayed lawn clippings. Then, each year, mulch planted areas with an inch or more of compost or organic mulch such as shredded or chipped bark. (For more on composting, see Chapter 24.)

Bad soil

If you find that your soil is not what it should be for the garden that you had in mind, now is the time to correct that problem. Be prepared to amend the entire garden area so that plant roots can grow freely without encountering a bewildering range of different soil blends. Dramatically different soil types can stop root growth cold. Adding organic matter makes a sandy soil hold more water and nutrients; it makes a clay soil easier to work, more fertile, and better draining. Apply at least a 2-to 4-inch-deep layer of compost and till it into the soil.

Plan to maintain your improved soil by adding several inches of organic material each year — even more in warm climates or particularly difficult soils. Compacted soils in perennial beds benefit from a yearly 1- to 2-inch-deep topdressing of compost. A compacted layer in annual gardens can be broken up by double digging (see "Double digging" later in this chapter) or by deeply tilling the soil below the hardpan layer and mixing in generous amounts of organic matter. In some soils, the thickness of the hardpan layer may require building raised beds. (See "Simple raised beds" later in this chapter.) Build a bed about 8 inches high — or even higher if you install a retaining wall. Cover the existing soil with commercial topsoil, preblended with sand if the topsoil is high in clay, and fortified with about 20 percent compost.

Changing pH

If you're growing pH-sensitive plants, you can adjust pH by adding sulfur to make a soil more acidic or ground limestone to make a soil more alkaline. But to maintain a suitable pH, you must continue to monitor and adjust the soil over the lifetime of the pH-sensitive plant. If you're not ready to commit to this ongoing maintenance, stick with plants that prefer the native soil pH.

Amending soil with organic matter such as compost gradually lowers pH. So does using fertilizers. But if your soil pH is significantly too low or too high for the kinds of plants you want to grow, you need to add ground limestone or soil sulfur, respectively. To increase or decrease your soil pH, do the following:

- **Add limestone to raise your soil pH from 5.0 to 6.5.** To each 1,000 square feet of sand, add 41 pounds; to each 1,000 square feet of loam, add 78 pounds; and to each 1,000 square feet of clay, add 152 pounds.

- **Add sulfur to lower your soil pH from 8.5 to 6.5.** To each 1,000 square feet of sand, add 46 pounds; to each 1,000 square feet of loam, add 57 pounds; and to each 1,000 square feet of clay, add 69 pounds.

Adding nutrients

If your soil is low in nutrients, which you can tell by having the soil tested or by seeing that plants grow poorly there, add extra nutrients now. If you haven't tested the soil, add a complete fertilizer according to package directions. If your soil has been tested, add amendments according to the lab's recommendations.

Fertilizers

Complete fertilizer contains nitrogen, phosphorus, and potassium, the major nutrients that all plants need. See Chapter 16 for more on fertilizers and fertilizing.

Compost

Composting is a way for gardeners to turn a wide variety of readily available organic materials — such as grass clippings, household garbage, and plant residues — into a uniform, easy-to-handle source of organic matter, increasing the soil's humus content, which in turn helps the soil hold more nutrients. Composting allows you to enrich your soil in an efficient, inexpensive way. See Chapter 24 for more on composting.

Green manures and cover crops

One easy way for gardeners to add organic matter and nutrients to the soil is to grow *green manure crops*. These are plants grown to be chopped and tilled or spaded into the soil when they are still green (before they blossom and produce seeds). The succulent plant material breaks down quickly, adding nutrients and improving soil texture. These crops are usually grown during the main gardening season — between crops or just after harvesting a crop.

Cover crops are often the same plants. However, the primary purposes of cover crops are to prevent soil erosion and choke out weeds, usually when the soil is bare of crops before and after the harvest.

The plants used as green manures and cover crops can be divided into two broad categories: *legumes* and *nonlegumes*. Examples of legumes are soybeans, vetches, cowpeas, and clovers. Legumes have special nodules on their roots that house nitrogen-fixing bacteria of the genus *Rhizobium*. If legumes are tilled back into the soil, succeeding crops benefit from the increased nitrogen.

Although nonlegumes don't add as much nitrogen to the soil as legumes do, many nonlegumes are very useful as green manures and cover crops simply for the organic matter that they add to the soil.

Loosening the Soil

The depth and techniques that you use to loosen the soil depend on which plants you intend to grow and the condition of your soil. For your average garden of annual flowers and vegetables, for example, you can break up the soil 8 inches deep with a rototiller or a spade.

Rototillers are wonderful to use on virgin soil and heavy or clumpy soils. But they do encourage fast breakdown of organic matter, so don't use them any more than necessary.

In existing gardens with light, fluffy soil, you may be able to turn the bed with a spade without too much difficulty and minimize organic matter loss. If you prepare the soil in autumn, let frost help break up the soil clumps. Then spade again in spring and finish up with a rake.

Roses, carrots, parsnips, and other deep-rooted plants grow best when you loosen the soil 12 inches deep or deeper. This calls for building a raised bed over the existing garden or for double digging.

When to work the soil

Have you ever grown your own mouth-watering melon, checking it daily to see whether it's perfectly ripe? Preparing the soil is similar. You need to wait until the soil is in the right condition — lightly moist, but not wet. If too wet, clays can dry into brick. If too dry, soil can turn into dust and blow away, leaving beneficial soil life to perish.

Fortunately, the right soil condition is easy to evaluate. Take a handful of soil and squeeze it in your fist. Tap the resulting ball with your finger. If it breaks up easily, the soil is ready. If it stays in a sodden clump, the soil needs to dry out more. If it doesn't cling at all, the soil is dry: Water the area, wait a day, and try again.

Simple raised beds

Raised beds are an ideal way to loosen the soil of the garden and define planting areas. To make a raised-bed garden, outline the beds with string. For vegetable gardens, a 3-foot-wide bed is best; for ornamental plantings, choose a size that best fits your design. After the beds are defined, loosen the soil in the bed by using a shovel or a garden fork. Then shovel soil from an adjacent path onto the bed. Figure 14-2 shows a basic raised bed and one edged with wood.

Figure 14-2: Make raised beds by drawing soil from walkway areas onto loosened soil (A). Leave them as is (B) or edge with wood (C) or other materials.

Double digging

Double digging works the soil more deeply than single digging and is useful for deep-rooted plants or areas where drainage needs to be improved.

1. **Mark out a bed 3 or 4 feet wide and as long as you want (but no more than 25 feet).**

2. **Across the width of the bed, remove a 6- to 8-inch-deep section of the topsoil layer in a 1- to 2-foot-wide trench and put the soil in your wheelbarrow.**

3. **With a digging fork, break up the subsoil at the bottom of the trench to the full depth of the tines — about 6 to 8 inches.**

4. **Step down the bed and dig the topsoil from the adjacent strip, moving it onto the exposed, loose subsoil of the first trench.**

5. **Break up the newly exposed subsoil with the garden fork.**

6. **Continue in this fashion until you break up upper and lower layers across the entire bed. The soil from the first trench, held in the wheelbarrow, goes into the last trench.**

After you've finished, the earth is mounded up high in the bed. Walk on the adjacent ground rather than on the raised bed. When you go to prepare the bed in subsequent planting seasons, you'll be amazed at how little work it takes to loosen the ground.

Finishing Touches

It's time to smooth everything over and prepare to plant. Use a garden rake to comb through the soil and remove rocks, clods, and any chunks of vegetation or plant roots that you missed previously. Now smooth the soil over the entire bed by raking. If you're making raised beds or double digging, you want to end up with a flat-topped raised bed.

Now it's time to plant! See Chapter 15.

Chapter 15

How to Plant

● (continued)

In This Chapter

▶ Knowing when to plant

▶ Making a planting plan

▶ Sowing seeds

▶ Transplanting seedlings

▶ Planting and transplanting trees and shrubs

▶ Planting bulbs

▶ Multiplying your own plants

▶ Hardening plants

● ●

*A*fter your garden bed is prepared, you're ready to plant as soon as the weather is right for the crops that you're dealing with. Most plants require moist and mild weather, although the specific timing varies according to the plant. (See Table 15-1 for some examples.)

When to Plant What

Table 15-1 lists general recommendations for planting. Ask your local nursery worker or Extension office for specifics regarding any particular crop in your area.

Table 15-1	A Planting Timetable	
Plant Type	*Warm Climates*	*Cold Climates*
Annuals	Year-round	Spring, summer
Bulbs, hardy	Autumn	Autumn
Bulbs, tender	Spring	Spring
Perennials	Autumn, winter, spring	Spring, late summer

(continued)

Table 15-1 *(continued)*

Plant Type	Warm Climates	Cold Climates
Shrubs	Autumn, winter, spring	Spring, autumn
Trees	Autumn, winter, spring	Spring, autumn
Vegetables, hardy	Autumn, winter	Spring, summer
Vegetables, tender	Spring, summer	Late spring

Making a Planting Plan

Before planting a decorative garden, fine-tune your garden layout so it will look as good as you planned. Set seedlings, bulbs, perennials, trees, and shrubs in the places you intend them to grow, spacing them so each plant can grow to its mature spread without overlapping a neighboring plant. (Closer spacing of bulbs and flowers results in an interwoven tapestry garden, which can be lovely but requires effort to keep in good condition.)

Once the plants are in place, stand back and give the layout a critical look. You may find that one color does not look as good next to another as you had hoped, or perhaps one cluster of plants needs a little extra space. Or you may want to place similar plants slightly closer together to leave a little open space between groupings. Massage your design now so it will be perfect when you plant.

Sowing Seeds in Your Garden

You can start a large number of plants for a small amount of money when you direct-sow seeds. *Direct-sowing* means planting seeds outdoors in the soil in the place where they are to stay and mature. Plant seeds in fine, level soil that's warm enough for the particular plants you're working with. For example, peas germinate nicely when the soil is about 60°F, but basil needs soil that is 70°F to sprout well.

Always check your seed packet before planting. Most are marked with the planting depth and space required between seeds and seedlings, as well as temperature suggestions. If you plant deeper than indicated on the packet, the seeds may not contain enough energy for the seedlings to reach the surface.

Pay attention to how you space the seeds so you get the best results. Some seeds are tiny and easy to sow too thickly. Instead of sprinkling these directly out of the seed packet, take a pinch between your thumb and forefinger and drop them one by one into the planting site. You can also mix small seeds with sand to make them easier to spread. Experiment a few times, and you'll begin to get the hang of this. Or, if you don't mind paying a bit more, look for seed tapes, which eliminate the need for you to guess about application rate.

Look on the seed packet for *germination percentages*. This number refers to the percentage of seeds that sprouted during quality-control checks. If the percentage is below 90 percent, plant more seeds than you really need so you have some extras on hand if necessary.

You have a choice of planting patterns to use. Plant small vegetables — carrots or lettuce, for example, or flowers that you want to transplant later — in wide beds that stretch a couple of feet across. Many gardeners find that 3-foot-wide beds are an ideal size for vegetable gardens because they adapt well to trellises and "season extenders" (see Chapter 26) and allow easy access to plants from either side of the bed.

Here are some tips on arranging your garden:

✔ If you like a neat, exact garden, use a wire grid to calculate your spacing. With carrots, for example, use wire mesh with inch-square openings. Lay the wire mesh across the bed and press a seed down into the soil through each opening. *Thin* when the seedlings arise so that each carrot has at least 3 square inches of space. For larger plants, such as lettuce, you can plant a seed every 4 or 5 squares to eliminate overcrowding.

✔ If you're a more casual gardener, you can *broadcast* your seeds (see the middle of Figure 15-1). Sprinkle them over the bed, dropping the seeds one by one and aiming to roughly meet the appropriate spacing. Then cover to the depth required by spreading soil gently over the top with a garden rake.

✔ Larger plants need more space. You can plant them in wide beds, alternating two or three plants across the bed in a diamond or triangular pattern (see the right side of Figure 15-1). Or place seeds of larger plants in single rows (see the left side of Figure 15-1). To make the rows straight, plant beside a string strung between two stakes. Run a hoe through the soil to dig a trench of the proper depth for the seeds you're planting. Set the seeds in the trench at the proper spacing. Then cover the seeds with soil.

Figure 15-1:
Typical planting patterns in a raised-bed garden.

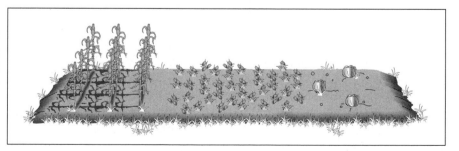

> ✔ In a decorative annual-flower garden, you can use wide-bed planting techniques to create clusters or "drifts" of flowers. Use a trickle of ground limestone to mark the place where you want a mass of seed-grown flowers, such as zinnias or nasturtiums. Set the seeds within that space as you would for a wide bed.

After the seeds are planted properly, label and water them. The best way to water is with a *soaker hose* or *drip irrigation*. Soaker hoses and drip irrigation systems are ground-hugging tubes that let moisture trickle out without splashing or compacting the soil. They also let you focus the water on just the seedbed. (See Chapter 16 for more discussion of watering systems.) If you don't have access to ground-watering systems, you can water from overhead as long as you do so gently with a fine spray from a hose or sprinkler. Avoid using a hose without a spray nozzle — the force of the water can compact the soil or splash the seeds out of place.

Transplanting Seedlings

Some plants don't start reliably from direct-sowing — perhaps their seeds take a long time to germinate and grow, or they struggle under unreliable outdoor conditions. Instead of direct-sowing them, start with seedlings that are already through the delicate seed-sprouting stage. If you purchase seedlings at a greenhouse or garden center, make sure that they're healthy. Or you can start your own at home (see "Starting Seeds Indoors" later in this chapter).

After your garden is established, you can also be on the lookout for self-sown seedlings of last year's flowers, vegetables, or herbs that you can transplant. These "volunteers" are easy to grow and cost you nothing.

Plants that start easily from seed

Some quick-growing plants are super-simple to start from seed. Other plants, though they grow easily from seed, are best direct-sown because they are sometimes damaged by transplanting.

✔ **Easy starters:** arugula, corn, cornflowers, cosmos, cucumbers, kale, kohlrabi, lettuce, muskmelons, nasturtiums, pumpkins, spinach, squash, sunflowers, sweet basil, watermelons, zinnias

✔ **Transplant resenters:** Beans, beets, black-eyed peas, carrots, dill, fennel, garden peas, lemon basil, radishes, Shirley poppies, sweet peas

To transplant seedlings:

1. **Use a hoe, spade, or trowel to make a small hole for each seedling.**

2. **Unpot the seedling by turning the pot upside down, cupping the seedling with your hand. Be sure to keep the root mass and soil intact.**

   If the seedling doesn't readily come out, gently rap the edge of the pot or gently press on the bottom of each cell with your hand — *don't* yank out the plant by its stem.

3. **Separate (spread out) the roots and check their condition. For larger plants, you can gently cut into the bottom of the rootball with a knife and "butterfly" the rootball apart.**

   If the roots are wound around the outside of the pot, work them loose with your fingers so they can grow out into the soil. Unwind larger roots and break smaller ones until their ends are all pointing outward.

4. **Fill each planting hole with water and a dilute liquid fertilizer that will help plants get off to a fast start.**

5. **Put each prepared seedling in the hole that you made.**

Most young vegetable seedlings should be transplanted up to their first true leaves (see Figure 15-2). Plant short, bushy seedlings or plants prone to *crown rot,* a disease that rots the base of the stems where they arise from the roots, at the same depth as they grew in the seedling pot.

If the seedling is tall and lanky with a barren base, you can sink the seedling a little deeper. Plants such as tomatoes grow extra roots along the lower portions of their stems and thrive with this treatment.

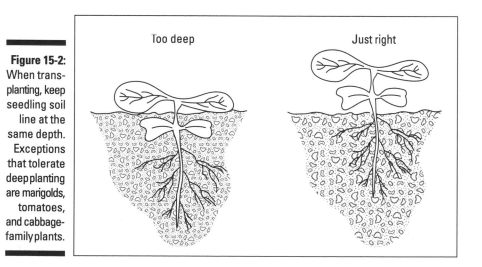

Figure 15-2: When transplanting, keep seedling soil line at the same depth. Exceptions that tolerate deep planting are marigolds, tomatoes, and cabbage-family plants.

Too deep

Just right

6. **With your hands, firm the soil around the roots. Make a small basin sloping toward the plant to hold water.**

7. **If the weather has been dry or your soil is sandy, you may want to water the entire bed. If not, you can wait until tomorrow for an overall watering. Keep the bed moist while the seedlings get established and begin to grow strongly. In extremely hot, dry weather, provide temporary shade for the transplants with paper tents or shingles pushed into the ground on the south or west side of the plant.**

Planting Trees and Shrubs

Planting your own trees and shrubs saves costs but does require stamina. Start with smaller, container-grown shrubs, which are not too heavy and can be planted any time the weather is mild. Large balled-and-burlapped trees are heavy and may require a crew of several strong people. Select your plants carefully and calculate placement plus hole width and depth in advance so you don't have to attempt last-minute corrections.

Here are some tips on planting the three basic types of trees:

✔ **Bare-root trees.** These trees are available for planting during the dormant season. They're lightweight and easy to handle — the most economical way to purchase trees. Check for damaged, soft, broken, mushy, or circling roots and prune back as necessary to the healthy, firm roots.

✔ **Balled-and-burlapped trees.** These trees are dug and sold during the dormant season with the rootball intact and wrapped. Check for major cracks or breaks in the rootball and make sure that the trunk doesn't rock in the soil ball or move.

✔ **Container-grown trees.** These trees are easy to handle and are available year-round. Check for circling or densely matted roots.

Set balled-and-burlapped, bare-root, or container-grown trees and shrubs so that they're buried at the same depth or slightly higher than they were in the nursery. In heavy, poorly aerated, or rocky soils that aren't well suited to planting, set the plant higher in the soil, digging the hole only $1/2$ or $2/3$ of the depth of the rootball. Then set the plant inside. Refill the hole and use good garden soil to build up a raised planting bed around the top of the ball.

Follow these steps for planting trees and shrubs:

1. **Dig a hole as deep as necessary (use a stick to determine depth) and three times as wide as the rootball. Slant the walls of the hole outward and loosen them with a shovel or garden fork to allow easy root penetration.**

Don't bother to amend the soil that you'll use to refill the hole; roots may not grow beyond the amended area if you do. If your soil is especially poor, work compost or organic matter such as composted fir bark into the planting bed. You can also build a raised bed that will provide a more expansive rooting area. Now you're ready to plant.

2. **Insert the tree or shrub.**

   • **Bare-root plants.** Set the base of the roots on a cone of soil in the middle of the hole, adjusting cone height so the plant's nursery soil line is even with the surface of the soil. Spread the roots in different directions and then refill the hole (see Figure 15-3).

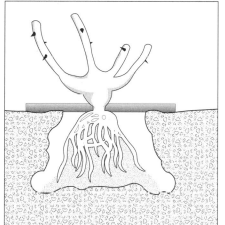

Figure 15-3: For bare-root shrubs, such as roses (shown here) or fruit trees, set the plant on a cone of soil in the middle of the hole.

   • **Container-grown plants.** Loosen any roots that have tangled inside the pot by spraying the soil off the outer few inches of the rootball. Cut off roots that are broken or permanently damaged. Work the roots through the soil as you refill.

   • **Balled-and-burlapped plants.** Remove the burlap, nails, and any twine or wire after setting the ball in place in the hole so that they won't interfere with future growth. If you can't get it all off, use a sharp knife to cut off everything except for what is directly underneath the ball.

3. **Water well by letting a hose trickle into the planting area until the area is soaked. To help direct irrigation and rainwater to the new roots, create a watering basin at least 4 to 6 inches high just outside the rootball.**

   Continue to water any time the soil begins to dry out for the next six months to a year.

4. Stake and mulch.

To *stake* the tree, drive two stakes into the soil beyond the roots. Attach ties to the tree at the lowest point at which the top remains upright. Tie loosely so that the tree can move in the wind and gain trunk strength.

A tree with a strong trunk stands on its own without staking. However, if the tree was staked in the nursery or if you are planting in a windy location, proper staking will support the tree during its first years in the ground.

Planting Bulbs

Always start your bulb garden with high-quality bulbs that are firm and free of disease. Plant spring- and early-summer flowering bulbs such as daffodils and tulips in autumn, giving them enough time to root so that they're ready to bloom when the weather warms. During frost-free weather, you can also plant tender bulbs, such as tuberous begonias and gladiolus, for a summer display.

Bulbs often look best when planted in clumps of five, seven, or nine of the same variety. Dig a broad, flat-bottomed hole and situate the cluster of bulbs inside so they don't touch. Ideally, large bulbs should be about 5 inches apart, and small bulbs should be about 2 inches apart.

Or if you want a naturalized bulb meadow, using a lot of bulbs in a large area, you can plant them individually or in drifts. Here's what you do:

✔ Avoid mixes or "economy" bulbs. They'll create a hodge-podge look of varying heights, shapes, and blooming periods. Plant in clumps of one type of bulb. Mimic nature, in which clumps will gradually mix with one another.

✔ Don't plant in rows but don't just scatter bulbs, either. Place bulbs over the area about 6 inches apart. Then get comfortable and dig.

  • For hard ground, loosen the base of each hole so that the bulb rests on soil, not above an air pocket.

  • For loose, sandy soil, open the ground with a *bulb planter,* a metal blade that slices into the ground. Drop your bulb in and push the earth back around the bulb.

  • For heavy but loose soil, use a cylindrical bulb planter that pulls out a core of soil to make the hole.

The depth of the hole varies with the kind of bulb. A general rule of thumb is to plant three to four times as deep as the bulb height. With this in mind, you can have fun layering large bulbs at the bottom of a hole and smaller bulbs at the top. Check with your nursery worker or Extension office for specific recommendations for your part of the country.

Getting Plants for Free

Raising your own plants from scratch is extremely satisfying and cheap. (Why buy perennials for $5 or so each when you can grow your own for little or no cost?) The best source for plant material for propagating is neighbors and friends. If your neighbor has a plant you'd like to grow (maybe a splendid azalea or a geranium that you can't find at the nursery), just *ask* to take cuttings (please note the emphasis on *ask!*). Gardeners on the whole are very generous people, especially when it comes to sharing their plants.

You have several techniques to choose from in raising your own plants. The simplest, described here, are painless and rewarding.

Dividing

As perennials become established in a garden, most develop into larger and larger clumps made up of small plants. Dividing these clumps and replanting is the easiest means of spreading and increasing perennials. Dividing works great with all but "tap-rooted" plants, namely plants with a main root that grows straight down, like a carrot.

To divide a perennial:

- ✔ Use a spade or digging fork to lift out a mature clump (usually three to five years old).

- ✔ Divide fine-rooted types, such as lamb's ears, by hand, gently teasing apart the clump into separate plants.

- ✔ Divide tough or fleshy-rooted types with a spade by cutting down through the roots, or use two garden forks back-to-back to pry the clumps apart.

Each new section for replanting should include several buds. Discard the older central section and replant the divisions as soon as possible.

Knowing the best season to divide perennials is important — and it varies by plant and climate. As a general guideline, divide spring-flowering perennials in very late summer or early autumn so that the new divisions can get established before winter. Divide summer- and autumn-flowering perennials in early spring, while new top growth is just 2 or 3 inches high.

In regions with severe winters, gardeners are often most successful when they dig and divide all their perennials in early spring, even though that year's spring flowers may be sacrificed.

Taking cuttings

Cuttings are plant pieces — stems, roots, and leaves — used to grow new plants. Stem cuttings are probably most useful, especially for starting perennials and shrubs. Softwood stem cuttings, taken from spring until late summer, are the quickest-rooting. At this time, plants are actively growing, and the stems are succulent and flexible.

Softwood stem cuttings

Here's how to take a softwood stem cutting:

1. **Use a sharp knife to cut a 4- to 5-inch-long stem (sideshoot) just below a leaf. Remove all but two or three leaves at the top.**

2. **Dip the cut end into *rooting hormone.***

   Rooting hormone is a powder or liquid containing growth hormones that stimulate root growth on cuttings. Some also contain a fungicide to control root rot. Check local nurseries or garden centers for the product. If you can't find it locally, you can order it from A. M. Leonard, Inc. (See Appendix C for the address.)

3. **Insert the cutting into a box or container (with drainage holes), filled with about 3 inches of moistened pure builder's sand.**

4. **Slip the container into a plastic bag and prop the bag up with something like toothpicks or short twigs so the plastic doesn't touch the leaves. Tie the bag closed to minimize water loss but open it occasionally to let in fresh air.**

5. **Place the covered container in indirect light.**

6. **When the cuttings are well-rooted (starting in 4 to 8 weeks, for most plants) and are putting on new growth, transplant them into individual containers of potting soil. As they continue to grow, gradually expose them to more light.**

7. **Once the plants are well established in the pots and continue to put on top growth, *harden them off* and plant in their permanent garden location.**

   For more details on hardening off, see "Getting on the (red) wagon: hardening plants" later in this chapter.

Here are some easy-to-root plants to grow from stem cuttings.

> ✔ **Perennials:** Begonia, candytuft, chrysanthemum, carnations or pinks *(Dianthus),* geraniums *(Pelargonium),* penstemon, phlox, sage, sedum

> ✔ **Woody plants:** Azalea, bougainvillea, fuchsia, gardenia, heather, honeysuckle, ivy, pyracantha, star jasmine, willow

Water-rooted stem cuttings

Some plants — fuchsia, coleus, English ivy, impatiens, and wandering Jew, for example — root directly in water. Just place the stems in a water-filled jar (some say opaque glass is best). There's no need to cover the plants. As soon as roots develop, transplant cuttings into containers filled with moistened potting soil.

Starting Seeds Indoors

Starting your own seeds indoors can seem like a hassle at first. "Why not simply buy seedlings at the nursery?" you ask. When you start your own plants from seeds, you become a much better gardener. Why? Having watched individual plants from the very beginning, you better understand their needs, and you are more invested in their success. You also become a better gardener because you can grow the varieties you want and sow and plant them outdoors at exactly the right time.

Annual vegetables and flowers tend to be the quickest and easiest to grow from seed. When you sow seeds for these plants in winter or early spring, they can be ready for the garden at the earliest possible planting dates for your region. In addition, many plants get off to a better start when they are sown indoors in containers and later transplanted into the garden.

Ask a dozen gardeners for their formula for successful seed starting, and you'll probably get a dozen different stories. Here's one basic method that works for us:

1. **Choose a container with drainage holes to hold the soil.**

   You can plant in flats or pots. They can be store-bought, or homemade from recycled aluminum foil pans, plastic cups, yogurt containers, or whatever.

2. **Buy a commercial planting mixture specifically formulated for starting seeds. Pour some in a bucket and thoroughly moisten it. Fill the container to 1 inch from the top with the mixture and level it.**

3. **Plant the seeds.**

   - **Small seeds.** *Broadcast* (refer to Figure 15-1) over the soil surface and cover with a fine layer of the moistened planting mix.

   - **Larger seeds.** Plant in shallow furrows (trenches) scratched or pressed into the soil surface or poke each one into the soil individually. Cover these seeds as recommended on the seed packet, usually to a depth equal to twice the seed diameter. Press the mixture gently yet firmly.

4. **Cover the container with an opaque plastic bag to conserve moisture and keep light out. (*Note:* Check the seed packet; a few seeds need light to germinate.) Place the container in a warm spot (between 75°F and 85°F is ideal), such as the top of a refrigerator or near another heat source.**

5. **Start checking for growth in about three days. As soon as plants emerge, remove the plastic and move the container to bright light. Water as needed to keep the planting mix moist.**

   You can find fluorescent bulbs that are specifically designed to provide plants with ideal light for growth. Adjust the height of the lights so that they're nearly touching the seedlings (raise the lights as the seedlings grow) and leave the lights on for 16 hours per day.

6. **When the seedlings have a second pair of true leaves, it's time to transplant them to small, individual pots filled with moist planting mix. (The first leaves a seedling produces are called *seed leaves*.)**

   Use a narrow spatula or similar tool to help scoop the plants from their original container. If necessary, gently pull the seedlings apart — hold the plants by the leaves rather than by their fragile stems.

7. **Place the container in bright, indirect light and keep the planting mix moist. As soon as the plants are growing well, move the container to increasingly brighter light. Begin feeding seedlings with liquid fertilizer. Follow label directions or, to be safe, begin feeding at half the recommended rate.**

8. **A few weeks to a month after transplanting, most plants are ready to be *hardened off* (see the next section) and planted in the garden.**

Getting on the (red) wagon: hardening plants

Seedlings and cuttings raised in comfortable indoor conditions need gradual adjustment to the more strenuous outdoor environment. This process of acclimating plants to the wind, strong light, and cooler temperatures outdoors is called *hardening off*.

The key word in the hardening-off process is *gradually*. Here's what you do:

1. **One week before you begin hardening your plants outdoors, cut back the amount of water you give them, stop their fertilizer habit, and keep temperatures slightly cooler.**

2. **Starting about ten days before transplanting into the garden, place plants outdoors in bright, indirect light for a couple of hours.**

Protect the plants from strong winds and be sure to keep them watered, as they'll dry out more quickly outside.

3. **Each day, increase the time that the plants are left outdoors and gradually expose them to more intense light and wind and a range of temperatures.**

4. **The last few days before transplanting, you can leave them outdoors overnight if weather permits.**

A cloudy, windless, warm day is best for easing the plants into their new home outdoors.

Part IV
Caring for Your Garden

In this part . . .

Yippee! You made a garden! (Or maybe you just inherited one.)

Do you need to water? How much? When? And what about weeds . . . and pruning or feeding? What kind of lawn is it, and how do you take care of it? What about pests?

All of these little ventures may sound like a lot to do, but they really aren't. And anyway, they're fun. Garden maintenance is a misnomer of sorts — there need be nothing janitorial about it.

Caring for your garden is, in fact, the essence of "gardening."

Chapter 16
Maintaining Your Garden

In This Chapter

▶ Pruning smart

▶ Watering just right

▶ Weeding easy

▶ Choosing and using fertilizers

Gardening is the most popular recreation in America. That's *recreation*, not drudgery. Experienced gardeners know how to maintain a visitor-friendly garden in the easiest, most pleasant way. This chapter tells you how to do the same.

Pruning Smart

Be lazy! Don't prune unless you must. To save work, always consider whether the plant really needs to be pruned. Many native or naturalized trees grow perfectly fine without pruning.

For example, severe pruning delays the time in a fruit tree's life that fruiting begins. And pruning reduces the harvest. Compared with an unpruned tree, a severely pruned tree bears nearly two-thirds fewer pounds of fruit in the first five years of its life.

However, if you don't want misshapen or partially dead trees in your yard, you'll probably need to prune. Here are some common reasons for pruning:

✓ Sculpting for decorative reasons

✓ Shaping the tree or shrub for strength and resistance to wind, snow, and ice damage (or to bear a bountiful crop)

✓ Keeping the plant healthy

To understand the "mystery" of how and when to prune, you need to know a bit about a plant's biology (and its inner struggles). Like a fast-growing teenager, a tree's growth is controlled by a mixture of hormones and food. A tree's food consists of carbohydrates that are generated in the leaves by photosynthesis. Some of the tree's important hormones — growth stimulators or regulators — come from the bud at the tip of each leafy shoot or branch. Biologists refer to this bud as the *apical* bud, or *leading* or *tip* bud. The tip bud stimulates new, lengthy, vertical growth and stifles the growth of lower potential shoots — called "dormant buds."

When you clip out any tip bud, you take away the stifling tip hormones and their dominance. The dormant buds below the cut burst into growth and begin to produce the tip hormones themselves as they vie for vertical dominance. The first dormant bud to grow the tallest becomes the new dominant tip bud.

On horizontal branches, the tip bud stops growing and loses its control over all growth and all dormant buds. Thus, the dormant buds at the base of each leaf sprout into vertical, unfruitful leafy shoots. So both vertical and horizontal branches are less likely to produce flower or fruit — each for different reasons.

When a branch is positioned at an angle between 45° and 60°, the flow of carbo-hydrates, hormones, and nutrients naturally favors the formation of flower buds. With many deciduous fruit trees, like apple, almond, and pear trees, the flower buds become long-term fruiting places, called *spurs*, in the following years.

Four kinds of pruning cuts

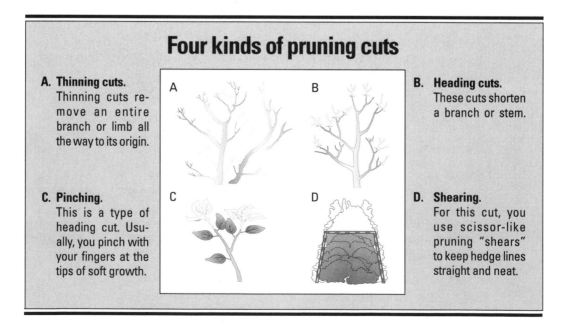

A. Thinning cuts. Thinning cuts remove an entire branch or limb all the way to its origin.

B. Heading cuts. These cuts shorten a branch or stem.

C. Pinching. This is a type of heading cut. Usually, you pinch with your fingers at the tips of soft growth.

D. Shearing. For this cut, you use scissor-like pruning "shears" to keep hedge lines straight and neat.

Pruning Basics

A few "rules of limb" apply when pruning all trees and shrubs:

- ✔ Remove dead or diseased wood as soon as possible. (Be sure not to spread certain diseases, like fire blight, with the pruning tools: Clean the blade with a 10-percent dilution of bleach after *every* cut.)
- ✔ Cut out one of two branches or shoots if they are rubbing together and causing an open wound.
- ✔ Prune in the winter to encourage new shoots and leafy growth.
- ✔ To remove unwanted shoots or limbs without stimulating too many new shoots, prune in the summer.

Details on these kindest cuts

Here's the scoop on the various pruning techniques:

- ✔ ***Heading back* a bud.** Always cut back to just above a dormant bud. Cut at a slight angle and leave less than $1/4$ inch of the shoot above the bud — not a long stub.
- ✔ ***Thinning out* a shoot or limb.** Cut nearly to the base of the season's growth. Don't cut absolutely flush to the remaining limb or branch. Leave the *branch collar* intact. The branch collar is slightly wider than the shoot you're removing, is marked with many compact wrinkles, and is usually a slightly different tone or texture than the shoot. Natural chemicals within the branch collar help prevent rot from entering the heart of the tree. Flush cuts allow the rot to slip past the collar and invade the very core of the tree or plant.
- ✔ **Sawing a medium-sized limb.** If the limb is small enough to hold so that it doesn't fall while cutting, only one cut with a pruning hand saw is required. Again, leave the larger and more noticeable branch collar intact. Don't let the limb drop as you cut through it, or the bark may be torn or ripped.
- ✔ **Sawing a large limb.** Large, heavy limbs need to be removed with three cuts. First, about a foot out from the branch collar, cut halfway through the limb from the underneath side. Then a few inches from the branch collar, cut all the way through the limb. If any bark begins to tear, it will stop at the underneath cut. Finally, make a proper trim cut at the branch collar. (See Figure 16-1.)
- ✔ **Treating your tree's wounds.** Throw away all your pruning paints, tars, or sprays. Modern research has shown that if the branch collar is left intact, all treatments to the pruning cuts are a waste of time. What a relief!

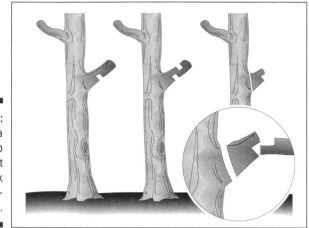

Figure 16-1:
Removing a
large limb
without
ripping bark
is a three-
cut process.

Pruning in winter

The traditional season for pruning is while all the buds are dormant — in late winter or very early spring before flowers or leaves open. Such pruning stimulates new vegetative shoots — which are less fruitful with fruit trees. Cutting back a dormant branch causes two or more side shoots to arise below the cut due to lost tip dominance. Winter pruning is especially helpful when you want to force new shoots to fill air space around the trunk with branches.

When you have many long, vertical shoots — erroneously called *suckers* or *watersprouts* — winter pruning only makes the problem worse. Thinning each vertical limb, even if cut to its base, usually multiplies the problem by causing two or more shoots to arise with the spring sap flow. This situation is remedied only with summer pruning.

Pruning in summer

Summer pruning can become the most valuable technique in a gardener's repertoire. Careful summer pruning has the effect of mildly stunting or dwarfing trees. The partial removal of the foliage in summer means fewer leaves to convert sunlight into stored carbohydrates.

Because summer pruning is so appropriate for removing unwanted branches, it is the preferred way to begin a program of restoration with neglected and overgrown trees.

Summer pruning is also the best time for thinning cuts. The active photosynthesis allows the trees to begin forming a *callus* over the cut. The well-knit callus tissue that forms a ring around the cut resists the sprouting of new shoots the coming spring.

Pruning too early in the season, during spring's burst of vegetative growth, has a stimulating effect more like dormant pruning. Summer-prune after the initial flurry of spring growth, as the weekly growth rate slows down.

In cold-winter climates, summer-prune by the end of summer because sometimes late summer pruning forces a few new, succulent shoots. These tender shoots don't harden off before freezing weather arrives and may be killed.

Pruning tools

Bad tools can cripple or maim a gardener. So pick a set of well-made, sturdy pruning tools. Here's a brief list of the essentials.

- ✔ **Hand pruner.** Hand pruners are usually reserved for cuts up to $1/2$ to 1 inch in diameter. Our favorite hand pruner is the Felco #8 — the most comfortable and easily used bypass pruner on the market.

- ✔ **Lopper.** Loppers can cut limbs up to several inches in diameter. You'll never need a lopping shear if your trees are well trained from the start. If you're restoring an abandoned tree or shrub, you need a lopper to remove older wood. We suggest choosing a 16- to 24-inch or 30-inch aluminum- or fiberglass-handled (not wood) lopper. Examples include the Felco F-20 or F-21 and the Sandvik P16-40 (16-inch) or P16-60 (24-inch).

- ✔ **Hand saw.** The one hand saw required is probably a 12-inch bladed, folding saw. Make sure that you get one with a locking mechanism for the open position. Good brands are the Felco #61 and the ARS #210-DX.

  If you're working on a disheveled or abandoned tree with large limbs slated for removal, you may want a large, 24- to 36-inch-long curved pruning saw with large 1- to 2-inch saw teeth. The bigger the saw's teeth and the wider the space between the teeth, the faster the saw cuts.

- ✔ **Ladder and pole pruner.** If you're caring for really large shade or fruit trees, you need a pruning ladder and/or a pole pruner.

  First buy a three-legged, aluminum (not wooden) orchard pruning and picking ladder. These ladders come in heights of 6, 8, 10, 12, 14, and 16 feet and cost from $75 to $200. Not cheap, but they are the most comfortable way to prune a large tree with hand pruners and a lopper.

  If ladders scare you, an extending pole pruner is your next best option. Buy one with fiberglass poles (no wood) that telescope from 6 to 12 feet. The only variety worth buying has a cast-metal head and a chain-and-gear-driven mechanism when. A good pole pruner will set you back $125 to $180.

Appendix C lists several mail-order companies that sell these tools.

Watering Just Right

Gardens seldom get just the right amount of rain. Thus the invention of irrigation. Here's how to select the best devices for watering your garden.

With irrigation, it's easy to get complicated fast. Be wise and start with the simplest watering method for your yard. You can always get fancy later. We explain basic ways to water first and then mention the more complicated ones.

Watering in furrows

Furrow irrigation uses narrow, shallow, water-flooded trenches snaking throughout the garden. This simple method has been used for thousands of years, even though it's not very efficient.

Make the furrows with a hoe. The sides of the wide, shallow (4 to 12 inches deep) trench should be no steeper than 45 degrees so the soil doesn't slide down to fill the furrow's bottom. Dig your furrows within 12 inches of any rows of vegetables, making sure that the base of the plant's stem is well above the high level of the water in the trench. With established shrubs and trees, hoe the furrow as far from the trunk as is the edge of the foliage (called the *dripline*).

Use a hose to slowly and completely fill a furrow. Then let the water soak in. Water can be diverted from one furrow to another by damming a furrow with soil or a board.

Sprinklers simplified

Sprinklers, which cover a wider area than furrows and don't flood the soil as rapidly, stimulate better plant growth.

These are the sprinklers our grandparents used:

- Sprinklers with a single, large-diameter hole at the top of a large metal dome
- A two-hole sprinkler with two metal domes
- A hollow metal cylinder on top of a spike with a large, frowning slot, making a fan-shaped spray of water

All of these are cheap and easy to move around and never clog due to the large openings.

Oscillating sprinklers

A more modern and popular sprinkler is the oscillating sprinkler, with its magnificent fan of water slowly sweeping back and forth. Although wind can steal plenty of moisture from oscillating sprinklers, they do cover a much larger area and are a frequent choice for watering lawns.

Oozing hoses

The modern form of soaker hose — which weeps, rather than sprays, water from tiny pores all over its surface — is called *porous hose*. You can snake porous hose throughout the garden to provide a wet spot as long and wide as the tubing, depending on the soil and how long the water is on. The slow, gradual soak is easier on root hairs than a sprinkler, so growth is better. Also, little moisture is lost to the sun or wind.

Don't use porous hose if you fall into one of these categories:

- Your water is high in dissolved minerals, especially calcium and iron. A filter takes care of the solid sediment, dirt, and sand. But water can be full of dissolved compounds that can precipitate (congeal) in the pores.

- You have well water without a chlorinator. In this case, graduate to true drip irrigation.

Drip irrigation

Wherever water is in seasonally short supply (such as Israel where the techniques of drip irrigation were first developed), drip irrigation is efficient and popular. The idea is simple: Apply the water no faster than the soil can absorb it.

Most drip irrigation systems are built around ³/₈-inch black tubing and specifically placed "emitters." The emitters may literally drip, or they may spray a fine mist.

Most hardware stores and nurseries in dry summer regions stock one or more varieties of drip systems, and attendants there can help you with design and construction. Or you can write or call mail order companies that specialize in drip irrigation, such as Gardener's Supply Co. and The Urban Farmer Store. The telephone numbers of both are listed in Appendix C.

How much water do plants need?

Irrigation hardware is useless if you don't have a clue about how much water your plant needs. The answer is to water just enough, but not too much. Easier said than done! So here are some guidelines for irrigation.

The best way to water is to replace what the plants are using, either daily, three times per week, or weekly. Plants lose moisture through their foliage due to *transpiration*. The soil also gives up water by evaporation. The combination of evaporation and transpiration is *evapotranspiration*.

Evapotranspiration is one way to figure how much water you need to apply. Hot, dry, and windy weather causes plants to use much more moisture than they do on a cool, overcast day. The evapotranspiration rate, measured as the total number of inches of water per week or month, tells how much water you can add to replace what the soil lost and the plants used. It's a more accurate way to judge how much to water than is the old-fashioned, and often inaccurate, "one inch per week" rule of thumb.

If you live in regions where irrigation is a fact of life, the local newspaper (usually on the page with the weather report) gives the recommended watering rate for lawns based on the evapotranspiration rate.

To convert "inches of water" to "how long to run the sprinklers," place containers at regular intervals throughout your sprinkler's spray pattern. Then run the sprinkler a specific length of time, such as one hour. With a metal ruler, measure the depth of water in each can and divide by the number of cans.

Now you can water by the newspaper's guideline. If, for example, the sprinkler test shows that your sprinkler puts out $3/4$ inch per hour and the paper says to apply $1^1/2$ inches of water this week, run your sprinkler for two hours. This same rate is a good starting point for trees, shrubs, annual flowers, and vegetables.

Weeding Made Easy

Weeds aren't inherently evil — they're just unwanted plants. In a vegetable garden, a rosebush may be out of place. In a field of corn, a single pumpkin vine may be uninvited and unceremoniously pulled out.

Every garden has plants labeled by the gardener as "weeds." So how to get rid of them?

Beware hitchhikers

Inspect all nursery plants for weeds to prevent hard-to-eradicate weeds from sneaking into your garden. Some of the nasty hitchhiking weeds to watch out for include the following:

- ✔ Grass with fleshy underground roots that travel sideways. These are called *runner roots,* and pieces sprout into new plants. Bermuda grass *(Cynodon dactylon)* is one example.

- ✔ Bindweed *(Convolvulus arvensis)*

- ✔ Creeping oxalis *(Oxalis corniculata)*

- ✔ Spurges *(Euphorbia* species*)*

After you bring the plant home, gently pull the plant and its roots from the container. Look for underground stems and roots not noticed at the nursery. Discard the roots of weeds.

If you're not planting that day, repot the plant with fresh, sterile potting soil. Remain vigilant against hitchhiking weeds and pests with every trip to a nursery!

Weeding by hand and by tool

Your best weeding tools are your hands. So don't be shy — drop to your knees and hand-weed. While kneeling, you can grab many weeds right at the base of the stem and yank them out, roots and all.

Not all weeds can be effectively hand pulled. Stubborn weeds require some special tools. The two best weeding tools are the hoe and the mattock.

A hoe is required for the rough-and-tumble weeds or a sea of young seedlings. The best modern hoes have long, white ash handles and forged-metal blades. Using the long handle — up to 5 feet long — means that you stoop less and your lower back remains stress-free. Forged hoe heads are the strongest; they have no bolts and are a continuous, seamless piece of metal from the blade (which does the cutting and hoeing) to the solid socket that wraps around the end of the handle.

Hoes come in many sizes and weights. Choose a hoe suited to the soil condition in your yard. Uncultivated, heavy soil requires a broad, heavy-duty grubbing hoe (also called *eye* or *Italian grading* hoe). After a year or two of soil improvement, you can move to a more traditional tool with a lightweight, small blade, such as a garden, nursery or planter hoe. In vegetable or flower beds with finely textured soil, an *oscillating* or *stirrup* hoe — shaped like a stirrup, with sharp edges on both sides so that it weeds and cuts in both directions — is the best choice. Keep a flat, smooth metal file handy to sharpen the edge of the blade as you hoe.

The hand mattock is our single favorite tool for weeding while kneeling. The head is shaped like a large garden mattock but is much smaller and has a shorter handle. This tool has a narrow, flat blade for chopping (which is different from the wider blade used for digging). The short handle also gives you a good reach. This tool is good for tracing down running roots and chopping out the crowns of blackberry roots.

Mulches

Mulch is any material, organic or not, placed over the surface of soil to conserve moisture, kill weed seedlings, keep soil temperatures down, or make the garden look more attractive — or all four at once. More and more folks are realizing the value of mulching. Mulch was traditionally thought to mean natural, organic materials such as leaves, wood chips, and sand. Now a multitude of plastic-based films or woven materials are sold to smother weeds.

A common goal of mulching is to reduce weeding. So it makes little sense to use a mulch chockfull of weed seeds. Instead, use these seed-free organic mulches or these inorganic mulches:

- Grass clippings (from a weed-free lawn)
- Leaves (shredded or composted)
- Newspaper (shredded or flat)
- Pine needles (for acid-loving crops)
- Salt hay (a generally weed-free plant from oceanside meadows)
- Shredded bark
- Wood chips

Inorganic mulches

Inorganic mulch holds in moisture and stops weeds but doesn't add fertility to the soil. Use it around perennials, shrubs, or trees that are naturally adjusted to your soil and don't require additional fertilizer. Examples of infertile mulch include gravel, landscape fabric, plastic film, sand, and stone.

Fertile mulches

Double your garden's pleasure by using fertile mulch, which controls weeds *and* provides small amounts of nutrients. All organic mulches made of plant material fit this group. Some quickly rot (decompose) and dissolve nutrients into the soil; these are green, fresh, and not too woody. Others are slow to decompose and release few nutrients; these are usually dry, woody, and very low in nitrogen. The mulches that quickly decompose can be used in the annual flower and vegetable beds. When sprinkled, or in rainy-summer areas, organic mulch that decomposes fairly quickly also leaches some nutrients while sitting on top of the soil. The woody mulches should not be tilled into the soil (unless they've fully rotted) and are best used with trees and shrubs.

Fertile mulches that quickly decompose but have weed seeds include cow and horse manure, hay, rabbit, goat, sheep, some poultry bedding, sewage sludge, and straw. Fertile mulches that also quickly decompose but have no weed seeds include clean grass clippings, leaves, and salt hay.

All these mulches are in addition to a nearly infinite selection of local specialties. Rice hulls, cocoa shells, sugar cane refuse, ground corncobs, peanut shells, and grape pomace are a few you may encounter.

Newspaper, shredded bark, and wood chips are not fertile and decompose slowly because they are high in carbon; they have no weed seeds.

Plastic films and woven plastic materials (called *landscape fabric*) act as a seedling barrier as well. But these effective materials are not attractive enough for some situations. Also, sunlight deteriorates these films and woven mulches. Therefore, it is best to cover these mulches with a weed-free organic mulch to block the sun's ultraviolet rays. The fabric will last longer and your garden will look better.

A well-read mulch

Newspapers provide the ultimate organic herbicide, a simple and cost-effective way to mulch out weeds. A thin layer of five to ten sheets of plain, black-and-white newspaper suppresses all sprouting weed seeds, stops some resprouting taproots, and makes life difficult for runner roots. The newspapers are best used around woody perennials, shrubs, and trees, but once you're familiar with the process, you can use them around flowers or vegetables.

To apply the newspaper, moisten the sheets so that they won't blow around while you're laying them out among the plants. Cover the papers with a thin layer of a weed-free, attractive mulch. The mulch helps the newspaper last for 6 to 18 months, depending on whether you have wet or dry summers, respectively.

Cardboard works even better than newspaper for the really tough weeds.

Plant Nutrients

Sixteen elements are known to be essential for healthy plant growth. Plants particularly need carbon, hydrogen, and oxygen in large quantities. Plants also need energy from sunlight for photosynthesis, the process by which green plants take carbon dioxide from the air and water from the soil to produce sugars to fuel their growth. Apart from watering plants, gardeners can trust nature to supply these big basic requirements.

Plants also need nitrogen, phosphorus, and potash in relatively large quantities. These three elements are often called *macronutrients.* Plants take up these three nutrients from the soil. If they are not present in the soil, you can supply them by using fertilizers. The percentages of these nutrients are the three prominent numbers on any bag or box of fertilizer, and the nutrients are always listed in the same order.

✔ **Nitrogen (N).** This nutrient is responsible for the healthy green color of your plants. It is a key part of proteins and *chlorophyll,* the plant pigment that plays a vital role in photosynthesis. Plants with a deficiency of nitrogen show a yellowing of older leaves first, along with a general slowdown in growth.

✔ **Phosphorus (P).** Phosphorus is associated with good root growth, increased disease resistance, and fruit and seed formation. Plants lacking in phosphorus are stunted, with dark green foliage, followed by reddening of the stems and leaves. As with nitrogen, the symptoms appear on the older leaves first.

✔ **Potash (K).** This nutrient promotes vigorous growth and disease resistance. The first sign of a deficiency shows up as browning of the edges of leaves. Older leaves are affected first.

✔ **Calcium, magnesium, and sulfur.** These are the *secondary nutrients.* They are needed in substantial quantities but not to the same extent as nitrogen, phosphorus, and potash. Where the soil is acid (areas of high rainfall), the secondary nutrients are important to lime soil, both to maintain a soil pH beneficial to plants and to supply calcium.

✔ **Iron, manganese, copper, boron, molybdenum, chlorine, zinc.** These are the *micronutrients,* meaning plants need only minute quantities for good health. These nutrients are often not lacking in the soil, but they may be unavailable to plant roots. The cause of this problem is usually a soil pH that is too acid or too alkaline. In this case, rather than adding the nutrient, adjusting soil pH is the remedy. Too much of any of these nutrients can be harmful.

See Chapter 14 for more about soils and soil needs.

Fertilizer Types and How to Use Them

After you decide to feed your plants, you're confronted by myriad _kinds_ of fertilizers at the nursery. How do you know which ones to buy?

When you buy a commercial fertilizer, its analysis is listed on the label with three numbers. These three numbers are helpful because they let you know which nutrients are in a particular fertilizer. The first number indicates the percentage of nitrogen (N), the second, the percentage of phosphate (P_2O_5), and the third, the percentage of potash (K_2O). A 5-10-10 fertilizer is 5 percent nitrogen, 10 percent phosphate, and 10 percent potash. A 100-pound bag of 5-10-10 contains 25 pounds of plant usable nutrients. Although the remaining 75 pounds may contain some plant usable nutrients, usually only _carrier_ or filler are left over from manufacturing.

Common fertilizer forms

- **Chelated micronutrients.** The word _chelate_ comes from the Latin word for _claw,_ and that's a useful way to understand these micronutrients' functions. These compounds bind to certain plant nutrients and essentially deliver them to the plant roots. Nutrients that plants require in minute quantities — such as iron, zinc, and manganese — are often available in chelated form.

- **Complete.** Any fertilizer that contains all three of the primary nutrients — nitrogen (N), phosphorus (P), and potash (K) — is a complete fertilizer. The garden term _complete_ has its basis in laws and regulations that apply to the fertilizer industry: It does not mean that the fertilizer literally contains everything a plant may need.

- **Foliar.** As the name implies, these fertilizers are sprayed over a plant's leaves. They contain nutrients that plant leaves can absorb directly. Although the nutrients in most foliar fertilizers can also be absorbed by plant roots, those absorbed via leaves have a quick effect. Don't apply foliar fertilizers in hot weather because leaves might be damaged.

- **Granular.** These fertilizers are the most common kind. They are commonly sold in boxes or bags. Most are partially soluble. For example, a 10-10-10 granular fertilizer is best applied to the soil about a month prior to planting in order for the nutrients to be available at planting time. You can also get special formulations, such as rose food or azalea food. They supply nutrients over a longer period of time than liquid or soluble fertilizers but not as long as slow-release kinds.

- **Liquid.** Most kinds of fertilizers are dry, but some come as liquid in bottles and jugs. On a per-nutrient basis, liquid fertilizers are more expensive than most dry fertilizers. Most liquid fertilizers need further dilution in water, but a few are ready-to-use. Liquid fertilizers are easy to inject into irrigation systems, which is the reason many professional growers prefer them.

✓ **Organic.** These fertilizers with nutrients are derived from something that was once alive. Examples are blood meal, fish emulsion, and manure. Usually, organic fertilizers contain significant amounts of only one of the major nutrients; for example, bone meal contains only phosphorus. Nutrients in organic fertilizers are made available to plant roots after breakdown by soil microorganisms. Activity of these microorganisms is fastest in summer when soils are warm. As a rule of thumb, half the nutrients in organic fertilizers are available to plants the first season.

✓ **Slow-release.** These fertilizers release the nutrients they contain at specific rates in specific conditions. For example, Osmocote fertilizers release nutrients in response to soil moisture. The nutrients inside the tiny beads "osmose" through a resin membrane. The coating around another type, sulfur-coated urea, is slowly acted upon by soil microorganisms until the nutrients are released. Some can release their nutrients for as long as eight months. Slow-release fertilizers are very useful for container plants that otherwise need frequent fertilizing.

Kinds of fertilizers for various plants

Here are our recommendations for fertilizers to use for different kinds of plants. Keep in mind that many exceptions exist.

✓ **Annual flowers:** Granular; supplemented by liquid soluble two weeks after planting

✓ **Bulbs:** Granular 8-8-8 or similar; applied at planting time

✓ **Fruit trees:** Organic; applied as necessary in spring only

✓ **Hanging baskets:** Slow-release

✓ **House plants:** Slow-release or liquid soluble

✓ **Lawns:** Granular 21-7-14 or similar, preferably slow-release; or an organic, high-nitrogen fertilizer

✓ **Perennials:** Organic; applied in autumn, supplemented by liquid soluble

✓ **Roses:** Organic; applied in spring and autumn for good growth

✓ **Trees and shrubs:** Organic; applied in autumn; supplement with complete granular — 10-10-10 or similar — if spring growth poor

✓ **Vegetables:** Organic; applied in autumn or at least one month prior to planting; continually enrich soil with organic fertilizers; supplement with granular 5-10-10 first two gardening seasons

Organic fertilizers

Organic or natural fertilizers such as manure and composts are more cumbersome and possibly more expensive than synthetic fertilizers, but nothing quite takes their place. In addition to providing some nutrient value, they improve soil structure, which increases the soil's ability to hold air, nutrients, and water.

Plants take up nutrients in specific forms, regardless of whether the source is organic or synthetic. You can supply all the nutrients that plants need by using only organic materials, but some care and effort are needed to ensure that sufficient amounts of nitrogen, phosphorus, and potash are available to the plants throughout the season.

Because the nutrients in organic materials are tied up in more complex molecules, these nutrients often take longer to become available to the plants, which can result in temporary nutrient deficiencies, especially in the spring.

Fresh manure can "burn" plants; woody materials (wood chips, sawdust, leaf piles, and so on) can cause a temporary nitrogen deficiency until they are sufficiently decomposed because the microorganisms that help the decay process may use up all the available nitrogen in order to break them down. You can counteract this effect somewhat by applying a little extra nitrogen in the spring. A rule of thumb is that when the material starts to resemble soil, it is ready for the garden.

Note: Manure and composts are not complete fertilizers because they are usually deficient in phosphorus and potash.

Here's an organic fertilizer recipe for a 30 × 33 foot garden (about 1,000 square feet):

✔ **Nitrogen:** 1,000 pounds of compost or 25 bushels rotted manure

✔ **Phosphorus:** 20 pounds or 10 quarts of bone meal

✔ **Potash:** 30 pounds or 15 quarts of wood ash

Work the materials into the top 4 inches of soil in early spring or the previous autumn. This practice should provide the equivalent of 40 to 50 pounds of 5-10-10, which is the amount of synthetic fertilizer recommended. (***Note:*** A wheelbarrow holds about two bushels.)

Chapter 17
Lawns and Lawn Care

· ·

In This Chapter

▶ Big lawn versus small lawn

▶ Putting in a new lawn

▶ Deciding which grass to grow

▶ Seeding

▶ Planting sod, plugs, or sprigs

▶ Overseeding for a winter lawn where winters are mild

▶ Reinvigorating an existing lawn

▶ Lawn maintenance

· ·

*F*or most people, the landscape isn't complete without at least some lawn. The lush color and smooth, uniform look are a practical and attractive way to complement our homes, trees, shrubs, and other plantings. And it's tough to beat a grassy area as a place for family and pets to relax and play. Many grasses can handle heavy foot traffic, and some even thrive in moderately shady areas. So lawns solve certain landscaping problems.

More Lawn or Less Lawn?

The utility of a well-kept lawn is undeniable. That's why for decades, putting in a lawn was the first thing that people did when they bought a new home. But recently, many people have started to question the amount of time, money, and resources that lawns demand. You should do the same.

Putting in a lawn is a lot of work. Then you must maintain it year after year. A lawn also uses resources — water, fertilizer, and pesticides — that may be in short supply in some areas or can be sources of pollution if not used correctly.

So do a little homework before you run down to the local seed-and-feed and purchase 50 pounds of seed. Figure out the minimum space that you need for a lawn and then determine which type of grass does best in your area.

If you have a newly built home and you're starting from scratch with the landscaping, think seriously about how much weekend time you want to spend pushing the lawn mower (or sitting on the riding mower) and what's appropriate water use for your part of the country. Size the lawn area accordingly. See Chapters 3 and 12 for help in deciding how else you might use the rest of your land and what to plant there.

Next, choose for your lawn one of the many new low-maintenance grass varieties available today. Selecting a grass adapted to your climate helps reduce the amount of work and resources required to keep your lawn looking good. For those of you who already have lawns, this chapter tells you how to easily reseed with one of these improved varieties and keep it in top shape.

With planning, you can satisfy your penchant for a lawn without putting too many demands on your leisure time or the environment.

Putting In a New Lawn

You create lawns by planting *turfgrasses* — grasses specially bred for this particular use — and this can be done in several ways.

The most common and economical way to plant grass is by spreading seed. Proper soil preparation and follow-up care are the keys to success here.

The fastest way to put in a new lawn is by *laying sod* — setting large sections of fully grown turf in place on the soil. The idea of an instant lawn certainly has its appeal, but sod is an expensive option, and you still have to prepare the soil as thoroughly and maintain the newly planted area as carefully as you would for a lawn from seed.

Some types of grass are available only as sod, or as *plugs* (chunks of turf) or *sprigs* (single plants or stems) that are set into little holes in the soil. It can take a couple of years before the grass completely fills the area and looks like a real lawn. Keeping weeds out of the bare soil until the lawn fills in is critical. Grasses that must be planted this way are noted in the following section, which describes the common turfgrasses.

Which grass is best?

Growing the appropriate variety of grass for your area of your country is critical. It'll make all the difference between a thriving lawn and one that doesn't survive the winter or languishes in the heat of your climate.

Turfgrasses fall into two broad groups: *cool season* and *warm season*. Cool-season grasses grow best between 60°F and 75°F and can withstand cold winters. Warm-season grasses, which grow vigorously in temperatures above 80°F, are planted in mild-winter regions. In general terms, cool-season grasses are grown in zones 6 and colder; warm-season grasses are grown in zones 7 and warmer.

Each type of grass has its named varieties, many of which have been bred for improvements like drought or shade tolerance or sheer ruggedness. Your local Extension office or garden center can recommend varieties for your area.

Turfgrass short list

The following sections describe cool-season and warm-season grasses. For details on how to discover your soil type, see Chapter 14.

Cool-season grasses

- **Fine fescue.** A fine-textured turfgrass. Quick to germinate and get established; does well in less-than-ideal growing conditions. The most shade tolerant of the northern grasses. Drought tolerant and requires little feeding. Newer varieties offer insect resistance.

- **Kentucky bluegrass.** The most common lawn grass for cold-winter regions. Slow to get established, but with its spreading habit, it fills in nicely. Fine texture with a rich green color. A heavy feeder. Very hardy; many disease-resistant varieties are available.

- **Perennial ryegrass.** This fine-textured grass is one of the quickest types to get established and will grow in up to 60 percent shade, but it doesn't tolerate the temperature extremes of bluegrass or hold up under mowing as well. Newer varieties offer insect and disease resistance.

- **Turf-type tall fescue.** This coarse-textured grass makes a lush, rugged lawn under difficult conditions. New varieties are resistant to everything: heat, drought, diseases, and insects.

- **Wheat grass.** A native grass of the Rocky Mountains and High Plains; very drought tolerant.

Warm-season grasses

- **Bahia grass.** This low-growing, coarse-textured grass is not as attractive as some of the other warm-season grasses, but it is low maintenance and grows in partial shade.

- ✔ **Bermudagrass.** The most common lawn grass in mild-winter climates. Texture ranges from coarse to fine, depending on the variety. This rugged, drought-resistant grass spreads quickly and can crowd out weeds. Needs frequent, close mowing. Some varieties offer disease and insect resistance. Common Bermudagrass can be grown from seed; the improved hybrids can be planted only as plugs or sod.

- ✔ **Blue grama grass.** A fine-textured grass with flat, gray-green blades. Native to the Great Plains; very drought resistant and requires little or no fertilization.

- ✔ **Buffalo grass.** Fine texture and curled, gray-green blades. Another heat- and drought-resistant Great Plains native. Requires little mowing and little or no fertilization.

- ✔ **Carpet grass.** Coarse texture and low-growing, pointed blades. Spreads quickly and does well in sandy soil.

- ✔ **Centipede grass.** Coarse to medium texture and flat, blunt blades. A low-maintenance, shade-tolerant grass that does well on soils that are acidic or low in fertility. Some disease resistance.

- ✔ **St. Augustine grass.** This coarse-textured grass tolerates partial shade. In general, susceptible to insect and disease problems, although some improved varieties have been introduced in the past few years. Planted from sod or sprigs.

- ✔ **Zoysia grass.** A coarse- to fine-textured grass with stiff blades. Slow growing but very tough once established. Drought resistant and shade tolerant. Planted from sod or sprigs.

Before you plant

The first step in preparing the area to be sown is to test your soil to see whether it's fertile and has the proper pH to grow grass. Turfgrasses prefer a nearly neutral soil pH of 6.5 to 7.5. If your soil is acidic, you may need to raise the pH by applying ground dolomitic limestone. To lower the pH of alkaline soil, you apply elemental sulfur. See Chapter 14 for more on testing soil and adjusting the pH. Your soil test will indicate how much of these soil amendments to use.

If you don't have reasonably fertile soil that can be worked to a depth of 6 to 8 inches, you'll need to purchase a load of topsoil — rich soil that's high in organic matter.

Spread the topsoil smoothly over the area to be seeded, mixing some of it in with the native soil below to prevent a water barrier. Make the topsoil layer 1 inch below the final level of the lawn if installing sod or $1/2$ inch below if sowing seed, and have it slope slightly away from the house for proper drainage.

Seeding a Lawn

The best time to seed a new lawn in cool climates is in the late summer or early autumn and in mild climates, in spring or early summer.

Shopping for seed

Your lawn is a landscape feature that you'll have for years to come, so skip the cheap stuff. How to recognize fine quality seed? Look for the following on the label:

- ✔ A variety name, such as 'Nugget' Kentucky bluegrass instead of generic Kentucky bluegrass

- ✔ Weed and other crop seed content of 0.5 percent or less; the highest-quality seed is free of weed and other undesirable crop seed

- ✔ *Germination percentage* (percentage of seeds in your bag that will sprout and begin to grow) of 85 percent or greater for Kentucky bluegrass and above 90 percent for all other grasses

Remember to measure the square footage of the area that you plan to seed; the label also indicates how large an area the package will cover.

Planting day

When you're ready to plant, assemble all the tools and equipment that you need: soil amendments, rototiller (see Chapter 4 for description), grass seed, lawn spreader (scatters seed evenly as you roll it over the soil — also called a mechanical spreader), board scraper (a board that you drag over the soil surface — see Figure 17-1) or rake, lawn roller (a large, heavy drum with a handle that you roll over the scattered seed to press it into the soil; the drum can be filled with water to increase the weight and mulching material such as straw. Large tools that you don't own can be rented locally for the day. Then follow these instructions:

1. **Spread over the soil any amendments required to correct the pH and apply a complete fertilizer recommended for new lawns in the amount given on the bag.**

   Chapter 14 has more information about soil.

2. **Rototill the soil a few inches deep to loosen it but don't overcultivate — leave small lumps and cracks to catch seed so it sprouts quickly. Remove stones and sticks.**

3. **Level the soil with a board scraper or rake to eliminate high spots where the mower would cut the grass too short as well as depressions where it might miss spots or where water could collect.**

   Figure 17-1 shows a board scraper in use. Try attaching a weight to the board scraper or rake to make the dragging easier.

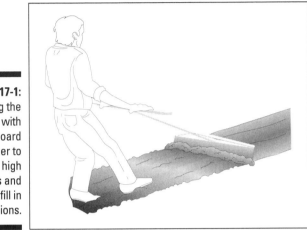

Figure 17-1:
Drag the surface with a board scraper to level high spots and fill in depressions.

4. **Roll the seedbed with the empty roller to firm the soil.**

   Make sure that the soil is dry before you roll; otherwise, it compacts, preventing seeds from sprouting.

5. **Sow the seed with a mechanical spreader or by hand.**

   Don't be tempted to oversow; if you do, the plants won't develop properly.

6. **Rake the surface lightly, barely covering about half the seed and leaving the rest exposed — it needs light to germinate.**

7. **Roll once more with the empty roller to press seeds in contact with the soil.**

8. **Lightly mulch the seedbed to keep the soil moist until the seeds germinate. The mulch also keeps the seeds from washing away in a heavy rain.**

   Chapter 16 discusses mulching.

9. **Give the newly seeded area a thorough initial soaking and then keep it well watered until the grass is established. Each watering should penetrate the soil to a depth of several inches to promote good root growth.**

Lawns from Sod

The best time to lay sod in cold-winter regions is in autumn; in mild-winter regions, the best time is early spring.

Buying sod

Sod is expensive, so buy from a quality supplier. Look for sections that are $3/4$ inch to 1 inch thick, with no brown patches or dried-out edges. Have the sod delivered on planting day so it doesn't sit in a pile and heat up.

Laying sod

When you're ready to lay the sod, assemble all the tools and equipment that you need: soil amendments, rototiller, board scraper or rake, and lawn roller. Prepare the planting area as you would for a lawn from seed (Steps 1 through 3 in the "Planting day" section of this chapter).

Then follow these instructions for laying sod:

1. **Roll out a piece of sod and press it into position. Fit the next section against it tightly but don't overlap.**

2. **Continue laying sections, staggering them slightly like bricks.**

3. **Use a roller over the newly laid turf, going back over it a second time at right angles to the first pass.**

4. **Rake the new lawn lightly to lift up the flattened grass, and keep the soil moist until the sod is well established.**

Planting plugs and sprigs

Prepare the planting area as you would for a lawn from seed (Steps 1 through 3 under "Planting day"). Then follow these instructions for planting plugs and sprigs:

1. **Dig holes 2 to 3 inches deep and 6 inches apart for zoysia grass, 12 inches apart for Bermudagrass. Set the plugs or sprigs in place. Water well.**

2. **Keep the bare soil weed free until the lawn is established.**

Overseeding to Improve Your Lawn's Looks

You can have two lawns in one by *overseeding* — planting seeds of two grasses in one lawn.

Lawn color where winters are mild

If your lawn is Bermudagrass, it'll turn brown when it goes into dormancy for the winter.

But you can still have a green lawn by overseeding with a cool-season grass, such as perennial ryegrass or a bluegrass, that will grow during the winter. The following summer, this cool-season grass will be the one to go dormant.

In the autumn, before the permanent lawn goes dormant, mow it about ¹/₂ inch to 1 inch high and rake it thoroughly. Your lawn may be so thick with *thatch* (the mat of clippings, roots, and stems that accumulates on top of the soil) that your mower won't cut into it. If so, rent a machine called a *power rake* — like a lawn mower with vertical blades that comb out heavy thatch as they slice into the soil. Overseed with 1¹/₂ times the amount recommended on the package. Once the Bermudagrass goes dormant, mow at a height of 3 inches through the winter.

Overseeding isn't recommended for zoysia grass lawns.

Don't like the lawn you've got?

You've got too many thin spots, weeds have gotten the upper hand, or the wrong type of grass is struggling to survive? Relax — you probably don't have to tear out the whole thing and start over. As long as your lawn is at least 50 percent grass (as opposed to weeds), you can give it a facelift by overseeding with an improved grass variety.

Overseed cool-season grasses in autumn and warm-season grasses in spring. Here's how:

1. **Mow your lawn closely and thoroughly rake out the thatch (as described in the "Lawn color where winters are mild" section).**

    Loosening compacted soil with a *coring machine,* a piece of power equipment that cuts out small plugs of soil to improve air and water circulation around the grass roots, also gets rid of some of the thatch.

2. **Adjust the soil pH if necessary and fertilize. Sow seed at 1$^1/_2$ times the rate recommended on the package. Sprinkle a light layer of topsoil over the lawn (called *topdressing*) and water thoroughly.**

   Chapter 14 describes soil testing. See Chapter 16 and also the upcoming section "Fertilizing" for information about fertilizers.

The Care and Feeding of Lawns

Your lawn requires some annual maintenance to keep it looking its best. Basic lawn care consists of weeding, mowing, and fertilizing. The following sections give you some tips on performing these chores.

Weeding and mowing

The best technique for keeping weeds under control in your lawn is to grow the right kind of grass and take good care of it. Weeds can't get established in a thick patch of healthy turf.

If you want to yank out the prime offenders, like dandelions, you can find tools for this purpose at most garden centers. But don't get obsessive — a few weeds won't spoil the overall look or purpose of the lawn.

The mowers available today make the inevitable task of mowing the lawn easier and more enjoyable. If you're in the market for a new mower, read about some of your options in Chapter 4.

Here are some tips:

✔ As a rule of thumb, keep cool-season grasses at a height of 2 inches during the summer and warm-season grasses at a height of 1 inch. Cutting too short affects the roots in their search for nutrients in the soil and reduces the nutrients manufactured by the leaves.

✔ Mow when the grass is 1 inch higher than its recommended height. Letting the lawn grow too long between mowings weakens the grass.

✔ Mow when the grass is dry.

✔ Avoid mowing in the same pattern — for example, always following horizontal paths — every time.

✔ As long as the clippings aren't too long, just leave them in place — they'll add nitrogen to the soil as they break down.

Fertilizing

Most grass varieties need to be fed regularly (except for the native grasses like blue grama and buffalo grass, which require very little to no fertilizing). A well-fed lawn is healthier, denser, and more weed free than a poorly fed or unfed one. Keep an eye on your soil pH and amend it if necessary (see the section on adjusting pH under "Before you plant" in this chapter). The plants can't make use of fertilizer when they're growing in soils that are too acidic or too alkaline.

Feed warm-season grasses in the spring and summer and cool-season grasses in the spring and autumn. Choose a slow-release organic fertilizer with a moderate amount of nitrogen — between 5 and 10 percent. (The first of the three numbers on the label is the percentage of nitrogen; see Chapter 16 for more on fertilizer labels.) Although different grasses vary in their fertilization requirements, as a general rule, you need 10 to 20 pounds of a 6 percent nitrogen fertilizer per 1,000 square feet of lawn.

Chapter 18
Pests and Diseases

In This Chapter

▶ Prevention: It's the best medicine, and it's free!

▶ Beneficial insects

▶ Put down that poison!

▶ Stopping 25 garden pests safely

▶ Using safe insecticides for vegetable gardens

▶ Cures for 12 plant diseases

*I*f you're a beginning gardener, you may find that keeping your landscape healthy and free of pests and diseases is a challenge. But problems often seem to disappear as you gain gardening experience. Why? Because you learn how to find the right plant for the right place and follow up with the proper care. Your plants begin to grow vigorously and are less susceptible to problems. And when you do have a pest or disease outbreak, you quickly and safely control it *before* it devastates your plants. This chapter gives you a start in that direction.

Preventing Pests and Diseases

With the right growing conditions, plants are less likely to get sick. Start by preparing a site with suitable soil, appropriate drainage and moisture, and the right amount of sun for the plant that you've selected.

Another trouble-free way to avoid pests and diseases is to grow only disease- and pest-resistant plants. These traits are clearly noted in most seed and nursery catalogs. If you simply must grow a plant that is prone to some problems, take steps in advance to avoid an outbreak. Monitor your plants regularly — look under, over, between, and around all the leaves, trunks, and stems for signs of infection or infestation. Don't panic if you see the nibblings of a few pests; these pests are food for garden predators such as ladybugs and birds. But if you find masses of crawling insects or rapidly spreading diseases, you need to act fast and take measures to prevent problems from getting out of hand.

Identify any suspicious pest, leaf spot, or growth that you find so you can determine whether it's a problem. For a start, consult our list of common pests and diseases coming up in this chapter. If you need more help, contact a full-service garden center that has a variety of reference books to consult as well as personal experience with local pests. Also check with a botanical garden, library, or your local Extension office.

At your nursery or library, ask to look at *The Ortho Problem Solver*. It's a 1,000-page encyclopedia of garden pest problems, each one with a color picture.

Look for the telephone number of your Extension office in your telephone book. Or buy the $23 book *County Agents* from Century Communication Corp., 6201 Howard St., Niles, IL 60714-3435; phone, 708-647-1200.

Gardening to prevent pest problems

Here's a list what of what to do for common-sense pest prevention:

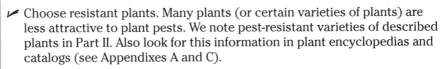

- ✔ Choose a proper site and soil so that plants are healthy, vigorous, and resistant to pests. For help, see Chapter 5 and Part III.

- ✔ Avoid planting the same crops in the same location year after year. *Crop rotation* prevents pests and diseases specific to certain crops from accumulating in the soil.

- ✔ Keep your garden clean and tidy! Sanitation eliminates problem plants and pests before they get started.

- ✔ Choose resistant plants. Many plants (or certain varieties of plants) are less attractive to plant pests. We note pest-resistant varieties of described plants in Part II. Also look for this information in plant encyclopedias and catalogs (see Appendixes A and C).

- ✔ Take steps to entice beneficial insects into your garden (see "Encouraging 'good' insects" in this chapter).

Beneficial insects are insects that prey upon or parasitize garden pests. In nature, beneficial insects keep plant-eating pests under control.

An insect or disease problem is often a symptom of something else being out of whack. Table 18-1 lists conditions and the pests that they promote. Treating the causes and not the symptoms makes good sense.

Table 18-1	Conditions That Promote Pest Problems
Condition	*Pest*
High or excessive organic matter in soil	Cutworms
Partially decomposed crop debris	Damping-off disease, cutworms
Poorly decomposed manure	Root maggots, weeds
Dry and dusty weather	Spider mites
Sandy soils	Root-knot nematode
Acid soils	Clubroot of cabbage, broccoli, and related crops
Too much water	Damping-off and other root rots, weeds
Too much nitrogen	Weeds, aphids

Encouraging "good" insects

In a garden, most of the insects that you see are neither "good" nor "bad," and many are (from our point of view, at least) distinctly beneficial.

To get the good insects to stick around, follow these tips:

- ✔ Avoid indiscriminate pesticide spraying, which kills beneficials as well as pests. If you must spray, use a product that specifically targets the pests you want to eliminate.

- ✔ Make sure that the beneficials have plenty to eat by allowing small numbers of pests to reside in your garden. Because some beneficials also feed on nectar and pollen, grow flowers.

- ✔ Provide beneficials with shelter. Grow a variety of plants — tall, short, spreading, and upright — to give beneficials many potential homes from which to choose.

- ✔ If beneficial insects are not as numerous in your garden as they could be, you can buy them from mail-order garden suppliers (several are listed in Appendix C). If you know when a particularly difficult pest is likely to appear, order in advance. That way, you can release the beneficials in time to prevent problems.

Here are some good insects that you can buy:

- ✔ **Chinese praying mantis.** General predator; interesting to watch but doesn't provide reliable control of pests.

- ✔ **Convergent lady beetle.** Feeds on small insects, such as aphids; release of adults generally not effective, as they disperse rapidly.

- ✔ **Fly parasites.** Various parasitic wasps can control manure-breeding flies, such as the common housefly; useful around feedlots and chicken houses.

- ✔ **Green lacewing.** Larval stage feeds on aphids, thrips, mites, and various other insect eggs; overall, the most useful in home gardens.

- ✔ **Parasitic nematodes.** Tiny worms that parasitize many soil-dwelling and burrowing insects, such as grubs, cutworms, and weevils.

- ✔ **Predatory mites.** Types of mites that feed on other spider mites.

- ✔ **Trichogramma wasps.** Tiny wasps that parasitize many kinds of caterpillars by laying eggs in them; effective against corn earworm, loopers, and tomato hornworm.

- ✔ **Whitefly parasite.** Tiny wasp that lays eggs on larvae of greenhouse whitefly.

Managing Pests

Think of pest management as a staircase. On the first step are innocuous, least disruptive actions, and on the top step are the most toxic and the most potentially harmful actions. This strategy is called *integrated pest management*, or IPM. That's a fancy-sounding label for something that is really basic common sense.

This list is an example of the actions you may take in your garden to keep a pest from getting the upper hand. We begin with the easiest and end with the most aggressive. If you come across unfamiliar words here, don't despair. We define them all as we go through this chapter.

- ✔ Water spray that knocks small pests such as aphids and spider mites off your plants

- ✔ Barriers — such as floating row covers (translucent, lightweight fabrics that cover plants) and cutworm collars (rings placed around seedlings) — to barricade pests away from plants

- ✔ Insect traps with lures and attractive baits or colors to draw pests to immobilizing traps

✔ Bacterial insecticides, such as Bt and milky spore disease

✔ Least toxic controls, such as insecticidal soaps and horticultural oils, which kill pests but cause minimal impact on the environment

✔ Botanical insecticides, such as pyrethrin and neem

When looking for a product to help control a pest or disease, read the label carefully to be sure that the product targets your plant's problem. Most botanical insecticides and organic fungicides can kill a variety of organisms, including beneficials. Use such products as a last resort.

The label tells you how often to reapply the product to kill future generations of pests and diseases. It also details what precautions to take to ensure that you're using the product safely so that it won't harm your plant or your family and pets.

Never store a pesticide in an unlabeled bottle, especially not in a breakable bottle, and follow proper disposal procedures for empty containers.

Dealing with pests in the vegetable garden

The materials and methods for controlling pests in a garden are doubly important in food gardens. For one thing, pesticide regulations are different for food than for ornamental gardens. But more important, who wants something greasy or potentially toxic in his or her salad bowl?

Table 18-2 lists the pests to watch out for in your vegetable gardens. We describe the diseases and pests in the sections "Insect pests that you're most likely to encounter" and "A dozen dirty diseases: what to do."

Table 18-2   Common Pests of Vegetable Seedlings

What the Problem Looks Like	Probable Cause
Seeds fail to germinate or appear	Seedcorn maggots, damping-off, birds
Seedling collapses	Damping-off, heat
Stems eaten at soil line	Cutworms
Leaves and stems chewed, torn	Snails, slugs, caterpillars, rabbits
Severely wilted plant (roots eaten)	Wireworms, root maggots, gophers
Small, round pits in leaves	Flea beetles
Threadlike, twisting lines in leaves	Leaf miners
Clusters of small, pear-shaped insects	Aphids
Plants completely removed	Animal pests such as birds or gophers

Cultural practices for avoiding diseases

✔ Mulch to prevent soilborne diseases from splashing onto flowers and vegetables. (But keep mulch away from trunks and stems to discourage collar rot.)

✔ Provide for good drainage of water through soil to discourage root rot.

✔ Rotate annual crops regularly so that disease problems can't build up.

✔ Provide good air circulation so that leaves dry quickly, preventing spores of some fungus diseases from growing.

✔ Water the soil, not the plants. Plants vary in their susceptibility to moisture-borne diseases. If a plant is prone to leaf diseases, avoid wetting its leaves.

✔ Choose plants or varieties of plants that are more tolerant of common disease problems.

✔ Keep your garden clean. Dispose of diseased plant parts in the garbage, not the compost pile. If necessary, sanitize pruning shears between cuts by spraying with Lysol or a bleach solution.

When a problem does occur, correctly identifying the cause is essential. The beetle that you see near a hole in a leaf may be a beneficial predator. But if it is damaging your plants, simply pick it off. Also consider that doing nothing at all — letting nature take its course — is often the best approach. Always use simple, noninvasive remedies first.

Insect pests you're most likely to encounter

Here are some common insect pests and what to do about them:

✔ **Aphids.** These tiny, soft-bodied, pear-shaped pests suck plant sap with their needlelike noses. Colors vary: They may be black, green, or even translucent. They leave behind sticky sap droppings that may turn black if covered with sooty mold. Aphids can proliferate quickly on weakened plants. Blast them off with a hose, control with beneficial insects or sticky yellow traps, or spray with insecticidal soap.

✔ **Black vine weevil.** This dark, crawling, 1- to 2-inch-long beetle chews on the foliage of evergreen trees and shrubs such as rhododendrons and yews, while the larvae attack from the other end, eating the roots. Black vine weevils also attack potted plants. Control adults and larvae with beneficial nematodes or spray with pyrethrin at night when the adults come out to feed.

✔ **Borers.** Several kinds of beetle and caterpillar larvae (they look like small worms and are usually less than 1 inch long) tunnel into the wood or stems of fruit trees, white birches, dogwoods, shade trees, rhododendrons, German irises, and squash vines. The boring weakens the plant and makes it more susceptible to diseases. It can also cut off nutrient flow to the affected limb or vine. Choose species that are less susceptible to borers. For example, try Siberian irises instead of German bearded irises. Keep susceptible plants growing vigorously and watch for signs of borer damage — dead bark, sawdust piles, and poor performance. Once you find borers, cut off and destroy severely infested limbs. Inject parasitic nematodes into the remaining borer holes. You also can use preventive insecticide sprays to kill mating adults or hatching larvae.

✔ **Caterpillars.** Moth and butterfly larvae are avid eaters that can cause damage to a variety of plants. However, you may decide to overlook the activities of some butterfly caterpillars so that you can enjoy the handsome butterflies later. (See Chapter 20 for more about gardening for butterflies.) Eliminate caterpillars such as the cabbage looper, tomato hornworm, and corn earworm before they do too much damage. If beneficial insects don't keep them in check, spray with Bt (a bacterial disease of caterpillars). You can also kill caterpillars with pyrethrin.

✔ **Chinch bugs.** These $^1/_4$-inch-long, brown or black insects suck grass sap, releasing toxins that make grass discolor and wilt. They can turn entire patches of lawn brown, especially in dry and hot areas. Dethatch the lawn (see Chapter 17) and let it grow a little longer than usual to discourage chinch bugs. For control, treat with neem.

✔ **Codling moths.** This 1-inch-long, pinkish-white caterpillar emerges from eggs laid on apples, peaches, pears, and other fruits. The caterpillars tunnel inside the fruit, making it unappealing. Use pheromone traps to monitor emergence of egg-laying females and spray with ryania or sabadilla as needed to prevent egg laying through the growing season. Eliminate wild or unsprayed trees nearby that shelter codling moth populations.

Pheromones are the perfumes of the insect world. Undetectable to us, tiny amounts of these chemicals released by female butterflies and moths are a siren song to a wandering male of the right type. Professionals use synthetic pheromones to monitor pest populations; you can use them to trap pests such as codling moth.

✔ **Colorado potato beetles.** This yellow-and-black-striped beetle ($^1/_3$ inch long, nearly round) is famous for obliterating potato plantings, but it also eats tomatoes, eggplant, petunias, and flowering tobacco. Discourage Colorado potato beetles by rotating planting sites. Cover potato plants with floating row covers to keep the beetles off. Spray with Bt formulated for Colorado potato beetles or with neem.

- **Spotted and striped cucumber beetles.** This $1/3$-inch-long beetle with yellow and black stripes (or spots) swarms on cucumber, squash, and melon plants. It may carry a bacterial wilt disease that will kill your vines — a good reason to keep the beetles away entirely. Cover young vines with floating row covers. Uncover when several flowers open, and spray as needed with pyrethrin or neem. Till soil in autumn to eliminate overwintering hideouts.

- **Cutworms.** These $1/2$-inch-long, grayish caterpillars emerge on spring and early summer nights to eat the base of young seedling stems, cutting the tops off from the roots. To control, surround seedlings with a barrier that prevents the cutworms from crawling close and feeding. These devices can be as simple as an empty cardboard toilet paper roll or a collar made from aluminum foil — just make sure that it encircles the stem completely and is set 1 inch deep in the soil.

- **Flea beetles.** These tiny black beetles feed on vegetable plants like eggplant, radish, and broccoli, sometimes riddling the entire leafy area of seedlings with holes. Cover susceptible plants with floating row covers as soon as you plant them. Keep them covered until the plants get fairly large and can hold their own. You also can spray with pyrethrin or neem.

- **Gypsy moths.** These 2-inch-long, gray (with brown hairs), foliage-eating caterpillars or their egg clusters hitchhike across the country on cars, campers, and trains. They eat foliage on a number of shade trees, including oaks, and can defoliate trees when their population gets large enough. Monitor population sizes with pheromone traps. Catch caterpillars as they attempt to crawl up tree trunks by using duct tape treated with a sticky barrier. Spray with Bt or neem.

Sticky pest barriers are just that — bands of goop that a crawling insect is unable to navigate. Buy this stuff at garden centers or from one of the mail-order suppliers listed in Appendix C.

- **Japanese beetles.** These beetles are $1/2$ inch long and metallic blue-green with coppery wing covers. They eat almost any plant with gusto. Their fat, white, C-shaped, $3/4$-inch-long larvae consume turf roots. To control, treat your lawn with milky spore disease, which takes several years to spread through the lawn, or with parasitic nematodes, a quicker-acting helper. Trap adult males with pheromone traps, set far downwind from your garden so that they don't draw extra beetles. Spray adult beetles with rotenone if necessary; use neem on prize plants to deter adults from feeding.

- **Leaf miners.** The larval form of tiny flies, these maggots tunnel randomly through leaves of plants such as columbine, peppers, beans, and lilacs. They mainly disfigure plants and are hard to eliminate because they are hidden inside the leaf. Prevent infestation by covering predisposed seedlings with floating row covers and removing and destroying infested leaves. Spray with neem in spring when adults begin to lay eggs.

✔ **Mealybugs.** These small sucking insects cover their bodies with a white, cottony substance that makes them easy to identify. Plus, they usually feed in groups. They're common on houseplants. You can wash off small numbers with cotton dipped in rubbing alcohol; for larger infestations, spray with insecticidal soap or neem.

✔ **Mexican bean beetles.** These ¹/₄-inch, round beetles are yellowish with black spots. They resemble ladybugs but are avid plant eaters. They can destroy an entire bean planting, enjoying snap beans most but also lima beans, soybeans, and other legumes. The spiny, yellow larvae that appear on the bean plants soon after the adults arrive are just as bad as the adults. Pull up and destroy infested plants, beetles and all, immediately after harvesting. Till the ground to kill beetles hiding there. If necessary, spray with pyrethrin or neem. (See Figure 18-1.)

✔ **Oriental fruit moths.** These small moths produce ¹/₂-inch-long, white-to-pink larvae that tunnel into the young wood or fruit of fruit and ornamental trees. In spring, work the soil shallowly around infested trees to kill overwintering larvae. Catch adult males in pheromone traps or use pheromones to confuse males and prevent breeding. You can kill moth eggs with horticultural oil.

✔ **Plum curculio.** These ¹/₄-inch-long beetles are easy to identify by the crescent-shaped, egg-laying cut they make in fruit. Unfortunately, after the eggs are laid, the fruit may be ruined. Shake tree branches to knock the beetles off and then step on them. Destroy prematurely fallen fruit, which may contain larvae.

✔ **Root maggots.** A variety of fly larvae (most are white and less than ¹/₄ inch long) attack the roots of carrots, the cabbage family, and onions. They can disfigure or destroy these plants. Look for resistant plants. Cover new plantings of susceptible types of cabbage, turnips, rutabagas, radishes, kohlrabi, carrots, parsnips, and onions with floating row covers.

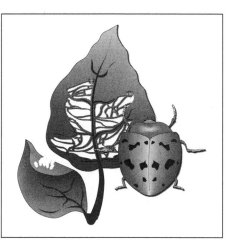

Figure 18-1:
Mexican
bean
beetles can
devastate
bean
plantings.

✔ **Scale.** Like bumps on plant stems and leaves, these tiny sucking insects cling to plant branches, hiding under an outer shellcover that serves as a shield. These pests suck plant sap and can kill plants if present in large numbers. Look for sticky, honeylike sap droppings, one clue that scale may be present. Remove and destroy badly infested stems. Clean off light infestations with a cotton ball soaked in rubbing alcohol. Spray with dormant oil in early spring or light horticultural oil in summer.

✔ **Snails and slugs.** These soft-bodied mollusks feed on tender leaves during the cool of night or in rainy weather. They proliferate in damp areas, hiding and breeding under rocks, mulch, and other garden debris. Clean up dark, damp hiding spots to relocate slugs elsewhere. Catch the ones that are left with saucers of beer set with the rim at ground level. Slugs crawl in and can't get out. Refill regularly. Or surround plants with *copper barriers* — metal strips that seem to shock slugs if they attempt to crawl across.

✔ **Spider mites.** These tiny arachnoids are almost microscopic, but when they appear in large numbers, you can begin to see the fine webs that they weave. They suck plant sap, causing leaves to discolor and plants to lose vigor. They are especially active in arid conditions. You find spider mites on fruit trees, miniature roses, potted begonias, and many houseplants. Indoors, wash houseplants often and spray with insecticidal soap. Outdoors, use dormant oil in early spring or light horticultural oil in summer.

✔ **Tarnished plant bugs (or lygus bugs).** These $1/4$-inch-long, yellow-to-brown plant eaters attack many kinds of plants — more than 400, including some of our most important economic crops — leaving behind dark, sunken leaf spots and wilting or dead shoots. They especially like the growing points of apples and strawberries. Catch them with white sticky traps. Prevent problems by covering susceptible plants with a floating row cover.

✔ **Tent caterpillars.** These caterpillars form tentlike webs full of teeming caterpillars on trees and shrubs. In large numbers, they can defoliate an entire tree. Cut off severely infested branches or knock off the tents. You also can spray minor infestations with Bt.

✔ **Tomato hornworm.** This large, 3- to 5-inch-long, green caterpillar is notable particularly for its white stripes and the threatening "horn" protruding from its rear. As dangerous as it appears, the horn can do no harm, which is why hand picking is one of the preferred controls. If you have lots of tomatoes (or peppers or potatoes), you may want to spray or dust with Bt in late spring or early summer.

✔ **Whiteflies.** Whiteflies look like small, white gnats, but they suck plant sap and can proliferate in warm climates or greenhouses. They can also spread diseases with their sucking mouthparts. Trap whiteflies with yellow sticky traps. Cure infestations with regular sprays of insecticidal soap, light horticultural oil, or pyrethrin.

Nine safe and effective pest remedies

Gardeners today have at their disposal a handful of effective and safe pesticides. All the following are safe to use on food crops as well as on ornamentals.

Bt

Bt exists naturally in most soils. Different strains of Bt occur that produce protein crystals toxic to certain insects. The strain for most caterpillars is *B.t.* var. *kurstaki*. Commercially prepared Bt spray or powder has no effect on adult butterflies or moths. Remember, however, that not all caterpillars are pests.

Strains of Bt have been developed for a few other pests. Some leaf-feeding beetles (including Colorado potato beetle) are susceptible to *B.t. tenebrionis,* for example.

Advantages: One advantage is safety — Bt is essentially nontoxic to humans, other mammals, and birds. The label specifies no waiting period between application and harvest. Bt is also highly selective and so easily incorporated with existing natural controls.

Disadvantages: A limitation of Bt is its slow action. After pests consume it, their feeding slows down. But their deaths may not occur for two to five days. Bt also breaks down quickly — if the caterpillars don't eat some while it's fresh, it probably won't work.

Because Bt is a near-perfect insecticide, there is danger of overuse. Any overused insecticide gradually becomes less effective as insects evolve defenses to it. Some insect pests, such as the diamondback moth and Indian meal moth, were once susceptible and are now at least partially immune to Bt.

How to use: Use Bt against cabbageworms, cutworms, and other caterpillars. Use *B.t. tenebrionis* against Colorado potato beetles. The bacterial toxin causes caterpillar death two to five days after it's eaten; the toxin dissipates in two days or less. It is available as liquid spray or dust. Apply in late afternoon and reapply after rain. Repeat applications as needed. Mix with insecticidal soap for greater effectiveness.

Diatomaceous earth (DE)

DE is a powderlike dust made of the silicate skeletons of tiny marine creatures called *diatoms*. Millions of years ago, as they died, their skeletons gradually accumulated into deep layers that are mined today from deposits where oceans or large lakes once covered the land. DE acts like ground glass, cutting into the waxy coat of insects and causing them to dry out and die.

Advantages: It is not toxic if eaten but is irritating if inhaled.

Disadvantages: It is not selective and kills spiders and beneficials as well as pests.

DE is available in two forms. One, which is used primarily in swimming pool filters, is not an effective insecticide and is dangerous to inhale (can cause a lung disease called silicosis). In your garden, use only the natural grade of DE. Still, wear goggles and a dust mask during application.

How to use: Dust DE onto leaves and stems to control pests such as aphids, immature Colorado potato beetles, immature forms of squash bug, immature Mexican bean beetles, and whiteflies. Or spread it as a barrier to slugs and snails. It works best in dry situations; reapply after rain. Don't overuse it.

DE is more effective when combined with pyrethrins.

Horticultural oils

Horticultural oils are most often highly refined extracts of crude oil. (Some vegetable oils, such as cottonseed and soybean oil, are also sometimes used.) They kill insects by plugging the pores through which the insects breathe.

Advantages: These oils are increasingly recommended for vegetable garden pest control because they present few risks to either gardeners or desirable species and integrate well with natural biological controls. Also, oils dissipate quickly through evaporation, leaving little residue.

Disadvantages: Oils can damage plants if applied at excessive rates or on particularly hot (above 100°F) or cold (below 40°F) days.

How to use: Spray oils in vegetable gardens to kill aphids, leafhoppers, spider mites, and whiteflies. A few drops of oil in the ear tips of corn control corn earworm.

Use highly refined horticultural oils and dilute according to label directions. Do not apply oils to drought-stressed plants, or on hot, cold, or very humid days. Don't apply horticultural oils to green plants at rates recommended for leafless, dormant plants.

Insecticidal soaps

Insecticidal soaps are specific fatty acids that have been found by experiment to be toxic to pests, primarily soft-bodied insects like aphids, mealybugs, spider mites, and whiteflies. Surprisingly, adult Japanese beetles are also susceptible.

Advantages: Insecticidal soap is one of the safest insecticides. Most nontarget insects are unaffected, and the soaps are not toxic to animals. Soap insecticides act fast and leave no residue. You can use them on vegetables up to the moment of harvest.

Disadvantages: Some plants, such as peas, are readily burned by soaps, and the soaps' effectiveness is greatly reduced when mixed with hard water.

How to use: Use against aphids, earwigs, grasshoppers, Japanese beetles (adults), leafhoppers, spider mites, and whiteflies. Apply diluted concentrate or ready-to-use liquid when the air is still. Mix with warm, soft water and be sure to cover both sides of leaves. Reapply after rain. Can burn leaves of certain plants during hot weather.

Neem

Neem is an extract derived from the crushed seeds of the tropical neem tree *(Azadirachta indica)*. Though intensely studied for many years now, it is still a new botanical insecticide. The primary active ingredient is the compound azadirachtin, although the oils and other ingredients also have some insecticidal effect.

Neem works both as an insecticide and as an agent that prevents insects from feeding. It kills insects in the juvenile stage by thwarting their development and is most effective against aphids, thrips, and whiteflies.

Advantages: Neem has no measurable toxicity to mammals and is harmless to most beneficial insects. (In some countries, neem extract is considered healthful to people and is added to various food and personal products.) Recently, the Environmental Protection Agency stipulated that neem was exempt from food crop tolerances because it is considered nontoxic.

Disadvantages: There is no quick "knock-down" with neem, but a week or so after application, you'll notice a steady decline in the number of pests. It is not effective against adult insects (though it may interfere with egg production) and has little impact on beneficial insects. Once beetle numbers build up on the plant, neem no longer discourages them.

How to use: Neem sprays degrade very quickly in water. Mix only the amount you need and apply all of it immediately. Reapply after rainfall. On the plant, neem retains its activity against juvenile insect pests for about one week.

Use neem to kill juvenile aphids, Colorado potato beetles, and thrips and to repel whiteflies, Japanese beetles, and adult Colorado potato beetles. Apply liquid spray morning or evening when humidity is highest. Repeat weekly; spray lasts on plants about one week. As a toxin, apply when pests are young. As an antifeedant, neem is effective against Japanese beetles; apply before the pests appear.

Pyrethrins

Derived from the painted daisy, *Chrysanthemum cinerariifolium,* pyrethrins are considered one of the most important natural insecticides. When you must either use a broad-spectrum insecticide in the vegetable garden or lose the crop, pyrethrins are among your best choices.

Broad-spectrum insecticides are products that kill a diversity of insects, pest and beneficial alike. If you need to use an insecticide to control a particular pest, it's better to use a product that targets that particular kind of pest without harming beneficial insects.

The terminology can be confusing, however. *Pyrethrum* is the ground-up flowers of the daisy. *Pyrethrins* (most always plural) are the insecticidal components of the flowers. *Pyrethroids*, such as cypermethrin, permethrin, and resmethrin, are synthetic compounds that resemble pyrethrins but are more toxic and persistent.

Though they're becoming increasingly popular commercially, home gardeners should avoid using pyrethroids.

Advantages: Pyrethrins are of low toxicity to mammals and kill insects quickly. In sunlight, they break down and are nontoxic within a day or less.

Disadvantages: Often, pure pyrethrins only stun insects, which is why they're often combined with a *synergist* (a chemical that enhances the effectiveness of the active ingredients) such as piperonyl butoxide or with another botanical insecticide, rotenone. Also, pyrethrin is toxic to honeybees — apply it in the evening after bees are in their hives.

How to use: Use against most vegetable garden pests, such as flea, potato, and bean beetles, including the hard-to-kill pests, such as beetles, squash bugs, and tarnished plant bugs. For best results, apply in the late afternoon or evening. Degrades within one day.

Sabadilla

This botanical insecticide is made by grinding the seeds of the sabadilla lily (*Schoenocaulon officinale*) into a fine powder.

Advantages: It's effective against a range of true bugs (insects of the order Hemiptera) as both a contact and stomach poison.

Disadvantages: Like most other botanical insecticides, sabadilla breaks down very quickly in sunlight but remains potent for many years if stored in a dry, dark place. And as with other toxic sprays, use it infrequently, as a last step in your vegetable garden IPM program. Sabadilla is highly toxic to honeybees (so don't spray it on flowers they visit) and highly irritating to mucous membranes of mammals.

How to use: Use against citrus thrips, green stinkbugs, harlequin bugs, leafhoppers, squash bugs, and tarnished plant bugs. Remains toxic for about two days.

Rotenone

Rotenone is often recommended for organic gardeners because of its botanical origin (derived from the roots of tropical legumes).

Advantages: It is approved for use in organic gardens and breaks down quickly in sunlight.

Disadvantages: It is more toxic than carbaryl and, like carbaryl, is toxic to pests and beneficials alike.

How to use: Use this broad-spectrum insecticide as a last resort against cabbageworms, Colorado potato beetles, flea beetles, fruit worms, Japanese beetles, loopers, Mexican bean beetles, thrips, and weevils. Apply in early evening when bees are inactive. It remains toxic up to one week.

Sevin (carbaryl)

One of the most widely used insecticides in home vegetable gardens, Sevin is controversial because it kills most kinds of insects. Sevin is a sledgehammer of a remedy. Use it sparingly, if at all.

Advantages: Aside from its effectiveness, Sevin's virtue is low toxicity to mammals and birds. It is less toxic than the botanical insecticide rotenone, and it is less toxic to birds than to mammals.

Disadvantages: Sevin requires two weeks or more to degrade, so it poses a significant hazard to a wide range of beneficial insects.

Sevin is particularly deadly to honeybees and wasps, several of which are parasites of other garden pests. Because it kills beneficial insects so effectively, Sevin often causes outbreaks of so-called secondary pests, such as spider mites. It is also toxic to earthworms.

How to use: Use only as a last resort and only after pyrethrin or perhaps rotenone have failed to be effective.

Least toxic disease remedies

Use the following time-tested fungicides to make a protective coating on susceptible plants. All are certified by most state organic gardening groups and are widely available at nurseries and garden centers.

✔ **Bordeaux mixture.** A mix of copper and sulfur, this old-time fungicide is less toxic than pure copper but has the same limitations.

✔ **Copper.** This strong, broad-spectrum spray can be toxic to some plants, especially when overused. Use only as a last resort.

✔ **Lime sulfur.** Powerful and caustic but highly effective for some problems, lime sulfur can burn the leaves of some plants.

✔ **Sulfur.** This naturally occurring mineral is nontoxic but is a potential skin or eye irritant.

Preventing Plant Diseases

If you know that disease is inevitably going to show up on your prized plant, take steps to prevent infection. Some diseases are difficult (and in some cases impossible) to cure. Find out when that disease is most likely to strike. Then identify the best product to prevent infection and use it on the plant as recommended on the product label.

If a disease strikes, identify it. You can get help at a full-service garden center, botanical garden, or Extension office. Occasionally, you can get products to eradicate or prevent further spread of the disease. To discourage reinfection, remove and destroy diseased plant parts, including spotted leaves, discolored and mushy roots, or branches that are dying. You should also remove weeds and neglected garden plants so they won't spread problems around.

Some insect pests — such as aphids, cucumber beetles, and tarnished plant bugs — can spread diseases. Keep them under control, and you'll prevent the disease. Make sure that *you* don't spread diseases, either. Don't walk amid plants when the foliage is wet, because you could spread disease spores from plant to plant. Also, don't handle cucumbers or tomatoes after handling tobacco.

A dozen dirty diseases: what to do

Here are some tips on how to prevent, identify, and — if possible — treat some common plant diseases:

- **Anthracnose.** This fungus can attack many trees, including dogwoods and sycamores, as well as tomatoes and melons. It begins by producing small, discolored leaf spots or dead twigs, which can spread to become serious. Avoid by choosing resistant plants. Destroy fallen diseased leaves and dead branches and twigs. Hire an arborist to spray susceptible trees.

- **Apple scab.** This fungus attacks apple and crab apple trees, producing discolored leaf spots and woody-brown fruit lesions. Avoid by planting scab-resistant varieties. Susceptible varieties need a preventive spray program during wet spring weather to prevent reinfection. (See Figure 18-2.)

- **Black spot.** This disease of roses causes black spots on foliage and can spread, causing complete defoliation. Avoid problems by growing disease-resistant roses and cleaning up and destroying any diseased leaves that fall to the ground. To prevent black spot on susceptible roses, use a preventive fungicide spray during damp weather.

Figure 18-2:
Apple scab is most prevalent in cool, humid regions. The best remedy is to plant resistant varieties, such as 'Liberty'.

- ✔ **Botrytis blight.** This fungus attacks a wide variety of plants, including peonies, tulips, geraniums, and strawberries. It causes discolored patches on foliage, browning and droopy stalks on flowers, and premature rotting of fruits. Discourage botrytis by allowing air to circulate freely around susceptible plants. Remove and destroy any infected plant parts.

- ✔ **Brown rot.** This fungus disease is common on peaches, nectarines, and other stone fruits. It can attack flowers and fruit, ultimately coating the infected parts with brown spores. The fruit rots and shrivels. To avoid, select disease-resistant plants or at least less susceptible types. Remove and destroy infected plant parts. You'll probably also need a preventive spray program.

- ✔ **Cytospora canker.** This bacterial disease attacks woody stems on susceptible plants, such as fruit trees, spruces, and maples, forming cankers that can kill infected branches. To avoid, plant resistant or less susceptible plants. Remove and destroy infected branches.

- ✔ **Damping-off.** This fungus disease attacks the base of seedling stems, cutting the stem off from the roots. Avoid damping-off by sowing seeds in sterile seed-sowing mix and spacing the seeds so they won't come up in a crowded mass. It also helps to cover the seeds thinly with *finely* shredded sphagnum moss, which has natural antibiotic action that helps prevent disease. Keep the soil moist but not soggy.

- ✔ **Mildew (downy and powdery).** These two fungi produce similar symptoms: white, powdery coating on leaves. A variety of plants are susceptible, including roses, grapes, bee balms, and lilacs, but each kind of plant is attacked by a different kind of mildew. A mildew that attacks lilacs won't harm roses. The fungi disfigure plants but may not kill them outright. Instead, they weaken plants, making them unattractive and susceptible to other problems.

Downy mildew attacks during cool, wet weather; powdery mildew comes later in the season during warm, humid weather and cool nights. Avoid mildews by planting resistant plants. Otherwise, you'll have to tolerate them or use a preventive fungicide.

✔ **Phytophthora blight.** This bacterial disease attacks a variety of plants, including rhododendrons. It causes leaves to discolor and stems to die, often killing the entire plant. Another form can cause root rot and rapid plant death. Start with healthy plants and provide them with well-drained soil. Work bark into the soil; it seems to discourage the fungus. Try not to wet the foliage in the afternoon or evening.

✔ **Rust.** This fungus disease is easy to identify: It forms a rusty coating on the foliage of susceptible plants, like snapdragon, hollyhock, and blackberry. Avoid susceptible plants or look for disease-resistant varieties. Provide good air circulation. Remove and destroy infected parts. Rust diseases are specific to individual plants and do not spread to unrelated plants.

✔ **Sooty mold.** Insect pests that release sticky drops of plant sap (honeydew), such as aphids, encourage this harmless but unattractive fungus disease. The black-colored mold grows on the honeydew, a sure sign that sucking insects are at work. Rinse off the mold and sap with soapy water and then control the insect pests.

✔ **Wilt — *Fusarium* and *Verticillium*.** These soilborne fungus diseases cause susceptible plants such as tomatoes, peppers, melons, cabbages, and strawberries to suffer leaf yellowing, wilting, and often death. Grow wilt-resistant or wilt-tolerant varieties and rotate susceptible plants with unrelated plants. Resistant tomato varieties have the letters VF as part of their name.

Part V
Creating Special Gardens

The 5th Wave   By Rich Tennant

"Well, Roger wanted to design the garden, and, of course, I _knew_ he was a paleontologist, but I had no idea..."

In this part . . .

A garden may be in a teacup or a barrel, or it may cover an acre or more. What makes a garden is the interest and intent of the gardener, not grandeur or super plantsmanship.

Inevitably, gardeners adopt specialties. Some like to grow their own food, while others cultivate only flowers. For some, a garden must be neat and orderly, while for others, the more casual the better.

Here are five of our favorite kinds of gardens (though admittedly, there are countless others). For inspiration, take a look at the color illustrations in this book.

Chapter 19

Gardens for Food and Flavor

. . . .

In This Chapter

▶ Making a vegetable garden

▶ Having veggies through the seasons

▶ Getting started with fruits and berries

▶ Sneaking edibles into your garden

▶ Encountering flavors of the flowering kind

. . . .

Growing good things to eat brings rewards that no other kind of gardening can offer: You can have your plants and eat them, too. Vegetables, herbs, fruits, and even a few flowers can make your yard taste as good as it looks, and many edible plants are super-easy to grow.

You don't need a lot of space or time, either. No rule says that vegetables must be laid out in long rows — many of them grow better in beds. You can even mix vegetables, herbs, fruits, and flowers together and end up with a little garden that pleases all your senses.

Growing a Vegetable Garden

You may find no greater pleasure in gardening than picking sun-warmed zucchini, peppers, tomatoes, lettuce, and green beans from your own patch of ground. Vegetable gardening has a reputation for being difficult and time-consuming. But really, it is simplicity itself — if you follow these guidelines.

Choose a sunny location

Most vegetables need daily six to eight hours of direct sun for best results. Leafy greens, like spinach and lettuce, can thrive with a bit less. Remember that trees that are leafless in winter will cast shadows as the seasons progress.

If possible, locate the garden so that access to and from the kitchen is easy and convenient — you'll be more apt to notice what needs to be tended and to take full advantage of the harvest.

Note: In many areas, the foundations of houses are drenched with pesticides to keep termites from eating the footings. Instead of growing edible plants right next to your exterior walls where their roots can contact death-wish chemicals, use those places for inedible flowers and shrubs.

The ideal garden location has loose soil that drains well. If your soil isn't perfect, see Chapter 14 for tips on testing and improving it.

Make the garden the right size

Start small. A 12 x 16-foot plot is sufficient for a garden sampler with a variety of greens, some herbs, a few tomatoes and peppers, beans, cucumbers, and even edible flowers such as nasturtiums for garnishes.

A 20 x 20-foot garden gives you room to grow a wide range of crops, including some tasty space hogs like corn and winter squash. By growing plants in succession and using 3-foot-wide beds with 18-inch paths, you should have plenty of luscious vegetables for fresh eating and even extras for friends.

Check out the color drawing in this book for a better look at the garden that we're describing here. Use the plan as a guide, substituting crops to suit your own tastes. The flowers add beauty and attract pollinating insects to the garden.

If you'd rather design your garden from scratch, plot it on $\frac{1}{2}$-inch graph paper. Outline the beds in pencil and then fill in the plant names.

Stake and weed the garden

As soon as you have a plan, you're ready to stake the garden. You need a tape measure, plenty of string, 12- to 18-inch stakes, and a hammer to drive the stakes into the ground.

For best sun exposure, orient the garden so the rows run east to west, with the tallest plants on the north end. Following your plan, drive a stake in each of the four corners of the garden and outline the beds with string.

At this point, you need to rototill or spade the garden by hand and remove existing weeds. If you haven't had your soil tested to determine the pH, do it now. Most vegetables require a pH between 6.0 and 6.8. (See Chapter 14 for more on soil testing and adjusting the pH.)

Raise the beds

To make a raised bed, first loosen the soil in the bed, using a spade or a garden fork, and then shovel soil from an adjacent path onto the bed. You can also stand in a pathway and use a rake to bring up soil from the next pathway. Or you can *double-dig* the beds. (See Chapter 13 for more on raised beds and double-digging.)

Feed the soil

As you build each bed, apply several inches of compost or natural fertilizers like decomposed chicken manure over the surface and work it into the soil with a rake. The nutrients from these organic products are released slowly, meeting the soil's long-term needs. Most garden centers sell these products in bags. Or you may find an ample supply from neighbors with livestock.

For a 12 x 16-foot garden (almost 200 square feet), use 30 pounds of aged chicken manure, 75 pounds of horse manure, or 75 pounds of commercial compost. If your garden is being created in previously uncultivated soil, we also recommend that you apply 5 pounds of an organic fertilizer (containing approximately 5 percent nitrogen) per 200 square feet. (The percent nitrogen is the first number of the three listed on the label. The second number is phosphorus and the third number is potash.) Fill a bucket with the total amount that you'll need for all your beds and then broadcast the material evenly over the beds (not in the paths). Rake the fertilizer into the top few inches of soil.

Decide what to grow and when

Many vegetables are best started from seeds sown directly in the ground *(direct-sown)*; others go in as young plants called *seedlings*. You can grow your own seedlings or buy them. (See Chapter 15 for specifics on raising your own seedlings and transplanting.) Two of your best sources of information about seeds and seedlings are free: seed packets and seed catalogs. To acquire several seed catalogs for free, you can subscribe to a garden magazine; you will begin receiving a selection of catalogs almost immediately. Or you can mail in the coupons bound inside the magazines.

Time it right

The average date of the last spring *frost* is the key date to use in garden planning. While frost may not always kill your young plants, it is damaging to most kinds of vegetables. If you don't know the date for your region, check with your local Extension office or nursery.

We've found that some of the most reliable crops are arugula, beets, chard, cucumbers, green beans, leaf lettuce, parsley, peppers, radish, summer squash, and tomatoes. All adapt unusually well to various regions.

Look for the packing date as carefully as you would if you were buying a carton of yogurt. Don't buy seed that's more than a year old.

Seed that has been treated with fungicides must say so on the label. Treated seeds cannot be eaten, and you'll need to wash your hands after handling them.

Tough or tender?

Here's a list of "tough" crops that you can plant one to two weeks before the last frost date:

Direct-sow	Transplant
Beets	Broccoli *
Carrots	Brussels sprouts *
Dill	Cabbage *
Peas	Parsley *
Radishes	
Salad greens	
Spinach	

Here's a list of "tender" crops to go into the garden after danger of frost is past:

Direct-sow	Transplant
Basil **	Eggplant
Beans	Peppers
Cucumbers **	Tomatoes
Melons **	
Squash **	

*   *These crops can be sown again later in the season: in midsummer for an autumn harvest, and in mild-winter climates, in autumn for a winter garden.*

** *In areas with a short growing season, these crops are often transplanted to give them a head start.*

Raise them right

Successfully planting seeds in the ground hinges on two factors: depth and moisture. The rule of thumb on depth is to plant the seeds twice as deep as they are wide. So you plant really big seeds like beans and squash 1 to 2 inches deep, medium-sized seeds like corn 1 inch deep, small seeds like beets and spinach $1/2$ inch deep, and itty-bitty lettuce, carrot, and turnip seeds no more than $1/4$ inch below the surface. You can also buy strips of paper with small seeds glued on at exactly the right spacing. You plant these strips, called *seed tapes,* and eliminate thinning. Most seed catalogs offer seed tapes.

Then you must keep the seeds moist. Water helps soften the seed's coat or shell so the sprout can break through. Either set up a sprinkler to help keep newly seeded beds moist or cover the bed with an old sheet in between daily watering. As long as the soil is not cold and clammy, the seeds should sprout within a week.

Whether you set out plants or sow seeds, weeds will appear all over your garden about three weeks after you plant. This is natural, but you do have to stifle those wild invaders. Get a comfortable pad to sit on and hand weed right around your plants. Then use a hoe to clear weeds from large areas of bare soil.

After you're through weeding, mulch over the weeded space to keep more weeds from taking the places of the ones you killed. You can use roll-out fabric mulch material, chopped leaves, grass clippings, hay, or even newspapers covered with enough leaves or grass clippings to keep them from blowing away. (See Chapter 16 for more on mulching.)

Put them together

Okay, let's walk through this thing. Suppose you live in an area like Kansas City, and your last spring frost comes around April 15. A week or two before that, you kick things off by planting three cool-season vegetables: lettuce (because it's easy), carrots (because they're pretty), and broccoli (because it's good for you).

After you get your taxes done, you cruise through the garden center and pick up some tomato and pepper plants. As soon as you get a confident feeling in your bones that the last frost is a done deal, you plant those plants.

Now it's a beautiful weekend in May, so you plant some warm-season stuff: bush beans, sweet corn, and cucumbers. Stash a few basil plants where you see gaps, and sow some dill seeds where the lettuce didn't come up. Now you have a diversified garden going, and if you get it weeded and mulched, you can trust it to behave while you take off on a well-deserved vacation.

Vacation's over and summer's midpoint has passed, so you choose some items, like spinach and more lettuce, from the cool-season list and get them going. See? By the time Jack and Jennifer Frost come to visit, you're sick of squash and tomatoes anyway, and your spinach really likes sitting around with the Frosts.

Have a happy harvest

If you plant what you like to eat, you'll have to hold yourself back to keep from picking your vegetables before their time. Fortunately, most veggies are best when picked on the young side, especially leafy greens, snap beans, peas, cucumbers, and squash. With some other vegetables, the old-timers taste better. Carrots wait until they reach full size to fill up with flavor, and tomatoes and peppers are best when allowed to hang on the plants until they're dead ripe.

When in question, take a bite! If you don't like what you tasted, spit it out, wait a few days, and try again. Not liking what you taste rarely happens — you'll probably be enthralled with the superior taste of really fresh vegetables from your own garden.

Is There Fruit in Your Future?

You don't need a lot of land to grow fruit. If you have just $^1/_4$ acre (100 x 100 feet) in your backyard or side yard, you can grow the full range of temperate tree fruits (apples, pears, cherries, peaches, and plums), plus berries and brambles. Instead of thinking in terms of an orchard, think in terms of a fruit *garden* — you really need only a handful of trees to get more than enough fruit. One full-grown peach tree, for example, gives you three or more bushels.

SOURCE

Get an agent

Extension office agents are people employed by your home state at county offices. They are gold mines of helpful information for farmers and regular people like you (and the information is usually free — you've already paid for it with your taxes). They don't have time to provide individual tutoring but will gladly give you literature on crucial topics like these:

- Average first and last frost dates for your area
- Home vegetable garden guide, including recommended varieties
- Home fruit production guide, including recommended varieties

Apples and pears are available as true dwarf varieties, so you can plant a large number of individual varieties without outpacing your ability to use the fruit. With careful pruning, you can keep the trees as small as 6 feet tall and spaced 2 feet apart — each will yield between 10 and 15 pounds of fruit.

Six steps to a fruit tree harvest

Here are some general tips on planting fruit trees:

- **Be patient.** Most fruit trees require at least two years from planting to the first harvest, although dwarf trees generally begin fruiting earlier.

- **Plant varieties adapted to your climate.** Cold temperatures limit the types of fruit that you can grow in cold climates, and lack of sufficient cold limits the varieties that you can grow in mild-winter regions. Most deciduous fruit trees need a minimum amount of *chill,* or number of hours below 45°F, while the tree is dormant in winter, to grow and fruit well the following season.

  Trees in northern regions get plenty of chilling hours, but in southern and western regions, gardeners need to choose varieties that have a low chill requirement. Double-check the chill accumulation for your area (shown in Figure 19-1) with chill requirements listed in fruit tree catalogs.

- **Provide pollinizers.** Many fruit trees need the pollen from a different but compatible variety — called *cross-pollination* — to produce a crop of fruit. Pears, sweet cherries, and Japanese plums are in this category. Exceptions include most peaches, figs, sour cherries, and the dwarf sweet cherry Stella. Some fruit trees, including most apples, are semi-self-fruitful. They make an adequate crop without cross-pollination, but yields increase with cross-pollination.

- **Plant in the right place.** This means full sun and fertile, well-drained soil. Avoid heavy clay. If you live in an area with strong winds, plant trees in protected locations. If spring frosts will threaten developing buds and flowers, plant on a gentle slope so that cold air will travel downhill and away from the trees.

- **Keep trees well watered and fed.** Water trees deeply every two weeks. The soil should be moist down to at least 2 feet for dwarf trees and 3 to 4 feet for full-sized trees. Use a mulch, like compost or straw, to help maintain even soil moisture. Apply an organic fertilizer, like compost or aged manure, or a complete commercial fertilizer, like 10-4-4, if growth is poor. But be aware that too much fertilizer can cause bland, soft fruit that's susceptible to brown rot.

✔ **Prune and thin.** The primary objectives of pruning fruit trees are to create a strong tree form and maximize the harvest. (See Chapter 16 for pruning guidelines.)

Thin the number of fruits that the tree sets after flowering to get larger, higher-quality fruit and to encourage steady, year-to-year production. The best time to thin is when fruits reach $1/2$ to 1 inch in diameter. In most cases, thin to allow 6 to 8 inches between fruits. For apples and Japanese plums, thin to one fruit per cluster.

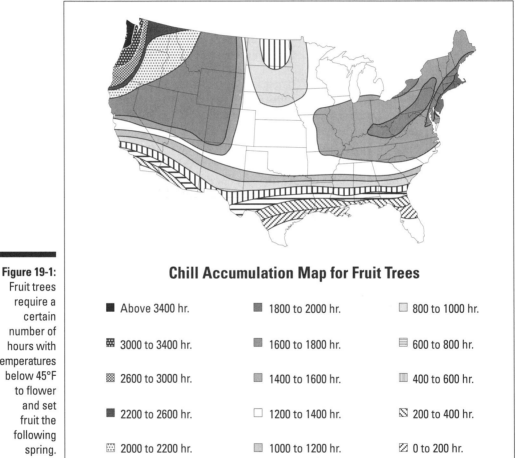

Figure 19-1: Fruit trees require a certain number of hours with temperatures below 45°F to flower and set fruit the following spring.

Chill Accumulation Map for Fruit Trees

- ■ Above 3400 hr.
- ▦ 3000 to 3400 hr.
- ▨ 2600 to 3000 hr.
- ■ 2200 to 2600 hr.
- ▦ 2000 to 2200 hr.
- ▦ 1800 to 2000 hr.
- ▦ 1600 to 1800 hr.
- ▦ 1400 to 1600 hr.
- ▢ 1200 to 1400 hr.
- ▦ 1000 to 1200 hr.
- ▢ 800 to 1000 hr.
- ▤ 600 to 800 hr.
- ▥ 400 to 600 hr.
- ▨ 200 to 400 hr.
- ▧ 0 to 200 hr.

Planning a fruit garden

It's tempting to immediately jump into fruit growing. After all, you have a two- to five-year wait between planting and first fruit, and you may well feel that time is too short to go slowly. But don't rush into it too fast. Think carefully about the many kinds of fruit and the number of trees you'll eventually want. You don't need to purchase and plant all the trees the first year, as long as you leave ample space for them.

Your fruit garden needs lots of sun, at least six hours at midday in summer. It's helpful to orient the rows north to south, if you can. That way, shade in the morning and evening falls on adjacent walkways rather than on adjacent trees. Plan to maintain walkways that are at least 4 feet wide between rows of trees. As for aesthetics, put lush, free-growing plants like peaches and apricots up front. Plan for as long a harvest season as you can by planting different kinds of fruit. And if you want fruit plantings nearer the house and among the vegetables, stick to the berries. They rarely need spraying and give you the earliest fruit. (See Chapters 6, 7, and 15 for details on planting trees and shrubs.)

Our mini-orchard shown in this book's color section provides space for fruit trees and berry plantings, as well as a good-sized vegetable garden. With these guidelines, you can design a custom fruit garden that provides an attractive landscape and a variety of fruit throughout the season.

Fruits for the home garden

The following sections describe some good choices for your mini-orchard.

Apples

Apples are easiest when you buy dwarf varieties, which grow 6 to 8 feet. Plant several varieties to provide a range of flavors and ripening times. Because apples need spraying more than other fruits, isolate these trees from vegetable gardens, patios, and pools. The yield of apple trees is 1 to 3 bushels per tree (late summer through autumn). Apples are hardy to zone 2a.

Scab is the most common disease problem of apples, especially in regions that get plenty of rainfall in summer. The following varieties are immune or resistant to scab, and they have excellent flavors:

- ✔ Dayton — deep red
- ✔ Enterprise — yellow covered with deep red
- ✔ Freedom — red

- GoldRush — pale yellow
- Jonafree — red like a Jonathan
- Liberty — very dark red
- Macfree — red and green
- McShay — red and green
- Nova Easygro — green-yellow striped with red
- Novamac — red and green like a McIntosh
- Prima — yellow-green with bright red areas
- Priscilla — yellow-green with red stripes
- Pristine — yellow with red blush
- Redfree — bright red over pale-yellow background
- Sir Prize — yellow with red blush
- Williams' Pride — bright red

Peaches

Peaches can be tricky but are worth the effort. Peach trees get big, so put them where you'll enjoy their profile and glossy green foliage. Mulch to thwart grass and nourish trees. Where it's too cold for peaches (–15°F, zone 5a), consider sour cherries or apricots for this spot in the landscape. The yield is 3 to 5 bushels per tree (mid- to late summer).

Pears

Pears are a bit easier than apples. On dwarfing rootstock, pears reach 8 to 10 feet tall. Train them as small pyramidal trees. Oriental pears, which are better adapted to the warmer regions, get one-third larger. You need two or more compatible varieties for pollination. The yield is 3 to 4 bushels per tree (late summer through autumn). Produce reliably to zone 3a.

Sweet cherries

Sweet cherries become medium to large trees. Stella is the only self-fertile variety. Tart cherries on a dwarf rootstock are scarcely larger than a bush, and because they're self-fertile, one is enough. The yield for sweet is 30 quarts, and for tart, 15 quarts (early summer). Produce reliably to zone 5b.

Plums

Plums make nice small- to medium-size trees for a yard. Japanese and Japanese-American hybrids need cross-pollination by another variety from either group. Most European plums need another European pollinator; a few are self-fertile. The yield is 2 to 3 bushels (mid- to late summer). Regularly produce to zone 4a.

Strawberries

Strawberries are the first fruits of the season, which may be why people treasure them so. An early and a late variety provide strawberries for two to three weeks. Grow them in 3- to 4-foot-wide beds and be ready to lay netting over the plants to keep out the birds. Strawberry beds need to be redug and rotated every two or three years. The yield is 1 quart per plant (late spring to early summer). Hardy to all zones.

Grapes

Grapes on a trellis are good for masking a fence or making a windbreak for vegetables or other tender plants. Traditionally, they are trained over arbors or trellises (see Chapter 13), but putting the vines so far overhead makes pruning and picking tough to do. The yield is 15 pounds per plant (late summer to early autumn). Productive to zone 3a.

Blueberries

Blueberries are a good candidate for a hedge because they grow in bushes. You need two varieties for cross-pollination — three or more are better and can extend the blueberry harvest two months. Some blueberries will grow nearly anywhere in America if you can provide acid soil rich in organic matter. The yield is 4 quarts per plant (mid- to late summer). Productive to zone 4a.

Bramble fruits

Bramble fruits — red and black raspberries and blackberries — are best grown as rambling hedges on large properties or trained to a wall or trellis on small ones. Of the group, raspberries are best adapted to cooler areas, and blackberries can grow in hotter areas. In temperate regions where all types grow, the bramble harvest can stretch from early summer into autumn. To get the most from red raspberries, plant at least two kinds: a main-crop variety for heavy early summer harvests and an autumn (or everbearing) type to close out the berry harvest. Productive to all zones.

Don't cut red raspberry canes back to make the canes self-supporting; the most fruitful buds are those nearest the top. But do train canes to two horizontal wires and prune out old growth after harvest. Black raspberries, however, should be cut back to 3 or 4 feet for best production. Blackberries must be restrained, or they'll become weeds. The yield is 2 quarts per plant.

Sneaking Edible Plants into Your Landscape

You can grow edible plants almost everywhere. If you're not ready to invest a lot of time into a separate space devoted exclusively to edibles, the following list offers some ways to sneak tasty plants into your landscape.

But, first, don't assume that because you can eat a plant's fruit, you can also eat its flowers. As you'll no doubt be told once you get to the emergency room, potato and tomato flowers are laced with poison, and foxglove can kill you.

✔ Adopt a few herbs to use as foliage plants in your flower beds. Parsley, dill, basil, oregano, and rosemary are simple to grow, especially if you buy ready-to-go transplants.

✔ If your landscape plan calls for an ornamental tree, make it an edible ornamental. Dwarf cherry trees and dwarf apples are lovely when they bloom in spring.

✔ Got a place for a good-sized shrub? Fill the space with a clump of blueberries, a fan trellis of thornless blackberries, or perhaps a mound of raspberries. Where it's hot, try blueberries and upright blackberries. Where it's cool, try raspberries. Anywhere, you might grow grapes aloft on a trellis and carpet the ground below with strawberries.

✔ If a high-visibility front yard bed is the only place you have to grow food plants, mix ornamental edibles with colorful flowers. Lettuce and other leafy greens offer above-average eye appeal, as do peppers and neatly staked tomatoes. Most of the easy annuals sold as bedding plants (petunias, marigolds, celosia) are fine companions for dressing up the edges.

Bon appétit!

Chapter 20

Gardens for Color and Cutting

- -

In This Chapter

▶ Enjoying flowers indoors and out

▶ Filling the season with flowers

▶ Staging a blooming concert in your yard

▶ Curing color shyness

▶ Fantasizing with wildflowers

▶ Growing wildflowers

▶ Identifying the best wildflowers for cutting

- -

*O*ne of the most popular things to do with a garden bed is to fill it with flowers. We introduce a number of garden-worthy plants in Part II; this chapter tells you how to put them together to create a beautiful bed or border.

Cutting some of your flowers to enjoy them indoors is not murder — it actually helps most plants. Cutting off the highest stems usually stimulates the plants to bush out and produce more flowering branches. In gardening lingo, this process is called *cut-and-come-again*. Most flowers with stems long enough to stick in a vase respond well to cutting.

As for the art of creating a beautiful bed or border, think of the whole thing as a concert, with each plant responsible for a certain instrument. The volume control is color, your overall design sets the tempo, and the site sets the mood.

Rooms with a View

What do you see when you look out your window? A lovely flower bed or your garbage cans? Most people look out their kitchen and living room windows more than any others in the house. Try to site your flower beds so you can enjoy them every time you look outside.

Try to find a spot in the front yard and another in back for your flower adventures. That way, you'll be able to experiment with two groups of flowers at a time and double your fun.

Consider the view from the street, too. Sit in your car at the curb and consider how a well-maintained flower bed can make your front yard look better.

Here's a visualization tip: Picture an asymmetrical triangle in which your house is one point, some feature on the horizon is another, and your beautiful, future flower bed is the third point. This is the Oriental concept of man (house) – heaven (skyline) – earth (beautiful flowers), and it makes a good starting point for drive-by flower bed design.

Make your design focus attention on the front door. Use flowers to give your entryway a "come hither" look, and you can't go wrong.

Swinging with the Seasons

All flowers grow, blossom, and rest, so your flower bed's appearance will be constantly changing. You'll see peak times, like late spring and midsummer, when the orchestra of plants reaches symphonic proportions, and other times, like the dead of winter, when nothing seems to be happening.

You can liven up the dead times by planting a few evergreens that offer something to gaze upon all year long. Shrubs that develop colorful berries or bark persisting into winter are prime possibilities. Small trees and shrubs with attractive limb structure can make every season more interesting, as can nonliving features like rocks, statuary, and reflecting pools.

Trees, shrubs, and other long-lived plants give a flower bed its structure. If your flower bed already has a sturdy backdrop of trees or evergreens, don't get hung up on this point. Your stage has already been set quite nicely by Mother Nature.

Don't Be Square

When was the last time you saw wild plants growing in a straight line? How about a perfect circle? Nature does not work in strict geometric shapes, and neither should you. Instead, think about curved edges, acute triangles, kidneys, or — the most fail-safe of all bed shapes — the teardrop.

The magic of the teardrop is motion. The teardrop — especially when its narrow end is farthest from the viewing angle and its bulbous end closest — suggests the same kind of whooshing movement that might be caused by wind and water.

Not every site can (or should) be molded into tears. The classic border is a long rectangle, but instead of giving it a straight front edge, pull it out into curves. The curves must fit the site, but they need not be symmetrical.

Symmetry — near-perfect balance in size, color, and texture between two equidistant landscape features — creates a formal look. Planned imbalances make the feeling more relaxed and informal. Because informal gardens allow plenty of room for experimentation, they tend to be more fun.

To keep an informal garden from getting wildly tacky, tame your fantasies with the concepts of *repetition* and *drift* (a *drift* is a grouping of plants — bulbs, perennials, ground cover — arranged in a naturalistic way).

- Repeating the same flower, or combination of flowers, at regularly spaced intervals gives the flower bed a unified look. Repetition shows that your flower bed has rhythm.

- Similar-looking plants look more natural in clumps or drifts than in rows; this arrangement draws the eye to whatever flower looks best at any given time. For example, when a cluster of sunflowers bursts into bloom, you'll be sufficiently captivated to see beyond the ragged drift of blown-out pansies right in front of it.

Simple designs composed of a few species planted repetitively in drifts look beautiful and are easy to maintain. If your list of wanna-grows can't be organized into a pattern, you need separate beds — not a more complex design.

How big is a drift? It can be one big shrub, three bushy marigolds, five zinnias, or seven daffodils. Using odd numbers is an old landscaping (and flower arranging) trick that keeps the eye excited.

While we're on the subject of size, don't let your bed get too wide. If you can't reach the middle without stepping on plants, either incorporate an access path (defined with stepping-stones, perhaps) or slim down the bed.

Small (and well maintained) is beautiful. If you can't maintain it, don't plant it. A weedy, overgrown flower bed can be a real eyesore.

Combining Congenial Flowers

Deciding which flowers will go where is rather like making a seating arrangement for a multicourse dinner. You want your guests to get along well with each other and have a good time, so you don't place a chemical company executive next to an environmental activist. In the same spirit, you want to place plants with the same needs together.

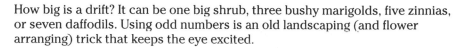

Here are some examples (see Chapters 9 and 10 for more on perennials and annuals):

- Plant tulips, daylilies, and irises together. They cover each other's defects and bloom at different times, yet all need to be dug and divided about every three years.

- If you live in a mild-winter area, rotate winter annuals (pansies, dianthus, poppies, and larkspurs) with summer annuals (marigolds, impatiens, and petunias).

- Grow perennials where they can be left alone — they need their peace. You can use a few annuals around your roses, tall phlox, daylilies, hostas, and other perennials as long as you keep digging to a minimum.

Another congeniality factor to consider is flower form. The majority of summer flowers have round, flat blossoms (like daisies). Nothing is wrong with round flowers, but a garden that's all round flowers is boring. Drama develops when you add flowers that form spikes (like salvias) or trumpets (like lilies).

Plant height controls the placement of some flowers (see Figure 20-1). Common sense tells you that tall ones must go in the back and short ones in the front. In between, you can put mid-sized flowers, clumps of accent plants, or something more solid, like a tree. If the tree is already there, celebrate its existence by surrounding it with flowers.

Figure 20-1:
Place the plants that will become tallest toward the rear of the flower bed and the ones that will remain low toward the front.

Coloring Your World

Color is the really fun part. The hot colors — red, orange, and bright yellow — are unsurpassed long-distance runners. Any flower bed that's viewed from far away benefits from a dash of fire. Hot colors also attract butterflies and hummingbirds.

Cool colors, including soft pink, blue, and white, set a more relaxed mood. They can also help light up shady places and outdoor living areas where you're likely to hang out at night.

Alternating abruptly from one color to another, or from one flower to another, creates tension, and that's good. But excessive tension leads to confusion and clash. These problems are easy to avoid if you follow a few simple guidelines:

✔ Beware of joining orange and pink — they look weird together. Instead, rescue orange with purple.

✔ Accessorize with gray, white, or light yellow — they go with everything, even orange. Quiet neutral colors won't quiet down loud human neighbors but are great for offsetting potential clashes between rowdy plants.

✔ Copy what other people do. Because flowers come in so many different hues, going with proven combinations is sometimes your best bet. Copy your neighbors or check out sure things at any botanical garden.

   Garden catalogs among the best places to look for good ideas and good information. Several are listed in Appendix C.

✔ Don't go with just one color for large plantings. For example, if you'll be planting a hundred impatiens, go with a mixture of pastel shades. If you'll be planting only a dozen, stick with one color.

✔ Include edges. Small edging plants soften the boundaries between garden and not-garden and hide the surprisingly ugly ankles often seen on otherwise beautiful flowering plants. Alyssum, *Nierembergia*, *Liriope*, *Ageratum*, and dwarf petunias make great edges.

Planting Your Rainbow

Enough rules and worries! Go ahead and plan a garden for color and cutting. The drawings in this book's color insert can give you some ideas to start with.

Table 20-1 lists flowers that are great for cutting. All varieties listed do well in full sun; an asterisk before the flower's name indicates that the flower does well in partial shade as well. You can find more about flowers of all kinds in Part II of this book, particularly Chapters 9 and 10.

Table 20-1	Top Flowers for Cutting			
Flower/ (Annual or Perennial)	Height in Inches	Color	Planting Season	Zones
Baby's Breath (*Gypsophila paniculata*)/P	18	White	Spring	4b–10a
Calendula/A	12–30	Yellow/Orange	Early spring	All
China Aster (*Callistephus chinensis*)/A	6–30	Many	Spring	All
Chrysanthemum/P	18–36	Many	Spring to autumn	3a–10a
Clove Pink (*Dianthus caryophyllus*)/P	8–18	Many	Spring to summer	3b–9a
Cosmos/A	24–84	Pink	Late spring	All
Daffodil/P	6–8	Yellow	Autumn	4a–11
Dahlia/P	12–20	Many	Spring	4a–10a
*Delphinium/P	18–24	Blue	Early spring	3b–9a
Gladiolus/P	24–36	Many	Spring	5a–10b
*Iris/P	12–18	Many	Early summer	3b–10a
*Larkspur/A	14–48	Blue	All seasons	All
Marigold/A	6–48	Yellow/Orange	Spring	All
Mealy-cup sage (*Salvia farinacea*)/A	8–36	Blue	Late spring	All
Stock/A	9–12	Many	Early spring	All
*Summer phlox (*Phlox paniculata*)/P	24–48	Many	Early spring	3a–9b
Sweet Pea/A	36–60	Many	Early spring	All
Tulip/P	6–28	Many	Late autumn	4a–10a
Zinnia/A	6–36	Many	Late spring	All

Wildflower Fantasies

Are you enticed by the carefree charm of a natural flowering meadow, the flamboyant colors, the sheer mass of blooms? You can create a miniature but lavish meadow for your private pleasure by planting wildflower seeds. (Of course, you'll probably want to share it with the birds, butterflies, and bees who will be drawn to the waves of blooms.)

A wildflower craze of sorts is going on these days, which means that you have many choices of seed types and seed sources. Mail-order wildflower seed companies (listed in Appendix C) offer pure seed of individual species as well as seed mixtures developed for various regions of the country and specific garden conditions, such as shade, lots of water, or little water. For best results, plant the appropriate wildflowers for your situation.

Wildflower mixes are not necessarily composed of native flowers. If you want to grow only species native to the United States or, more specifically, to your region of the country or world, then be an eco-smart shopper: Read the descriptions of mixes carefully to see whether the plants are identified as native. (These plants will help sustain the myriad creatures that live in your area and depend on native plants.)

You can also create your own seed mix by combining seeds for plants that you know are native. Several suppliers of wildflower seeds are included in Appendix C. Their catalog descriptions usually indicate the region of origin.

Growing wildflowers

Here are some rules of (green) thumb for growing wildflowers:

- ✔ **Timing is everything.** Ideally, you should sow seeds to coincide with the rainy season so that rainwater will irrigate the planting for you. In mild, winter-rain areas, sow seeds in autumn for flowers in late winter, spring, and early summer.

  In cold-winter climates where rain occurs throughout the summer, plant in spring two weeks prior to your last expected frost. The flowers will bloom later in spring and early summer.

- ✔ **Be prepared.** Your efforts in soil preparation (see Chapter 14) will truly pay off. Most important, start with a clean seedbed by clearing weeds and grasses that might compete with the wildflowers. Turn the soil to a depth of a few inches and then rake to smooth it.

- ✔ **Sow as you go.** Carefully scatter the seeds by hand onto the prepared soil, first walking in one direction and then in the perpendicular direction. Small seeds are easiest to handle when you first mix them with sand (one part seed to four parts sand). Ask for clean builders sand at any building supply store.

  Press the seeds into the soil with your footsteps. Or lightly rake the area, taking care not to bury the seeds more than $1/8$ inch deep.

✔ **Let it rain.** If your timing is right and you've planted during the rainy season, you can wait for rain to sprout the seeds. Without rain, you must water regularly to keep the seeded area consistently moist until the seedlings are up and growing.

✔ **Keep on weedin'.** Pull weeds that appear in your new planting. At first, distinguishing them from the wildflowers will be difficult. Just be highly suspicious of any plant that's growing much faster than everything else.

Just so you know: wildflower facts

✔ Generally, ¼ pound of seed covers 1,000 square feet of garden space, but differences are dramatic: Some seeds are large, others tiny.

✔ Wildflower seed mixes are usually composed of annuals and perennials, which means that the flower show will change from year to year. The annuals are most dramatic the first year; some will reseed and flower in subsequent years. While the annuals are stealing the show the first year, the perennials are establishing themselves for their big debut a couple of seasons down the road.

✔ Under the right conditions, many wildflowers do naturalize and come back year after year. Even so, filling in with a little fresh seed each year may be necessary, just to keep the flowers coming on strong.

✔ If you want your wildflowers to reseed and come back again the following year, you must let the flower heads mature their seeds and die naturally. For a more "kept" look, you can mow the flowers after the seeds have matured and dropped.

✔ A large expanse of wildflowers will turn from looking gorgeous in bloom to appearing dead and dried up as the flowers finish blooming. Keep this in mind when you plan your garden. You might be wise to plant the wildflowers on a hillside or in an area of the garden that is viewed from a distance. Or combine wildflowers with garden backbones, like shrubs, that hold their shape and look good beyond the wildflower season.

Chapter 21

Gardens for Birds and Butterflies

• •

In This Chapter

▶ A garden's wild side

▶ Bird-friendly plants

▶ Heavy-drinking butterflies

• •

*I*f you plant a garden, the birds come. Butterflies, too, and lots of other insects for the birds to eat, which, of course, brings the birds back for more. In this chapter, we cover ways you can fine-tune your landscape so that birds and butterflies find your yard irresistible. See the special color section in this book for some ideas for your own bird and butterfly garden.

Why bother? Birds love to talk, and their chatter and songs bring sound to the garden. Butterflies don't talk, but their flitting movements put the garden scene in motion.

The engaging little shows staged by birds and butterflies change with the seasons. Butterflies, being solar-powered creatures, perform only during the warm months, while the bird circus is most evident in the autumn, winter, and spring. This seasonal sequence of wildlife activity is the first angle to exploit when attracting birds and butterflies to your yard. And because birds and butterflies, like other creatures, mostly hang around places where their needs for food, water, and shelter is met, providing these three necessities is your primary means for attracting them.

Making Birds an Offer They Can't Refuse

North American birds, and birds in other parts of the world, are in crisis; growing towns and cities have taken away many of the trees they used as homes. Sparrows, blackbirds, and a few other species have rolled with the punches and built nests in buildings and power switchboxes. Most other birds *must* have trees.

There's a food shortage, too. If you're a finch, finding thistle and weed seeds in a condominium complex isn't easy, and chickadees cannot survive in a concrete jungle where there are few insects to eat. You can help solve the housing and food shortage by planting or preserving bird-friendly trees and bushes, particularly native species that host native birds. From a bird's-eye point of view, here are some of the best trees and shrubs:

- ✔ **Trees:** pines and other evergreens (whatever species grow best in your area), wild cherries, serviceberries (*Amelanchier* species), hawthorns, cedars, and mulberries

  Be careful not to plant trees that produce juicy berries close to your house, or you'll get berry goo all over your shoes.

- ✔ **Shrubs:** junipers, hollies, native viburnums, and cotoneaster; when planted in clumps or hedges, provide habitat and food for birds

Hungry birds are not finicky eaters. Almost every species loves black oil sunflower seeds (the common type sold as birdfood), so a feeder stocked with these seeds gets birds interested in your yard in a hurry. When birds get used to finding sunflower seeds at your feeder, they go to great lengths to find acceptable nesting sites in or near your yard.

When summer comes, you can ease up on the birdseed; most birds crave protein-rich insects while raising their young, and they can probably find plenty of palatable creatures in and around your garden. On the other hand, if you want to attract woodpeckers year-round, keep a supply of commercial suet in your yard (see Figure 21-1).

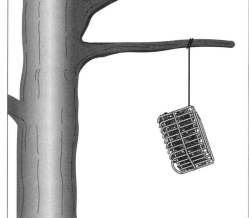

Figure 21-1: Insect-eating birds such as woodpeckers are attracted to suet.

Also, provide a yearlong supply of water for birds in a birdbath or set out shallow dishes of water. If your house is near a pond, stream, or river, don't worry too much about water — the birds will know where to go.

If you live where water in birdbaths freezes, you can keep the water ice-free by changing it frequently or by using an immersion-type water heater designed for outdoor use (see Figure 21-2).

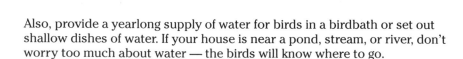

Figure 21-2:
Birds need water year-round. Use an immersion-type heater to keep birdbaths thawed in cold-winter areas.

Feeders and watering sites for birds can be plain or fancy, but they must be placed out of reach of cats. Your beloved kitty is probably adept at assassinating birds, and you don't want to be an accomplice to such crimes. Suspend feeders from secure limbs or place them atop a stout unclimbable pole.

Different types of birds live in different places, and you can network with other bird lovers to learn more about helping the winged ones that live in your area. Check your telephone directory or ask your Chamber of Commerce for information about local birdwatching clubs. Or find a local chapter of the National Audubon society; the headquarters address is 700 Broadway, New York, NY 10003; 212-979-3000.

Keeping Pest Birds at Bay

The sounds and movements brought by birds come at a cost. If you plan to grow fruits, you need to take precautions to keep birds from eating them. Birds especially love berries, and some birds eat corn and tomatoes. Effective deterrents include the following:

- ✔ **Polyester bird netting.** Sold at most garden centers. By far the most reliable way to protect your fruits and vegetables. Drape the netting over fruit-bearing plants as soon as their fruits begin to ripen (see Figure 21-3).

- ✔ **Birdscare Flash Tape.** Looks like metallic ribbon. Decorate the tops of plants with the stuff and trick birds into thinking the plant is on fire.

- ✔ **Fake predators.** Includes plastic snakes, polystyrene owls, and good old scarecrows. Rearrange these phony spooks often to keep the birds baffled.

✔ **Noisemakers.** Includes wind chimes, bells, rattling aluminum pie pans, and other items that make sounds when bumped by birds or jostled by the wind (just use your imagination).

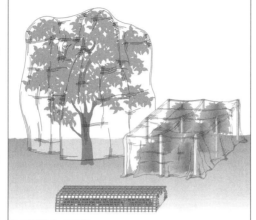

Figure 21-3:
Covering plants with bird netting is the only sure way to protect ripening crops from pest birds.

Beckoning Butterflies to Your Garden

Inviting butterflies (and moths) into your yard is as easy as growing flowers. Both will probably find your yard no matter what kinds of flowers you grow, but there are lots of easy ways to make sure they'll flit in your direction.

First, you need some sun. Butterflies can feed in shade, but they must have sun to charge their energy batteries. On cool mornings, have you noticed how butterflies stand around, slowly opening and closing their wings, and how they don't fly away when your six-year-old grabs at them? This is called *basking,* and it's how cold-blooded butterflies gather solar energy. If your yard is basically shady, put some flat, dark colored stones in a spot that gets morning sun and watch the butterflies use the sun-warmed stones as their warm-up room.

Next, grow flowers that produce nectar. Butterflies and moths consume the juices of flowers, and flower nectar is becoming a rare commodity these days. Like native birds, native butterflies and moths are struggling amid burgeoning urbanization. The weeds, clovers, and wildflowers they used to find everywhere are in increasingly short supply. You can help set things right by growing flowers that butterflies like a lot and planting the flowers in ways that make it impossible for minibrained butterflies to miss them.

Plants that are native to your region not only are more likely to grow and survive, but also provide the specific foods that native birds and butterflies rely upon. By using native plants, you'll help sustain native wildlife.

A butterfly sips flower nectar by sticking its long tongue (properly called a *proboscis*) down the throats of nectar-rich flowers. Some flowers are much more slurp-able than others, both because they have a lot of nectar and because the flowers are shaped just right. No butterfly garden should be without at least one of the following three plants — your aces-in-the-hole for attracting butterflies:

- **Butterfly weed** *(Asclepias tuberosa)*. This native perennial weed is hardy to zone 3a (–40°F). The seeds are hard to sprout, so it's better to start with nursery-propagated plants. Butterfly weed needs plenty of sun, blooms orange from midsummer onward, and seldom grows more than 1 to 2 feet tall. Once planted, it likes to stay put.

- **Butterfly bush** *(Buddleia davidii)*. This hardy shrub has become so popular that pot-grown plants are now easy to find. They are hardy to zone 5a (–20°F); come in many shades of purple, pink, and white; and, depending on conditions, grow 3 to 6 feet tall. When they freeze, you may cut them down to the ground; they'll revive to grow and bloom again. It's not unusual to find several species of butterflies sipping at a buddleia bush all at the same time.

- **Lantana** *(Lantana camara)*. This tender perennial survives winter only in zones 8 (10°F) through 10 (30°F), but you can buy bedding plants in the spring and grow them as summer annuals. You encourage the most flowers by growing lantana in full sun. Almost all butterflies like lantana.

Okay, so you don't have all three of the butterfly biggies. As long as your garden includes plenty of flowers, preferably the nectar-rich types with fewer petals (properly called *single* flowers), you will still see plenty of butterflies.

Why singles? When a blossom is jam-packed with petals, butterflies have a hard time getting to the nectar hidden in the middle. Single flowers that are relatively flat give butterflies a solid place to land and easy access to nectar. Among easy annuals, single cosmos, marigolds, and zinnias are of great interest to butterflies. Where you can use more height, try tithonia, also known as Mexican sunflower or torch flower.

Some other good plants to incorporate into your butterfly haven include any type of verbena, salvias, cosmos, phlox, coneflowers, and rudbeckias. Always keep your eyes peeled for flowers that attract butterflies in your area — butterflies often show strong regional preferences for certain plants.

Designing for butterflies

If you splash flower color around in broad strokes, butterflies have an easier time finding the flowers. The color of the flowers is not as important as the size of the clump, which should include at least three plants of any individual flower.

For a long time, gardeners were advised to use bright reds and oranges to lure butterflies, but it turns out that pink, purple, lavender, and yellow work just as well. The key is to keep similar colors more or less together. Butterflies are not very smart. A big jolt of color or fragrance is often necessary to get their attention.

Most buddleias produce lavender or purple flowers, so use that hue as a starting point for choosing the colors of your other flowers. Orange or yellow contrasts nicely with purple, and many butterfly gardens use either purple and yellow or purple and orange as their basic color scheme.

Mixing a butterfly cocktail

If you're a butterfly, you don't want to hang out around deep or moving water, where a good gust of wind may turn your beautiful wings into a sopping mess. But you and your friends like to get together for a drink, so you're always on the lookout for a nice watering hole. Your idea of a friendly bar is an almost-puddle of soaked soil, where you can stand firmly (without getting your feet too wet) and slurp up soupy water by sticking your proboscis in the ground.

It's a fact of butterfly life that males (and an occasional female) like to drink together in puddle clubs. To create such a pub in your butterfly garden, mix some sand, soil, and pebbles together and use the mixture to fill a small shallow basin lined with smooth stones. From time to time, fill the basin with water until it's puddly. Neon signs are not necessary — the butterflies will find it on their own.

Most pesticides are toxic to butterflies, which is one more reason to use gentle biological controls for pest management and to use them only when absolutely necessary. That's why we think it's best to simply handpick the plant-eating caterpillars that you encounter. (See Chapter 18 for more information on wise use of garden pesticides.)

When winter comes, most butterflies have already taken care of the business of ensuring the welfare of the next generation. Monarchs migrate to California, Mexico, and beyond; swallowtails end the season by laying dormant eggs; and several species wrap themselves in leaves and sleep through winter as mummy-like larvae, called *hibernaculi*. A few wait out winter as adults, hidden away in tree crevices or perhaps your attic.

The last thing we need to say is that birds eat butterflies. But don't worry — making your yard bird-friendly does not sentence your butterflies to certain death. There are plenty of other insects that birds would rather eat, and they'll bypass a dozen butterflies to get at a feeder filled with sunflower seeds.

Be sure and see the color illustrations later in this book for more about what these gardens look like.

Chapter 22
Gardens in Containers

In This Chapter
▶ Choosing plantable pots
▶ Creating order from chaotic containers
▶ Soil and planting specifics
▶ A menu of container compositions
▶ Custodial care of pot-bound plants

*T*he logical place to grow plants is in the ground. Many spots that cry out for plants, however, may not offer the best soil. The solution? Planters and pots!

Even in well-grounded landscapes, containers spilling over with plants are eye-catching. And if you like to rearrange things, container gardening may be your niche. (Then again, perhaps you bought an incredibly tacky urn at a yard sale, and you can't wait to display it.) Some of the most creative garden projects come to life in pots.

Choosing the Right Pots

The only thing a plant container absolutely *must* have is a drainage hole in the bottom — and the more the merrier. Here are some of the most popular choices of pots, along with some handy suggestions for what to do with them:

✔ **Terra cotta clay pots.** Cheap and plentiful, red clay pots drain really well and look great near brick and masonry with a hint of orange. But they dry out fast, so you need to check the soil regularly for moisture. Matching saucers prevent excess water from spilling on decks and other surfaces.

✔ **Concrete urns and boxes.** Heavy and hard to move, concrete containers are semipermanent and are therefore preferred as homes for perennials. They're also great for use in places where kids and dogs may knock over a lightweight planter.

✔ **Foam-formed plastic (terra cotta or concrete look-alikes).** Comparatively lightweight and crack-resistant, these new containers can really lighten your load — and they look just like the real thing. They dry out more slowly than pottery, too.

- **Plastic pots, boxes, and baskets.** Plastic is plastic, which is bad if you're throwing it in a landfill but good if you're looking for clean, lightweight, moisture-holding plant pots or window boxes. Semiflexible plastic lasts the longest, and pots with built-in saucers are easy to move around. You can also use black plastic nursery pots (which many people throw away) as planters. If you can't stand looking at them, slip them into more attractive containers, such as ceramic urns or wooden boxes.

- **Hanging baskets.** The classic material for hanging baskets is a wire form that is lined with a 1-inch-thick layer of sphagnum moss and then filled with potting soil and plants (see Figure 22-1). Overlap the moss so that it contains the soil mix and fill the basket to within a $1/2$ inch of the top, inserting plants through the sides and into the top layer of potting soil.

- **Wood boxes.** The great thing about wood boxes is that you can build them yourself. You can then put your plants right inside the boxes themselves (if the boxes contain drainage holes), or you can tuck ugly black pots inside (filled with beautiful flowers, of course) and camouflage the tops of the pots with moss or straw. If your wood boxes are big, install rollers on the bottom so that you can move them around. All wood boxes should stand an inch or so above the ground or floor, placed on bricks or small strips of wood, to help the boxes drain and to keep their bottoms from rotting.

- **Ceramic pots.** Beautiful yet delicate, ceramic pots are best if filled with plants you intend to pamper, such as indoor houseplants.

Figure 22-1:
Transform decks and entryways with hanging baskets, which you can easily make at home for less than nurseries charge.

Making a Garden in a Pot

Container gardening is too much fun to gum up with a lot of rules, but some tried-and-true arrangements are worth keeping in mind.

✔ Place three similar containers planted with similar plants together, with a taller contrasting pot behind them. For example, flank a concrete urn with three terra cotta pots.

✔ In multiple window boxes, repeat the same plant combinations over and over to create unity and rhythm.

✔ Group bright colors together where you want a bold look. Five pots of neon-pink petunias or three window boxes with red geraniums get a lot of attention.

✔ Use light colors (white and light pastels) for natural contrast in dark places.

✔ Don't forget foliage. Dressy leaves of ivies, for example, often look every bit as good as flowers.

✔ Let vines and cascading plants spill over the edges of big containers. (It's an "ooh-ahh" thing.)

✔ Where horizontal space is tight, go vertical. Flowering vines can be grown in containers and trained up a trellis attached to a wall; tall evergreen shrubs can stand at attention like great green pillars; or you can attach hanging baskets to the walls at different heights. The sky is the only limit!

A primer on soil for pots

Most people who grow plants in containers use bagged potting soils or soilless mixtures made up of *peat* plus *perlite* or *vermiculite* (see the following list if you don't know what these are). These products are (or should be) free of microorganisms that cause plant diseases, already have their pH corrected with the appropriate addition of lime, and hold just the right amount of moisture. The reigning favorite is Pro-Mix, which is widely available at garden centers. If you can't find it locally, call 800-667-5366. The downside is that soilless mixtures contain few, if any, plant nutrients, so you must feed your plants regularly with some kind of fertilizer.

Rather make your own potting soil? Sooner or later, you may delve into creating special mixtures for ferns, cacti, or some other plants that have strange tastes in soil. The following list describes your basic ingredients and the flavor that each one brings to the stew:

✔ **Peat moss.** Basically rotted moss, peat moss is soft-textured and almost never hosts diseases, and it's like a feather bed to delicate plant roots. Final content of peat in the mixture can run as high as 80 percent (for ferns), or 40 to 75 percent for other plants. Peat has an acidic pH and contains negligible plant nutrients. Be sure to moisten it to make it easier to work with.

✔ **Sand.** Sand drains fast and doesn't hold water worth a flip, which makes it a good addition to pots planted with cacti, herbs, and bulbs. Sand content of the mixture rarely — if ever — exceeds 20 percent.

✔ **Vermiculite or perlite.** These popcornlike mineral particles lighten up a mixture and help keep it porous yet damp. For potted plants, 20 percent of one or the other of the 'lites is right, or maybe use a little of each.

✔ **Lime.** Ground-up dolomitic limestone corrects the acidic pH of peat, and plants that prefer neutral-to-alkaline conditions (such as wallflowers and clematis) need an extra dose. Always add lime with restraint. One teaspoon per gallon of potting mix is the max.

Fill 'er up

Ready to get your fingers dirty? Follow these steps to plant a pot (or box, or urn, or shoe), one step at a time, using bedding plants:

1. **Cover the drainage holes in your container.**

   If you cover the holes with a small section of window screen, water can't puddle up in the bottom of the pot, and the soil won't gush out through the holes. Note the difference between *covering* holes and plugging them up. Avoid the outdated practice of putting a layer of gravel in the bottom of the container.

2. **Fill the container ²/₃ full with soil.**

3. **Plant plants about ¹/₂ inch deeper than they grew in their baby pots, adding more soil almost to the top of the pot.**

   A few gentle tamps help settle everything in nicely.

4. **Place the whole thing in a small tub (or your kid's wagon), water thoroughly, and fill the tub (or wagon) with water ¹/₂ inch deep.**

5. **Wait 15 minutes and then water your plants again.**

6. **Finally, set the plants on the ground and let them drip dry.**

Deciding What to Grow

This is the gardener's eternal burning question, and seldom does the fact that you're growing something in a pot become a serious limitation. But because summer annuals and bulbs are downright easy, why not start with one or both of them? If all this talk of potting has made you hungry, we've thrown in some edible ideas as well.

Annuals all summer

All the flowers listed in Table 22-1 are team players that also make good solo performers if planted alone. Match numbers to find plants that combine well in containers. For example, combine alyssum with fibrous begonia, celosia, lobelia, and pansies. If you're combining different plants, place the tallest, most upright ones in the center.

Table 22-1	**Annuals to Combine in Pots**	
Flower	*Combinations*	*Uses*
1. Alyssum	(2, 3, 5, 7, 8, 10)	Pots, boxes, baskets
2. Begonia (fibrous)	(1, 4, 7)	Pots, boxes
3. Celosia (plume)	(1, 9, 10)	Pots, boxes
4. Coleus	(1, 2, 6, 7)	Pots, boxes, baskets
5. Geraniums	(1, 7, 9, 10)	Pots, boxes, baskets
6. Impatiens	(4, 7)	Pots, boxes, baskets
7. Lobelia	(1, 2, 4, 5, 6, 7, 8, 9)	Pots, boxes, baskets
8. Pansy	(1, 7)	Pots, boxes, baskets
9. Petunia	(3, 5, 7)	Pots, boxes, baskets
10. Verbena	(1, 3, 5)	Pots, boxes, baskets

How many will fit?

With annuals, plant no more than three plants in a 10-inch-wide pot or six in a 14-inch-wide pot. In window boxes, start with plants 4 inches apart.

Perennial accents

To have year-round fun in an all-container garden, you need some evergreens to hold the fort from autumn to spring. As long as you use big pots (more than 14 inches wide), dwarf conifers, spreading junipers, dwarf boxwoods, and other small shrubs are happy to serve as permanent features. You can underplant them with a few little bulbs (such as crocus or muscari) or pave over their soil with ivy. Figure 22-2 shows a window box filled with a variety of annuals, perennials, and bulbs.

In cold climates — zones 5 and colder (see Chapter 5 for more about growing zones) — perennials and bulbs can't survive through the winter in a container outdoors. If possible, move the pots into a garage or basement that stays cool but protects the plants from frigid outdoor temperatures and winds.

Of course, you can grow tender plants outdoors in containers during warm weather and then winter them indoors near a bright window. Hibiscus and lemon trees are commonly grown like this in regions far colder than their native ones. Additionally, many plants live long lives in containers. These include shrubs, living Christmas trees, and large perennial plants.

Figure 22-2:
Add a
variety of
plants —
annuals,
perennials,
and bulbs
— to a
window box.

Delectable edibles

Your adventures in containers don't need to stop with flowers. Try some tastier side trips: Carrots, herbs (chives, marjoram, parsley, and thyme are good choices), red- and green-leaf lettuces, dwarf or cherry tomatoes, peppers, and radishes are our suggestions.

Is Everybody Happy?

Plants growing in containers can't let their roots wander about in search of food and water, so you must take care of these needs. In mild spring weather, you probably don't need to water your plants more than once a week, but as temperatures rise and the plants get bigger, you may need to water almost every day. Big plants need more water than little ones do.

As for food, many mix-with-water plant foods are available for your use. You can also spoon-feed your plants with composted manure or another organic fertilizer or use some time-release granular stuff. But as long as you're watering anyway, the liquid diet is easy to follow. If you earmark a certain weekday as fertilizer day, your plants will never go hungry.

When the end finally comes and your plants are dying or are frozen to death, dump plants from the pots and clean up the pots before stashing them away until next year. Of course, you can leave pots out all winter just to remind everyone that you're a container gardener, but if you're like most pot-bound folks, your friends have already heard the fascinating details of your green adventures.

Chapter 23

Rose Gardens

In This Chapter

▶ Learning the language of roses

▶ Pleasant company in the rose bed

▶ The many kinds of roses

▶ Planting roses with ease

▶ Primping and pruning your roses

A natural romance between people and roses has been going on since the first human fell on a rosebush and discovered the pleasure that came with the pain. Above their thorny stems, roses produce sensual, intoxicating blossoms that most gardeners find irresistible.

Then you run into rabid rose hobbyists, known as *rosarians*, who tell you that you must follow a hundred rules before you can possibly grow roses. "Wait," you say, "I just want to grow a few roses." The rabid rosarian shakes his head, makes funny clicking noises, and mutters on about things you must *always* do or *never* do.

Bah, humbug! You can bend or break many of the rules of rose growing, have gorgeous flowers for modest effort, and enjoy your home-quality roses as much as the rosarian loves exhibition-quality roses. You can also gain insight into the passionate pursuit of perfection that drives rosarians half-crazy.

Rose gardening is easy — it's the lingo that's hard. The entire Northern Hemisphere came equipped with several hundred species of roses, and over the centuries, those species have been selected, crossed, and recrossed to form numerous *types*, or *classes*, of roses. If you aspire to become a rabid rose hobbyist, you need to learn about polyanthas and noisettes and other historical strains; but if you just want to grow some roses, jump right into the following pool of varieties in the following section "Kinds of Roses."

As you jump into the world of roses, be sure to check in with the American Rose Society. (Insiders refer to it as *The ARS*.) The ARS is located at P.O. Box 30,000, Shreveport, LA 71130-0030; 318-938-5402. Annual membership in the ARS, which includes a one-year subscription to the monthly magazine, *American Rose*, costs $32.

Kinds of Roses

Roses are hardly any *one* thing. There are literally thousands of kinds, short to tall, big to little flowers, fragrant or not — you name it. Here's a crash course on the kinds of roses out there and what you can expect of them.

Trying out teas

The blossoms of *hybrid tea roses* look like the roses that come from a florist, yet usually smell much better. The plants are upright and rather angular, and their distinctive flowers and buds on long stems have come to typify what a rose is for most people. The hybrid tea is the latest development in the history of the rose and is by far the most popular rose today. The big plus of hybrid teas is that they're ever-blooming (bloom all summer).

You can use hybrid teas as specimen shrubs in mixed flower beds or group them in a special rose bed. Some varieties are relatively hardy. Most varieties, however, require special attention to keep the plants vigorous where winters are severe.

The following hybrid teas have earned consistently superior ratings from the ARS for their lovely flowers, healthy, disease-resistant leaves, and cold hardiness:

- ✔ **'Double Delight'.** White blushed with red
- ✔ **'Olympiad'.** Velvety red blossoms
- ✔ **'Peace'.** Ivory with pink blush
- ✔ **'Pristine'.** White tinged with pink
- ✔ **'Touch of Class'.** Coral pink

Fun with floribundas

Floribunda roses, crosses of *polyantha roses* (cluster-flowering roses) with hybrid teas, were developed in an attempt to bring larger flowers and repeat bloom (bloom early in the season, stop, and then bloom again later) to winter-hardy roses. Floribunda roses have blossoms shaped like those of hybrid teas, but the flowers are usually smaller and often are grouped in loose clusters. (Hybrid teas typically carry their blossoms singly on long stems.) Yet floribundas are comparatively rugged and make great specimen shrubs or hedges. Following are three fantastic floribundas with superior ARS ratings:

- ✔ **'Europeana'.** Deep red
- ✔ **'Iceberg'.** Pure white
- ✔ **'Sexy Rexy'.** Light pink

Here comes the queen

The class called *grandiflora* was invented to describe stately 'Queen Elizabeth', which came about as a cross between a pink hybrid tea and a red floribunda. The flowers have the size and form of hybrid teas but are more freely produced, singly or in clusters, on taller, exceptionally vigorous plants. Subsequent breeding efforts to expand the grandiflora class have yet to produce roses as fine as the queen herself, with the possible exception of 'Gold Medal', a colossal yellow rose.

Climbing high with roses

Climbing roses are very long-branched roses that you can tie onto (or weave into) a support structure so that the roses look as though they're climbing. Climbing roses can be old-fashioned roses, hybrids, or chance variants of hybrid teas. The supporting structure can be anything from a chain-link fence to a fancy iron archway. Tie climbing roses gently with pieces of stretchy cloth or old pantyhose. Some great climbers are 'Altissimo' (deep red) and 'America' (bright pink).

"Honey, I shrank the roses!"

Miniature roses have small leaves, short stems, and small flowers; they usually grow less than 2 feet tall. Miniatures are easy to fit into small beds and make great edging plants. Or you can grow them in containers. The following four varieties are remarkably hardy, fragrant, disease-resistant, and long-blooming:

- ✔ **'Magic Carousel'.** Red edged in white
- ✔ **'Party Girl'.** Apricot-yellow and salmon-pink
- ✔ **'Rise 'n Shine'.** Yellow
- ✔ **'Starina'.** Orange-red

". . .Honey, now I've stretched the roses"

Another fun trick rosarians have played on the hapless rose is turning it into a tree. These are called *standards,* and you can buy most any kind of popular rose this way. Imagine a regular rose, but on stilts. We like standards because they raise the flowers to nose height. So-called *patio* roses are the same idea, but smaller.

Shrub varieties proliferate

The terms *shrub rose* and *landscape rose* are loose designations for a catchall class of modern roses. A rose gets assigned to the shrub roses class when it doesn't fit precisely in one of the preceding classes. This clan of merry misfits is getting bigger all the time and includes some of the most carefree and profusely blooming of all roses. Shrub roses are freely integrated into the landscape, according to their size and shape.

Many kinds of shrub roses have been introduced in recent years, especially the so-called *ground covers*, such as 'Cliffs of Dover', 'Flower Carpet', and 'Jeepers Creepers'. These are ideal for slopes and large vistas. In smaller gardens, try these and other ground cover roses as specimens in containers and hanging baskets.

Hedge roses, such as 'Bonica', 'Carefree Delight', and 'Simplicity', have become very popular in recent years. Compared with their fancier, larger-flowered cousins, hedge roses are humble members of the rose family. But they are extremely disease-resistant, and they flower throughout the season.

Some new shrub roses are reliably hardy in cold climates. The Morden and Explorer series are hardy to –25°F, and some repeat-blooming varieties of *Rosa rugosa* are hardy to –30°F. In addition to their hardiness to cold, the rugosa roses also thrive in coastal regions under the constant assault of salty wind.

David Austin roses

At the other end of the spectrum are David Austin's English roses. The name of the English rose breeder David Austin is a household word in rose circles. Austin mixed the blossom shapes and scents of almost-forgotten old roses with the disease resistance and everblooming qualities of newer strains, and he came up with a bunch of wonderful — if unpredictable — new roses. You are very likely to hear about the following three:

- ✔ **'Gertrude Jekyll'.** Strongly fragrant shell-pink blossoms on a plant that can be pruned into a bush or trained as a climber

- ✔ **'Graham Thomas'.** Pinkish buds open to shockingly fragrant yellow blossoms, on a big plant that likes to sprawl and demands elbow room

- ✔ **'Heritage'.** Extremely well-behaved pink rose with a citrusy scent; perfect as a specimen shrub in a mixed border

Old-fashioned roses

When we talk about an old rose, we mean old in the sense that it was popular among Victorians. And some types, such as the *centifolias,* have been grown for centuries. The plants you buy are, of course, only a couple of years old, same as for any rose purchased. Here are a few "old" roses:

- **Alba.** Tall, vigorous, thorny; fragrant, usually pale-colored flowers. Blooms once per season.

- **Bourbon.** Tall, vigorous plants. Blooms more than once per season.

- **Centifolia.** Arching, thorny stems. Fragrant flowers come in spring only.

- **China.** Delicate plants with lots of twiggy growth. Blooms more than once per season.

- **Damask.** Thorny, arching stems. Flowers usually pink and very fragrant. Blooms once per season.

- **Gallica.** Small plants. Fragrant roses in clusters. Blooms once per season.

- **Hybrid perpetual.** Tall, stiff shrubs. Fragrant flowers bloom more than once per season.

- **Moss.** Shrub is stiffly upright. Flower buds have "mossy-looking" growth. Blooms once per season.

- **Portland.** Small shrub. Flowers are fragrant. Blooms more than once per season.

- **Tea.** Delicate plants. Flowers have classic florist shape. The parent of modern "hybrid" teas. Blooms more than once per season.

Roses by many other names. . .

Finally, numerous roses don't easily fit an existing category or group. These roses include 'Iceberg', 'Lady of the Dawn', 'Simplicity', and 'Festival Fanfare'. Officially classed as floribundas (shrubbier versions of a hybrid tea), these roses meet or exceed all the requirements of a shrub rose. Another example is 'Magic Carpet'. Classed as a large-flowered climber, 'Magic Carpet' serves beautifully as a ground cover.

Older roses that fit the shrub category include the Kordesii, musk, and Buck hybrids, ancestors of some of the new shrubs listed here. Kordesii hybrids include the 8-foot-tall 'Dortmund', which is hardy to −15°F and is very disease resistant. The nearly everblooming musks, such as 'Buff Beauty' and 'Kathleen', grow 5 to 10 feet tall and produce 2-inch fragrant flowers in clusters; their plants are hardy to 0°F. Buck hybrids, such as 'Apple Jack' and 'Prairie Princess', grow 3 to 5 feet high and are hardy to −15°F.

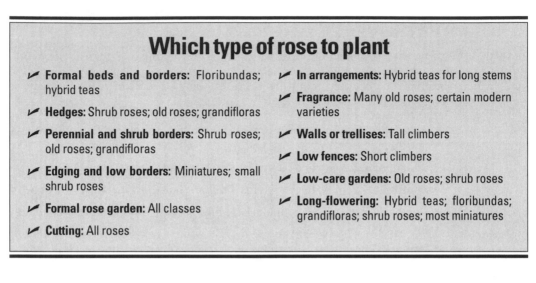

Which type of rose to plant

- **Formal beds and borders:** Floribundas; hybrid teas

- **Hedges:** Shrub roses; old roses; grandifloras

- **Perennial and shrub borders:** Shrub roses; old roses; grandifloras

- **Edging and low borders:** Miniatures; small shrub roses

- **Formal rose garden:** All classes

- **Cutting:** All roses

- **In arrangements:** Hybrid teas for long stems

- **Fragrance:** Many old roses; certain modern varieties

- **Walls or trellises:** Tall climbers

- **Low fences:** Short climbers

- **Low-care gardens:** Old roses; shrub roses

- **Long-flowering:** Hybrid teas; floribundas; grandifloras; shrub roses; most miniatures

Landscaping with Roses

Roses are sun-loving plants, so place your roses where they can get at least six hours of sun each day. In cool, cloudy climates, roses grow best with all-day sun; in really hot regions, afternoon shade gives them a much-needed break.

Like most other plants, roses need very good drainage and sufficient air circulation to help their leaves dry out fast whenever they get wet. Almost all roses need periodic grooming, so make sure that you can reach your roses easily when the time comes to trim and prune them.

You can put several roses together in a special rose bed, plant a group of the same kind of rose in a line to create a hedge, or work your roses into a mixed bed or border with other flowers. In all three of these situations, you soon discover that roses are not beautiful all of the time. Solve this problem by using companion plants that look great while your roses aren't blooming. In most climates, your roses look bad three times during the year — winter, early spring, and midsummer.

- **For winter allure.** Keep the scene lively with small evergreen shrubs, ground cover junipers, or ornamental grasses.

- **For spring excitement.** Punctuate your rose planting with small clumps of daffodil, muscari, or crocus bulbs; or incorporate mounds of creeping phlox (or perennial candytuft) or an edging of pansies.

- **For midsummer color and contrast.** Choose one or more of these as possible partners: perennials such as geraniums, blue salvias, dwarf daylilies, and moss rose *(Portulaca)*, and foliage herbs, like rosemary, thymes, artemisias, and lamb's ears *(Stachys)*.

Buying, Planting, and Growing Roses

The best selection of roses hits the garden centers in late winter, when plants are sold bare-root (see Figure 23-1) with their roots tightly wrapped in plastic. Such roses look dead, but they're merely sleeping.

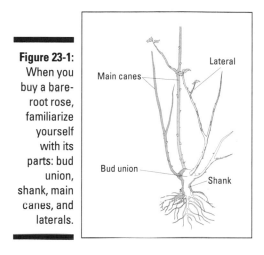

Figure 23-1:
When you buy a bare-root rose, familiarize yourself with its parts: bud union, shank, main canes, and laterals.

If you want your roses to hit the ground running, spend a couple of extra bucks for #1 grade plants, which have more stems and roots than cheaper #2 grade plants. Most roses are really two plants — the first plant is the hardy, vigorous root, and the second plant is the fancy rose grafted onto that root. The graft union should look like a solid bulge just above the roots, and the plant should have at least three main canes reaching for the sky.

The latest and greatest roses are usually patented. This is fair because if the rose is successful, the hybridizer who invested years of cross-breeding into its development is rewarded. By the same token, you can look for nonpatented roses. The plants should be as healthy and vigorous, and you'll save a few dollars.

If you pay any attention to roses at all, sooner or later you'll come across the acronym *AARS*, which stands for All-American Rose Selections. While AARS serves primarily as a public relations arm of the rose industry, rose varieties that win the AARS designation are generally among the best.

Roses like a near-neutral soil pH of 6.5 to 7.0 (see Chapter 14 for details on testing and adjusting your soil pH) but beyond that, they are not picky about the kind of soil in which they are planted.

To plant a bare-root rose in good, rich topsoil, dig a hole wide enough to extend the roots without bending them. If the roots are damaged, trim them as needed.

(See Figure 23-2.) Spread the roots over a low cone of soil in the center of the planting hole. Backfill with the soil removed from the hole, firming the soil in place with your hands. Finally, water thoroughly to settle soil and eliminate air pockets.

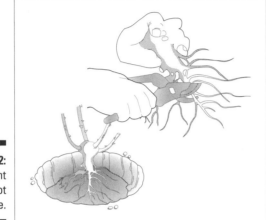

Figure 23-2:
How to plant
a bare-root
rose.

To plant a rose in tight clay or porous sand, dig a roomy planting hole about 14 inches square, put the excavated soil in a wheelbarrow, and mix the excavated soil with one-fourth part peat moss, one-fourth part bagged compost or aged manure, and a couple of handfuls of bone meal. Partially refill the hole, spread out the roots of your rose, add some more soil, and water well. Then finish dumping in your enriched soil.

If you live where winter temperatures are 20°F or above, plant so that the bud union of grafted roses is at soil level. Unless otherwise noted, most roses die to ground level at temperatures around –20°F. Where winter temperatures range between 20°F and –20°F, set the bud union deeper, 2 or more inches below the soil surface. In climates where winter temperatures reach lower than –20°F, choose nongrafted roses grown on their own roots. Own-root roses are more likely to survive and regrow after severe cold. Several own-root roses are available, including the Morden series, the Explorer series, and specific varieties, such as 'Simplicity'. Plant own-root roses at the previous soil line, which is indicated by the color change on the thick shank above the roots.

If you buy your plants at a nursery or garden center during the growing season, the plants will be growing in containers. When transplanting a potted rose to the garden, dig a hole that is twice the width and about the same depth as the container. Use a utility knife to cut the pot away so that the roots are disturbed as little as possible.

Roses planted while winter still rages can be damaged if the graft union freezes hard. Cover the graft union with a mound of extra soil; then remove the extra soil when winter finally ends.

As soon as spring warms up, tufts of leaves sprout from little buds on the canes. That's when you should begin to fertilize your roses lightly with a specially blended rose fertilizer (following label instructions) and prune off canes that have died. Continue to fertilize your roses about once a month all summer, until early autumn. If you live where rainfall during the growing season is slight or nonexistent, give the young plants a deep, thorough soaking once or twice weekly throughout the summer.

Pruning Roses

The following sounds hokey, but when it comes to knowing exactly how to prune a rose, you must discuss the matter with your plant. The first year with any rose is like a blind date — you don't know what the rose thinks of you; you don't know what you think of it. Here are some things to look for when you think that your rose is subliminally telling you that it wants to be pruned:

- ✔ **Long, skinny canes with a tuft of leaves at the end.** Carefully examine the canes for tiny, pinkish, pointed bumps called *leaf buds.* Find a good leaf bud that faces away from the center of the plant and is no more than halfway down the cane. Prune ¹/₄ to ¹/₂ inch above that bud.

- ✔ **Branches that come up out of the ground below the graft union.** Gently dig to where these guys begin and cut them off with a sharp knife. These are shoots from the rootstock, usually an ultra-vigorous but unattractive type of rose. If you don't cut them out, they'll take over the rose plant.

- ✔ **Sickly looking branches where most of the leaves show black circular freckles.** This combination of symptoms indicates a common disease called black spot (see Chapter 18). Prune off badly affected branches to keep black spot from spreading out of control.

- ✔ **Dead canes.** Prune them away.

Hybrid teas require somewhat more pruning to bring out their best performance. In early spring, cut back vigorous hybrid tea canes to the height of the other canes on the plant. Make cuts at a 45° angle, about ¹/₄ inch above a bud (see Figure 23-3). Remove suckers and any dead or crowded branches. All this keeps the center of the plant *open,* meaning free of twiggy growth, and allows sunshine to reach all parts of the plant.

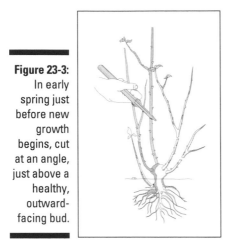

Figure 23-3:
In early spring just before new growth begins, cut at an angle, just above a healthy, outward-facing bud.

You also need to prune off dead blossoms. If your rose blooms very heavily and then looks as if it's ready to die, prune the whole plant back by one-third, fertilize the plant lightly, and water it well. Within two weeks you should see lots of new branches budding all over the plant, and within a month you should once again be smelling like a rose.

Helping roses survive winter

Where winter temperatures often go below 25°F, mulch the base of every plant to keep the base from freezing, thawing, and refreezing over and over. Wait until early winter, when the plant seems to be nodding into dormancy, and cut the canes back halfway (unless the rose is a climber). Dump a cone of soil, sawdust, compost, or other insulating material, 6 to 10 inches deep, over the base of the plant. Then, encircle the base of the plant with a wire cage or cardboard box and stuff it with shredded leaves. The goal is to preserve the leaf buds on the bottom 8 inches of each cane. Remove whatever insulation you use in spring so sun can reach the soil and warm it up.

You know that you have chosen good roses for your climate and are giving them suitable care if the plants get bigger and stronger with each passing year. But a certain amount of trial and error exists in growing roses. If at first any rose does not succeed, you can always try again.

Part VI
The Part of Tens

The 5th Wave — By Rich Tennant

"Before I show you the rest of 'Castle Dracula', let me show you my garden. It's a hobby with me. I do most of the work myself; however, Renfield helps keep the garden free of bugs."

In this part . . .

We had great fun with this part because it includes some (although not always ten) of the most specific and useful ideas and information we think you'll find in any book about gardening. Here we share our many years' experience about composting (or in the current jargon, "recycling").

Think you don't have enough space to garden? With our tips, you'll harvest a bounty of fruits and flowers, even in the smallest yard.

And what about fragrance? For some of us, delightful scent is the criterion for choosing which flowers to grow.

Let your mind wander among these gardens . . . for ideas on making your piece of paradise perfect.

Chapter 24

Composting and Recycling Yard Waste

• •

In This Chapter

▶ All about composting and composting aids

▶ Tips on turning yard waste into treasure

▶ Mulches from your own backyard

• •

*1*n this Part of Tens chapter, we deviate a little because nearly everything there is to know about recycling yard waste might be summed up in one word: *compost.* Composting is really not at all complicated. After all, that's what nature does. But you probably have questions about the quickest, most convenient, or most attractive way to compost, and all of that is what this chapter is mostly about.

Another way to manage yard waste is to recycle by finding uses for various materials. Sometimes, it's hard to see a twig or branch that you've just pruned as useful. But consider that expensive, rustic, "twig" as furniture. Sometimes the humblest objects become the most chic.

Finally, consider all that stuff you rake and throw away year after year — the leaves, grass clippings, or pine needles. It's valuable. It's good for your soil; it can feed your plants; *and* to throw all of it away and then buy something else for the same purpose is expensive. We're talking about *mulches,* especially the ones you already own.

How the Piles Stack Up

As we visit the gardens of friends and neighbors around the country, interestingly enough, a stop at the compost pile is included in almost every garden tour. Meeting a gardener who shows off a rich, dark, earthy compost as eagerly as towering dahlias with their 10-inch blossoms is not at all unusual.

Not so long ago, we gardeners hid our compost piles. In privacy, we'd witness the magic of composting, the transformation of garden and yard waste into sweet-smelling black gold. We feared that others (especially neighbors) would judge our passion as a waste of time and space.

Attitudes have changed. Landfills are filling up, and some states even ban yard waste from landfills. Composting is now widely recognized as an easy, effective way to reduce solid waste at home.

More to the heart of gardeners is the fact that compost is a valuable natural soil amendment. Adding compost to garden beds and planting holes enhances nutrients and improves soil texture. Compost helps to loosen heavy clay soils, and it increases the water-holding capacity of sandy soils (see Chapter 14 for more about soils).

A *compost pile* is a collection of plant and sometimes animal materials, combined in a way to encourage quick decomposition. Soil microorganisms (bacteria and fungi) do the work of breaking down this organic material into a soil-like consistency.

These organisms need oxygen and water to survive. Turning the pile provides oxygen, and an occasional watering helps keep it moist. If the pile is well made and the organisms are thriving, it heats up quickly and doesn't emit any unpleasant odors. Finished compost that looks and feels like dark, crumbly soil can thus take as little as a month to produce.

From refuse to riches: composting

Whether you make your compost in an elaborate store-bought bin (one that closes tightly) or simply build a freestanding pile, the essentials of good composting are the same. To get fast results, follow these steps:

1. **Collect equal parts by volume of dried, brown, carbon-rich material (like old leaves or straw) and fresh, green, nitrogen-rich material (fresh-cut grass, green vegetation, and vegetable kitchen wastes are examples).**

   A few materials should *not* be used in an open compost pile. Although farm animal manures are a safe source of nitrogen for the pile, dog and cat waste can spread unhealthy organisms. Meat, fats, bones, and cooked foods decompose slowly, may be smelly, and may attract animal pests — add these only to compost bins that close tightly. Finally, keep out pernicious weeds that spread by runners and roots, such as Bermuda grass.

2. **Chop or shred the organic materials into small pieces.**

   Pieces that are $^3/_4$ inch or smaller are ideal.

3. **Build the pile about 3 feet × 3 feet × 3 feet (1 cubic yard), alternating layers of the carbon-rich material with the green material.**

4. **Wet the pile as you build it.**

   Keep the material moist, not soaked. (It should be about as moist as a wrung-out sponge.) A well-built pile heats up in approximately a week, peaking between 120°F and 160°F.

5. **After the temperature begins to decrease, turn the pile, wetting it as necessary to keep it moist.**

   If you don't have a compost thermometer, just turn the pile every week or so the first month.

Bin or no bin?

A compost pile cares not whether it's caged or freestanding. An enclosure, called a *compost bin,* mostly keeps the pile neat and can help retain moisture and heat. Depending on its design, a compost bin also keeps out animal pests. For these reasons, especially in urban settings, a bin is a good idea.

Often, city or county recycling programs have a home demonstration site that displays a variety of compost bins in use, including homemade and commercial types. Some cities offer compost bins at a reduced price; others provide plans for making your own. (A few enlightened cities collect garden waste, compost it, and then make it available to gardeners.)

To build or buy?

Bins are available by mail order and, increasingly, through nurseries, garden centers, and even discount stores. You can spend up to $400 or more for a commercial compost bin, or you can make your own with scrap materials.

A *wire bin* is perhaps the easiest type to make. You need an 11-foot length of 36-inch-wide welded reinforcing wire with a grid of about 2 × 4 inches. Simply bend the wire to form a hoop and tie the ends together with strong wire. This bin will hold about a cubic yard when full.

To use the bin, fill it with the appropriate balance of organic material. When the pile is ready to turn, lift off the wire mesh and set it next to the pile; then, turn the material and fork it back into the enclosure.

Another option is a *wooden compost bin,* made with wooden pallets, wooden scrap boards, and wire or — for the more elaborate model — 2 × 4 and 2 × 6 lumber. The Cadillac of the wooden compost bins utilizes three bins arranged side by side. Though it can be time consuming to construct, some gardeners prefer the convenience of a three-box bin. Each bin is for compost at a different stage of maturity. For example, fresh material is added to the far-left bin, turned into the middle one after a few weeks, and then turned into the bin at the far right to finish.

Among commercial bins are four basic types:

✔ **Containers for hot compost.** Usually made out of recycled plastic, these bottomless boxes or cylinders are designed to be used in much the same way as the wire bin, described in the preceding paragraphs. You completely fill the bin with the right blend of materials and let the pile heat up. To "turn" the compost, when the bin is full, you lift off the top section of compost and place it on the ground (the section on top now becomes the section on the bottom). Then you reach in with a fork and lift some of the lower compost, making it the top section of compost, and so on.

Some of these containers are stackable, which makes removing them and turning the compost easier (see Figure 24-1). With sufficient turning, this type of bin delivers fast results.

Figure 24-1: This stackable, plastic, bottomless bin makes turning the compost pile easy.

✔ **Bins for a static pile.** With these plastic units (which usually have air vents along the sides), you make a compost pile by putting a balance of waste materials in the top of the bin and letting the mixture sit. As the waste decomposes, you remove the finished compost from the bottom of the bin and add more waste to the top (see Figure 24-2).

This type of bin is the most commonly available bin, though not necessarily the best. Although no turning is required and you can add waste at any time, decomposition is slow and you get only small amounts of compost at a time. Because the pile does not get very hot, weeds, seeds, and plant diseases may survive.

Figure 24-2:
Vents at the side of a static compost pile provide air to the maturing pile. The finished compost empties at the bottom.

✓ **Tumblers.** With a tumbler, you place your compost inside the container and then turn the entire bin to toss the compost inside. Some tumblers have crank handles for turning. One tumbler system is designed to roll on the ground, tumbling the compost inside as it goes.

With these units, you make a hot compost by balancing the waste materials and turning the bin frequently. Tumblers are generally the most expensive type of bin, but the ease of turning and the fast results may be worth the money. Choose one with at least a 1-cubic-yard capacity and test it for ease of loading and turning before you buy.

✓ **Anaerobic containers.** These sealed, closed-to-air compost bins require no turning or aerating. You simply fill the container with organic material and close the lid. Compost is ready in six months or more.

Although no maintenance is required, this type of bin often has insect and odor problems. The decomposed product is slimy and requires drying before use, and shoveling the compost out of the bin is difficult. We give this product low marks for home gardeners.

Composting aids . . . who needs them, anyway?

No store-bought gadgets are required to make compost happen. With or without accessories, you can create a perfect pile. A few supplies, however, do make composting faster, more exacting, and perhaps easier. Here's a rundown of these handy items for your consideration. All are available through mail-order garden supply catalogs (see Appendix C).

✔ **Compost starters.** Manufacturers claim that these products, sometimes called *inoculants* or *activators,* accelerate the composting process and improve the quality of the finished compost. Many compost starters are currently on the market; most are blends of bacteria, fungi, and enzymes, sometimes combined with products high in nitrogen and protein. The powdery substance is either mixed in or sprayed onto the pile.

As an alternative to buying a commercial starter, throw in a few shovelsful of rich garden soil when you first build your pile.

✔ **Compost thermometer.** This thermometer consists of a face dial and a steel probe (about 20 inches long). It is used to accurately monitor the temperature of compost. The instrument measures temperatures from 0°F to 220°F and enables you to know when your pile is cooking and when it is cooling down and ready to turn. After you insert the steel probe into the pile, the temperature reading becomes visible on the face dial.

✔ **Compost aerating tool.** You push a galvanized steel tool, which is about 36 inches long, into the compost pile. As you pull the tool out, two paddles open, creating a churning action that enables oxygen to enter the pile.

✔ **Compost sifter.** Because different materials decompose at different rates, you may end up with some large chunks of not-yet-decomposed material in compost that is otherwise ready for the garden. The sifter separates out the large pieces, which you can then toss back into a new compost pile to further decompose.

You can save a few bucks by making your own sifter. To do so, use ¹/₄-inch window screen stapled or nailed to a wooden frame made of lumber. Make the frame large enough so that you can position it over a wheelbarrow and sift compost through it.

✔ **Pitchfork.** This long-handled tool, with tines about 10 to 12 inches long, is the best instrument to use for turning compost.

Heap it on

So what else can you put in your compost pile besides the obvious? The following list describes several other materials found around the home and garden that make good additions to any compost pile:

✔ Ashes from the wood stove (sprinkle them lightly between layers; *don't* add them by the bucketful)

✔ Chicken or rabbit manure

✔ Coffee grounds

✔ Eggshells (crush them before adding)

✔ Flowers

- ✔ Fruit and vegetable peels, stalks, and foliage (everything from salad leftovers to old pea vines)

- ✔ Fruit pulp from a juicer

- ✔ Grass clippings (mix them thoroughly to prevent clumping)

- ✔ Hedge clippings

- ✔ Leaves

- ✔ Pine needles (use sparingly; they are acidic and break down slowly)

- ✔ Sawdust

- ✔ Sod and soil

- ✔ Wood chips (chipped very small for faster decomposition)

If it smells bad, fix it

Don't be alarmed if your compost pile gives off a foul odor. It's simply calling for attention. Odors occur if the pile lacks oxygen or has too much wet green material and too little dry brown material. You can alleviate the odor by turning the pile and mixing in equal parts of brown and green stuff. If it's really wet and slimy, open the pile up a bit in the middle to let it dry out some.

Treasures from Twigs

Consider yourself lucky if you are trimming a vine, grooming a hedge, or pruning a tree here and there and find yourself with a few piles of twigs and branches. These bits of woody materials have many uses in the home and garden, both utilitarian and aesthetic. Using these materials saves money. So before you start hacking away with a machete or hauling this stuff off to the dump, consider the possible alternatives for dealing with the following:

- ✔ **Brush cuttings.** Use prunings that are about $1/4$ to $1/2$ inch thick at the base to support bush peas.

- ✔ **Straight branches.** Branches about 3 feet long and $1/2$ inch wide make sturdy plant supports. To keep blooms of large-flowering perennials such as peonies from toppling over, drive stakes into the ground to form a ring around the plant. Connect the stakes with twine tied at the appropriate height to support top-heavy stems.

  You can also handcraft rustic trellises from straight, sturdy branches (see Figure 24-3). Allow 18 inches at the base to push into the soil for support. Weave rope or twine as shown to connect the branches and provide supports for plants.

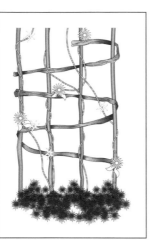

Figure 24-3:
Straight, sturdy branches can be used to make a rustic trellis.

✔ **Tall stems.** Use wispy, branching stems about 24 inches long to support stems of paper white narcissus growing in pebbles and water.

✔ **Twigs.** Use thin twigs to support cut flowers in arrangements. Place groups of twigs at different angles in the vase and then insert flowers.

✔ **Vines.** To form decorative wreaths, bend and weave together fresh-cut vines from dormant grapes, bittersweet, or willow. Bind the ends together with wire and let the vines dry out.

Mulching Matters

Mulch is any loose material, organic or not, placed over the soil surface. Ground bark, leaves, straw, and, yes, even compost are commonly used. Mulch is a good thing; it helps smother weeds (making your work easier), reduces moisture loss from the soil (conserving water resources), and insulates the soil from rapid temperature changes. Plus, a good-looking mulch makes the garden tidy, and organic mulches improve the soil as they decompose. You can find more about mulch and mulch options in Chapter 16.

As a general guideline, apply 2 to 4 inches of organic mulch to garden beds and around trees and shrubs. Keep the mulch several inches away from the stems of plants (trees and shrubs included).

Chapter 25

Ten Quick "Garden" Projects

In This Chapter

▶ Cooking up herb vinegars

▶ Making a flowering centerpiece

▶ Creating a water garden in a tub

▶ Forcing a pot of fragrant narcissus

▶ Cleaning old terra cotta pots

*H*ere are ten (well, almost ten) easy projects that will get you into your garden or make being in your garden even more enjoyable.

Cooking Up Herb Vinegars

Herb vinegars are so easy to make that they ought to be illegal to sell. You can flavor and mellow vinegars with many kinds of fresh garden herbs — fennel, sage, rosemary, garlic, and chives, to name a few. Our favorite herb vinegar is one made with purple basil. In addition to its spicy basil flavor, this vinegar turns a gorgeous orchid pink.

As a general guide, use 1 cup of fresh-picked herbs to flavor 1 quart of vinegar. Depending on your taste, use white, cider, or wine vinegar. (White vinegar works best with purple basil.)

Here's all there is to it, though the variations are endless:

    1. Loosely fill a glass jar with clean herbs.

    2. Cover with vinegar and cap with plastic or a cork (don't use metal).

    3. Store in a cool, dark place for two to six weeks.

    4. Strain to remove the herbs when the flavor satisfies your taste.

Making a Flowering Centerpiece

This living centerpiece makes an impressive table decoration, indoors or out. The process takes about half an hour.

For a picnic table in summer, you might combine begonias, ageratum, and sweet alyssum, the combination that we've based this set of steps on. A winter centerpiece, for indoor decoration, might combine moth orchids and African violets with ivy and diminutive ferns. You may need a small bag of potting soil to fill in gaps between plants. If need be, put loose perlite (that white, light, popcornlike soil amendment you can get at nurseries) underneath plant pots to raise them up in the basket.

1. **Choose an oblong basket (about 15 to 20 inches long, 8 to 10 inches wide, and 4 or so inches high).**

2. **Line the basket with a heavy plastic trash bag and trim the edges.**

3. **Fill the basket with a combination of flowering and foliage plants in small, 2- to 4-inch containers. Place the tallest plants (like begonias) in the center and lower-growing plants (like ageratum and sweet alyssum) toward the outside. Trailing plants, including small-leafed ivies, can be squeezed in at the edges. Fill all gaps with potting soil. Use Spanish moss to hide pots.**

4. **To maintain the centerpiece, water plants individually, using a narrow-spouted watering can. Feed the plants regularly. Refresh the centerpiece with new plants as needed.**

For a very full look, squeeze in more plants by removing some of the smaller ones from their containers and slipping the rootball of each plant into a zipped sandwich bag (partially close the bag around the base of the plant). Then gently squeeze the bagged plants between the potted plants. Water the plants just enough to keep them moist.

Creating a Water Garden in a Tub

What better project for a hot summer afternoon? While the thought of building a traditional garden pond may be overwhelming, creating a soothing water feature in a tub is quite achievable. Though small in scale, your tub garden will teem with life: fish, flowers, and even the birds that come to drink. Figure 25-1 shows water lilies in a large pot of water — an example of a simple water garden.

Display the water garden where it will receive two to three hours of shade during the hottest part of the day.

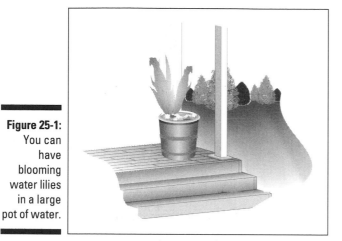

Figure 25-1:
You can have blooming water lilies in a large pot of water.

Here are the materials you need:

- Sturdy, plastic or glazed ceramic pot without a drainage hole

  New, durable faux terra cotta containers (Choose one about 30 inches in diameter and about 20 inches high.)

- Water plants: one water iris, one water lily, one free-floating water hyacinth, and a clump of parrots feather, a common water plant

- Half-dozen fish: mosquito fish, minnows, or goldfish

- Empty 5-gallon plastic pot

Here's what you do:

1. **Fill the large tub about ²/₃ full with water and place the 5-gallon pot, inverted, to one side of the tub.**

2. **Place the iris on top of the inverted 5-gallon pot.**

3. **Place the water lily, in its own container, on the bottom of the tub.**

   Its leaves and flowers will rise above the water surface.

4. **Plant the clump of parrots feather in the soil in the iris container.**

5. **Add the floating water hyacinth and fill the tub with water.**

6. **Acclimatize fish by placing them — still in their plastic bag — in the water for about 20 minutes. Then release them from the bag.**

   You don't need to give them supplemental food — they'll feed on algae and insect larvae in the water.

Aquatic plants are becoming more readily available at nurseries. If you can't find them locally, order them by mail. (See Appendix C for mail-order sources.)

Forcing Narcissus Indoors

On blustery winter days when the garden is dull and quiet, a pot of home-grown bulbs gracing the dining room table is truly gratifying. In winter, flowers are a feast for the eyes. Setting up narcissus to bloom takes little effort. All they need are water and several weeks to work their magic.

The two varieties of narcissus that are most available and reliable for water culture are paper-whites and yellow Soleil D'Or. Paper-whites flower in only five to six weeks after planting; Soleil D'Or take a bit longer.

Here's what you do:

1. **Choose a fairly shallow waterproof bowl or pot, at least twice as deep as the size of the bulbs.**
2. **Fill the container to within several inches from the top with pebbles.**
3. **Set the bulbs on the pebbles about $1/2$ inch apart with the broad ends down.**
4. **Fill the container with water so that the water just touches the bottom of the bulbs.**

   See Figure 25-2.

5. **To hold the bulbs in place, fill the spaces between them with more pebbles.**
6. **Put the planted container in a cool, dark place to encourage root growth.**
7. **In two to three weeks, when the leaves are about 3 inches high, move the container to a warmer, bright location.**
8. **As the plants develop, add water from time to time, keeping it at the base of the bulbs.**

Figure 25-2: Set bulbs of paper-white narcissus into a pot filled with small pebbles. Maintain water level at bulbs' base.

If you want blooms for Thanksgiving, start paper-whites about the middle of September. For Christmas blooms, start them in mid-November. For continuous flowers through winter, start the first pot of bulbs in late October and continue planting at two- to three-week intervals. Fore more on growing bulbs in containers, see Chapter 11 and the color illustration of bulbs.

Cleaning Containers

By cleaning used terra cotta containers before replanting, you help prevent spreading plant diseases and pests.

Using a stiff wire brush, scrape off soil and fertilizer residue, algae, and salt crust inside and outside the pot. Then scrub the pots with a 10-percent bleach solution and rinse well.

If you've had a perennial or a shrub growing in the same container for several seasons, the outside surface of the container may be dirty and discolored. To freshen it up, brush the surface and using an old rag, rub on linseed oil.

Preparing a Salad Basket

You're probably familiar with *mesclun* — those expensive mixes of tender gourmet salad greens. Why buy mesclun when you can easily grow it? Why grow it in a garden when you can have it in a basket? That's what we thought.

Many mesclun greens germinate just a few days after planting and are ready for harvesting in two to four weeks. More good news for gardeners: After you cut mesclun greens, they grow back for a repeat harvest.

You can buy a premixed mesclun seed blend or mix your own by combining your favorite greens. Typical ingredients include loose-leaf lettuces, arugula, chicories, mizuna, red mustard, and curly cress. The Cook's Garden and Shepherd's Garden Seeds are two excellent sources for mesclun greens (mixed or not); addresses are in Appendix C.

Here's how to grow a basket of mesclun that you can harvest after three weeks:

1. **Choose a large, sturdy basket that can support the weight of wet soil. Line it with a heavyweight plastic trash bag. To provide drainage, use scissors to poke holes through the plastic at the bottom of the basket.**

2. **Fill with moistened peat moss and perlite-type potting mix (several kinds are available commercially) to 2 inches below the rim (trim off any plastic that extends beyond the rim).**

3. **Scatter seeds thinly over the soil surface, cover with about $1/4$ inch of potting mix, and then water.**

4. **Cover the basket with a piece of plastic until the seeds germinate.**

5. **When seeds sprout, remove the plastic and move the basket to a sunny location. Keep the soil moist as the plants grow and feed weekly with a complete liquid fertilizer.**

6. **Start harvesting when the seedlings are about 3 inches tall by cutting with scissors $1/2$ inch above the soil surface.**

Drying Flowers

The essence of summer is easily preserved when you pick a bunch of flowers and hang them to dry for winter bouquets. It's time to harvest flowers for drying when the garden is nearing full, glorious bloom.

You can effectively air-dry the annuals listed here simply by hanging them upside down in bundles, from the ceiling or from a drying rack. Remove the foliage, group them in small bunches, and tie them with a rubber band. Keep the drying flowers in a warm, dark place with good ventilation. Most flowers are dry when the stems snap. Store dried flowers in covered boxes or paper bags (away from dust and light).

Some dried flowers, such as strawflowers, have weak stems and must be wired if used in arrangements.

Here are a dozen annuals that you can count on to hold their shape and color:

- **Winged everlasting** *(Ammobium alatum)*. Colors are white and yellow with yellow centers. Cut when buds start to open.

- **Safflower** *(Carthamus tinctorius)*. Cut yellow-orange flowers in bud or just at peak color.

- **Cockscomb** *(Celosia cristata)*. Colors are intense and warm. Cut when heads reach full color.

- **Larkspur** *(Consolida ambigua)*. Colors are pink, blue, purple, and white. Cut stems when about two-thirds of the flowers are open and one-third are in bud.

- **Globe amaranth** *(Gomphrena globosa)*. Colors are orange, white, pink, purple, and red. Cut when heads are plump and in full color.

- **Strawflower** *(Helichrysum bracteatum)*. Colors are mixed and vibrant. Cut when buds start to open.

- **Pink paper daisy** *(Helipterum)*. Colors in shades of pink and white. Cut partially open blooms.

- ✔ **Statice** *(Limonium sinuatum)*. Colors range from purple to orange. Cut when most of the florets are open.

- ✔ **Love-in-a-mist** *(Nigella damascena)*. Grown for attractive seed pod. Cut when mature.

- ✔ **Pink pokers** *(Psylliostachys suworowii)*. Cut lavender pink flowers when fully open.

- ✔ **Starflower** *(Scabiosa stellata)*. Cut decorative seed pods as soon as petals fade.

- ✔ **Immortelle** *(Xeranthemum annuum)*. Colors are lavender, white, and shades of pink and purple. Cut open flowers after they show full color.

Creating an Autumn Harvest Wreath

You don't need to be an artist to pull off this craft project successfully. After just a couple of hours of collecting and arranging leaves, seed pods, and fruits from your garden and grocery store, you have a beautiful wreath for your Thanksgiving celebration. It lasts anywhere from several days to several months, depending on the plants you use.

The object is to cover a polystyrene foam wreath base (available at craft and floral supply stores) with garden goodies. You need about two large grocery bags full of plant material to cover a 12-inch wreath. Combine foliage like magnolia, eucalyptus, and dusty miller leaves with colorful accents like rose hips, seed pods, and pyracantha berries. If you're short on home-grown plants, use accent material like baby corn, lady apples, and miniature pumpkins purchased from your grocery store.

Here's what you do:

1. **Attach a wire to the wreath base to hang the wreath. Slide the wire through the base, leaving a looped hook on top; twist and cut the ends.**

2. **Cover the wreath base with dry leaves, using hairpins to hold it in place. Work in one direction around the base from the inside of the wreath outward. Attach thin-stemmed leaves in clusters and large leaves individually. For pizzazz, combine foliage of different colors and textures.**

3. **After you cover the base, add accents. Secure small fruits and berries with hairpins or glue. Secure larger fruits, such as baby pumpkins or lady apples, by using floral picks (available at craft and floral supply stores). Place these larger items sparingly as focal points.**

Making Cut Flowers Last

If you're cutting flowers for arrangements, care in harvesting and handling helps them last — which means that you can enjoy them longer.

- Use sharp shears and cut the flowers in the early morning (before too much moisture has transpired from the plant).

- As you cut, put stems directly into water — carry a water-filled bucket into the garden with you.

- As soon as you bring the flowers indoors, remove the lower leaves that will be below the water in your vase. Submerged leaves cloud the water and can give off an unpleasant odor.

- Recut stems under water before placing them in the vase.

- Use flower food in the vase water. It promotes water uptake and helps control microorganisms that cloud the water.

- Change the vase water every couple of days.

- Place your bouquet in a cool spot, out of direct sunlight and away from heating vents.

Some large flowers with hollow stems, such as delphiniums and amaryllis, last longer if you first hold the stems upside down and pour water into them. Then plug the base of the stem with cotton.

Experience has shown that certain flowers, including Iceland poppies, euphorbias, and hollyhocks, need to have their stems sealed by searing to prevent them from drooping. Immediately after cutting, hold each stem over a flame for a few seconds or dip the stems in boiling water for a couple of minutes.

Plants with woody stems, such as lilacs, forsythias, and pussy willows, require a slightly different treatment. Their stems need to be split or smashed to help with the uptake of water. One way to accomplish this is to pound the bottom few inches of each stem with a hammer. As an alternative, use a sharp knife or clippers to cut several times an inch or so deep into the stem (see Figure 25-3).

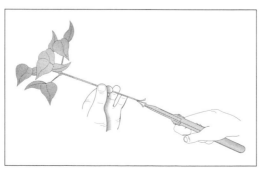

Figure 25-3:
Use clippers or a sharp knife to slice woody stems.

Chapter 26

Ways to Stretch the Garden Season

In This Chapter

▶ Getting a jump on spring

▶ Using cold frames and season extenders

▶ Holding back autumn

*W*hen you live in a northern climate, you're stuck with a short growing season. If you want to increase your garden bounty, you need to squeeze in a few extra weeks of plant growth both earlier and later in the year. By utilizing some of the techniques described here, you can enjoy the advantages of gardeners one or two zones milder.

Planting Earlier in the Year

Gardeners are master manipulators and have devised all sorts of ways to get a jump on spring. The first is simply to plant early. Here's how to get away with it:

✔ **Start plants indoors.** Cool-season plants, such as lettuce and broccoli, tolerate light frosts. Start them indoors, timed so they'll be ready for transplanting about three to four weeks before the average last frost date.

You can start frost-tender plants — such as tomatoes, peppers, squash, and eggplant — early, too. Plan on transplanting them under protective cover (described later in this section) about two weeks before the average last frost date.

✔ **Use a cold frame.** A *cold frame* speeds seed germination and shelters plants from frost. The frame is a bottomless box, usually constructed from wood. It has a slanting, tight-fitting top made of old windows or other transparent or translucent materials such as plastic or fiberglass. A typical frame is approximately 3 feet wide and 6 feet long with an 18-inch-high back sloping down to 12 inches high in the front. (See Figure 26-1.)

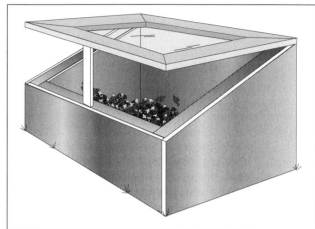

Figure 26-1:
Use a cold frame to protect young plants in early spring.

Place the frame outdoors, over a garden bed or against the south wall of your home. Orient it so it slopes to the south. The sun warms the air and soil inside, creating a cozy environment for plants. Sow seeds for transplants directly in the cold frame. (Or grow crops such as radishes, spinach, beets, and lettuce to maturity in the frame.)

Prop the top open during the day for ventilation and lower it at night to conserve heat. If you can't check the frame regularly, consider buying a thermostatically controlled vent opener as insurance against cooking or freezing your plants.

If you like the idea of a cold frame but want even greater temperature control, consider a *hot bed*. It's essentially a cold frame with a heat source (commonly electric heating cable) to warm the soil. The cable usually includes a built-in soil thermostat preset for about 75°F, ideal for germinating most seeds. Cable with a thermostat and plug is sold by wattage and length.

When tender plants are ready for the garden, you'll need to protect them from frost. Here's a rundown of useful frost guards:

✔ **Why not hot caps?** These are individual covers that work like miniature greenhouses. They can be homemade or store bought. To make your own, cut the bottom out of a plastic gallon milk jug. Anchor it in the ground with a stake and leave the cap off so your plant doesn't bake inside. Commercially produced hot caps are made of translucent wax paper, plastic, or fiberglass.

✔ **Set up a Wall O' Waters.** A ring of connected, water-filled plastic tubes forms a small teepee, which is used to enclose an individual plant. During the day, the water in the tubes absorbs solar heat. As the water cools down at night, it releases heat slowly, protecting the plant inside from temperatures down to 16°F. Use them to protect seedlings from late spring frosts.

✔ **Use row covers.** Drape lightweight synthetic fabrics, called *floating row covers,* over the plants. They let light and water pass through while protecting plants from temperatures as low as 24°F (depending on the fabric used). The fabrics are available in a variety of widths and lengths. (See Figure 26-2.)

Row covers of slit plastic are cheaper but usually require more work because they need to be supported by hoops or a frame. You also have to pull the plastic aside to water. Plastic covers create higher daytime temperatures than fabric, which may be advantageous when you're trying to give heat-loving plants, like peppers, a boost in cool weather.

✔ **What about junk from your house?** Every so often, an unexpected late spring frost catches you off guard. Usually, the frost prediction comes about the time the garden is dotted with green, tender, young plants. To save plants, rummage around for anything that may protect them without crushing them. Cardboard boxes, old sheets, empty buckets, or even newspaper spread over the plants lend a few degrees of protection. Just remember to remove the stuff the following day, or the plants may bake.

In addition to providing frost protection, serious cold-climate gardeners often warm the soil in early spring before planting. They spread a soil-warming, plastic-type mulch over the soil surface and cut holes in it for the transplants. After planting, they protect plants with floating row covers.

Clear plastic has traditionally been the mulch of choice for heating the soil, but weeds really thrive under it. Now you can use a new high-tech option called *IRT mulching film.* This green film heats up the soil as well as clear plastic but blocks the portion of the light spectrum that supports weed growth. (Clear plastic is used to *solarize* soil in summer, that is, heat the soil sufficiently to destroy insects, fungi, and weed seeds.)

Figure 26-2:
Lay lightweight row covers directly over seedlings or support them with wire hoops. Plastic row covers develop more heat and must be vented.

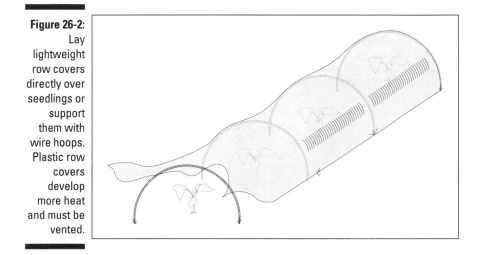

Extending the Season into Autumn (and Beyond?)

Now that you've got a jump on spring, consider these tips on foiling the first frosts of autumn:

- ✔ **Cover up again.** You'll often face an occasional light frost before the first big killer. On those crisp, clear evenings when a light frost is forecast, throw a few bedsheets or floating row covers over tender crops. With little effort, you can prolong the harvest of summer crops.

- ✔ **Spray-on frost protection.** What if you forget — or are just too tired — to cover up crops on a chilly evening? Well, you have a second chance to save them (after you've rested, of course). Turn on your garden sprinkler during the late-night hours (as soon as the temperature drops below 33°F). Leave the water on until the sun has warmed the air above freezing. A fine spray of water is more effective than large water droplets.

- ✔ **Plant again.** Remember those cool-season plants that tolerate frost? You can plant a second crop of those vegetables in mid- to late-summer for a late autumn or winter harvest. They grow fast in the still-warm soil of summer and start maturing about the time tender crops are declining. Kale, beets, chard, and turnips are among the stars of the post-frost harvest.

Gardening All Year

Frost is the culprit that usually dictates the beginning and end of the gardening season. Planting dates revolve around the first and last average frost dates. If you don't know the dates for your area, ask a nursery professional or call your Extension office. The Extension system number is usually listed in the phone book among the state university numbers or under *Extension* in the business section.

In mild-winter regions, where an occasional light frost is as bad as it gets, the best way to stretch the season is to keep on gardening right through winter. Winter gardening has many benefits: Pest and disease problems are fewer; you don't have to water much, if at all; and winter crops are varied, nutritious, and delicious. In addition to the cool-season vegetables (see Chapter 19 for more on vegetables), annual flowers such as calendula, stock, and primula thrive in winter. Autumn is prime planting time for winter gardening, although some crops, such as lettuce and beets, can be planted in succession throughout the winter.

If you want to reap every last tomato in autumn but don't want to hassle with protecting individual plants from frost, you have a couple of other options:

- ✔ Pick your green tomatoes right before the first frost. Arrange them in a single layer on a shelf or table and cover them loosely with newspaper. Check frequently for ripeness and toss any that start to rot.

- ✔ When frost is predicted, cut or pull your plants and pile them together. Cover the pile with plastic. The tomatoes will continue to ripen.

One important strategy for getting your tomatoes, eggplants, peppers, and melons before the frost gets them is to grow what are called *short season* or *early* varieties. These plants mature much more quickly than their "long season" relatives. An 'Ichiban' Japanese eggplant, for example, takes only 61 days to reach maturity, while the Italian heirloom, 'Rosa Bianca', takes 75 days.

Chapter 27

How to Support Climbing Plants

In This Chapter

▶ Using naturally ascending plants (and helping those that don't)

▶ Checking out freestanding plant supports

▶ Gardening with trellises

Although the chief purpose of trellises and other supports is to hold up climbers, trellises and their kin also add height to the garden and maximize ground space. These structures can be decorative as well as practical when they turn a plain wall into a vertical garden, frame a view, or create a privacy screen.

Some climbing plants naturally cling to their supports, but others must be trained and tied. Examples of plants that attach naturally are sweet peas (with coiling tendrils), clematis (with coiling leaf stalks), bittersweet (with twining stems), English ivy (with rootlike holdfasts), and Boston ivy (with adhesive discs). Jasmine and climbing roses are examples of plants that require tying.

Recycled nylon hosiery, cut into strips, is one of the very best materials for tying plants to their supports. Nylons are strong, yet stretchy, so they won't bind and cut plant stems.

The most important guideline for choosing a structure is that it be large and sturdy enough to support the plant when fully grown. Choose a simple garden structure that harmonizes with your home and existing garden features.

Raising Canes

Most types of vines may be grown on one or more of the supports described here. (The exception is vines with adhesive disks, which grow best on stone or brick walls.) When choosing a structure for your garden, first consider the type of plant that you are growing and how it will fit and look on the structure. After that, your choice is a matter of personal taste, maintenance considerations, and budget.

Bamboo teepees

Perhaps you remember bamboo teepees from your childhood. Bamboo teepees have long been popular in vegetable gardens for supporting climbing green beans. Teepees are quick and easy to make, and the bamboo stakes can be reused for many garden seasons. (See Figure 27-1.)

Figure 27-1: Bamboo teepees are popular for supporting vegetables like peas and beans.

To make a teepee, arrange three or four 12-foot bamboo stakes around a -3 to 4-foot circle. Space them at least 18 inches apart. Push each stake into the ground at least 12 inches deep. Lash the top of the stakes together with twine.

Plant beans (or other annual climbers) at the base of each stake. As the beans start to grow, direct them up the stakes; once started, the plants won't need additional training or tying. At the end of the season, clean off the bamboo and store it indoors.

Teepees can serve double-duty when they provide support for climbers and create shade beneath for plants, such as lettuce, that prefer cooler temperatures.

Mini-teepees of $1/4$- or $1/2$-inch-diameter bamboo canes (often dyed green and sold at garden centers) are useful supports for annual climbers in containers. Try planting sweet peas or nasturtiums at the teepee's base.

Chain-Link Fences

Okay, so chain-link fence is not the most attractive plant support, but such fencing is strong and durable. Chain-link's industrial appearance practically screams to be cloaked in greenery. For an attractive barrier or privacy screen, plant a climbing rose at the base of a chain-link fence. (The links provide both air circulation and spaces for tying branches.) Or cover the fence with a dense climber (such as evergreen *Hardenbergia*) or an annual vine (such as morning glory).

Metal Trellises

Chic, freestanding metal trellises come in many shapes and sizes. Such trellises are whimsical to formal in design and are made from a variety of materials, including copper tubing, epoxy-coated wrought iron, and galvanized steel (with a hardened oil finish). Metal trellises are sturdy and easy to install (simply push their feet into the soil), but they're not very wide (most are less than 2 feet wide). Metal trellises look most attractive when placed in front of simple walls, and then draped with a single vine. Expect to pay $50 to $100 (or more!) for each trellis.

For an impressive selection of decorative metal trellises, check the catalogs in Appendix C.

Latticework Trellises

Premade lattice trellis is usually constructed of wood, although trellises made of plastic are also available. Lattice is designed for mounting on walls or fences; or attach it to fence posts to make inexpensive screens. Look for lattice at lumberyards and home-building centers.

When securing lattice directly to a solid surface, extend connecting supports several inches beyond the solid surface so that the trellis does not lie directly upon the surface. This extra space improves air circulation around the plant, which helps reduce pest and disease problems.

To make house painting or other maintenance easier, fasten the latticework to hinges at the bottom so that you can lay the trellis back for easy access to the wall. Use metal hooks and eyes to attach the lattice to the wall at the top. Many vines, including star jasmine *(Trachelospermum jasminoides)* and winter jasmine *(Jasminum nudiflorum)* are flexible enough to bend as you raise and lower the lattice.

Sturdy lattice is also suitable for attachment to the top of a wooden fence; such lattice adds height to the fence and extends the growing area. Two vines useful for topping fences are evergreen clematis *(Clematis armandii)* and Spanish jasmine *(Jasminum grandiflorum)*. The latter plant gives an open, airy effect.

Fan Trellises

Made from wood or plastic, store-bought fan trellises come in many sizes. Each fan trellis generally supports a single climber. You can use fan trellises in much the same way as you would use lattice. A fan trellis can also be used to support a climber in a container. Try to secure the fan trellis to the inside of container before planting in the container. (This task is easiest to accomplish if you use a wooden trellis and a wooden container.) Grow annual vines, such as sweet peas or black-eyed Susan vine.

Plastic Netting

Lightweight plastic netting (often in an unobtrusive green) is a quick fix for vining vegetables like pole beans, peas, and cucumbers. Plastic netting is easy to install: just suspend it between vertical posts. Although some types of plastic netting are ultraviolet-resistant and can last for years, patience is required to remove old vines and tendrils without cutting or ripping the mesh.

Pillars

Simply put, a pillar is a sturdy, rot-resistant wood or metal post set in the ground. (Perhaps you have a lamp post just waiting for a vine.) Pillar dimensions can vary, but the pillar's base should be buried at least 2 feet deep. Climbing roses are a traditional pillar plant. Examples of good pillar roses are 'Dortmund' (cherry red with white eye), 'Cl. Iceberg' (white), and 'Sombreuil' (white). You need to use ties to train roses up a pillar.

Wall-Mounted Supports

If you have masonry walls, you can create a sturdy support system with galvanized wire. Thread 14- or 16-gauge wire through eye bolts attached to the wall with expanding anchors. Arrange the wires horizontally, vertically, or in a fan shape, depending on the space and the plant to be grown. This system is sturdy and supports heavy climbers like roses and honeysuckles.

As an alternative, simply attach plant ties through the eye screws and eliminate the wires. Either way, extend the eye screws a couple of inches beyond the wall to provide air circulation.

Arbors

Decked with wisteria, bougainvillea, climbing roses, or clematis, an arbor raises the garden to new heights. Arbors may be works of art in their own right, or they may have simple designs, so as to highlight plants without competing with them. A heavy-duty arbor anchors the landscape, creating a feeling of permanence as well as a feeling of comfort. Placed over a path at the garden's entrance, an arbor becomes a welcoming doorway.

Arbors may be homemade or prefabricated. Above all else, they must be sturdy. To avoid damaging the growing plant while working, put the trellis or support in place before planting.

Chapter 28

Tips for Gardeners without Much Garden

● ●

In This Chapter

▶ Finding garden space you didn't know you had

▶ Unifying garden parts

▶ Creating an illusion of space

▶ Using space savers

▶ Planting for small gardens

● ●

*J*ust because your yard is small doesn't mean you have to give up your dreams of a truly satisfying garden. In fact, if you've ever lingered in a small garden that is well-planned and carefully put together, you've probably noticed that the garden has a sense of intimacy and enclosure that most large, sprawling landscapes lack.

Smallness need not dictate the style of garden that you create nor the type of gardening that you do. Whether you are aiming for a serene Japanese-style meditation garden or the country charm of an English cottage garden, the basic techniques for successful small-space gardening are the same.

The following tips and techniques will help you on your way; but before you start digging, review Part 1 of this book on garden planning. Because every inch of available space is critical in small gardens (and every element is seen close up), starting with a cohesive plan is doubly important.

Simple Pleasures

A small garden feels most spacious and harmonious when the design is simple and all the elements work together. Choose a single style or theme for your garden and use this style to connect all the parts, from paving to plants and structures and ornaments. Just imagine how distracting a spewing Goliath of a fountain would be in a tiny, contemplative Japanese-style garden. In contrast, a bamboo spout trickling water onto stone would feel soothing and appear quite natural in such a setting.

To help keep things simple and avoid a hodgepodge, repeat garden elements. For example, rather than planting a wide assortment, use a few types of plants repeatedly in different areas of the garden. Rely on two or three colors that best express the garden's mood. Choose one or two types of paving for walkways and use those same materials throughout the garden to create a visual, as well as a physical, connection.

Details Make the Difference

In a little garden, everything shows. Each plant, ornament, structure, and surface becomes an integral part of the whole. One goal of small-garden design is to create interest and intrigue without adding extraneous *stuff*.

One of the advantages of smallness is that it encourages you to focus on quality rather than quantity. Just a few carefully chosen and well-placed plants or ornaments can transform an otherwise bland plot into an evocative haven. Consider using the following lures (and invent some of your own) to attract attention and keep the viewer from taking in your entire garden at a glance:

- ✔ Bent willow chair flanked by a large pot of tulips in bloom

- ✔ Wall-mounted fountain (saves more space than a freestanding one)

- ✔ Ornamental waterspout protruding from a wall and flowing onto a pebble surface

- ✔ Small pond in a large antique ceramic pot

- ✔ Stone sculpture

- ✔ Clipped boxwood topiary

- ✔ Single raised urn set in brick paving and filled with white daisylike marguerites and geraniums at the urn's base

- ✔ Apple tree trained to a decorative pattern against a fence or wall

Illusions of Grandeur

Visual trickery lies at the very heart of successful small-space gardening. Employ the following strategies to help defy garden boundaries and make your small space feel larger:

✒ **Use plants to blur walls and fences.** Doing so ensures that your eye doesn't abruptly stop at the garden's boundaries.

✒ **Construct gently curving paths.** By curving your paths, you can make them "disappear" at the garden's edge (perhaps at a false gate in a fence) to suggest that more lies beyond. (See Figure 28-1.)

✒ **Vary levels.** Add vertical texture to the garden by using berms, steps, or terraces. Changes in levels add dimension and lengthen the route through the garden, which makes the space appear bigger. Level changes also divert the eye from the garden's boundaries and add an element of surprise as you move through the garden.

✒ **Create depth.** Layer plants at the garden's periphery. Put light-colored or variegated plants in front of taller, darker green ones. Or place shrubs or small trees in front of a vine-covered wall or fence.

✒ **Position cool colors.** Use cool colors, such as blue and violet, toward the farthest edges of the garden. These colors tend to recede and give an impression of distance.

✒ **Install a wall-mounted mirror.** Such a mirror can reflect an intriguing view.

✒ **Draw attention inward and downward.** Use decorative paving or an eye-catching living ground cover.

Figure 28-1:
A curving path, leading out of view, gives the illusion of a larger garden beyond and adds an element of mystery.

  ✔ **Borrow a view.** Expand the boundaries of your garden visually to incorporate a view beyond your property line into your garden design. If, for example, your neighbor has a gorgeous flowering shade tree, situate a bench in your yard to take advantage of the view.

Outer-Space Exploration

There's no such thing as having no space to garden. Take a cue from dandelions: They make room for themselves in the cracks of asphalt-surfaced parking lots. If you feel as though you have no growing space, then create some — on walls and overhead, in containers and window boxes, between pavers and in raised beds. Here's how.

  ✔ **Plant in gaps.** Gardening in the crevices between bricks or stone not only gives you more growing space but also softens the hard look of these surfaces. And plants within paving create a visual link, connecting the hard surfaces with adjacent flower beds or other plantings. (See Figure 28-2.)

  Good gap plant choices provide a thick, low carpet of greenery that stands up to some foot traffic. Certain ground covers add flowers or fragrance as well. See "Top gap plants" later in this chapter for information about plants best suited for gaps.

  ✔ **Create window boxes.** These wall-hung mini-gardens provide a view from inside and outside your window. Mix in a few sweet-scented plants and enjoy the wafting fragrance as well.

  ✔ **Build raised beds.** When space is at a premium, room for large flower beds and borders may be unavailable. Rather than plant large beds and borders, squeeze in a few raised beds spilling over with annuals, perennials, or even vegetables.

Figure 28-2:
Planting
between
steps or
paving has
a softening
effect.

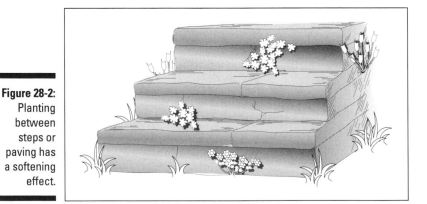

✔ **Cover up with climbers.** Save valuable ground space by growing plants vertically. Use annual or perennial climbers or use wall shrubs — shrubs you can prune until they are nearly flat against a wall. For ideas on how to choose and train climbing vines, see Chapters 8 and 27. For information about good wall shrubs, turn back to Chapters 6 and 7.

✔ **Plant overhead.** Encourage plants up and over arbors and arches to create a cool, green ceiling or a dramatic canopy of blooms. Deciduous plants provide welcome filtered shade in summer and let the warming sun shine through in winter.

Start with simple, sturdy structures that can support the weight and bulk of heavy, woody vines at maturity. A classic plant for garden ceilings is wisteria with its fragrant violet flowers in $1^1/_2$-foot-long clusters. Among edibles, the kiwi vine (with branches to 30 feet long) is a favorite patio cover. Check Chapter 8 for additional ideas.

Use light-weight containers to suspend plants from tree branches or overhead structures. Chapter 22 explains container gardening in detail.

Diamonds in the Rough

Select plants for your small garden as though you were choosing gems for your lover. A plant with the right style, fit, size, and color has the potential to dazzle, just as an inappropriate choice will look and feel awkward. When you select plants, consider the big picture — consider how each plant will contribute to the whole. Bear in mind the following tips when making your choices:

✔ Choose plants that fit your soil type, site (shady, sunny, wet, dry), and climate.

✔ Choose plants in proportion to your house and garden.

✔ Consider the mature size of plants so that you're not eventually faced with either constant shearing or a huge tree devouring the entire garden.

✔ Select plants with well-mannered roots that won't rob their neighbors of garden space, water, and nutrients.

✔ Because flowers are transitory, use them as color accents in a garden well-clothed in trees, shrubs, and vines that remain attractive year-round.

✔ Consider plant forms. Rounded shrubs are good backdrops for spiky accent plants. Pendulous or weeping plants direct attention downward. Use pyramidal or columnar plants for height.

✔ Limit the number of plant varieties and plant forms, and plant in groups to give your garden order.

✔ At the garden's edges, group plants of different sizes, shapes, and textures to create a sensation of depth.

✔ Because too many plants with strong personalities can make the garden's space appear cluttered, choose a few show-offs as accents.

By now, you must be assured that a garden is a garden, no matter what size it is. Even with room for only a few containers of plants and a chair, your garden can be inspiring and satisfying. So go forth and seek out the nooks and crannies.

Top gap plants

Ten excellent plants for planting in crevices are ajuga *(Ajuga reptans)*, blue star creeper *(Laurentia fluviatilis)*, creeping speedwell *(Veronica repens)*, crane's bill *(Erodium chamaedryoides)*, dichondra *(Dichondra micrantha)*, Indian mock strawberry *(Duchesnea indica)*, moneywort *(Lysimachia nummularia)*, partridgeberry *(Mitchella repens)*, sandwort *(Arenaria montana)*, and spring cinquefoil *(Potentilla tabernaemontanii)*.

For fragrance underfoot, thymes are quite reliable. Plant gray-green woolly thyme *(Thymus pseudolanuginosus)*, lemon thyme *(T. citriodorus)*, or mother-of-thyme *(T. praecox arcticus)*. Other fragrant choices include chamomile *(Chamaemelum nobile)*, Corsican mint *(Mentha requienii)*, and yerba buena *(Satureja douglasii)*.

Chapter 29

Best Plants for a Perfumed Garden

In This Chapter

▶ Herbs with the best-scented foliage

▶ Most fragrant annuals and perennials

▶ Perfumed surprises

▶ Trees, vines, and shrubs to grow for fragrance

▶ Sweet-scented bulbs

▶ Award-winning fragrant roses

*F*ragrance has a way of lifting our spirits and stirring good memories as nothing else can. Growing fragrant plants is a sure way to enrich the sensory pleasure of gardening. Sweet scents come with all types of plants — from annuals to shrubs to vines and trees. We tend to focus on flowers when we think of scent, yet many garden plants have luscious-smelling leaves. Certainly the fragrant foliage of lemon verbena or a mint-scented geranium rivals that of many a rose. Although flower fragrances waft on high, leaf fragrance often must be discovered. Only when you rub or crush the leaves of such fragrant delights as Corsican mint or rosemary do they release their aromas.

Here's a sampling of some of the best herbs for fragrant foliage (in addition to smelling great, thyme, lavender, and rosemary are extremely useful and rugged landscape plants):

    Lemon verbena *(Aloysia triphylla)*

    Chamomile *(Chamaemelum nobile)*

    Lavender *(Lavandula)*

    Corsican mint *(Mentha requienii)*

    Scented geraniums *(Pelargonium* species, including *P. citrosum, P. graveolens, P. nervosum, P. odoratissimum, P. quercifolium,* and *P. tomentosum)*

    Rosemary *(Rosmarinus officinalis)*

    Thyme *(Thymus)*

Getting the Most for Your Whiff

Much current garden literature encourages readers to cluster fragrant plants together in a collection. But the most sensual gardens of all are infused with perfumed plants through and through. Cultivate sweet-scented plants in prime locations so that you are certain to catch their drift. Target the following areas:

- ✔ Locate potted plants under windows or on your balcony so that you can enjoy the aromas indoors and out. Perfumed annuals (such as sweet alyssum, carnations, and stocks, which release their fragrance at night) or bulbs (such as freesias and paper-white narcissus) are excellent choices.

- ✔ Frame your front door or garden entrance with a sweet-smelling vine, such as Arabian jasmine or goldflame honeysuckle. Or plant the thornless climbing rose 'Zephirine Drouhin'. Its cerise-pink blooms are strongly perfumed.

- ✔ Cover a sturdy arbor or patio with a robust climber like the old-fashioned wisteria; its fragrant blooms in 1- to 2-foot pendulous clusters are legendary.

- ✔ Edge pathways with fragrant herbs (like lavender and thyme), annuals (mignonette, for example), and perennials (such as chocolate cosmos and lemon daylily).

Flowers Most Possessed with Scent

Don't be shy about cultivating fragrance. In a single gardening season, you can work aroma magic simply by planting fast-growing annuals and perennials. Enjoy the instant fragrance gratification of these plants while your slower-growing perfumed trees and shrubs become established.

Sweet sultan *(Centaurea moschata)*. An annual with erect branching stems to 2 feet with thistlelike, 2-inch, musk-scented flower heads; common colors include lilac, rose, yellow, and white. Sweet sultan is good for cutting.

Chocolate cosmos *(Cosmos atrosanguineus)*. A perennial with deep brownish-red fragrant flowers, nearly 2 inches wide, atop stems to $2^1/_2$ feet. Some say the fragrance is chocolate — others say vanilla!

Pink *(Dianthus)*. Several kinds of strongly fragrant perennial pinks, or border carnations, are available. Tops for fragrance are cheddar pink *(D. gratianopolitanus)*, cottage pink *(D. plumarius)*, maiden pink *(D. deltoides)*, *D.* 'Rose Bowl', and *D.* 'Tiny Rubies'.

Carnations *(Dianthus caryophyllus)*. Perennial, usually grown as an annual. Choose spicy sweet border carnations, which are bushier and more compact than the florist type. Some varieties to look for are 14-inch-high 'Fragrance' in shades of crimson, rose, pink, and white; 1-foot-tall 'Juliet' with scarlet flowers; and 2-foot-tall 'Luminette', also with scarlet flowers.

Common heliotrope *(Heliotropium arborescens)*. A tender perennial, usually grown as an annual. This plant's delightful sweet fragrance comes from clusters of rich purple flowers on 3- to 4-foot-tall stems. The veined leaves have a darkish purple cast.

Sweet peas *(Lathyrus odoratus)*. The old-fashioned varieties are the most fragrant by far. Look for 'Old Spice' and 'Painted Lady'. Other truly fragrant sweet peas are 'Mammoth Mix' and the 'Old Royal' series.

Stock *(Matthiola incana)*. Spicy sweet flowers cluster along erect stems, which are from 1 to 3 feet tall, depending on variety. Flowers of this annual come in shades of pink, rose, purple, yellow, and white and are good for cutting.

Mignonette *(Reseda odorata)*. An old-fashioned annual, considered one of the most fragrant of all flowers. It's been described as having a sweet-pea-raspberry-tangerine scent. The plant itself is not showy; it reaches from 1 to 1^1/$_2$ feet with inconspicuous flowers in dense spikelike clusters. The compact forms are the most fragrant.

Sweet violet *(Viola odorata)*. A perennial, long cherished for its sweet oils, which were extracted for perfumes. It has dark green, heart-shaped leaves and depending on the variety, grows 2 to 12 inches. The plant's flowers (see Figure 29-1) come in shades of deep violet, bluish pink, and white. Sweet violet spreads by runners near the soil surface, and in mild climates it can become a pest.

Some types of flowers are not usually sought after for fragrance, yet particular species or varieties among them are quite nicely scented. So if you're planting peonies, for example, look for 'Myrtle Gentry' with its exceptional tea rose fragrance. Daylilies noted for fragrance include the lemon daylily *(Hemerocallis lilioasphodelus)* and hybrids such as 'Fragrant Light', 'Hyperion', 'Ida Jane', and 'Citrina'. Among tulips, some single early types have a sweet scent. Examples are butter-yellow 'Bellona' and golden-orange 'General De Wet'. Also, the multiflowered *Tulipa sylvestris* has a pleasant, sweet fragrance; the blossoms are yellow with a hint of green on the outer petals.

Figure 29-1:
Old
fashioned
sweet
violets are
deliciously
scented.

Fragrance after Dark

Certain plants release their heady scents only near or after dark. Plant them near the spots where you hang out on summer nights — close to porches and bedroom windows and beside your most comfy garden bench.

Dame's rocket *(Hesperis matronalis)*. Annual in regions with frigid winters; perennial in temperate winter regions. Excellent for the wild garden where it often self-sows. Its branching plants reach 2 to 4 feet high with rounded clusters of richly fragrant phloxlike blooms in lavender or purple. The blossoms are most fragrant at night.

Moonflower *(Ipomoea alba)*. A perennial vine grown as a summer annual. The fragrant white trumpet blooms open to 6 inches wide at sunset.

Evening stock *(Mathiola longipetala bicornis)*. Only 3 to 12 inches tall, this inconspicuous annual with small purplish flowers is extraordinarily fragrant at night.

Flowering tobacco *(Nicotiana alata)*. This wild species has large white flowers that open toward evening on 2- to 3-foot stems. The variety 'Grandiflora' is exceptionally fragrant. (See Figure 29-2.)

Fragrant evening primrose *(Oenothera caespitosa)*. A low-growing perennial with gray-green fuzzy leaves and white, 4-inch blooms that open in the evening.

Night phlox *(Zaluzianskya capensis)*. A perennial where frosts are light and infrequent, but treated as an annual in colder climates. Fragrant 2-inch flowers are dark red with white interiors; the blossoms grow in clusters on wispy stems to 18 inches high.

Figure 29-2:
Plant the 'Grandiflora' variety of flowering tobacco to experience a rich perfume wafting on an evening breeze.

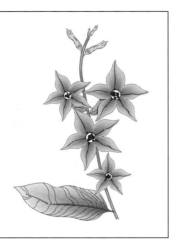

Heavenly Scented Trees, Shrubs, and Vines

We conducted an informal survey among our trusty garden gurus across the country, asking them to name the most pleasantly fragrant trees, shrubs, and vines they grow. Here are 11 of their favorite perfume-packed plants:

Butterfly bush *(Buddleia davidii)*. Sometimes called summer lilac, this deciduous or semi-evergreen shrub grows fast to 10 feet. In summer, small fragrant flowers develop in arching spikelike clusters to 12 inches long. Typical flower color is lilac with an orange eye, although (depending on variety) flowers can be pink, blue, purple, or white.

Daphne *(Daphne species)*. These shrubs can be a bit temperamental, but the flowers' seductive scent encourages serious fragrance fanciers to persist. You can choose from several species, including *D. burkwoodii* (white flowers fading to pink), *D. cneorum* (rosy-pink flowers), *D. mantensiana* (purple flowers), and *D. odora* (flowers pink to deep red with creamy pink throats).

All parts of this plant are poisonous.

Gardenia *(Gardenia jasminoides)*. The classic corsage flower. Depending on variety, these evergreen shrubs grow from 3 to 8 feet high. Gardenias tolerate temperatures of 20°F or even lower, but they need summer heat to grow and bloom well.

Arabian jasmine *(Jasminum sambac)*. A tender shrub that's hardy at best to 25°F and yet is among the most highly scented plants. Known as *pikaki* in Hawaii, it is used for necklace leis, and its essence is distilled to make perfumes. Grows about 5 feet high, and the white flowers are $^3/_4$ to 1 inch wide. The variety 'Grand Duke' has larger flowers with more petals.

Goldflame honeysuckle *(Lonicera heckrottii)*. A sweet-smelling vine that grows up to 12 feet with rose-pink and pale yellow flowers.

Michelia *(Michelia champaca)*. An evergreen tree that grows to 30 feet and has large, glossy leaves and deliciously fragrant, 3-inch, pale orange flowers.

Banana shrub *(Michelia figo)*. A slow-growing evergreen shrub that reaches 8 feet or more. Small creamy-yellow flowers with purplish shading exude a powerful fruity fragrance resembling the smell of ripe bananas.

Sweet olive *(Osmanthus fragrans)*. An evergreen shrub that grows up to 10 feet or more. Easily trained as a small tree or espalier (a plant trained to grow flat against a support). The tiny, inconspicuous white flowers exude a powerfully sweet apricotlike fragrance.

Plumeria *(Plumeria rubra)*. A tender deciduous shrub or small tree with long, pointed leaves and clusters of 2- to $2^1/_2$-inch-wide fragrant flowers. Depending on the variety, plumeria's flowers may be red, purple, pink, yellow, or white.

Cleveland sage *(Salvia clevelandii)*. A rounded, drought-tolerant shrub that grows to 4 feet and has intensely fragrant gray-green foliage. The shrub's lavender-blue flowers are also fragrant.

Lilac *(Syringa)*. Best known is the common lilac *(S. vulgaris)*, with many named varieties. Lilacs grow best in cold-winter regions.

Best Bulbs for Fragrance

Among the bulbs are some of the most highly scented flowers. For more about bulbs, including some of the following, see Chapter 11.

Naked lady *(Amaryllis belladonna)*. Evocatively named because 3-foot-high flowering stalks emerge in later summer, but not leaves. Its pink, trumpet-shaped shaped flowers are about 3 inches in diameter. It is a native of South Africa, hardy to zone 8b (15°F).

Lily-of-the-valley *(Convallaria majalis)*. This hardy and resilient bulb is easy (perhaps too easy) to get started in your own garden. The tiny, hanging, bell-shaped flowers that appear in early spring are wonderfully scented. Many gardeners are introduced to it first by a neighbor who just happens to have some freshly dug clumps. It spreads aggressively, making a good ground cover beneath shrubs such as rhododendrons (see Chapter 7).

Freesia *(Freesia)*. Not all are fragrant, but 'Safari' (yellow), 'Snowdon' (double white), and the red and yellow Tecolote hybrids emit the strong, spicy-sweet scent associated with these spring bloomers.

Hyacinth *(Hyacinthus orientalis)*. These large bulbs are easily forced indoors, (see chapter 11 for details on forcing bulbs)—and you can get special vases to fit them. Several colors are available, and all are equally fragrant. They are so strongly scented that one flowering hyacinth is enough to perfume an entire house. Or plant them outdoors in clumps or in containers.

Lily *(Lilium)*. Lily species include gold-banded lily *(L. auratum)*, Madonna lily *(L. candidum)*, and trumpet lily *(L. longiflorum)*, as well as Oriental lilies, such as 'American Eagle', 'Blushing Pink', 'Imperial Silver', 'Journey's End', and 'Everest'. (Figure 29-3 shows an Easter lily.)

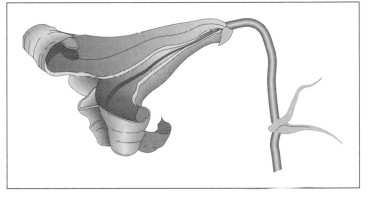

Figure 29-3: The well-known and highly scented Easter lily is the best known type of trumpet lily.

Grape hyacinth *(Muscari azureum)*. It's incongruous: You put your nose next to this flower and smell a glass of fresh grape juice. Flower spikes are about 8 inches high, with clusters of blue flowers.

Narcissus *(Narcissus jonquilla, N. tazetta)*. Jonquils are the shorter narcissus that produce 2 to 4 flowers per flowering stalk. The tazettas include the pure white paper-whites and the golden 'Soleil d'Or'. As is often the case with these highly scented flowers, a single paper white can perfume an entire house, but it's not a scent that's universally loved. Try it for yourself.

Tuberose *(Polianthes tuberosa)*. These tender summer-to-autumn flowering bulbs are native to Mexico. Flowers are heavy and waxy — almost unreal looking. The scent is equally unbelievable. Plant in spring, after frost danger is past.

Tulip 'Bellona'. A bright-yellow, single early tulip hybrid that grows about 12 inches tall.

Redolent Roses

Writing a chapter on gardening for fragrance without acknowledging the plant most associated with fragrance — the rose — is impossible. Nothing is quite like sniffing an old rose (meaning an antique type) for the most intense floral-fragrance experience. Fragrance aficionados can even identify the class of old rose — Tea, China, Damask, and Bourbon, for example — by its characteristic perfume. Entire books are devoted to old roses, and we recommend one in particular that describes and rates flower fragrance (and offers excellent rose-gardening advice): *Landscaping with Antique Roses* by Liz Druitt and G. Michael Shoup (The Taunton Press, 1992).

Modern roses are another story. In their quest for improved flower color and growth habits in modern roses, breeders have sacrificed the fragrance of the older varieties. Some dedicated rose lovers, however, have managed to develop garden rose varieties with the attributes of a modern rose *and* a delicious fragrance. So by choosing varieties carefully, you can have your hybrid tea and smell it, too. The following modern roses have received awards for their intense fragrance (see Chapter 23 for definition of these rose types):

- ✓ **'Chrysler Imperial'** (hybrid tea; rich crimson with darker shadings)
- ✓ **'Crimson Glory'** (hybrid tea; deep crimson aging to purplish)
- ✓ **'Double Delight'** (hybrid tea; cherry-red surrounding creamy center)
- ✓ **'Fragrant Cloud'** (hybrid tea; orange-red)
- ✓ **'Granada'** (hybrid tea; yellow flushed with pink and red)
- ✓ **'Papa Meilland'** (hybrid tea; bright, dark crimson)
- ✓ **'Sundowner'** (grandiflora; orange and salmon-pink)
- ✓ **'Sunsprite'** (floribunda; yellow)
- ✓ **'Sutter's Gold'** (hybrid tea; yellow with red shading on outer petals)
- ✓ **'Tiffany'** (hybrid tea; soft pink with yellow at the petal base)

One last note here on experiencing your favorite floral fragrance: A flower's perfume is usually strongest on warm and humid days and weakest when the weather is hot and dry. For an intense rush of flower fragrance, bring the blossom to your face and lightly breathe into it before inhaling. The warmth of your breath releases the flower's volatile oils.

Part VII
Appendixes

The 5th Wave   By Rich Tennant

"NOW, THAT WOULD SHOW HOW IMPORTANT IT IS TO DISTINGUISH 'FERTILIZING PRACTICES' FROM 'FERTILITY PRACTICES' WHEN DOWNLOADING A VIDEO FILE FROM THE INTERNET."

In this part . . .

*W*e like to think we've answered every question you might have about gardening. But in case we haven't or if, as we hope, you've been bitten by the gardening bug and just have to know even more, here are the resources you'll need. From Appendix A, you can choose books and magazines about all kinds of gardening. If you want to go online and chat with others who share your hobby, check out Appendix B.

Appendix C is your entrée to the world of gardening. Among the listed companies you can find just about anything related to gardening. We also took pains to include some e-mail addresses and Web sites.

Appendix A

Books and Magazines about Gardening

• •

Sooner or later, most gardeners get hooked on books and magazines. There are publications for all gardeners, from those just beginning to those who specialize in a particular type of plant, such as rhododendrons or orchids or wildflowers, or a particular type of gardening, such as edible landscaping or rock gardening or indoor gardening. Because their natures differ, books and magazines tend to treat the various gardening topics in different but complementary ways. Books are ideal for treating broad subjects in depth and for bringing together in one place information that would otherwise be scattered. Magazines are ideal for reporting new trends and seasonal topics and for approaching specific topics from interesting and unusual angles. Using books and magazines together, you can easily form an impressive knowledge base.

The resources included here are predominantly North American, the territory we know best. On every continent — not to mention in every region — you can find gardening information targeted directly to plants and conditions there. Also, international trade rules are still complex enough to discourage easy exchange. All the prices noted here are in U.S. dollars and assume U.S. delivery. We encourage you to seek out the resources where you live, beginning perhaps at local botanical gardens.

Books

Gardeners love gardening books, which not only contain essential information but are a joy to read and to handle. A book exists for every gardener, including those known as armchair gardeners, and for every skill level, type of gardening, and style of garden. Many gardeners turn into passionate book collectors and build extensive libraries of both old and new books.

Gardening books fall into two basic categories: *practical* and *inspirational.* *Practical* books are both how-to books that show you how to do the basic tasks of gardening and reference books that you will refer to over and over. Essential reference books include encyclopedias of plants, dictionaries of gardening terms and practices, and directories of sources. Sources include nurseries and mail-order companies for obtaining seeds and plants, lists of organizations that provide information, and descriptions and addresses of gardens to visit and events to attend.

Gardens are very personal, and your favorite books will be a very personal selection also. Nevertheless, you should watch for the following things when considering the practical type of book:

- ✔ **Plant requirements.** Make sure that any book of plants you buy includes the light, moisture, soil type, and temperature requirements for growing them successfully. It can be frustrating to discover that the "perfect" plant in terms of size, shape, color, and seemingly every other aspect is not cold hardy or heat tolerant for your area.

- ✔ **Plant names.** Beginning gardeners are intimidated by botanical names of plants and find it much easier to use common names, but common names of plants are so ambiguous that planning gardens or buying plants based on common names alone isn't wise. Don't buy a book of plants that doesn't also give the Latin name, or you'll never be sure of getting the plant that you saw in the book.

- ✔ **Conditions in your geographical region.** Climate, soil, and temperature vary; thus, the plants that grow well and the cultivation methods used to make them flourish vary. A book that tells you how and particularly *when* to do tasks such as planting and mulching must address your particular region.

- ✔ **Qualifications of the author.** Look for authors who have experience in the type of gardening that you want to do or the style of garden that you want to create.

- ✔ **Quality and number of illustrations.** Are gardening steps illustrated and clearly labeled? Are photographs in focus and true to color? Are they illustrating the subject, or are they merely big, beautiful pictures? Are they accompanied by captions? If the book is on garden design, are there plans? Are the plans labeled? Do they show plant names? Is the scale clear?

- ✔ **Size and type of index.** Good books have indexes, usually at the back of the book. The best indexes include names of gardens, organizations, nurseries, people, and plants as well as the topics mentioned in the book. Dictionaries and encyclopedias avoid the need for an index by arranging entries in alphabetical order.

Inspirational books are those that stimulate and invite you to stretch your thinking. They are the books that feed your dreams. Inspiration can be visual, with books of exciting full-color photographs, or literary, with works that capture the imagination through the excellence of their writing.

We recommend that beginning gardeners start with one or two general how-to books and a few reference books. When your skill level progresses and your tastes develop, you can branch out and read in-depth treatments of your specific subjects. We selected the practical books in this list because they are both easy for beginners to understand and have content substantial enough to be useful as gardening skill grows.

Where-to-Find-It Books

✔ *Gardening by Mail: A Source Book,* 4th Edition. Barbara J. Barton. Houghton Mifflin, 1994. $18.95 (paperback). If you can afford only one source guide, this is it. Through this book, you can find enough plant and seed sources, garden suppliers and services, professional societies, trade associations, conservation and umbrella groups, horticultural and plant societies, magazines and newsletters, libraries, and books to support any kind of gardening.

✔ *North American Horticulture: A Reference Guide,* 2nd Edition. Compiled by the American Horticultural Society. Thomas M. Barrett, editor. Macmillan Publishing Co., 1992. $75.00. The Cadillac of source guides, it lists organizations, garden clubs, garden centers, programs, educational institutions, museums, gardens open to the public, herbaria, libraries, magazines, and newsletters, but it does not list commercial nurseries. Check out this book at the library.

Basic Gardening Primers

✔ *The 400 Best Garden Plants: A Practical Encyclopedia of Annuals, Perennials, Bulbs, Trees and Shrubs.* Elvin McDonald. Random House, 1995. $40.00. The author lists plants that he believes have the best chance of thriving in your garden. Each entry has a detailed description of the plant, a clear photograph, the conditions that the plant likes, and notes for planting, fertilizing, pruning, and performing other care, with particular attention to regional variations.

✔ *The Garden Primer.* Barbara Damrosch. Workman, 1988. $24.95 (hardcover); $16.95 (paperback). A superb manual for beginners, it gives clear, hands-on instructions for doing every type of gardening. Good descriptions for planting and caring for 300 plants and notes on ones you shouldn't plant. Great value.

✔ *Organic Gardener's Basics.* Barbara P. Lawton and George F. Van Patten. Van Patten Publishing, 1993. $12.95. Two masters deliver what the title says in a small, economical book. Covers irrigation well — one of the most important aspects of gardening that you'll encounter.

✔ *Patios and Decks.* Sunset Publishing Corp., 1979. $9.99.

✔ *Readers' Digest Illustrated Guide to Gardening.* 1978 (reprinted regularly). $30.00. Good line drawings of gardening techniques make this manual especially easy to understand and follow. Good section on identifying plant disorders. Still one of the best overall guides around, though somewhat less tuned to environmental concerns.

✔ *Rodale's All-New Encyclopedia of Organic Gardening: The Indispensable Resource for Every Gardener.* Fern Bradley and Barbara Ellis, editors. Rodale Press, 1993. $29.95. A great manual and plant guide. Includes a section on crafts.

✔ *Sunset Western Garden Book.* Sunset Publishing Corp., 1995. $24.95 (paperback). Sunset has been a pillar of Western gardening for many years, developing 24 climate zones in detailed maps and championing water-wise and earth-friendly techniques. This is an excellent gardening guide, with an extensive plant encyclopedia, a plant selection guide illustrated with color photographs, and a resource directory of gardens to visit and mail-order sources. Not just for the West.

✔ *Taylor's Guide to Gardening Techniques.* Houghton Mifflin, 1991. $18.95 (paperback). A complete guide to planning, planting, and caring for your garden. Very compact — it can be taken to the garden in a big pocket.

✔ *Taylor's Master Guide to Gardening.* Frances Tenenbaum, editor-in-chief. Houghton Mifflin, 1994. $60.00. An authoritative guide to creating and caring for a pleasing home landscape. Gardening manual plus plant encyclopedia that describes 3,000 plants that do well in the U.S. Cold-hardiness ratings are mentioned, as are special plant characteristics such as tolerance of, or sensitivity to, summer heat, humid or dry air, drought, drainage, and lean or rich soil. Includes 1,000 clear color photographs of outstanding plants organized into categories for easy selection. Pays attention to regional and environmental concerns and has a useful bibliography for further reading.

Beyond basic books

After you have been gardening for a while, you will begin to understand the importance of good design and to develop preferences for certain styles of gardens or types of plants. You will probably want to add to your garden — more plants, more decorative ornaments or structures, or even more gardens, perhaps an herb garden, a water garden, or another theme garden. You'll distinguish between ornamental and edible gardens. You'll have more and more questions on how to maintain a healthy garden with less work. You may develop an interest in the history of gardening or succumb to the charm of old books. You'll probably want to travel to see other gardens. You'll want to read more on each of the topics that you're interested in, and you'll be confronted by the seemingly daunting task of choosing the best from among hundreds of books.

Avid gardener Jan Dean has already done a lot of the work for you. In her book *The Gardener's Reading Guide: The Best Books for Gardeners*, published in 1993 by Facts on File, New York, N.Y., she lists 3,000 books by category and gives a brief description of each.

A good way to test books without going broke is to get to know and use your public library or specialized horticultural library. Ask your librarian for recommendations. Borrow books and then buy the ones you like best.

A word about British books

There is a definite cachet to British gardens and British gardeners. Great Britain, with good reason, has been called the garden capital of the world. British gardens are emulated around the world, and some of the best gardeners and garden writers are British.

Gardening in Great Britain, however, is not like gardening in the United States, Australia, Canada, South Africa, or anywhere else, for that matter. Some things that are different are climate, soil, pests, diseases, light, and availability of plants, and how and when to best perform garden tasks. Indoor conditions are different, too. For example, in winter, people in the United States tend to keep their houses hotter and drier. We use different terminology.

Beginning gardeners find some of the how-to advice in British books confusing and the results disappointing. Beginning gardeners seeking how-to books should buy books by authors familiar with the conditions where they will be gardening. Experienced gardeners are better able to filter out advice not appropriate to their situations and, thus, to benefit from exposure to new ideas and different ways of doing things. As you gain gardening skills, we recommend that you do explore the full and wonderful world of garden books, but be cautious at first.

Many plant varieties grown in Great Britain are not available in the United States and strict regulations govern international trade of live plants. So a British book about plants is more useful to you if it has been "Americanized" that is, the author lists alternative plant varieties that give the same effect and gives North American sources for obtaining the plants. Look for books that give plant cold-hardiness temperatures as well as other requirements, such as type of soil preferred and shade, heat, and drought tolerance.

The British excel in matters of taste, plant collecting, and plant breeding. British books on gardens, garden history, garden design, garden ornamentation, floral arrangement, plant exploration, plant breeding and propagation, biography, and essays can be used with far fewer caveats than books whose main intent is to show you how to do it yourself.

Sources of books

Most bookstores have gardening sections, as do many garden centers and nurseries. Here are several mail-order sources:

- ✔ American Horticultural Society, P.O. Box 0105, Mount Vernon, VA 22121; 800-777-7931, extension 36. Sells books at discount to members.
- ✔ Capability's Books, 2379 Hwy. 46, Deer Park, WI 54007; 800-247-8154. Small independent bookstore with a large selection.
- ✔ Edward R. Hamilton, Bookseller, Falls Village, CT 06051-5000. Discounted books are a specialty.
- ✔ The Garden Book Club, 3000 Cindel Dr., Delran, NJ 08075; 800-257-8345.
- ✔ The Organic Gardening Book Club, P.O. Box 4514, Des Moines, IA 50336; 800-678-5661.

Magazines, Newsletters, and Newspapers

Magazines, newsletters, and newspapers are important sources of both information and inspiration and are good values for the money. Magazines publish feature-length articles that cover a wide variety of topics and situations. They usually also give very practical information, such as sources for obtaining plants or seeds, and generally are illustrated with full-color photographs as well as plot plans, diagrams, and botanical drawings. Many do reviews of garden books, a very useful service in helping you decide which books are right for you. Many have regular columns for presenting news, discussing trends, or answering readers' questions.

Magazine issues are published frequently, so articles are often more up to date than books.

Newsletters usually have fewer pages than magazines and look less glossy. They also tend to be more text oriented, generally having fewer illustrations or simple black-and-white drawings and fewer or no advertisements. And they're usually more focused, as they're frequently devoted to a certain style of gardening or a particular region, and may express the opinion of one individual. Most newspapers have gardening columns that appear regularly on a certain day and are good sources of local information. Reading a few of each gives you a good balance of ideas plus sources and means to make those ideas happen.

Hundreds of periodicals publish articles about plants and gardens. Like books, a magazine or newsletter exists for every skill level and type and style of garden imaginable. Start with a few of the most popular national magazines and then add subscriptions to specialty periodicals as you find appropriate. For lists of periodicals and where to obtain them, look at *Gardening by Mail: A Source Book,* 4th Edition (see the "Books" section of this appendix for details).

Some of the leading national magazines are as follows:

✔ *American Horticulturist*. Published monthly. American Horticultural Society, 7931 E. Boulevard Dr., Alexandria, VA 22308-1300; 703-768-5700. Available with membership. $45. Every other month is a news edition.

✔ *Brooklyn Botanic Garden: Handbook*. Published quarterly. Brooklyn Botanic Garden, 1000 Washington Ave., Brooklyn, NY 11225; 718-622-4433. Available with membership. $25. Each issue covers a different topic.

✔ *Fine Gardening*. Published bimonthly. The Taunton Press, 63 S. Main St., P.O. Box 5506, Newtown, CT 06470-5506; 800-283-7252 or 203-426-8171. Subscriptions $28. Articles about flowers and ornamental gardens.

✔ *Flower & Garden*. Published bimonthly. KC Publishing, Inc., 700 W. 47th St., Ste. 310, Kansas City, MO 64112. $14.95. Subscriptions: P.O. Box 7507, Red Oak, IA 51591-0507; 800-444-1054.

✔ *Garden Design*. Published bimonthly. Meigher Communications, 100 Avenue of the Americas, New York, NY 10013; 212-334-1212. $24. Subscriptions: P.O. Box 55458, Boulder, CO 80322-5458; 800-234-5118. Splashy and fun.

✔ *Garden Gate*. Published bimonthly. August Home Corp., 2200 Grand Ave., Des Moines, Iowa 50312; 800-978-9631. $19.95. Articles about home gardening and design.

✔ *Horticulture: The magazine of American gardening*. Published ten times a year. 98 N. Washington St., Boston, MA 02114; 617-742-5600. $26.

✔ *National Gardening*. Published bimonthly. National Gardening Association, 180 Flynn Ave, Burlington, VT 05401; 802-863-1308. $18. Subscriptions: P.O. Box 52874, Boulder, CO 80322-2874; 800-727-9097. Articles about all aspects of home gardening.

✔ *Organic Gardening*. Published nine times a year. Rodale Press, 33 E. Minor St., Emmaus, PA 18098; 215-967-5171. $25. Vegetable gardening. Subscriptions: Box 7320, Red Oak, IA 51591-0320; 800-666-2206.

Many fine periodicals specialize in a type of plant or style of garden. Some examples are *Herb Companion, Rock Garden Quarterly, American Cottage Gardener,* and *Wildflower*.

Some of our favorites are the region-specific periodicals. These include *Pacific Horticulture, Chicagoland Gardening, Southern California Gardener, Rocky Mountain Gardener, Texas Gardener, Carolina Gardener, Green Scene, New England Gardening News,* and *Minnesota Horticulturist*.

Some general-interest magazines publish articles on gardening. Good ones are *Better Homes & Gardens, House Beautiful, Country Journal, Southern Living,* and *Sunset: The Magazine of Western Living*.

Inquisitive gardeners and travel-minded gardeners also read magazines published in Great Britain, the garden capital of the world. Some good ones are *The Garden, The New Plantsman* (both published by The Royal Horticultural Society), and *Gardens Illustrated*.

Three good newsletters to keep you up to date with what's new in plants, tools, techniques, books, and trends are

- ✔ *The Avant Gardener*. Published monthly. Horticultural Data Processors, Box 489, New York, NY 10028. $20.

- ✔ *HortIdeas*. Published monthly. Greg and Pat Williams, 460 Black Lick Rd., Gravel Switch, KY 40328. $20.

- ✔ *Plants & Gardens News*. Published quarterly. Brooklyn Botanic Garden, 1000 Washington Ave., Brooklyn, NY 11225-1099; 718-622-4433. Available with membership. $25.

Most gardening magazines publish annual indexes to articles appearing in their own magazines. You can also purchase indexes that cover several magazines. Two such indexes are *Garden Literature: An Index to Periodical Articles and Book Reviews* (Garden Literature Press, 398 Columbus Ave, Suite 181, Boston MA 02116, 617-424-1784), and *Gardener's Index* (Compudex Press, P.O. Box 16313, Kansas City, MO 64112).

Appendix B
Gardening Online

• •

▶ America Online
▶ CompuServe
▶ Internet newsgroups and listservs
▶ Gardening sites on the World Wide Web

• •

*W*hen we're not digging, planting, weeding, or harvesting, we're reading about gardens, looking at pictures of gardens, or talking to other gardeners. By connecting to commercial online services or to the Internet, we get a lot of useful information and — sometimes — manage to solve problems that stump the local, over-the-fence experts.

Online gardening information falls mostly into four categories:

✔ Discussion with other gardeners

✔ Reference material, such as Extension office pamphlets and plant dictionaries

✔ Connections to commercial (and nonprofit) sources for tools, seeds, and specialty equipment

✔ Pictures of gardens and specimen plants

Tying into this online world has never been easier. Basically, all you need are a Macintosh or a PC running Windows 3.1 or Windows 95, a modem, and the appropriate software. You can buy this software at any bookstore or any computer store, or you can get it free by contacting America Online (AOL) or CompuServe. The software connects you to both their services and the Internet. Expect to pay charges based on the number of hours you're online.

Call AOL customer relations at 800-827-6364. Call CompuServe at 800-848-8199.

Online conversations come in three forms: sending messages directly to another person's online address (electronic mail, or *e-mail*), chatting with someone in real time by typing messages back and forth in electronic conference rooms, and posting messages on the electronic equivalent of a bulletin board (or *message board*).

In this appendix, we don't cover how to use the Internet or commercial online services. For that information, some great books in the *...For Dummies* series can get you going in a hurry — like *America Online For Dummies,* 2nd Edition, by John Kaulfeld, and *CompuServe For Dummies,* 2nd Edition, by Wallace Wang (both published by IDG Books Worldwide, Inc.). Check out those books if you don't understand some of the terminology used in this appendix. But don't let your lack of knowledge deter you from sampling the pleasures of online life.

Commercial Online Services

You can find many commercial online services, but AOL and CompuServe offer the best gardening resources. They also supply access to e-mail, Usenet newsgroups, and the World Wide Web on the Internet. You can pretty much have access to the entire online world, with either service.

America Online

AOL has a slick, easy-to-use interface that compensates for limited resources and sporadic connection problems. A good starting point is The Garden Spot (keyword: **Garden**), which includes a handful of short articles from *Home* magazine (*Home* magazine's "Home & Garden"), about two dozen columns on lawn and garden care (UHA's Garden & Landscape), a spot to order books (Gardening Bookstore), and three gardening message boards: Flower Talk (sponsored by 800-FLOWERS), The Garden Club (sponsored by *Woman's Day*), and The Gardening Message Center. In addition, other AOL sponsors, such as *Sunset* magazine, provide gardening-specific information. An additional button links you to garden-related sites on the World Wide Web.

To access information, click on an interesting subject, and you'll find yourself reading strings (*threads* in online jargon) of messages. In The Garden Club, each new subject receives its own folder, which holds replies to the original message. Because The Garden Club's message area is not very active, weeks sometimes pass without responses, although interesting discussions feature new contributions almost every day.

The Gardening Message Center is more useful, if more chaotic. Each message is listed as its own subject, and no real sorting exists. In practice, this setup can mean scrolling through hundreds of messages, looking carefully at the subject lines. Fortunately, the message center permits searching messages by date and subject. The strength of the Gardening Message Center lies in regular contributors who share their expertise.

CompuServe

CompuServe is a vast but well-organized service. It can be harder to navigate than AOL, but it offers much better reference material, sometimes for an extra charge. For example, Magazine Database Plus (**GO MAGDB**) supplies indexes and full text from several hundred consumer magazines (including *Horticulture, Sunset,* and *Organic Gardening*), in many cases going back a decade or more. Retrieving or reading each article costs $2.50.

A better bet on CompuServe is The Gardening Forum (**GO GARDEN**), operated by, *ahem, National Gardening* magazine. Like most CompuServe forums, it is divided into three areas: conference rooms for live chat, a library section, and a message section. The library and message areas are further divided by 21 subjects that range from vegetables, herbs/mushrooms, orchids, and fruits/ nuts/berries to areas dealing with greenhouses, seed swaps, soil, and fertilizers. Many libraries stock articles from past issues of *National Gardening* magazine, while others feature handy software tools. For example, in the library "Tools/ Books/Software," you'll find a comprehensive list of gardening Web sites.

In addition, some of the libraries feature some great pictures; the Roses library, for example, features close-ups of various roses. Because the message areas are organized by subject and then by topic, you'll find it easier here to follow (or join) discussions on a gardening subject than anywhere else in cyberspace. Each message area is directed by an expert, which generally means that the information is more reliable than the blather that appears on unsupervised bulletin boards. Figure B-1 shows a sample of the Gardening Forum.

Figure B-1: CompuServe's Gardening Forum is divided into two broad categories: a bulletin board (left) for messages and chat and a library (right) for reference material.

Library 11 (Tools/Books/Software) is one of the easiest places online to find and try shareware and freeware programs for garden design. The corresponding message area (bulletin board) is the best place to get help making the software work.

The Internet

The Internet is a vast, sprawling, anarchic network of millions of people, including every science or math professor who made your college years a living hell and scores of bureaucrats and university researchers, thanks to its roots in the academic and government worlds. Fortunately for gardeners, some of those bureaucrats work for the U.S. Department of Agriculture or state departments of agriculture, and some of the researchers are attached to the best agriculture schools in the world. As an upshot, the Internet is packed with information about gardening, horticulture, and botany. And you'll even find people to talk to about the fat, green, creepy-crawlies on your eggplants or the sap-sucking dust on the underside of your snapdragon leaves.

The Internet is actually a collection of networks and services. The World Wide Web is the most glamorous service of the Internet, providing those cool graphics and Web pages to your *Web browser* (see the "Web Sites" section of this appendix). *Gophers* are huge archives of text. *Usenet newsgroups* are worldwide discussions of a single topic. And e-mail, while considerably less glamorous than these other features, is actually the most popular offering of the Internet.

Check out *The Internet For Dummies,* 3rd Edition, by John Levine or *Netscape and the World Wide Web For Dummies,* 2nd Edition, by Paul Hoffman (both published by IDG Books Worldwide, Inc.) for instructions and information.

Talking (or typing): Usenet newsgroups for gardeners

Depending on your software and personal preferences, you can join conversations on any number of subjects, either by reading and posting messages to a Usenet newsgroup or by getting and sending e-mail, usually from a program named *listserv.*

You reach newsgroups by typing an address (see the bulleted list coming up for a look at some addresses). Newsgroups are organized by subjects, some broad and some very narrow. When you read through the postings on a newsgroup, you're reading through a query and the responses. (However, many Internet users reply to messages directly to the sender via e-mail instead of leaving responses in the postings; therefore, newsgroups and lists often resemble heaps of unanswered questions.) If you have a question, you can jump right in and submit your own posting. Luckily, some of the newsgroups are moderated, which means that a designated person looks through the potential messages and weeds out the unnecessary ones.

Three main newsgroups take care of most gardeners' needs:

- ✔ rec.gardens. Busiest of garden-related bulletin boards, sometimes getting several hundred messages per day. In its raw form, rec.gardens is chaos. Tame it by searching the index at Prairienet's Web site (see the "Web Sites" section of this appendix).

- ✔ rec.gardens.orchids. Deals with growing, hybridizing, and caring for orchids. Most common question is "How do I get my orchid to bloom?"

- ✔ rec.gardens.roses. For those who don't believe that a rose will smell as sweet by any other name.

Other newsgroups for gardeners are:

- ✔ alt.folklore.herbs
- ✔ alt.landscape.architecture
- ✔ alt.sustainable.agriculture
- ✔ bionet.plants
- ✔ rec.arts.bonsai
- ✔ sci.agriculture
- ✔ sci.agriculture.beekeeping

Cutting through the clutter

A newsgroup can be a rather chaotic source of information, especially with some of the broader groups. Unless you have several hours a day to read through newsgroup postings, you'll want to tame that beast through some careful planning. That's why you should begin any newsgroup participation by reading through the group's *Frequently Asked Questions,* or FAQs, which distill the collective wisdom of the newsgroup into one easily read document. Chances are pretty good that someone else has attempted to solve the same problem you're having and that someone else knew the answer. In these cases, the newsgroup moderator plucks the problem and the solution from the general discussion and places them in the FAQ. By solving your problem through the FAQ rather than posing the question of the entire newsgroup, you're saving the time of other newsgroup participants, who tire of reading the same questions endlessly. You can often find FAQs in messages sent to the entire group; you can also find them on other Internet sites (such as many of the Web sites that we list later in this chapter). Very often, you can bypass the vast majority of messages in a newsgroup in favor of a FAQ.

Mailing lists

Another method of taming newsgroups is by subscribing to a *mailing list,* which takes the contents of a newsgroup and sends it out via e-mail. This isn't always a good thing — subscribing to the rec.gardens mailing list, for example, will swamp your mailbox unless you ask for a *digest,* which is a condensed version of the newsgroup.

Not every newsgroup has a mailing list; those that do usually include subscription information in its FAQ. However, it's not very difficult to subscribe: You send an e-mail message to an e-mail address (the address usually begins with *listserv,* which is the software that handles the mailing) with the single line message

```
SUB LIST-L Your Name
```

where *LIST-L* is the name of the list and *Your Name* is, well, your name. The software is smart enough to figure out your e-mail address.

You'll know that you've successfully subscribed when you get an acknowledgment from the listserv. If you weren't successful, check the postings of the newsgroup for specific instructions on subscribing. After you've subscribed, ask for the list in digest form (a whole day's messages in one e-mail) — it's much easier to download and read offline than online, provided that the list supports a digest. To do that, send the listserv the single line message

```
SET LIST-L DIGEST
```

Posting a message to the list is simplicity itself: Send it as an e-mail message to the listserv address.

Table B-1 lists some mailing lists that you may want to subscribe to.

Table B-1	Some Key Gardening Mailing Lists	
Name	**Focus**	**Address**
gardens	Main list for everyone	listserv@ukcc.uky.edu
hga-l	Hobby greenhouses	listserv@ulkyvm.louisville.edu
bonsai	All permutations of growing artistic little trees	listserv@cms.cc.wayne.edu
brom-l	Discussion of Bromeliaceae plant family	listserv@ftpt.br
cacti_etc	Discussion of cacti and succulents	listproc@opus.hpl.hp.com
chile-heads	Essential forum for *Capsicum* fanatics	listserv@chile.ucdmc.ucdavis.edu
mgarden	Master Gardeners discussion list	listproc@listproc.wsu.edu
mherbs	Medicinal herb mailing list	listserv@trearnpc.ege.edu.tr
herb	Basil, horehound, and other medicinal and aromatic plants	listserv@vm3090.ege.edu.tr
orchids	All manner of orchids	mailserv@scuacc.scu.edu
res-gard	About gardening in Texas	listserv@tamvml.tamu.edu

Chile-heads is a popular list. To get the digest form, send a message to listserv@chile.ucdmc.ucdavis.edu with the single line

```
SUBSCRIBE chile-heads-digest
```

Web Sites

The World Wide Web is a graphical window on Internet resources. Point and click, and away you go. You need a *Web browser* — a tool for navigating the Web. Some Web browsers are Netscape Navigator, Microsoft Internet Explorer, and NCSA Mosaic. However, most Web browsers basically do the same thing, and you'll find that any of the popular Web browsers out there will fill your needs. The chief advantage to using the Web to find gardening information is that the wonderful people who wrote the Web pages did most of the hard work. You mostly click on buttons and occasionally type a search term.

Most gardening sites on the Web have an overload of graphics that can slow you down when you're looking for information. Unless you're deliberately viewing photographs (some great shots of show gardens are available), turn off the graphics on your browser.

Six major gardening centers (and dozens of smaller ones) inhabit the Web. These big ones will point you to the rest:

- AGropolis, The Texas A&M University System Agriculture Program: `http://agcomwww.tama.edu/agcom/agrotext/visitor.html`

  Still under construction, AGropolis not only links to everything else in the universe but also provides terrific Texas A&M publications, most in the Adobe Portable Document Format (.PDF). Most popular Web browsers, such as Netscape Navigator, can read PDF files.

- Garden Gate on Prairienet: `http://www.prairienet.org/ag/garden/homepage.htm`

  Karen Fletcher's gardening resource list and her column about online gardening — "Garden Spider's Web" — are very helpful. She also provides good information for Midwestern gardeners.

- GardenWeb: `http://www.gardenweb.com`

  GardenWeb offers a limited bulletin board area of garden messages broken down into many categories. It's also home to Barry Glick's enthusiastic column "The Cyber-Plantsman" and a good representation of the Brooklyn Botanic Garden and its publications.

- GardenNet: `http://www.olympus.net/gardens/welcome.html`

  Cheryl M. Trine keeps up-to-date links on most new Internet garden resources, including a good selection of botanical gardens that you can visit online.

- Ohio State University's WebGarden: `http://hortwww-2.ag.ohio-state.edu/hvp/Webgarden/Webgarden.html`

  This site includes all the fascinating columns and info — along with thorough information for Ohio gardeners and a super database with 4,000-plus links to horticultural fact sheets from the United States, Canada, and the Netherlands.

These six sites will get you started, but they may not point you directly to any information that you need. When you need more information, use an Internet *search engine*. A search engine takes a word or phrase from you and returns the Web resources containing the word or phrase. Of course, this means that you'll want to be as precise as possible when submitting information to the search engine.

A good search engine is Alta Vista (http://altavista.digital.com/). It's run by Digital Equipment, which claims that it's the most complete index to the Internet. Here's an example: Alta Vista took the term *Bromeliaceae* and returned the addresses and summaries of 110 Web pages containing the term, including http://www.shsu.edu/~stddct/html3/brom/new.html, which happens to be the Bromeliaceae Web Page (really!). By clicking on the address or the title of the page, you're directly connected to that Web page. Access to those 110 Web pages should satiate your need for Bromeliaceae information.

Other popular Internet search engines include Yahoo (http://www.yahoo.com), Inktomi (http://inktomi.berkeley.edu/), InfoSeek (http://www.infoseek.com), and Lycos (http://www.lycos.com).

Appendix C
Where to Find It

● ●

*I*f you're lucky enough to live down the street from a Home Depot, a Lowe's, or some great garden center, you can find just about everything you need to garden. Buying plants from locally owned nurseries is preferable because the plants will be better adapted to your climate. It's different if you live out in the boondocks, or if you're looking for any plant or product that isn't mainstream — and that includes most of the nifty stuff that makes gardens and gardening fun. It's when you're looking for something special that you'll love the following companies. These are our favorite mail-order suppliers of plants, gardening tools, and equipment. Through them, you can find the latest and the weirdest, as well as the run-of-the-mill.

We have noted in the lists that follow which suppliers charge a fee to send a catalog. Most refund the catalog cost with your first order. If no fee is listed, the catalog is free.

Bulbs

Breck's, 6523 N. Galena Rd., Peoria, IL 61632; phone 309-691-4610, fax 309-691-1544. Bulbs direct from Holland.

Caladium World, P.O. Box 629, Sebring, FL 33871; phone 941-385-7661, fax 941-385-5836. More than 20 varieties of fancy strap- and dwarf-leaf varieties.

Connell's Dahlias, 10616 Waller Rd. E., Tacoma, WA 98446; phone 206-531-0292, fax 206-536-7725. Catalog $2. More than 350 varieties.

The Daffodil Mart, 85 Broad St., Torrington, CT 06790; phone 800-255-2852, fax 800-420-2852. More than 1,000 different flower bulbs. Wholesale and retail.

Dutch Gardens, P.O. Box 200, Adelphia, NJ 07710; phone 800-818-3861, fax 908-780-7720. Spring and summer bulbs; perennials.

John Scheepers, 23 Tulip Dr., Bantam, CT 06750; phone 860-567-0838, fax 860-567-5323. Tulips, daffodils, allium, lilies, amaryllis, and hard-to-find bulbs.

McClure & Zimmerman, 108 W. Winnebago, P.O. Box 368, Friesland, WI 53935; phone 414-326-4220, fax 800-692-5864. Wide selection of spring- and autumn-blooming bulbs.

Schipper and Company, USA, P.O. Box 7584, Greenwich, CT 06836; phone 203-625-0638, fax 203-862-8909. Catalog $1. Classic color combinations of tulips.

Swan Island Dahlias, P.O. Box 700, Canby, OR 97013; phone 503-266-7711, fax 503-266-8768. Catalog $3. More than 250 varieties.

Van Bourgondien Brothers, 245 Farmingdale Rd., P.O. Box 1000, Babylon, NY 11702; phone 800-622-9997 (orders) or 800-622-9959 (customer service), fax 516-669-1228. Importers and distributors of bulbs and perennials.

Flowers and Vegetables

W. Atlee Burpee & Co., 300 Park Ave., Warminster, PA 18974; phone 800-333-5808, fax 800-487-5530. Home page: `http://garden@burpee.com`. Wide selection of flower and vegetable seeds and supplies.

The Cook's Garden, P.O. Box 535, Londonderry, VT 05148; phone 802-824-3400, fax 802-824-3027. Wide selection of culinary vegetables, herbs, and flowers, including European and hard-to-find salad greens.

Filaree Farm, 182 Conconully Hwy., Okanogan, WA 98840; phone 509-422-6940. Catalog $2. More than 350 varieties of garlic.

Fragrant Path, P.O. Box 328, Fort Calhoun, NE 68023. Catalog $2. Seeds of fragrant, rare, and old-fashioned plants.

Garden City Seeds, Room 1, 778 Hwy. 93 N., Hamilton, MT 59840; phone 406-961-4837, fax 406-961-4877, e-mail `gcseeds@aol.com` or `gdnctysd@cyberport.net`. Wide selection of seeds. Specialist in open-pollinated, short-season vegetable seeds.

Gurney Seed Company, 110 Capital St., Yankton, SD 57079; phone 605-665-1930, fax 605-665-9718. Full-line seed and nursery catalog.

Harris Seeds, 60 Saginaw Dr., P.O. Box 22960, Rochester, NY 14692-2960; phone 800-514-4441 or 716-442-0100, fax 716-442-9386. Vegetable and flower seeds and gardening accessories.

Johnny's Selected Seeds, Foss Hill Rd., Albion, ME 04910; phone 207-437-4301, fax 207-437-2165. Vegetable, herb, and flower seeds.

Jung Seeds, 335 S. High St., Randolph, WI 53957; phone 800-247-5864, fax 800-692-5864. Wide selection of garden plants and products.

Liberty Seed Company, P.O. Box 806, New Philadelphia, OH 44663; phone 216-364-1611, fax 216-364-6415. More than 1,000 varieties of annual and perennial flowers and vegetables.

Nichols Garden Nursery, 1190 N. Pacific Hwy., Albany, OR 97321-4598; phone 541-928-9280, fax 541-967-8406. Asian and unusual vegetables and herbs.

Park Seed Company, Cokesbury Rd., Greenwood, SC 29647-0001; phone 800-845-3369, fax 800-275-9941. More than 1,800 kinds of bulbs and seeds.

Pinetree Garden Seeds, P.O. Box 300, New Gloucester, ME 04260; phone 207-926-3400, fax 207-926-3886. More than 750 varieties of seeds; also, tools and books.

Ronniger's Seed Potatoes, Star Route, Moyie Springs, ID 83845. Catalog $2. More than 60 varieties of potatoes.

Seeds of Change, P.O. Box 15700, Santa Fe, NM 87506-5700; phone 800-957-3337, fax 505-438-7052. Organic, open-pollinated vegetable, flower, and herb seeds.

Select Seeds — Antique Flowers, 180 Stickney Rd., Union, CT 06076-4617; phone 860-684-9310, fax 860-684-9310. Catalog $1. Vintage flowers for color or cutting; vines for arbors.

Seymour's Selected Seeds, Dept. 92, P.O. Box 1346, Sussex, VA 23884-0346; phone 803-663-9771, fax 803-663-9772. Seeds of cottage garden plants from England.

Shepherd's Garden Seeds, 30 Irene St., Torrington, CT 06790; phone 860-482-3638, fax 860-482-0532. Catalog features European and Asian gourmet vegetables, herbs, recipes, and old-fashioned flower varieties.

R. H. Shumway's, P.O. Box 1, Graniteville, SC 29829; phone 803-663-7271. Wide selection of vegetable seeds.

Southern Exposure Seed Exchange, P.O. Box 170, Earlysville, VA 22936; phone 804-973-4703, fax 804-973-8717. Catalog $2. Over 500 varieties of heirloom and traditional vegetables, flowers, and herbs.

Stokes Seeds, Inc., P.O. Box 548, Buffalo, NY 14240; phone 716-695-6980, fax 716-695-9649. Complete listing of flower and vegetable seeds, including cultural information.

Sunrise Enterprises, P.O. Box 1960, Chesterfield, VA 23832; phone 804-796-5796, fax 804-796-6735, e-mail sunrise@visi.net. Catalog $2. Oriental vegetable seeds and flowering plants.

Territorial Seed Company, 20 Palmer Ave., Cottage Grove, OR 97424; phone 541-942-9547, fax 541-542-9881. Home page: http://www.territorial-seed.com. Vegetable, herb, and flower seeds, especially varieties suited to the Pacific Northwest.

Thompson & Morgan Seed Co., P.O. Box 1308, Jackson, NJ 08527-2225; phone 800-274-7333 or 908-363-2225, fax 908-363-9356. Wide selection of English flowers and vegetables.

Tomato Growers Supply Co., P.O. Box 2237, Fort Myers, FL 33902; phone 941-768-1119, fax 941-768-3476. More than 375 kinds of tomatoes and peppers.

Totally Tomatoes, Dept. 84, P.O. Box 1626, Augusta, GA 30903; phone 803-663-0016, fax 803-663-9772. More than 350 varieties of tomatoes and peppers.

Vermont Bean Seed Company, 32 Garden Ln., Fair Haven, VT 05743; phone 802-273-3400. More than 100 varieties of beans, plus other vegetable seeds.

Herbs

Al's Farm, P.O. Box 1282, Crystal Beach, TX 77650; phone or fax 409-684-8201. Herb, spice, and pepper seeds.

Companion Plants, 7247 N. Coolville Ridge Rd., Athens, OH 45701; phone 614-592-4643. Catalog $3. Wide selection of plants and seeds.

Rasland Farms, NC 82 at US 13, Godwin, NC 28344; phone 910-567-2705. Catalog $3. Herb plants and products for potpourri, teas, and baths.

Richters Herb Company, Goodwood, ONT LOC 1AO, Canada; phone 909-640-6677, e-mail orderdesk@richters.com. Extensive selection of herb seeds, plants, books, and products.

The Rosemary House and Gardens, 120 S. Market St., Mechanicsburg, PA 17055; phone 717-697-5111, e-mail rosemaryhs@aol.com. Catalog $3. Everything for and about herbs.

Sandy Mush Herb Nursery, 316 Surrett Cove Rd., Leicester, NC 28748-9622; phone 704-683-2014. Catalog $4. Unusual culinary herbs and fragrant and native plants.

The Thyme Garden, 20546-N Alsea Hwy., Alsea, OR 97324; phone 541-487-8671. Catalog $2. More than 460 varieties of herb seeds and plants.

Well-Sweep Herb Farm, 205 Mt. Bethel Rd., Port Murray, NJ 07865; phone 908-852-5390. Catalog $2. Unusual and old-fashioned herbs and flowering perennials.

Fruits and Berries

Indiana Berry & Plant Co., 5218 W. 500 South, Dept. NG-96, Huntingburg, IN 47542; phone 800-295-2226, fax 812-683-2004. Strawberries, blueberries, raspberries, blackberries, asparagus, and grapes.

Ison's Nursery & Vineyards, 6855 Newnan Hwy., Brooks, GA 30205; phone 800-733-0324, fax 770-599-6970. Mucho muscadines (grapes for warmer climates), plus dozens of other fruits, large and small.

Lawson's Nursery, 2730 Yellow Creek Rd., Ball Ground, GA 30107; phone 770-893-2141. Wide selection of apples, cherries, peaches, pears, and plums.

Miller Nurseries, 5060 West Lake Rd., Canandaigua, NY 14424; phone 800-836-9630 or 716-396-2647, fax 716-396-2154. Complete selection of fruiting plants, including many varieties of antique dwarf apples.

Northwoods Retail Nursery, 27635 S. Oglesby Rd., Canby, OR 97013; phone 503-266-5432, fax 503-266-5431. Unique fruits and ornamentals.

Pacific Tree Farms, 4301 Lynwood Dr., Chula Vista, CA 91910; phone 619-422-2400. Catalog $2. Extensive collection of citrus, other exotic fruit plants, and rare and unusual trees and shrubs.

Raintree Nursery, 391 Butts Rd., Morton, WA 98356; phone 360-496-6400, fax 360-496-6465. Fruits, nuts, berries, and bamboo.

Stark Bro's. Nursery, P.O. Box 10, Hwy. 54 W., Louisiana, MO 63353; phone 800-325-4180, fax 573-754-5290. Fruit trees and landscape plants.

Womacks Nursery, Rt. 1, Box 80, DeLeon, TX 76444-9631; phone 817-893-6497, fax 817-893-3400. Fruit and pecan trees.

Perennial Plants

Ambergate Gardens, 8015 Krey Ave., Waconia, MN 55387-9616; phone 612-443-2248, fax 612-443-2248. Catalog $2. Many new hardy perennials.

Andre Viette Farm & Nursery, Rt. 1, Box 16, Fishersville, VA 22939; phone 540-943-2315, fax 540-943-0782. Catalog/resource guide/landscaping kit $5. Top perennials from around the world.

Bluestone Perennials, 7211 Middle Ridge Rd., Madison, OH 44057; phone 800-852-5243, fax 216-428-7198. More than 400 perennials.

Busse Gardens, 5873 Oliver Ave. S.W., Cokato, MN 55321-4229; phone 612-286-2654, fax 612-286-6601. Catalog $2. Cold-hardy and unusual perennials and native plants.

Carroll Gardens, 444 East Main St., P.O. Box 310, Westminster, MD 21158; phone 800-638-6334 or 410-876-7336, fax 410-857-4112. Catalog $3. Wide selection of rare and unusual perennials, herbs, vines, roses, and shrubs.

Gilson Gardens, 3059 Rt. 20, P.O. Box 277, Perry, OH 44081; phone 216-259-4845, fax 216-259-2378. Perennials, ornamental grasses, and ground covers.

Goodwin Creek Gardens, P.O. Box 83, Williams, OR 97544; phone 541-846-7357, fax 541-846-7357. Catalog $1. Herbs, everlastings, scented geraniums, plants and seeds for hummingbirds and butterflies.

Heronswood Nursery, Ltd., 7530 N.E. 288th St., Kingston, WA 98346; phone 360-297-4172, fax 360-297-8321. Catalog $4. Rare and hard-to-find trees, shrubs, vines, and perennials.

Klehm Nursery, 4210 N. Duncan Rd., Champaign, IL 61821; phone 800-553-3715, fax 217-373-8403. Peony specialist.

Kurt Bluemel, 2740 Greene Ln., Baldwin, MD 21013-9523; phone 410-557-7229. Catalog $3. Bamboo, ferns, ornamental grasses, perennials, and water plants.

Milaeger's Gardens, 4838 Douglas Ave., Racine, WI 53402-2498; phone 800-669-9956 or 414-639-2371. Catalog $1. Many varieties of hostas, daylilies, and other perennials.

Shady Oaks Nursery, 112 10th Ave. S.E., Waseca, MN 56093; phone 800-504-8006, fax 507-835-8772. Specialist in hostas and other shade perennials.

Spring Hill Nurseries, 6523 N. Galena Rd., Peoria, IL 61656; phone and fax 800-582-8527. Perennials, roses, shrubs, and vines.

Wayside Gardens, Hodges, SC 29695-0001; phone 800-845-1124, fax 800-817-1124. Bulbs, perennials, roses, trees, and shrubs.

Weiss Brothers Nursery, 11690 Colfax Hwy., Grass Valley, CA 95945; phone 916-272-7657, fax 916-272-3578. More than 400 varieties of perennials and herbs.

White Flower Farm, P.O. Box 50, Litchfield, CT 06759-0050; phone 800-503-9624 or 860-496-9600, fax 860-496-1418. Lavishly illustrated catalog includes more than 700 varieties of annuals, perennials, bulbs, and shrubs.

Roses

Antique Rose Emporium, Rt. 5, Box 143, Brenham, TX 77833; phone 800-441-0002, fax 409-836-0928. Catalog $5. Specialist in easy-to-grow old garden roses.

Blossoms & Bloomers, E. 11415 Krueger Ln., Spokane, WA 99207; phone 509-922-1344. Catalog $1. Old roses, perennials, and plants for birds.

Edmunds' Roses, 6235 S.W. Kahle Rd., Wilsonville, OR 97070; phone 503-682-1476, fax 503-682-1275, e-mail edmdsroses@aol.com. Specialist in exhibition and European varieties of modern roses.

Jackson & Perkins, 1 Rose Ln., Medford, OR 97501; phone 800-292-4769, fax 800-242-0329. World's largest producer of new roses.

Justice Miniature Roses, 5947 S.W. Kahle Rd., Wilsonville, OR 97070; phone 503-682-2370. Specialist in miniature roses.

Lowe's Own-Root Roses, 6 Sheffield Rd., Nashua, NH 03062-0328; phone 603-888-2214, fax 603-888-6112. Catalog $2. Many kinds of roses, including climbers and rare varieties.

Nor'East Miniature Roses, Inc., 58 Hammond St., P.O. Box 307, Rowley, MA 01969; phone 800-426-6485 or 508-948-7964. Also: P.O. Box 473, Ontario, CA 91762; phone 800-662-9669 or 909-984-2223. Large selection of miniature roses.

The Roseraie at Bayfields, P.O. Box R, Waldoboro, ME 04572; phone 207-832-6330, fax 800-933-4508. Home page: http://www.olympus.net/gardens/rosebay.htm. Free consultations by phone and $6 video available. Practical roses for hard places.

Roses of Yesterday and Today, 803 Browns Valley Rd., Watsonville, CA 95076; phone 408-724-3537, fax 800-980-7673. Catalog $3. Old, rare, and unusual roses.

Royall River Roses, 70 New Gloucester Rd., N. Yarmouth, ME 04097; phone 207-829-5830, fax 207-829-6512. Catalog $3. 250 varieties of hardy bare-root roses.

Wayside Gardens, Complete Rose Catalog, 1 Garden Lane, Hodges, SC 29695-0001; phone 800-845-1124, fax 800-817-1124. Wide variety of modern, shrub, and antique roses.

Tools and Supplies

Bozeman Biotech, P.O. Box 3146, Bozeman, MT 59772; phone 800-289-6656 or 406-587-5891, fax 406-587-0223, e-mail ewayne@pop.mcn.net. Environmentally friendly products for lawn, garden, and farm.

Garden Trellises, Inc., P.O. Box 105N, LaFayette, NY 13084; phone 315-498-9003. Galvanized steel trellises for vegetables and perennials.

Gardener's Eden, P.O. Box 7307, San Francisco, CA 94120-7307; 800-822-9600. Stylish garden supplies and accessories.

Gardener's Supply Company, 128 Intervale Rd., Burlington, VT 05401; phone 800-863-1700, fax 800-551-6712, e-mail info@gardeners.com. Home page: http://www.gardeners.com/gardeners. Hundreds of innovative tools and products for gardeners.

Gardens Alive!, 5100 Schenley Pl., Dept. 5672, Lawrenceburg, IN 47025; phone 812-537-8650, fax 812-537-5108. One of the largest organic pest control suppliers.

Harmony Farm Supply, P.O. Box 460, Graton, CA 95444; phone 707-823-9125, fax 707-823-1734. Catalog $2. Drip and sprinkler irrigation equipment, organic fertilizers, beneficial insects, power tools, and composting supplies.

Hoop House Greenhouse Kits, Dept. N, 1358 Rt. 28, South Yarmouth, MA 02664; phone 800-760-5192. Hoop house greenhouse kits.

IPM Labs, P.O. Box 300, Locke, NY 13092-0300; phone 315-497-2063. Specialist in beneficial insects.

Kinsman Company, River Rd., FH, Point Pleasant, PA 18950; phone 800-733-4146, fax 215-297-0450. Gardening supplies and fine-quality tools.

Langenbach, P.O. Box 1420, Lawndale, CA 90260-6320; phone 800-362-1991, fax 800-362-4490. Fine-quality tools and garden gifts.

A. M. Leonard, Inc., P.O. Box 816, Piqua, OH 45356; phone 800-543-8955, fax 800-433-0633. Professional nursery and gardening supplies.

Mellinger's, Inc., 2310 W. South Range Rd., North Lima, OH 44452; phone 800-321-7444, fax 216-549-3716. Broad selection of gardening tools, supplies, fertilizers, and pest controls as well as plants.

Natural Gardening, 217 San Anselmo Ave., San Anselmo, CA 94960; phone 707-766-9303, fax 707-766-9747. Organic gardening supplies; tomato seedlings.

Peaceful Valley Farm Supply, P.O. Box 2209 #NG, Grass Valley, CA 95945; phone 916-272-4769, fax 916-272-4794. Organic gardening supplies and fine-quality tools.

Plow & Hearth, P.O. Box 5000, Madison, VA 22727; 800-627-1712. A wide variety of products for home and garden.

Smith & Hawken, 2 Arbor Ln., P.O. Box 6900, Florence, KY 41022-6900; phone 800-776-3336, fax 606-727-1166. Home page: http://www.smith-hawken.com. Wide selection of high-end tools, furniture, plants, and outdoor clothing.

The Urban Farmer Store, 2833 Vicente St., San Francisco, CA 94116; phone 800-753-3747 or 415-661-2204. Catalog $1. Drip irrigation supplies.

Walt Nicke Co., P.O. Box 433, Topsfield, MA 01983; phone 800-822-4114, fax 508-887-9853. Good selection of gardening tools.

Trees, Shrubs, and Vines

Fairweather Gardens, P.O. Box 330, Greenwich, NJ 08323; phone 609-451-6261, fax 609-451-6261. Catalog $3. Trees and shrubs. Large selection of camellias, witch hazel, magnolia, holly, and viburnum.

Forestfarm, 990 Tetherow Rd., Williams, OR 97544-9599; phone 541-846-7269, fax 541-846-6963. Catalog $3. More than 4,000 varieties of native and rare plants, with particular emphasis on plants for wildlife.

Greer Gardens, 1280 Goodpasture Island Rd., Eugene, OR 97401-1794; phone 800-548-0111 or 541-686-8266, fax 541-686-0910. Catalog $3. Specialist in rhododendrons, but offers other rare and unusual plants.

Hughes Nursery, P.O. Box 7705, Olympia, WA 98507-7705; phone 360-352-4725, fax 360-352-1921 or 360-249-5580. Catalog $1.30. Specialists in dwarf, Japanese, and other maples.

Musser Forests, Inc., Dept. 12-B96, P.O. Box 340, Indiana, PA 15701-0340; phone 800-643-8319, fax 412-465-9893. Northern Hemisphere-grown ornamental shrubs, nut trees, evergreen trees, and hardwood trees.

Roslyn Nursery, 211 Burrs Ln., Dix Hills, NY 11746; phone 516-643-9347, fax 516-484-1555. Catalog $3. Many rare and unusual plants.

Siskiyou Rare Plant Nursery, 2825 Cummings Rd., Medford, OR 97501; phone 541-772-6846, fax 541-772-4917. Catalog $3. Hardy perennials, shrubs, and smaller conifers; alpine and rock garden plants.

Water Garden Plants and Supplies

Lilypons Water Gardens, 6800 Lilypons Rd., P.O. Box 10, Buckeystown, MD 21717-0010; phone 800-723-7667, fax 800-879-5459. Specialist in all aspects of water gardening.

Paradise Water Gardens, 14 May St., Whitman, MA 02382; phone 617-447-4711, fax 617-447-4591. Catalog $3. All supplies for water gardening.

Slocum Water Gardens, 1101 Cypress Gardens Blvd., Winter Haven, FL 33884-1932; phone 941-293-7151, fax 800-322-1896 or 941-299-1896. Catalog $3. A nursery of aquatic plants.

VanNess Water Gardens, 2460 N. Euclid Ave., Upland, CA 91784-1199; phone 800-205-2425 or 909-982-2425, fax 909-949-7217. Wide selection of water plants and supplies.

Wildflowers

Agua Viva Seed Ranch, Rt. 1, Box 8, Taos, NM 87571; phone 800-248-9080 or 505-758-4520. Hardy perennials and bulbs in addition to wildflowers.

Clyde Robin Seed Company, P.O. Box 2366, Castro Valley, CA 94546; phone 510-785-0425, fax 510-785-6463. Catalog $2. Wildflower specialists.

Moon Mountain Wildflowers, P.O. Box 725, Carpinteria, CA 93014-0725; phone 805-684-2565. Catalog $3. Wildflower mixes and individual annual and perennial varieties.

Native Gardens, 5737 Fisher Ln., Greenback, TN 37742; phone or fax 423-856-0220. Catalog $2. Native perennials.

Prairie Moon Nursery, Rt. 3, Box 163, Winona, MN; phone 507-452-1362. Catalog $2. Native plants and seeds for wetlands, prairies, and woodlands.

Vermont Wildflower Farm, P.O. Box 5, Rt. 7, Charlotte, VT 05445-0005; phone 802-425-3500, fax 802-425-3504. Seeds of meadow and prairie wildflowers.

Wildseed Farms, 1101 Campo Rosa Rd., P.O. Box 308, Eagle Lake, TX 77434; phone 800-848-0078, fax 409-234-7407. Wildflower seeds by the packet or pound.

Index

• A •

A. M. Leonard, Inc., 33, 150
Aaron's-beard, 113
AARS (All-American Rose Selection), 241
Abelia grandiflora, 69
Abies koreana, 75
Abies nordmanniana, 75
Acanthus mollis, 54
Acer plamatum, 62
Acer platanoides, 62
Acer rubrum, 62
Acer saccharum, 62
Achillea filipendulina, 90
Achillea tomentosa, 112
acidity, 135
action hoe, 34
African daisies, 112
Agapanthus orientalis, 105
AGropolis site, 304
ajuga, 278
Ajuga reptans, 278
alba rose, 239
Alchemilla mollis, 54
alkalinity, 135
allspice, 56
alt.folklore.herbs newsgroup, 301
alt.landscape.architecture newsgroup, 301
alt.sustainable.agriculture newsgroup, 301
Alta Vista, 305
'Altissimo' climbing rose, 237
Aloysia triphylla, 279
alyssum, 93, 233
amaryllis, 262
Amaryllis belladonna, 284
amending soil
   adding nutrients, 137–138
   bad soil, 136–137
   changing pH, 137
   compost, 137

cover crops, 138
fertilizers, 137
good soil, 136
green manure crops, 138
legumes, 138
nonlegumes, 138
organic matter, 136–137
'America' climbing rose, 237
America Online (AOL), 297–298
American Cottage Garden, 295
'American Eagle' lily, 285
American Horticultural Society, 294
American Horticulturist, 295
American Rose, 235
American Rose Society, 235
amethyst, 55
Ammobium alatum, 260
amount of sun
   full sun, 17
   heavy shade, 18
   latitude, 19
   light shade, 17
   position of sun in sky, 19
andromeda, 56
Andromeda polifolia, 56
annual chrysanthemum, 95
annual vinca, 97
annuals, 91–92
   alyssum, 93
   amethyst flower, 55
   annual chrysanthemum, 95
   annual vinca, 97
   bedding begonia, 96
   black-eyed Susan vine, 55
   California poppy, 95
   Canterbury bells, 55
   care, 94
   Chinese forget-me-not, 95
   coleus, 55, 97
   container gardens, 94, 232–233
   cool-season, 91–96

cosmos, 97
drying, 260–261
dusty miller, 95
English primrose, 96
fairy primrose, 96
fertilizers, 170
flowering cabbage or kale, 95
flowering tobacco, 97
forget-me-not, 55
geranium, 96
impatiens, 55, 97
   landscaping with, 93–94
larkspur, 95
'Little Sweetheart' sweet peas, 95
lobelia, 55, 93, 97
love-in-a-mist, 55
Madagascar periwinkle, 97
marigolds, 92, 98
mixing types, 93
monkey flower, 55
nasturtium, 96
nicotiana, 55
pansies, 55, 92, 96
petunias, 92, 97
planting, 92–93
pot marigold, 95
primroses, 92, 96
reseeding themselves, 92
sage, 97
scarlet sage, 55
shade-loving, 55
snapdragon, 94
'State Fair' zinnia, 98
stocks, 96
sunflowers, 97
'Sunspot' sunflowers, 97
sweet alyssum, 96
sweet peas, 94–95
'Thumbelina' zinnia, 98
verbena, 98
violas, 92, 96
warm-season, 91–92, 96–98

annuals *(continued)*
  waxleaf begonia, 55
  when to plant, 141
  wishbone flower, 55
  zinnia, 92, 98
'Anthony Waterer' spiraea, 73
anthracnose, 198
Antirrhinum majus, 94
aphids, 185, 187–188
apical bud, 158
'Apple Jack' rose, 239
apple scab, 198
apples, 211–212
Aquilegia, 55
Arabian jasmine, 283
arboretums, 58
arbors, 31, 128, 272
Arctostaphylus uva-ursi, 112
Arenaria montana, 278
'Argenteo-marginata' holly, 71
aristocrat pear tree, 64
artemisia, 87
Asclepias tuberosa, 227
ash trees, 63
Aster frikartii, 87
asters, 87
Astilbe, 55
'Aurea' fir, 75
'Aureo-variegata' euonymus,
  71
'Aureus' red cedar, 76
Aurin saxatilis, 87
'Aurora' flowering dogwood,
  63
Austin, David, 238
autumn harvest wreath, 261
Avant Gardener, The, 296
Azadirachta indica, 195
azaleas, 72–73, 150

• *B* •

B. t. kurstaki, 193
B. t. tenebrionis, 193
baby gladiolus, 106
baby's breath, 220
Bahia grass, 175
balled-and-burlapped trees,
  146–147
'Baltica' English ivy, 81

bamboo tepees, 270
banana shrub, 284
'Bar Harbor' junipers, 114
barberries, 69–70, 112
bare-root trees, 146–147
bark paths, 121
Barrett, Thomas M., 291
Barton, Barbara J., 291
basket-of-gold, 87
bear's breech, 54
bedding begonia, 96
bee balm, 55
Begonia semperflorens, 96
*Begonia semperflorens-
  cultorum*, 55
Begonia tuberhybrida, 105
begonias, 100, 102–103, 105,
  150, 233
'Belgian Indicas' azaleas, 73
bellflower, 55, 87
'Bellona' tulip, 281, 285
beneficial insects, 184–186
Berberis mentorensis, 70
Berberis thunbergii, 69, 112
bergenia, 55
Bergenia crassifolia, 55
Bermuda grass, 165, 176
berries, 311
Better Homes & Gardens, 295
Betula pendula, 62
bigleaf hydrangea, 71
bindweed, 165
bionet.plants newsgroup, 301
birch trees, 59
birds, 187
  feeding, 224
  gardens for, 223–226
  keeping pest birds away,
    225–226
  watering sites, 224–225
  woodpeckers, 224
bittersweet, 269
black plastic mulch, 131
black spot, 198
black vine weevil, 188
black-eyed Susan, 55, 90, 271
blackberries, 213–214
blanketflower, 88
bleeding heart, 55

blood-red geranium, 89
bloodgood maple, 62
blue fescue, 113
blue grama grass, 110, 176
blue oat grass, 89
blue salvias, 240
blue-leaf plantain lily, 89
blueberries, 213–214
'Blushing Pink' lily, 285
board scraper, 177–178
'Bonica' hedge rose, 238
books about gardening
  advanced, 292–293
  British, 293
  inspirational, 290
  mail-order sources, 294
  practical, 290
  primers, 291–292
  where-to-find-it books, 291
Bordeaux mixture, 197
borders, 83–84
borers, 189
boron, 168
Boston ivy, 77, 81, 269
botanical gardens, 58
botrytis blight, 199
bougainvillea, 80, 150, 272
bourbon rose, 239
boxwoods, 70
Bradley, Fern, 292
bramble fruits, 213
branch collar, 159
brick, stone, or concrete
  pavers, 120–121
bridal wreath spiraea, 73
British gardening books, 293
broad-spectrum insecticides,
  196
broadcasting seeds, 143
broadleaf evergreens, 65–66
*Brooklyn Botanic Garden:
  Handbook*, 295
Browallia, 55
brown rot, 199
Bt, 193
Buck hybrid rose, 239
Buddleia davidii, 227, 283
budget and planning garden,
  24

'Buff Beauty' rose, 239
buffalo grass, 110, 176
bulb bark, 104
bulb food, 102
bulb pans, 104
bulb planter, 148
bulbs, 99
  baby gladiolus, 106
  begonias, 100, 102–103, 105
  bulb food, 102
  buying, 101
  calla lily, 108
  cannas, 106
  caring for, 102–103
  chilling, 101
  common hyacinth, 106
  container forcing, 101,
    104–105
  corms, 99
  crocuses, 103–104
  daffodils, 99–101, 103, 107
  dahlias, 100–103, 106
  dividing, 103–104
  dwarf daffodils, 104
  English bluebell, 100
  fancy-leaf caladium, 105
  fertilizers, 170
  freesia, 106
  giant snowdrop, 106
  gladiolus, 103–106
  grape hyacinth, 100, 107
  hyacinths, 104
  iris, 107
  King Alfred daffodils, 107
  lilies, 103–104, 107
  lily-of-the-Nile, 105
  lily-of-the-valley, 106
  narcissus, 107
  naturalizers, 100
  Persian buttercup, 107
  planting, 101–102, 148
  propagating, 103–104
  replanting, 100
  rhizomes, 99
  scented, 284–285
  snowdrops, 106
  snowflake, 107
  tuberous roots, 99, 104
  tubers, 99
  tulips, 99–101, 104, 107
  when to plant, 141
  where to find, 307–308
  where to plant, 100–101
'Burfordii' holly, 71
bush cinquefoil, 72
butterflies, 218
  basking, 226
  color, 227–228
  drinking, 228
  flower clumps, 227
  pesticides, 228
  proboscis, 227
butterfly bush, 227, 283
butterfly weed, 227
Buxus microphylla japonica,
    70
Buxus microphylla koreana, 56
Buxus sempervirens, 70

• _C_ •

cabbage looper, 189
calcium, 168
Caldium hortulanum, 105
calendula, 220
Calendula officinalis, 95
caliche, 134
California poppy, 95
calla lily, 108
Callistephus chinensis, 220
Calycanthus, 56
camellia, 56, 70
Camellia japonica, 56, 70
Camellia sasanqua, 70
Campanula medium, 55
Campanula persicifolia, 87
Campanula portenschlagiana,
    55
Campanula poscharskyana,
    87-88
camphor trees, 65
candytuft, 89, 150
cannas, 106
Canterbury bells, 55
Capability's Books, 294
'Capital' pear tree, 64
'Carefree Delight' hedge rose,
    238
carnations, 13, 150, 281
Carolina Gardener, 295
carpet bugle, 112
carpet grass, 176
carrier, 169
carrots, 138
Carthamus tinctorius, 260
caterpillars, 187, 189
Catharanthus roseus, 97
cedar trees, 65
  dwarf conifers, 75
Cedrus deodara, 75
celosia, 233
Celosia cristata, 260
Centaurea cineraria, 95
Centaurea moschata, 280
centifolia rose, 239
centipede grass, 176
ceramic pots, 230
Ceris canadensis, 62
Ceris occidentalis, 62
chain-link fences, 270–271
Chamaecyparis lawsoniana, 75
Chamaemelum nobile,
    112–113, 278–279
chamomile, 112 113, 278–279
cheddar pinks, 280
chelated micronutrients, 169
Chicagoland Gardening, 295
chicken-wire fences, 124
China aster, 220
China rose, 239
chinch bugs, 189
Chinese forget-me-not, 95
Chinese jasmine, 81
Chinese juniper, 71
Chinese pistache tree, 64
Chinese praying mantis, 186
Chinese wisteria, 82
chlorine, 168
chlorophyll, 168
chocolate cosmos, 280
chrysanthemum, 88, 150, 220
Chrysanthemum
    cinerariifolium, 195
Chrysanthemum coccineum, 88
Chrysanthemum frutescens, 88
Chrysanthemum paludosum,
    95

Chrysanthemum superbum, 88
'Chrysler Imperial' rose, 286
Cinnamomum camphora, 65
cinnamon basil, 13
'Citrina' daylilies, 281
'Cl. Iceberg' climbing roses,
    272
clay, 20, 132
clearing site, 129
    black plastic mulch, 131
    stripping sod, 130–131
    tilling and cover crop
        method, 131
clematis, 11, 80, 269, 272
Clematis aramandi, 81, 271
Clethera alnifolia, 56
Cleveland sage, 284
'Cleveland Select' pear tree,
    64
'Cliffs of Dover' shrub rose,
    238
climbing plants
    naturally attaching, 269
    supporting, 269–272
climbing roses, 11, 77, 82, 237,
    269–270, 272
clinging vines, 77
clove pink, 220
clubroot, 185
coast live oak, 66
cockscomb, 260
codling moths, 189
cold frame, 263–264
coleus, 55, 97, 151, 233
Coleus hybridus, 97
coolibah tree, 65
Colorado potato beetles, 189
columbine, 55, 87
common heliotrope, 281
common hyacinth, 106
common lilac, 74, 284
'Compacta' cedar, 75
'Compactum' viburnum, 74
complete fertilizers, 169
compost, 137, 171, 247–253
    activators, 252
    aerating tool, 252
    aids for making, 251–252
    compost bins, 249–251

hot cycle, 121
innoculants, 252
odors, 253
pitchfork, 252
rules, 248–249
sifter, 252
starters, 252
thermometer, 252
what else you can put into,
    252–253
compost bins, 249
    anaerobic containers, 251
    building or buying, 249
    hot compost containers, 250
    static piles, 250
    three-bin boxes, 250
    tumblers, 251
    wire, 249
    wooden, 249
compost piles, 247–248
'Compressa' juniper, 75
CompuServe, 297, 299–300
concrete urns and boxes, 229
'Conica' spruce, 76
conifers, 65
Consolida ambigua, 95, 260
'Constellation' flowering
    dogwood, 63
container gardens
    annuals, 232–233
    fertilizer, 234
    perennials, 233
    planting, 232–234
    pots, 229–230
    rules, 230–231
    soil, 231–232
    watering, 234
container-grown trees,
    146–147
continental zones, 46–51
Convallaria majalis, 106, 284
convergent lady beetle, 186
Convolvulus arvensis, 165
Cook's Garden, 259
cool-season
    annuals, 91–92, 94–96
    turfgrasses, 175
copper, 168, 197

copper barriers, 192
coral bells, 89
coreopsis, 88
Coreopsis grandiflora, 88
coring machine, 180
cork oak trees, 65
corms, 99, 103
corn earworm, 189
Cornus florida, 63
Cornus sericea, 56
Cornus stolonifera, 69
Corsican mint, 278–279
cosmos, 97, 220, 227
Cosmos atrosanguineus, 280
Cosmos bipinnatus, 97
cotoneaster, 70, 113, 224
Cotoneaster divaricatus, 70
Cotoneaster horizontalis, 113
Cotoneaster lacteus, 70
Cotoneaster microphyllus, 113
cottage pinks, 280
Country Journal, 295
cover crops, 138
crab apples, 59
crane's bill, 278
crape myrtle trees, 64
creeping fig, 81
creeping oxalis, 165
creeping phlox, 240
creeping speedwell, 278
creeping St. John's wort, 113
creeping thyme, 114
'Crimson Glory' rose, 286
crocuses, 103–104, 240
crop rotation, 184
crops, 13
crown rot, 145
cucumbers, 272
cut-and-come again, 215
cuttings, 150–151
cutworms, 185, 187, 190
Cynodon dactylon, 165
Cynoglossum amabile, 95
cypresses, 75
cytospora canker, 199

• *D* •
D.I.Y. (Do It Yourself)
    projects, 118

daffodils, 99–101, 103, 107, 220, 240
dahlias, 100–104, 106, 220
daisies, 13
damask rose, 239
dame's rocket, 282
damping-off disease, 185, 187, 199
Damrosch, Barbara, 291
daphne, 283
Daphne burkwoodii, 283
Daphne cneorum, 283
Daphne matensiana, 283
Daphne odora, 283
daylilies, 89, 217–218
'Dazzler' holly, 71
deadheading, 85–86
Dean, Jan, 293
deciduous
  hedges, 10
  plants, 11
  rock cotoneaster, 113
  shrubs, 56
  trees, 59, 62–65
decks, 117, 126–127
delphiniums, 220, 262
dianthus, 88, 218
Dianthus barbatus, 88
Dianthus caryophyllus, 220, 281
Dianthus deltoides, 280
Dianthus gratianopolitanus, 280
Dianthus plumarius, 280
diatomaceous earth (DE), 193–194
diatoms, 193
Dicentra spectabilis, 55
dichondra, 278
Dichondra micrantha, 278
digging bar, 118
direct-sowing, 142–144
direct-sown seeds, 205
dirt. *See* soil
discount stores, 42
diseases, 198–200
  preventing, 183–184, 188
dividing perennials, 149
documenting property size and shape, 16

'Dolga' flowering crab apple, 64
'Dortmund' climbing roses, 239, 272
'Double Delight' hybrid tea rose, 236, 286
double digging, 136, 140
drainage, 21, 133–135
drainage tiles, 21
drawing goose eggs, 16–17
drift, 217
drip irrigation, 144, 163
dripline, 162
Drosanthemum floribundum, 113
Druitt, Liz, 286
drying flowers, 260–261
Duchesnea indica, 278
dusty miller, 95
dwarf
  apple trees, 214
  cherry trees, 214
  conifers, 74–76
  daffodils, 104
  daylilies, 240
  periwinkle, 114

• E •

'Earlyred' pear tree, 64
Easter lily, 285
eastern redbud, 62
Echinacea purpurea, 90
edible plants, 213–214
Elaeagnus angustifolia, 63
electric bulb-planting drill, 41
electric fences, 124
electric rotary mowers, 37
electric string trimmers, 39
Ellis, Barbara, 292
'Ellwoodii' cypress, 75
English bluebell, 100
English boxwood, 70
English holly, 71
English ivy, 77, 79, 81, 113, 151, 269
English oak trees, 65
English primrose, 96
English roses, 238

entertaining, 11–12
Erodium chamaedryoides, 278
Eschscholzia californica, 95
Eucalyptus microtheca, 65
Eucalyptus nicholii, 65
eucalyptus trees, 65
Euonymus alata, 70
Euonymus europaea, 70
Euonymus fortunei, 71, 113
Euonymus japonica, 71
euonymus shrubs, 70–71
euphorbias, 262
European spindle tree, 70
European white birch, 62
'Europeana' floribunda rose, 236
evapotranspiration, 164
evening stock, 282
'Everest' lily, 285
evergreen clematis, 81
evergreen hedges, 10
evergreen rockspray cotoneaster, 113
evergreen shrubs, 56, 76, 240
evergreen trees, 62
evergreens, 11, 224
Extension offices, 184
  help from agents, 208
  information about trees, 58
  testing soil, 135
eye hoe, 165

• F •

fairy primrose, 96
false spiraea, 55
fan trellises, 271
fancy-leaf caladium, 105
farm and feed stores, 42
fences, 10, 31, 117, 123–125
fertile mulch, 166–167
fertilizers, 137
  carrier, 169
  container gardens, 234
  forms, 169, 170
  fruit gardens, 209
  lawns, 182
  organic, 171
  roses, 243
  vegetable gardens, 205

'Festival Fanfare' rose, 239
Festuca ovina glauca, 113
Ficus pumila, 81
fifteen flowering perennials
    for shady sites, 54–55
fine fescue, 175
Fine Gardening, 295
fir trees, 65
firethorn, 72
firs, 75
five deciduous shrubs for
    shady sites, 56
flea beetles, 187, 190
flea control, 13
Fletcher, Karen, 304
flooring, 11
floribunda roses, 236, 239
Flower & Garden, 295
'Flower Carpet' shrub rose,
    238
flower gardens
    color, 218–219
    congenial flowers, 217–218
    cut-and-come again, 215
    drift, 217
    edging plants, 219
    entertaining, 12
    flower form, 218
    flowers for cutting, 220
    peak times, 216
    plant height, 218
    repetition, 217
    shapes, 216–217
    small trees and shrubs, 216
    symmetry, 217
    teardrop, 216
    view, 215–216
    wildflowers, 220–222
flowering cabbage or kale, 95
flowering centerpiece, 256
flowering crab apples, 64
flowering dogwood, 63
flowering perennials, 54–55
flowering tobacco, 97, 282
flowers, 13
    annual, 91–98
    drying, 260–261
    lasting cut flowers, 262
    most-scented, 280–281

perennial, 83–90
    single, 227
    where to find, 308–310
fly parasites, 186
foam-formed plastic pots, 229
foliar fertilizers, 169
forcing narcissus indoors,
    258–259
forget-me-not, 55
forsythias, 262
*400 Best Garden Plants: A
    Practical Encyclopedia of
    Annuals, Perennials,
    Bulbs, Trees and Shrubs*,
    291
fourteen annuals for shady
    sites, 55
'Fragrance' carnations, 281
'Fragrant Cloud' rose, 286
fragrant evening primrose,
    282
'Fragrant Light' daylilies, 281
Fraxinus oxycarpa 'Raywood',
    63
free plants, 149
    cuttings, 150–151
    dividing perennials, 149
freesia, 106, 285
French sorrel, 13
front tine rotary tillers, 39
frost, 266
fruit gardens
    apples, 211–212
    blueberries, 213
    bramble fruits, 213
    grapes, 213
    patience, 209
    peaches, 212
    pears, 212
    planning, 211
    planting, 209
    plums, 212
    pollinizers, 209
    pruning and thinning, 210
    strawberries, 213
    sweet cherries, 212
    watering and fertilizing, 209
fruit trees and fertilizers, 170

fruits, where to find, 311
full sun, 17, 52
furrow irrigation, 162
fuschia, 150–151

• *G* •

Gaillardia grandiflora, 87
Galanthus elwesii, 106
'Galaxy' flowering dogwood,
    63
gallica rose, 239
ganzanias, 112
Garden Book Club, The, 294
garden cart, 35
Garden Design, 295
Garden Gate, 295
Garden Gate on Prairienet
    site, 304
garden hose, 34
garden penstemon, 89
Garden Primer, The, 291
Garden, The, 296
garden projects
    autumn harvest wreath, 261
    cleaning containers, 259
    drying flowers, 260–261
    flowering centerpiece, 256
    forcing narcissus indoors,
        258–259
    herb vinegars, 255
    lasting cut flowers, 262
    salad basket, 259–260
    water garden in tub,
        256–257
garden tractors, 38
*Gardener's Reading Guide:
    The Best Books for
    Gardeners*, 293
Gardener's Supply Co., 163
gardenia, 71, 150, 283
Gardenia jasminoides, 71, 283
gardening, 1
    beneficial insects, 185–186
    books, 289–294
    magazines, newsletters,
        newspapers, 294–296
    online, 297–305
    preventing pests, 184–185

Gardening by Mail: A Source Book, 291
gardening gloves, 35
gardening tools, 36–42. *See also* tools
GardenNet site, 304
gardens
  arbors, 128
  arranging, 143
  birds and butterflies, 223–228
  borders, 83–84
  container, 229–234
  D.I.Y. (Do It Yourself) projects, 118
  decks, 117, 126–127
  drawing features on paper, 26
  entertaining, 11–12
  fences, 117, 123–125
  flea control, 13
  flower, 13, 215–222
  frost, 266
  fruit, 208–213
  gazebos, 128
  growing crops, 13
  heavy work, 25
  hiring help, 118
  light work, 25
  maintenance, 157–171
  making places for people, 117–128
  moderately strenuous work, 25
  outdoor rooms, 117
  paths, 14, 119–123
  patios, 117, 126–127
  paving walkways, 117
  perfumed, 279–286
  perimeter walls, 124
  pets, 13
  places to sit, 14
  planning, 23–31
  plant order, 30
  play area, 12
  practical work area, 12
  privacy, 9–11
  private nooks, 127–128
  raised beds, 139

rose, 235–244
row covers, 265
scenic views, 21
screens, 127–128
small, 273–278
stretching season, 263–267
sunny or shady, 14
terraces, 126–127
toolkit for building projects, 118
vegetable, 203–208
walkways, 119
year-round, 266–267
Gardens Illustrated, 296
GardenWeb site, 304
gasoline-powered string trimmers, 39
gazebos, 128
'General De Wet' tulips, 281
Geranium sanguineum, 87
geraniums, 96, 150, 233, 240
  scented, 279
germination percentages, 143
'Gertrude Jekyll' English rose, 238
giant snowdrop, 106
gladiolus, 103, 106, 220
Gladiolus colvillei, 106
Glick, Barry, 304
Global ReLeaf, 58
globe amaranth, 260
globeflower, 55
gloriosa daisy, 90
glossy abelia, 69
'Gold Medal' grandiflora rose, 237
gold-banded lily, 285
'Golden Spreader' fir, 75
goldflame honeysuckle, 284
Gomphrena globosa, 260
goose eggs, 16–17
gophers, 187
'Graham Thomas' English rose, 238
'Granada' rose, 286
'Grand Duke' Arabian jasmine, 283
grandiflora roses, 237
granular fertilizers, 169

grape hyacinth, 100, 107, 285
grapes, 11, 77, 82, 213
grass, 174–176
  germination percentage, 177
  paths, 119–120
  runner roots, 165
  variety names, 177
gravel paths, 121
gray-green woolly thyme, 278
'Green Beauty' boxwood, 70
green lacewing, 186
green manure crops, 138
Green Scene, 295
ground cover junipers, 240
ground covers, 15, 69, 109–110
  Aaron's-beard, 113
  African daisies, 112
  'Bar Harbor' junipers, 114
  barberries, 112
  blue fescue, 113
  blue grama grass, 110
  buffalo grass, 110
  carpet bugle, 112
  chamomile, 112–113
  cotoneasters, 113
  creeping St. John's wort, 113
  creeping thyme, 114
  'Crimson Pygmy' barberries, 112
  deciduous rock cotoneaster, 113
  dwarf periwinkle, 114
  English ivy, 113
  evergreen rockspray cotoneaster, 113
  ganzanias, 112
  ice plants, 113
  Japanese spurge, 114
  junipers, 114
  Kinnikinnick, 112
  lily turf, 114
  low-growing prairie-type plants, 109–110
  mondo grass, 114
  native grasses, 109–110
  planting, 110–112
  rosea ice plant, 113
  'San Jose' junipers, 114

ground covers (continued)
  shrub roses, 238
  spring cinquefoil, 114
  star jasmine, 114
  trailing African daisy, 112
  trailing ice plant, 113
  wheat grass, 110
  winter creeper, 113
  woolly yarrow, 112
gypsy moths, 190
Gysophila paniculata, 220

• H •
'Hahn's Self-Branching'
    English ivy, 81
Hamilton, Edward R., Book-
    seller, 294
hand pruner, 161
hand saw, 161
hand shears, 35
hand tools, 33–35
hand trowel, 34
hand-held tiller/cultivators, 40
hanging baskets, 230
  fertilizers, 170
hardening off, 150, 152–153
hardiness, 46–51
hardpan, 134, 137
hardscapes, 29, 31
hardware stores, 42
hawthorns, 59, 63
heading back buds, 159
heading cuts, 158
heather, 150
heavenly bamboo, 71
heavy shade, 18
Hedera helix, 81, 113
hedge roses, 238
hedges, 69
heirloom tomatoes, 13
Helianthus annuus, 97
Helichrysum bracteatum, 260
Helictotrichon sempervirens,
    89
Heliotropium arborescens, 281
Helipterum, 260
Hemerocallis lilioasphodelus,
    281
hemlocks, 65

Herb Companion, 295
herb vinegars, 255
herbs, 214, 240, 279
  where to find, 310
'Heritage' English rose, 238
Hesperis matronalis, 282
Heuchera sanguinea, 88
hiring
  heavy jobs, 25
  help for projects, 118
hitchhiking weeds, 165
hoes, 34, 165
holly, 71, 224
holly oak, 66
hollyhocks, 262
home-building centers, 42
Homelite trigger start
    trimmer, 38
honeysuckle, 150, 272
horizontally spreading plants,
    29
horse chestnut, 60
Horticulture: The magazine of
    American gardening, 295
horticultural oils, 194
HortIdeas, 296
Hosta sieboldiana, 89
hostas, 55, 218
hot bed, 264
hot caps, 264
hot composting cycle, 121
House Beautiful, 295
house plants and fertilizers,
    170
hummingbirds, 218
hyacinths, 104, 285
Hyacinthus orientalis, 106, 285
hybrid perpetual rose, 239
hybrid tea roses, 236
  pruning, 243
hydrangea, 71
Hydrangea arborescens, 56
Hydrangea macrophylla, 71
Hypericum calycinum, 113
'Hyperion' daylilies, 281

• I •
Iberis sempervirens, 88
ice plants, 113

'Iceberg' floribunda rose, 236,
    239
Iceland poppies, 262
'Ichiban' Japanese eggplant,
    267
icons used in this book, 5–6
'Ida Jane' daylilies, 281
Ilex aquifolium, 71
Ilex cornuta, 71
Ilex glabra, 56
immortelle, 261
impatiens, 55, 97, 151, 233
Impatiens wallerana, 55, 97
'Imperial Silver' lily, 285
Indian hawthorn, 72
Indian mock strawberry, 278
InfoSeek, 305
Inkberry, 56
Inktomi, 305
inorganic mulch, 166
Ipomoea alba, 282
Iris sibirica, 55
insecticidal soaps, 194–195
insecticides, 185
  broad-spectrum, 196
integrated pest management
    (IPM), 186
Internet
  mailing lists, 302–303
  Usenet newsgroups,
    300–303
iris, 107, 217, 220
iron, 168
IRT mulching film, 265
Italian grading hoe, 165
ivy, 150

• J •
Japanese barberry, 69
Japanese beetles, 190
Japanese boxwood, 70
Japanese camellia, 70
Japanese flowering crab
    apples, 64
Japanese maple, 62
Japanese photinia, 72
Japanese snowball, 56
Japanese spurge, 114
jar soil test, 133

jasmine, 269
Jasminum grandiflorum, 271
Jasminum polyanthum, 81
Jasminum sambac, 283
'Jeepers Creepers' shrub rose, 238
Jerusalem artichokes, 10
jonquils, 285
'Journey's End' lily, 285
'Juliet' carnations, 281
junipers, 65, 71, 75, 114, 224
Juniperus chinensis, 71, 114
Juniperus communis, 75
Juniperus horizontalis, 114

• K •

Kalmia latifolia, 56
'Kathleen' rose, 239
Kentucky bluegrass, 175
King Alfred daffodils, 107
Kinnikinnick, 112
'Knap Hill-Exbury Hybrid' azaleas, 73
Kordesii rose, 239
Korean boxwood, 56
Korean spice viburnum, 74
Krauter's Vesuvius purple-leaf plum, 64
'Kurumes' azaleas, 73
Kwanzan flowering cherry trees, 64

• L •

labor, 24
ladder, 161
'Lady of the Dawn' rose, 239
lady's mantle, 54
Lagerstroemia indica, 64
'Lalandei' firethorn, 72
lamb's ears, 90
Lampranthus spectabilis, 113
landscape fabric, 111, 167
landscape rose, 238
landscaping
  construction before planting, 24
  edible plants, 213–214

listing priorities, 24–25
removing bad features, 24
soft and natural, 17
unsuitable areas for plants, 24
Landscaping with Antique Roses, 286
lantana, 227
Lantana camara, 227
larkspur, 95, 218, 220, 260
Lathyrus odoratus, 95, 281
latitude, 19
latticework trellises, 271
lavender, 279
Lavandula, 279
lawn and garden tractors, 38
lawn mowers, 36–38
lawn rake, 34
lawn roller, 177
lawn spreader, 177
lawns
  before planting grass, 176
  best grasses, 174–176
  cutting grass, 36–38
  deciding size of, 173–174
  fertilizers, 170, 182
  laying sod, 174
  mowing, 181
  new, 174
  overseeding, 180–181
  plugs, 174
  seeding, 177–178
  sod, 179
  sprigs, 174
  testing soil, 176
  thatching, 180
  topsoil, 176
  turfgrasses, 174–176
  weeding, 181
Lawton, Barbara P., 291
laying sod, 174
leading bud, 158
leaf buds, 243
leaf miners, 187, 190
least toxic disease remedies, 197
legumes, 138
lemon daylily, 281
lemon thyme, 278
lemon verbena, 279

light shade, 17
light. *See* amount of sun
lightweight tiller/cultivators, 40
lilacs, 262, 284
lilies, 103–104, 107, 285
Lilium auratum, 285
Lilium candidum, 285
Lilium longiflorum, 285
lily turf, 114
lily-of-the-Nile, 105
lily-of-the-valley, 106, 284
lime, 232
lime sulphur, 197
limestone, 137
Limonium sinuatum, 261
liquid fertilizers, 169
Liquidambar styraciflua, 64
liquidambar trees, 59, 64
Liriope muscari, 114
Liriope spicata, 114
listing landscaping priorities, 24
literal screens, 10
'Little Sweetheart' sweet peas, 95
loam, 20, 132
lobelia, 55, 93, 97, 233
Lobelia erinus, 55, 97
Lobularia maritima, 96
Lonicera heckrottii, 284
loosening soil, 138–140
lopper, 161
lopping shears, 35
love-in-a-mist, 55, 261
low plants, 30
low-growing prairie-type plants, 109–110
'Luminette' carnations, 281
lungwort, 55
Lycos, 305
lygus bugs, 192
Lysimachia nummularia, 278

• M •

McDonald, Elvin, 291
macronutrients, 168
Madagascar periwinkle, 97
Madonna lily, 285

magazines, 294–296

'Magic Carousel' miniature rose, 237

'Magic Carpet' rose, 239

magnesium, 168

Magnolia grandiflora, 65

Magnolia soulangiana, 64

magnolia trees, 64

maiden grass, 10

maiden pinks, 280

mail-order gardening book sources, 294

mail-order tools, 42

mailing lists, 302–303

maintaining gardens

  fertilizers, 169–171

  plant nutrients, 168

  pruning, 157–161

  watering, 162–164

  weeding, 164–167

'Majestic Beauty' Indian hawthorn, 72

Malus sargentii, 64

Malus zumi calocarpa, 64

'Mammoth Mix' sweet peas, 281

manganese, 168

manure, 171

maple trees, 62

marguerites, 88

marigolds, 92, 98, 220, 227

Matthiola incana, 96

Matthiola longipetala bicornis, 282

mattock, 165–166

meadow rue, 55

mealy-cup sage, 220

mealybugs, 191

mechanical spreader, 177

Mentha requienii, 278–279

mesclun, 259–260

metal trellises, 271

metal-rod test method, 134–135

Mexican bean beetles, 191

michelia, 284

Michelia champaca, 284

Michelia figo, 284

microclimates, 46

micronutrients, 168

mignonette, 281

mildew, 199–200

Mimulus hybridus, 55

mini-tillers, 40–41

Minnesota Horticulturist, 295

miniature roses, 237

Miscanthus sinesis, 89

Mitchella repens, 278

'Mojave' firethorn, 72

'Mollis Hybrids' azaleas, 73

molybdenum, 168

Monarda didyma, 55

mondo grass, 114

moneywort, 278

monkey flower, 55

moonflower, 282

'Moonshine' yarrow, 90

morning glory, 270

moss rose, 239–240

mother-of-thyme, 278

mound-shaped plants, 30

mountain laurel, 56

mowing lawns, 181

mugho pine, 72

mulberries, 224

mulch, 254

  fertile, 166–167

  inorganic, 166

  newspaper, 167

  paths, 119–120

mulching rotary mowers, 37

muscari, 240

Muscari azureum, 285

musk rose, 239

Myosotis sylvatica, 55

'Myrtle Gentry' peonies, 281

• *N* •

naked lady, 284

'Nana' pine, 76

'Nana' yew, 76

Nandina domestica, 71

narcissus, 107, 285

  forcing indoors, 258–259

Narcissus jonquilla, 285

Narcissus tazetta, 285

nasturtium, 96

National Audubon Society, 225

National Gardening, 295

National Gardening Association, 4

native grasses, 109–110

native plants, 53

native viburnums, 224

natural features, 15

naturalizers, 100

naturally rounded plants, 30

neem, 195

'Nellie Stevens' holly, 71

Nerium oleander, 71–72

New England Gardening News, 295

New Plantsman, The, 296

newsletters, 294–296

newspaper mulch, 167

newspapers, 294–296

Nichol's willow-leaf peppermint, 65

nicotiana, 55

Nicotiana alata, 55, 97, 282

Nigella damascena, 55, 261

night phlox, 282

night-time perfumed gardens, 282

nitrogen (N), 138, 168

nonlegumes, 138

North American Horticulture: A Reference Guide, 291

'Northern Lights Hybrid' azaleas, 73

Norway maples, 62

nurseries

  information about trees, 58

  tools, 41

nutrients, 137–138

• *O* •

oak trees, 65–66

Oenothera caespitosa, 282

'Old Royal' sweet peas, 281

'Old Spice' sweet peas, 281

old-fashioned roses, 239

oleander, 71–72

online gardening

  America Online (AOL), 297–298

CompuServe, 297, 299–300
Internet, 300–303
WWW (World Wide Web)
    sites, 303–305
'Olympiad' hybrid tea rose,
    236
Ophiopogon japonicus, 114
organic fertilizers, 170–171
Organic Gardener's Basics, 291
Organic Gardening, 295
Organic Gardening Book Club,
    294
organic matter, 20, 136–137
organic mulch, 111
oriental fruit moths, 191
ornamental grasses, 89, 240
Ortho Problem Solver, 184
oscillating sprinklers, 163
oscillating hoe, 34, 165
Osmanthus fragrans, 284
Osteospermum, 112
outdoor rooms, 117
overseeding lawns, 180–181
Oxalis corniculata, 165

• *P* •

Pachysandra terminalis, 114
Pacific Horticulture, 295
painted daisy, 88, 195
'Painted Lady' sweet peas,
    281
pansies, 55, 92, 96, 218, 233,
    240
'Papa Meilland' rose, 286
paper-white narcissus, 258
parasitic nematodes, 13, 186
Park Seed Co., 41
parks departments, 58
Parney cotoneaster, 70
parsnips, 138
Parthenocissus quinquefolia,
    81
Parthenocissus tricuspidata, 81
Patios and Decks, 291
Patriania, 13
partridgeberry, 278
'Party Girl' miniature rose,
    237

paths, 14, 31, 119
  bark, 121
  black lawn edging, 120
  brick, stone, or concrete
      pavers, 120–121
  easier to climb, 121–123
  grass, 119–120
  gravel, 121
  mulching, 119–120
  naturalistic, 119–120
  permanent edging, 120
  steps, 121–123
  stopping weeds, 122
  width, 119
patio roses, 237
patios, 117, 126–127
'Peace' hybrid tea rose, 236
peach-leaf bellflower, 87
peaches, 13, 212
pears, 212
peas, 272
peat moss, 231
Pelargonium citrosum, 279
Pelargonium graveolens, 279
Pelargonium nervosum, 279
Pelargonium odoratissimum,
    279
Pelargonium quercifolium, 279
Pelargonium tomentosum, 279
Pennisetum setaceum, 89
penstemon, 150
Penstemon gloxinioides, 89
percolation test method, 134
perennial candytuft, 240
perennial ryegrass, 175
perennials, 83–84
  artemisia, 87
  asters, 87
  basket-of-gold, 87
  bellflower, 87
  black-eyed Susan, 90
  blanketflower, 88
  blood-red geranium, 89
  blue oat grass, 89
  blue-leaf plantain lily, 89
  borders, 83–84
  candytuft, 89
  caring for, 85–86
  chrysanthemum, 88

columbine, 87
container gardens, 233
coral bells, 89
coreopsis, 88
cutting back, 86
daylilies, 89
deadheading, 85–86
dianthus, 88
dividing, 87, 149
favorite, 87–90
fertilizers, 170
garden penstemon, 89
gloriosa daisy, 90
lamb's ears, 90
marguerites, 88
'Moonshine' yarrow, 87
ornamental grasses, 89
painted daisy, 88
peach-leaf bellflower, 87
pinching out new growth, 85
plantain lily, 89
planting, 85
'Powis Castle' artemisia, 87
purple coneflower, 88
purple fountain grass, 89
'Rubrum' purple fountain
    grass, 89
salvias, 90
Serbian bellflower, 87
Shasta daisies, 88
softwood stem cuttings, 150
stacking, 86
summer phlox, 90
sweet William, 88
tall, 10
when to plant, 141
where to find, 311–312
yarrow, 87
'Zebrinus' variegated eulalia
    grass, 89
perfumed gardens
  bulbs, 284–285
  flowers with most scent,
      280–281
  night-time, 282
  roses, 286
  shrubs, 283–284
  trees, 283–284
  vines, 283–284
  where to put plants, 280

pergola, 128
perimeters walls, 124
perlite, 232
permanent fences, 125
permanent path edging, 120
Persian buttercup, 107
pest birds, 225–226
pesticides, 228
pests
  aphids, 188
  beneficial insects, 184
  black vine weevil, 188
  borers, 189
  caterpillars, 189
  chinch bugs, 189
  codling moths, 189
  Colorado potato beetles,
    189
  crop rotation, 184
  cutworms, 190
  flea beetles, 190
  gardening to prevent,
    184–185
  gypsy moths, 190
  insecticides, 185
  Japanese beetles, 190
  leaf miners, 190
  lygus bugs, 192
  managing, 186–187
  mealybugs, 191
  Mexican bean beetles, 191
  oriental fruit moths, 191
  plum curculio, 191
  preventing, 183–184
  root maggots, 191
  safe and effective remedies,
    193–197
  scale, 192
  slugs, 192
  snails, 192
  spider mites, 192
  spotted and striped
    cucumber beetles, 190
  sticky barriers, 190
  tarnished plant bugs, 192
  tent caterpillars, 192
  tomato hornworm, 192
  vegetable gardens, 187–188
  whiteflies, 192

pets, 13
Petunia hybrida, 97
petunias, 92, 97, 233
'Pfitzerana' junipers, 71
pH, 137
  tests, 135
pheromones, 189
phlox, 150
Phlox paniculata, 90, 220
Photinia fraseri, 72
Photinia glabra, 72
phosphorus (P), 168
photinia, 72
phytophthora blight, 200
Picea glauca, 76
pick, 118
pikaki, 283
pillars, 272
pinching, 158
pines, 65, 224
  dwarf conifers, 76
pink paper daisy, 260
pink pokers, 261
'Pink Spires' flowering crab
    apple, 64
pinks, 150, 280
Pinus mugo mugo, 72
Pinus strobus, 76
Pistacia chinensis, 64
pitchfork, 252
places to sit, 14
planning gardens, 23
  budget, 24
  drawing features on paper,
    26
  elements, 29–31
  hardscape, 29, 31
  hiring heavy jobs, 25
  labor, 24
  listing landscape priorities,
    24–25
  photos of your property, 26
  plants, 29–30
  quality plants, 24
  scaled plan of property,
    26–29
Plant Hardiness Zone Maps,
    47–51
plant nutrients, 168

plant requirements, 45
  continental zones, 46–51
  matching plants to planting
    site, 46
  native plants, 53
  room to grow, 52
  shade, 53–56
  soil and water, 52
  sun or shade, 51–52
plantain lily, 89
planting, 141–142
  bulbs, 148
  container gardens, 232–234
  fruit gardens, 209
  patterns, 143
  plan, 142
  roses, 241–243
  seedlings, 144–146
  shrubs, 146–148
  site, 46
  sowing seeds, 142–144
  starting seeds indoors,
    151–153
  trees, 146–148
  when to plant what, 141–142
  wide-bed techniques, 144
plants
  chlorophyll, 168
  color, 30
  copper barriers, 192
  easily started from seed, 144
  evapotranspiration, 164
  form and shape, 29
  free, 149–151
  hardening off, 150, 152–153
  hardiness, 46–51
  horizontally spreading, 29
  how much water they need,
    164
  leggy, 52
  low and spreading, 30
  names of, 4–5
  naturally rounded or
    mound-shaped, 30
  order, 30
  planning gardens, 29–30
  preventing disease, 198–200
  protecting from frost,
    264–265

quality, 24
repetition and rhythm, 30
resenting transplanting, 144
shade-loving, 53–56
site inventory, 15
size, 29
small gardens, 277–278
starting indoors, 263
style, 30
texture, 30
thinning, 16, 143
transpiration, 164
upright or spiky, 29
wet or soggy soil, 21
zones, 46–51
Plants & Garden News, 296
plastic netting, 272
plastic pots, boxes, and
baskets, 230
play area, 12
plot plan, 16, 18
Platycladus orientalis, 76
plugs, 174, 179
plum curculio, 191
plumeria, 284
Plumeria rubra, 284
plums, 212
pole beans, 272
pole pruner, 161
polyantha roses, 236
Polianthes tuberosa, 285
poppies, 218
porous hose, 163
Portland rose, 239
posthole digger, 118
pot marigold, 95
potash (K), 168
Potentilla fruticosa, 72
Potentilla tabernaemontanii,
114, 278
power cultivators, 40
power rake, 180
power tools, 35
lawn mowers, 36–38
rotary tillers, 39–41
string trimmers, 38
tilling soil, 39
power-reel mowers, 36–37
'Powis Castle' artemisia, 87
'Prairie Princess' rose, 239

predatory mites, 186
prefabricated fences, 125
preparing soil
amending, 136–138
clearing site, 129–131
loosening soil, 138–140
raking, 140
testing, 131–136
primroses, 55, 92, 96
primula, 55
Primula malacoides, 96
Primula polyantha, 96
'Pristine' hybrid tea rose, 236
privacy, 9–11
privacy fences, 123
private nooks, 127–128
private retreat in shade, 54
property
amount of sun, 17–18
controlling water move-
ment, 20–21
documenting size and
shape, 16
drainage, 21
drawing goose eggs, 16–17
evaluating potential, 15–21
meeting potential, 22
photos of, 26
plot plan, 16
scaled plan, 26–29
scenic views, 21
site inventory, 15–16
size of, 16
soil, 18–20
tips for scale drawing, 28
unsuitable for plants, 24
property fences, 123
pruners, 34
pruning, 157–158
basics, 159
fruit gardens, 210
heading back buds, 159
heading cuts, 158
hybrid tea roses, 243
pinching, 158
roses, 243–244
sawing limbs, 159
shearing, 158
suckers, 160

summer, 160–161
thinning cuts, 158
thinning out shoot or limb,
159
tools, 161
watersprouts, 160
winter, 160
psychological screens, 10
Psylliostachys suworowii, 261
Pulmonaria, 55
purple coneflower, 88
purple fountain grass, 89
push rotary power mowers,
37
push-reel mowers, 36
pussy willows, 262
pyracantha, 150
Pyracantha coccinea, 72
Pyrus kawakamii, 65
pyrethrins, 195–196
pyrethroids, 196

• Q •

quality plants, 24
'Queen Elizabeth' grandiflora
rose, 237
Quercus agrifolia, 66
Quercus ilex, 66
Quercus robur, 65
Quercus rubra, 65
Quercus suber, 65
Quercus virginiana, 66

• R •

rabbits, 187
raised beds, 139, 276
rakes, 177
tines, 34
raking, 140
Ranunculus asiaticus, 107
raspberries, 213–214
Raywood ash, 63
*Readers' Digest Illustrated
Guide to Gardening*, 292
rear tine rotary tillers, 39
rec.arts.bonsai newsgroup,
301
rec.gardens newsgroup, 301

rec.gardens.orchids newsgroup, 301
rec.gardens.roses newsgroup, 301
recycling yard waste, 253–254
red cedars, 76
red oak tree, 65
red-osier dogwood, 56
redbuds, 62
repetition, 30, 217
'Redspire' pear tree, 64
Reseda odorata, 281
Rhaphiolepis indica, 72
rhizomes, 99
rhododendrons, 56, 72–73
rhythm, 30
ribbons and bows soil test, 133
riding mowers, 37
'Rise 'n Shine' miniature rose, 237
Rock Garden Quarterly, 295
Rocky Mountain Gardener, 295
Rodale's All-New Encyclopedia of Organic Gardening: The Indispensible Resource for Every Gardener, 292
room to grow, 52
root maggots, 185, 187, 191
root-knot nematode, 185
rooting hormone, 150
'Rosa Bianca' eggplant, 267
Rosa rugosa, 238
rosarians, 235
'Rose Bowl' pinks, 280
rose gardens, 235–244
rosea ice plant, 113
Rosemarinus officinalis, 279
rosemary, 279
roses, 73, 138, 218, 235
  AARS (All-American Rose Selection), 241
  buying, 241
  classes, 235
  climbing, 237
  companion plants, 240
  English, 238
  fertilizer, 170, 243
  floribundas, 236, 239

  grandiflora, 237
  hedge, 238
  hybrid tea, 236
  landscape, 238
  landscaping with, 240
  leaf buds, 243
  miniature, 237
  old-fashioned, 239
  patented, 241
  patio, 237
  planting, 241–243
  polyantha, 236
  pruning, 243–244
  scented, 286
  shrub, 238
  soil, 241
  standards, 237
  surviving winter, 244
  trees, 237
  types, 235
  when they look bad, 240
  where to find, 313
  which type to plant, 240
rotary tillers, 39–41
rotenone, 196–197
rototillers, 138
row covers, 265
'Rubrum' purple fountain grass, 89
Rudbeckia hirta, 89
rugosa roses, 73
runner roots, 165
Russian olive trees, 63
rust, 200

• S •

sabadilla lily, 196
'Safari' freesia, 285
safe and effective pest remedies
  Bt, 193
  diatomaceous earth (DE), 193–194
  horticultural oils, 194
  insecticidal soaps, 194–195
  neem, 195
  pyrethrins, 195–196

  rotenone, 196–197
  sabadilla, 196
  sevin (carbaryl), 197
safflower, 260
sage, 97, 150
St. Augustine grass, 176
'Saint Mary' dwarf magnolia, 65
salad basket, 259–260
Salvia azurea grandiflora, 90
Salvia clevelandii, 284
Salvia farinaea, 220
Salvia splendens, 55
Salvia superba, 90
salvias, 90
'San Jose' junipers, 114
sand, 19, 132, 231
sandwort, 278
Sargent crab apple, 64
Sasanqua camellia, 70
Satureja douglasii, 278
sawing limbs, 159
Scabiosa stellata, 261
scale, 192
scale drawing, 27
scaled property plan
  computer entry, 27–29
  sketching in existing features, 27
  tips, 28
Schoenocaulon officinale, 196
Scarlet sage, 55
scenic views, 21
scented geraniums, 279
sci.agriculture newsgroup, 301
sci.agriculture.beekeeping newsgroup, 301
screens, 10–11, 69
scuffle hoe, 34
search engines, 304–305
secondary nutrients, 168
sedum, 150
seed leaves, 152
seed tapes, 207
seedcorn maggots, 187
seeding lawns, 177–178
seedlings, 144–146
  crown rot, 145

seed leaves, 152
vegetable gardens, 205
seeds
    broadcasting, 143
    depth for vegetable gardens, 207
    germination percentages, 143
    planting patterns, 143
    plants easily started from, 144
    sowing, 142–144
    spacing, 142–144
    starting indoors, 151–153
    watering, 144
    wide-bed planting techniques, 144
self-propelled rotary mowers, 37
Senecio cineraria, 95
Serbian bellflower, 87
seven essential tools, 33–34
sevin (carbaryl), 197
'Sexy Rexy' floribunda rose, 236
shade, 51–53, 55–56
    entertaining, 12
    from trees, 59
    private retreat in, 54
shade-loving plants
    annuals, 55
    deciduous shrubs, 56
    evergreen shrubs, 56
    flowering perennials, 54–55
Shady Oaks Nursery, 54
Shasta daisies, 88
shearing, 158
Shepherd's Garden Seeds, 259
Shoup, G. Michael, 286
shovels, 34
shrub roses, 238
shrubs, 67
    accents, 69
    'Anthony Waterer' spiraea, 73
    'Argenteo-marginata' holly, 71
    'Aurea' fir, 75

'Aureo-variegata' euonymus, 71
'Aureus' red cedar, 76
azaleas, 72–73
background, 69
barberries, 69–70
barriers, 69
'Belgian Indicas' azaleas, 73
bigleaf hydrangea, 71
boxwoods, 70
bridal wreath spiraea, 73
'Burfordii' holly, 71
bush cinquefoil, 72
camellias, 70
Chinese juniper, 71
common lilac, 74
'Compacta' cedar, 75
'Compactum' viburnum, 74
'Compressa' juniper, 75
'Conica' spruce, 76
cotoneaster, 70
'Dazzler' holly, 71
design considerations, 68
dwarf conifers, 74–76
'Ellwoodii' cypress, 75
English boxwood, 70
English holly, 71
euonymus, 70, 71
European spindle tree, 70
evergreen, 76
favorite, 69–76
fertilizers, 170
firethorn, 72
flowering, 69
foundation plantings, 68
gardenia, 71
glossy abelia, 69
'Golden Spreader' fir, 75
'Green Beauty' boxwood, 70
ground cover, 69
heavenly bamboo, 71
hedges, 69
holly, 71
hydrangea, 71
Indian hawthorn, 72
Japanese barberry, 69
Japanese boxwood, 70
Japanese camellia, 70
Japanese photinia, 72

junipers, 71
'Knap Hill-Exbury Hybrid' azaleas, 73
Korean spice viburnum, 74
'Kurumes' azaleas, 73
'Lalandei' firethorn, 72
'Majestic Beauty' Indian hawthorn, 72
'Mojave' firethorn, 72
'Mollis Hybrid' azaleas, 73
mugho pine, 72
'Nana' pine, 76
'Nana' ycw, 76
'Nellie Stevens' holly, 71
'Northern Lights Hybrid' azaleas, 73
oleander, 71–72
Parney cotoneaster, 70
'Pfitzerana' junipers, 71
photinia, 72
planting, 146–148
repeating, 68
rhododendrons, 72–73
roses, 73
rugosa roses, 73
Sasanqua camellia, 70
scented, 283–284
screens, 69
selection, 68–69
'Silver King' euonymus, 71
'Southern Indicas' azaleas, 73
'Spartan' junipers, 71
spiraea, 73
'Teton' firethorn, 72
'Torulosa' junipers, 71
'Variegatum' viburnum, 74
viburnum, 74
when to plant, 142
where to find, 313–314
winged euonymus, 70
'Winter Gem' boxwood, 70
'Winter's Beauty' camellia, 70
'Winter's Interlude' camellia, 70
'Winter's Star' camellia, 70

shrubs *(continued)*
  'Winter's Waterlily'
    camellia, 70
  'Wintergreen' junipers, 71
Siberian Iris, 55
silt, 20, 132
'Silver King' euonymus, 71
'Simplicity' hedge rose,
    238–239
single flowers, 227
site inventory, 15–16
six evergreen shrubs for
    shady sites, 56
slow-release fertilizers, 170
slugs, 187, 192
small gardens
  arbors and arches, 277
  choosing plants, 277–278
  climbing vines, 277
  details, 274
  planting in gaps, 276
  raised beds, 276
  simple design, 273–274
  visual trickery, 274–276
  window boxes, 276
smooth hydrangea, 56
snails, 187, 192
snapdragon, 94
snow fence, 124
'Snowdon' freesia, 285
'Snowdrift' flowering crab
    apple, 64
snowdrops, 106
snowflake, 107
soaker hose, 144, 163
sod, 179
softwood stem cuttings, 150
soil, 18–20
  acidity, 135
  adding nitrogen, 138
  alkalinity, 135
  amending, 129, 136–138
  caliche, 134
  changing pH, 137
  clay, 20, 132
  container gardens, 231–232
  double digging, 140
  drainage, 133–135
  hardpan, 134, 137
  limestone, 137

loam, 20, 132
  loosening, 138–140
  percolation rate, 134
  preparing, 129–136
  Pro-mix, 231
  raised beds, 139
  requirements, 52
  roses, 241
  sand, 19, 132
  silt, 20, 132
  sulfur, 137
  testing, 19, 131–136, 176
  tilling tools, 39–41
  types, 19–20
  warming, 265
  wet or soggy, 21
  when to work it, 139
soil structure, 133–135
'Soleil d'Or' narcissus, 258,
    285
'Sombreuil' climbing roses,
    272
sooty mold, 200
Southern California Gardener,
    295
'Southern Indicas' azaleas, 73
southern live oak, 66
Southern Living, 295
southern magnolia trees, 65
Spanish jasmine, 271
'Spartan' junipers, 71
spider mites, 185, 192
spiderwort, 55
spiky plants, 29
spiraea, 73
Spiraea bumalda, 73
Spiraea vanhouttei, 73
spotted and striped cucum-
    ber beetles, 190
sprawling vines, 77
spreading plants, 30
sprigs, 174, 179
spring cinquefoil, 114, 278
sprinklers, 162–163
spruce trees, 65
  dwarf conifers, 76
spurges, 165
spurs, 158
Stachys byzantina, 89

staking trees, 148
star jasmine, 77, 82, 114, 150,
    271
starflower, 261
'Starina' miniature rose, 237
starting seeds indoors,
    151–153
'State Fair' zinnia, 98
statice, 261
steel bow rake, 34
'Stellar Pink' flowering
    dogwood, 63
sticky pest barriers, 190
stiff-tined rake, 34
stirrup hoe, 165
stocks, 96, 281
strawberries, 13, 213
strawflower, 260
stretching garden season
  extending season into
    autumn, 266
  planting earlier, 263–265
  protecting plants from frost,
    264–265
  year-round gardens,
    266–267
string trimmers, 38–39
stripping sod, 130–131
structures, 15
subsoil, 134
suckers, 160
sugar maples, 62
sulphur, 137, 168, 197
summer phlox, 90, 220
summer pruning, 160–161
summersweet, 56
sun, 51–52
'Sundowner' rose, 286
sunflowers, 97
Sunset Western Garden Book,
    48, 292
*Sunset: The Magazine of
    Western Living*, 295
'Sunspot' sunflowers, 97
'Sunsprite' rose, 286
supplies, where to find,
    315–316
supporting climbing plants
  arbors, 272

bamboo tepees, 270
chain-link fences, 270–271
fan trellises, 271
latticework trellises, 271
metal trellises, 271
pillars, 272
plastic netting, 272
wall-mounted supports, 272
'Sutter's Gold' rose, 286
sweet alyssum, 96
sweet cherries, 212
sweet olive, 284
sweet peas, 94–95, 220, 269, 271, 281
sweet sultan, 280
sweet violet, 281
sweet William, 88
symmetry, 217
synergist, 196
Syringa vulgaris, 74, 284

• T •

tall perennials, 10
tall phlox, 218
tape measure, 35
tarnished plant bugs, 192
Taxus cuspidata, 76
Taylor's Guide to Gardening Techniques, 292
Taylor's Master Guide to Gardening, 292
tea rose, 239
Tecolote freesia, 285
ten quick garden projects, 255–262
Tenenbaum, Frances, 292
tent caterpillars, 192
terra cotta clay pots, 229, 259
terraces, 126–127
testing soil, 131, 136
    Extension office, 135
    jar test, 133
    metal-rod method, 134–135
    percolation method, 134
    pH tests, 135
    ribbons and bows method, 133
    structure, 133–135
    texture, 132–133

'Teton' firethorn, 72
Texas bluebell, 13
Texas Gardener, 295
Thalictrum, 55
thatching lawns, 180
thinning cuts, 158
thinning out shoot or limb, 159
thinning plants, 16, 143
'Thumbelina' zinnia, 98
Thunbergia alata, 55
thyme, 279
Thymus, 279
Thymus citriodorus, 278
Thymus praecox arcticus, 114, 278
Thymus pseudolanuginosus, 278
'Tiffany' rose, 286
tilling and cover crop method, 131
tilling soil, 39–41
tines, 34
'Tiny Rubies' pinks, 280
tip bud, 158
tomato hornworm, 189, 192
tomatoes, 13
toolkit for building projects, 118
tools
    coring machine, 180
    digging bar, 118
    discount stores, 42
    farm and feed stores, 42
    hand pruner, 161
    hand saw, 161
    hand tools, 33–35
    hardware stores, 42
    hoe, 165
    home-building centers, 42
    ladder, 161
    lopper, 161
    mail-order, 42
    mattock, 165–166
    nurseries, 41
    pick, 118
    pole pruner, 161
    posthole digger, 118
    power rake, 180

power tools, 35–41
    pruning, 161
    seven essential, 33–34
    weeding, 165–166
    where to find, 313–315
    where to shop for, 41–42
topsoil, 19, 134, 176
Torenia fourneiri, 55
'Torulosa' junipers, 71
'Touch of Class' hybrid tea rose, 236
Trachelospermum jasminoides, 82, 114, 271
Tradescantia virginiana, 55
trailing African daisy, 112
transpiration, 164
transplanting seedlings, 144–146
trees, 57–61
    apical bud, 158
    aristocrat pear, 64
    ash, 63
    attractive bark, 59
    balled-and-burlapped, 146–147
    bare-root, 146–147
    birch, 59
    branch collar, 159
    broadleaf evergreens, 65–66
    callus, 160
    camphor, 65
    'Capital', 64
    cedar, 65
    Chinese pistache, 64
    choosing, 57–58
    'Cleveland Select', 64
    coast live oak, 66
    colorful fruit, 59
    conifers, 65
    container-grown, 146–147
    coolibah, 65
    cork oak, 65
    crab apples, 59
    crape myrtle, 64
    deciduous, 59, 62–65
    'Earlyred', 64
    eastern redbud, 62
    English oak, 65
    eucalyptus, 65

trees *(continued)*
European white birch, 62
evergreen, 62
evergreen pear, 65
fast-growing, 61
favorite, 62–66
fertilizers, 170
firs, 65
flowering crab apples, 64
flowering dogwood, 63
growth, 158
hawthorns, 59, 63
healthy from nursery, 63
hemlocks, 65
holly oak, 66
horse chestnut, 60
information about, 58
Japanese flowering crab
apples, 64
junipers, 65
Krauter's Vesuvius purple-
leaf plum, 64
Kwanzan flowering cherry,
64
liquidambars, 59, 64
magnolia, 64
maple, 62
maximizing effectiveness of,
58
messy, 61
Nichol's willow-leaf peppermint, 65
oak, 65–66
'Pink Spires' flowering crab
apple, 64
pines, 65
planting, 58, 60, 146–148
pruning, 157–160
Raywood ash, 63
red oak, 65
redbuds, 62
'Redspire', 64
roses, 237
Russian olive trees, 63
'Saint Mary' dwarf magnolia,
65
Sargent crab apple, 64
scented, 283–284
seasonal color, 59

shade from, 59
'Snowdrift', 64
southern live oak, 66
southern magnolia, 65
spruce, 65
spurs, 158
staking, 148
too big at maturity, 60–61
too close to paving, 61
weeping willow, 60
western redbud, 62
what not to do with, 60–61
when to plant, 142
where to find, 315
'Whitehouse', 64
windbreaks, 59
trellises, 31
trichogramma wasps, 186
Trine, Cheryl M., 304
Trollus, 55
Tropaeolum majus, 96
trumpet lily, 285
tuberose, 285
tuberous roots, 99, 104
tubers, 99
Tulipa clusiana, 107
Tulipa sylvestra, 281
tulips, 99–101, 104, 107, 217,
220
turf-type tall fescue, 175
turfgrasses, 174–176
Turkish eggplants, 13
twining vines, 77

• U •

universities, 58
upright plants, 29
Urban Farmer Store, The, 163
USDA Plant Hardiness Zone
Maps
United States and
Alaska, 48–49
Canada, 47
Usenet newsgroups
FAQs (Frequently Asked
Questions), 301–302
mailing lists, 302–303

• V •

Van Patton, George F., 291
'Variegatum' viburnum, 74
vegetable gardens
direct-sown seeds, 205
fertilizers, 205
harvesting, 208
last frost date, 205–206
moisture, 207
pests, 187–188
raising beds, 205
seed depth, 207
seed tapes, 207
seedlings, 205
size, 204
staking and weeding, 204
sunny location, 203–204
tender crops, 206
tough crops, 206
weeds, 207
vegetables, 214
early varieties, 267
fertilizers, 170
short season, 267
when to plant, 142
where to find, 308–310
verbena, 98, 233
Verbena hybrida, 98
vermiculite, 232
Veronica repens, 278
viburnum, 74
Viburnum carlesii, 74
Viburnum plicatum, 56, 74
Viburnum tinus, 74
Vinca minor, 114
vine-covered trellis or fence,
11
vines, 77
'Baltica' English ivy, 81
Boston ivy, 77, 81
bougainvilleas, 80
Chinese jasmine, 81
Chinese wisteria, 82
clematis, 80
climbing rose, 77, 82
clinging, 77
creeping fig, 81

English ivy, 77, 79, 81
evergreen clematis, 81
favorite, 80–82
grapes, 77, 82
growing where they
    shouldn't, 79
maximizing effectiveness,
    79–80
'Hahn's Self-Branching'
    English ivy, 81
pruning, 80
recycling, 254
scented, 283–284
sprawling, 77
star jasmine, 77, 82
supporting, 78–79
twining, 77
Virginia creeper, 79, 81
where to find, 313–314
Viola ordorata, 281
Viola wittrockiana, 55
violas, 92, 96
Virginia creeper, 79, 81

• *W* •

walkways, 31, 117, 119
Wall O' Waters, 264
wall-mounted supports, 272
wandering Jew, 151
warm-season
    annuals, 91–98
    turfgrasses, 175–176
water, 20–21
    requirements, 52
water gardens
    plants and supplies, 315–316
    tub, 256–257
water wand, 35
water-rooted stem cuttings,
    151
watering
    container gardens, 234
    drip irrigation, 163
    dripline, 162
    fruit gardens, 209
    furrow irrigation, 162
    how much plants need, 164
    porous hose, 163
    soaker hoses, 163

sprinklers, 162–163
    vegetable gardens, 207
watersprouts, 160
waxleaf begonia, 55
WebGarden site, 304
weeding, 185
    by hand, 165–166
    hitchhiking weeds, 165
    lawns, 181
    mulches, 166–167
    tools, 165–166
    vegetable gardens, 204, 207
weeping willow, 60
western redbud, 62
wheat grass, 110, 175
whiteflies, 186, 192
'Whitehouse' pear tree, 64
wild cherries, 224
Wildflower, 295
wildflowers, 220–222
    where to find, 316
willow, 150
wilt, 200
window boxes, 276
winged euonymus shrubs, 70
winged everlasting, 260
winter creeper, 113
'Winter Gem' boxwood, 70
winter jasmine, 271
winter pruning, 160
'Winter's Beauty' camellia, 70
'Winter's Interlude' camellia,
    70
'Winter's Star' camellia, 70
'Winter's Waterlily' camellia,
    70
'Wintergreen' junipers, 71
wireworms, 187
wishbone flower, 55
wisteria, 272
Wisteria sinensis, 82
wood boxes, 230
woodpeckers, 224
woody plants, 150
woolly yarrow, 112
work area, 12
WWW (World Wide Web)
    gardening sites, 303–304
    search engines, 304–305

• *X* •

Xeranthemum annuum, 261

• *Y* •

Yahoo, 305
yard waste, 247–253
yarrow, 87
year-round gardens, 266–267
yerba buena, 278
yews, 76

• *Z* •

Zaluzianskya capensis, 282
'Zebrinus' variegated eulalia
    grass, 89
zinc, 168
Zinnia elegans, 98
zinnias, 92, 98, 220, 227
zones, 46–51
zoysia grass, 176

IDG BOOKS WORLDWIDE REGISTRATION CARD

Visit our Web site at http://www.idgbooks.com

ISBN Number: 1-56884-644-4

Title of this book: Gardening For Dummies ™

My overall rating of this book: ❑ Very good [1] ❑ Good [2] ❑ Satisfactory [3] ❑ Fair [4] ❑ Poor [5]

How I first heard about this book:

❑ Found in bookstore; name: [6] .

❑ Advertisement: [8]

❑ Word of mouth; heard about book from friend, co-worker, etc.: [10]

❑ Book review: [7]

❑ Catalog: [9]

❑ Other: [11]

What I liked most about this book:

What I would change, add, delete, etc., in future editions of this book:

Other comments:

Number of computer books I purchase in a year: ❑ 1 [12] ❑ 2-5 [13] ❑ 6-10 [14] ❑ More than 10 [15]

I would characterize my computer skills as: ❑ Beginner [16] ❑ Intermediate [17] ❑ Advanced [18] ❑ Professional [19]

I use ❑ DOS [20] ❑ Windows [21] ❑ OS/2 [22] ❑ Unix [23] ❑ Macintosh [24] ❑ Other: [25]

(please specify)

I would be interested in new books on the following subjects:

(please check all that apply, and use the spaces provided to identify specific software)

❑ Word processing: [26]

❑ Data bases: [28]

❑ File Utilities: [30]

❑ Networking: [32]

❑ Other: [34]

❑ Spreadsheets: [27]

❑ Desktop publishing: [29]

❑ Money management: [31]

❑ Programming languages: [33]

I use a PC at (please check all that apply): ❑ home [35] ❑ work [36] ❑ school [37] ❑ other: [38]

The disks I prefer to use are ❑ 5.25 [39] ❑ 3.5 [40] ❑ other: [41]

I have a CD ROM: ❑ yes [42] ❑ no [43]

I plan to buy or upgrade computer hardware this year: ❑ yes [44] ❑ no [45]

I plan to buy or upgrade computer software this year: ❑ yes [46] ❑ no [47]

Name: Business title: [48] Type of Business: [49]

Address (❑ home [50] ❑ work [51]/Company name:)

Street/Suite#

City [52]/State [53]/Zip code [54]: Country [55]

❑ **I liked this book!** You may quote me by name in future
IDG Books Worldwide promotional materials.

My daytime phone number is _____

IDG BOOKS
WORLDWIDE
THE WORLD OF
COMPUTER
KNOWLEDGE®

☐ YES!

Please keep me informed about IDG Books Worldwide's World of Computer Knowledge. Send me your latest catalog.